The

DAUGHTER

outcast | rebel | survivor

SUZANNE BETH JORDAN

PUBLISHED BY SILVER WOLF PRESS

The Deviant Daughter: outcast | rebel | survivor
by Suzanne Beth Jordan

Published by Silver Wolf Press, California

Narrative editor: Laurie Chittenden
Editor: Megg Mueller
Cover concept design: Suzanne Beth Jordan
Book design: Book Savvy Studio

Library of Congress Control Number:
ISBN: 979-8-9957624-0-9 (paperback)
ISBN: 979-8-9957624-1-6 (eBook)
ISBN: 979-8-9957624-2-3 (hardcover)

First Edition
Printed in the United States of America

Dedication

For all of you big-energy children, full of bodacious feelings, may you know your gifts and enjoy them all the days of your lives.

To my stunning five siblings, Megg, Tom, Mike, Pete and Kris, we weathered turbulent storms and emerged loving and laughing. You are all extraordinary.

For my beautiful mother, Mary. You are, and always have been, the beating heart of our family. Thank you for a lifetime of love.

My parents, Tom and Mary at his parent's home in Saratoga, California in 1969.

acknowledgements

Huge appreciation to my 11th grade teacher, Sandy Macias, who inspired my first writings. I still have the journal pages I wrote for your class in 1975.

To Gail Schiewe, the frangipani teenager who influenced me greatly though I was only around her for a mere twenty days of my life. I'm forever grateful for the care and concern you showed me as a young girl.

Graciela Casillas, warrior woman and trailblazer. Without you, I might never have regained my freedom. Thank you for helping me to wake up and thank you for the lifeline.

Lisa Solwold, my dear friend for forty years. Thank you for decades of unconditional love and the gift of your deep listening. You summoned the winds of change when you sweetly suggested that I say a prayer.

Sean Thomas Harmon, my spiritual godson. Being in your corner has brought me immense joy and oh so many riveting moments. I admire your mighty heart and fierce loyalty. Thank you for years of inimitable encouragement as I worked on this book.

Douglas James Ryan, my grandfather, who passed away in 1993. You gave the love my father was incapable of giving. You were the rock beneath us, the always steady presence amid the storms of chaos. Your love made so much more possible for us all. Thank you.

Linda Humphreys, thank you for your tireless support and friendship as this manuscript progressed.

Nicole Harvey, thank you for your boundless enthusiasm, huge generosity and ever sharp legal counsel. You have a heart of gold.

Peter Blachy, you are one of the few Renaissance men I've ever met, your boundless creativity is inspiring. Thank you for all the heartfelt conversations along the way.

To all the followers of Yogi Bhajan who won't read this book: Truth requires far more courage than stagnating in a lie.

To the fantastic humans in the *Beyond the Cage* Facebook group, thank you for your brilliant presence and sharing these last seven years as we supported one another. I'm a profoundly better person from sharing virtual space with you.

My narrative editor, Laurie Chittenden, thank you for your insightful counsel that made such a difference and galvanized my commitment to complete this memoir.

My big sister Kris, thank you for your final read through and for your unparalleled attention to detail.

Megg, my sister and my person. Thank you for always being safe and loving me through my darkest times. Thank you also for your editing expertise and narrative guidance.

To my brothers, Tom and Pete, despite dad's horrid example, you both grew up to be admirable men and loving fathers. You amaze me.

To my brother Mike, I miss you every day and only wish with all my heart that you could have stayed with us longer.

A shout out from the mountaintops to my Self for facing all that I had to face to write this book. I found the "magic something" to complete my manuscript in the Scottish Highlands while staying at the home of my lovely friends, Alan and Carol.

And finally, to my sweet mother, Mary. Thank you for allowing me to tell painful parts of your story as I told mine. I know at times it wasn't easy or pleasant for you and I honor your courage in permitting me to do so.

contents

introduction

My first inclination that I would someday tell this story happened in 1986 when I was twenty-six years old. My first timeline notes for this book are from that year. At some point during the process of writing this memoir I realized the impetus for writing my story was quite private: I needed to sit with my younger self and remember her experiences, to see the world again through her eyes. There was healing that needed to happen so that I could feel whole.

I could not have foreseen how difficult a task lay ahead. I had no idea how much pain I held in my body for her or how many tears I had never cried. Back then, any notion of therapy or processing my feelings was a luxury I could not afford. I existed in survival mode twenty-four hours a day.

This book is an invitation to witness that story. It begins at summer camp, when I'm eleven. It was important to me to begin there, to record the powerful fluctuations of my childhood. To witness the place where the seeds of self-loathing and shame were planted. These younger years laid the foundation for the kinds of decisions and consequences that would follow. My younger years serve as a map to cultville.

Because the world is changing at warp speed, I also wanted to record the details of my analog childhood, a kind of life now strictly relegated to the past.

For those of you reading now, I am deeply moved and honored to have you share this journey with me.

The latter section of this book reflects the time I spent in the Healthy, Happy, Holy Organization (3HO) which was founded by

Yogi Bhajan. In documenting my experiences with Yogi Bhajan's teachings and practices, I want to ensure that I do not inadvertently mislead readers into believing that Sikhism incorporates Hindu elements. Sikhism is a distinct, monotheistic religion and is completely separate from Hindu caste, ritual, and theology.

Historically and presently, many mainstream Sikhs have objected to 3HO specifically due to this Hindu-Sikh conflation introduced by Yogi Bhajan and not native to the Sikh faith. This conflation is a distortion specific to 3HO rather than a feature of the original religion.

In addition to these religious distortions, his teachings are infused with his own homophobia and misogyny, along with dubious child-rearing practices, extreme diets, and a form of yoga with a questionable lineage.

Some call 3HO a new religious movement while myself and many like me call it a cult. Members of 3HO refer to themselves as Sikhs and/or kundalini yogis. 3HO issues forth spiritual monikers to anyone who wants one. They use the Sikh tradition of adding Singh (lion) and Kaur (princess) as middle names. For easier reading, I used first names as much as possible. A couple of names have been changed to accommodate anonymity requests.

Yogi Bhajan spoke in non-native English which is rendered faithfully here. Unusual syntax is not a typo, it accurately depicts the way he spoke.

Internal dialogue is in italics for clear differentiation. Journal entries are left unedited and have some typos.

Profanities abound. They authentically reflect what I heard and how we spoke.

Possible Trigger Warnings are hereby issued for some portions of this book. Please take good care of yourself while reading and be sure to get support if you need it.

Well I left my happy home
to see what I could find out
I left my folk and friends
with the aim to clear my mind out

~ Cat Stevens,
"On the Road to Find Out."

prologue

Floundering in the wake of a relentless series of stressful events—my husband's betrayal and our subsequent divorce; moving back home after thirty-five years; getting fired from my job and not being able to find work; and the death of my beloved King Charles Spaniel, Toby, I was in a desperate state about my life. Having invested financially for decades in new-age seminars, books, and healing sessions, my dismay lodged itself as a heavy lump in the center of my chest.

While I observed my contemporaries retiring, taking vacations around the world, and basking in newfound freedom, I was filled with consternation about the future. My father, who for decades watched my spiritual forays with skepticism and frustration, had recently bellowed unkindly into the phone, "You don't have a pot to piss in!" as I grumbled about the predicament I was in. As if that wasn't enough, he added, "You could very well end up being a bag lady, living in the gutter."

I didn't disagree with him and told him so. We got off the phone and I wept on my bed, curled up in a tight ball.

My future felt fucked, primarily because I had never given it any thought.

The chaos of my teenage years produced a young woman with a low sense of worth and little hope for what lay ahead. Searching for something to believe in, at some point I heard the new-age affirmation *things are always working out for me* and for decades, I clung to those words like a life raft. However, things weren't working out for me and with each passing year, my fears loomed larger. I was out of ideas and exhausted from the neverending, relentless struggle to survive.

After blowing through a box of tissues, I called my close friend, Lisa, for support. She listened as I shared my misery and grim conclusion that I didn't want to be on the planet anymore—a new-age euphemism for suicide. I had already tried looking up ways to kill myself. I searched the internet for what pill combination might do the trick and got endless page results for suicide hotlines. I searched for the precise timing of when to jump off a bridge to make sure an oncoming 18-wheeler would finish me off. Again, I got endless page results for suicide hotlines. I chuckled telling her how the internet did not cooperate as I contemplated various ways to off myself.

When I stopped talking, Lisa paused and then rather softly said, "Suz, why don't you pray on it?"

"Pray on it?" I complained, "I haven't prayed since I left the ashram over thirty years ago."

"Nonetheless," she said, undeterred, "why not pray on it?"

I value her friendship and advice to such a degree that I stopped resisting and considered her suggestion.

"What would that even look like anymore?" I said, becoming emotional at the absence of faith in my life.

"Well," Lisa suggested, "it might look like kneeling down at your bedside and talking about your circumstances."

Her suggestion didn't seem like too difficult a thing to do, so I promised her I'd give it a try. Before I got into bed that night, I knelt down and said a prayer. It went something like this:

Dear whoever,

I no longer feel relevant in my life. I have no plan for my future. I have no savings, no investments, no home, no health insurance, no money, no job, no husband, no children and no hope for any solution. I feel like a big fucking loser who fucked up her life and I feel like it's time for me to go.

I'd like to feel like it matters that I am alive. I'd like to feel relevant, like I have something meaningful to contribute, otherwise I don't see the point in being here anymore.

If you exist, and you can help, that would be great.

This was right before midnight on New Years Eve, 2019.

A few weeks later, a memoir titled *Premka: White Bird in a Golden Cage* by Pamela Saharah Dyson popped up in my social media feed. It chronicled her involvement with Yogi Bhajan and his Happy, Healthy, Holy Organization.

I'd also been involved with 3HO and lived in the same community in Los Angeles as Pamela. I read her book and contacted her. We reminisced about those days and the abuses of Yogi Bhajan. She had a Facebook page to promote her memoir and asked if she could hire me to manage it. I said yes.

Within weeks it became obvious that the page was morphing into something else. We already had a couple thousand members, but the focus had veered away from Pamela's book. Because of this, she suggested we delete the page as it wasn't giving her the results she wanted and she no longer wanted to pay to have it managed.

"Oh no, I definitely don't think we should do that," I replied.

Instead, I offered to assume sole responsibility for the page, saying, "Something is happening here, people are gathering to share their stories of abuse by Yogi Bhajan. This is important."

As a result, the page transformed into a private Facebook group called *Beyond the Cage: The 3HO | Yogi Bhajan | Kundalini Yoga Aftermath*. This newly focused group reached 6,000 members by summer.

Never before had I been a part of something this raw and dynamic. These were painful stories: women who were raped and sexually abused, followers who were brutalized on many levels and the second generation of children—born into 3HO or introduced to it at a young age—were sharing truly horrific accounts of abuse.

Those early days were unadulterated chaos. Huge divisive arguments, name-calling, accusations, denials, deep emotional upset and harmful communications were the norm.

This will sound strange, but for me, the unprecedented nature of this undertaking was exhilarating. There is nothing I love more than swimming in the deep waters of humanity, exploring what makes us tick and why.

The group was volatile. Raw. Real. Messy. Complicated. Heartbreaking. People wanted to share what had happened to them. They wanted to feel seen and heard.

Then, Covid hit.

I was unemployed and at home. For several years, I spent up to sixty hours a week dedicated to the group. By the end of the first year, I was contacted by four different production teams interested in making a documentary about Yogi Bhajan's cult. It was madness and unprecedented. It was a zeitgeist offshoot of the #metoo movement at a fever pitch.

Many people asked me, "How do you manage the group? It's

so intense!" Each time I was asked this, it perplexed me, because it was easy for me to manage the group. It was giving as much to me as I was giving to it. I felt needed, I felt I had something unique to contribute, and I felt relevant.

One might even go so far as to conclude that my prayer offering on New Year's Eve had been answered.

The ease of managing it intrigued me. Why was it easy? As I sat one evening enjoying a cup of Earl Grey tea it came to me: I am *really* good at chaos. Chaos has been a lifelong companion of mine. I can sit in the center of a raging hurricane of emotions and feel calm. In fact, I thought to myself, *I've been cavorting with chaos my entire life.*

This memoir tells the story of how the chaos and trauma of my childhood compelled me to find answers. Often I went looking in terrible places. It is a journey of reclamation, driven by my longing to experience the oneness I felt as a child.

Chaos:
Formless primordial matter,
the true foundation for reality.

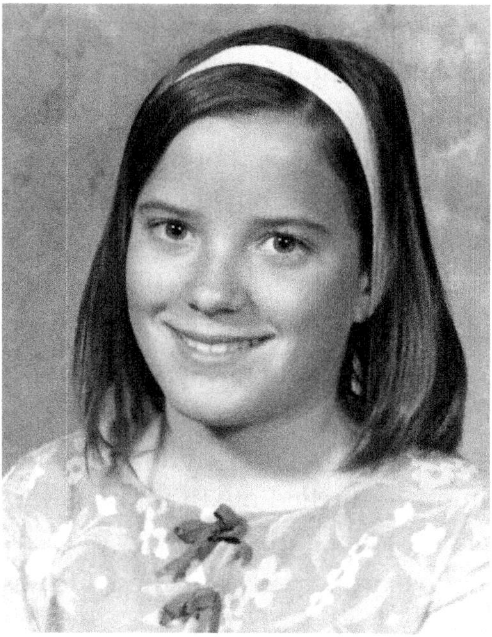

My 6th grade picture from Christ the King School in Richland, Washington. Still full of wonder.

1
awakening

Wonder was the vast and edgeless playground I frolicked in as a child, a kind of placeholder for questions neither parent nor religion could answer. It nurtured my sensuality and held my memories close until I was old enough to use language to ponder them. When I was fifteen, this innate conduit was severed. My natural elation and innocence were obliterated and the course of my life was irrevocably altered.

However, on this first day of my story in 1971, I am an excited eleven-year-old girl, returning to summer camp. Ten precious days of uninterrupted fun lay ahead. Each day would be a flurry of arts and crafts, horseback riding, swimming, archery, singing and bedtime ghost stories. All was promised to "be enjoyed in a Christian atmosphere" in the Catholic Youth Organization camp advertisement. Father O'Grady's Sunday mass was mandatory.

Nothing in the advertisement indicated the promise of a peak experience in consciousness. Psychologist Abraham Maslow prolixly defined this as "rare, exciting, oceanic, deeply moving, exhilarating, elevating experiences that generate an advanced form of perceiving reality."

Likewise, the ad did not hint at the convergence of my youthful wonderment with the unripe sexuality of the teenaged camp counselors with whom I would soon be smitten.

Nestled near the quaint Bavarian-style village of Leavenworth, Washington, Camp Field welcomed approximately one-hundred girls for each of the three 10-day sessions during the summer.

As soon as camp ended the year before, I pleaded with my parents to let me return. It was my younger brother Tommy's turn to go, but as luck would have it, he wasn't interested. Thus, my parents said yes. My father required payment, however, so I promised to weed around the base of the twenty evergreen trees lining our property all year to earn the forty-three dollar tuition.

All those months on my knees, pulling weeds among the roly-polies and earwigs were worth it as my friends and I waited for the bus in the school parking lot. I had just completed the sixth grade. My heart was hopscotching beats as I swayed back and forth in anticipation.

My first time at Camp Field, I was injured. I ignored a camp rule by running on the wooden deck of our lodge without shoes on. A splintered board drove a four-inch fragment deep into the sole of my left foot. An emergency trip to the hospital resulted in a painful extraction. For the remainder of camp, I struggled with crutches and a plastic bag tied over my foot so I could attend swim class.

That year, when honor certificates were given out at the end of camp, mine read THE BEST CRIPPLE, which was meant to be humorous, but having my injury singled out as the thing that was significant about me felt awful. I envied the other girls whose certificates featured "best storyteller," "best runner," and "best smile" epithets.

This year will be different, I told myself; because I would mind the rules. When the bus rattled into the parking lot at noon, I was tingling with excitement.

After we boarded, a bubbly counselor stood in the aisle to teach us traditional camp songs. We made multiple stops, picking up more campers and counselors at each location. After what seemed like an eternity, we finally arrived and were separated into lodges based on our age. The lodges had names taken from various indigenous languages: Waconda, Chiwaukum, Okanogan, Tamanawas, and Kamiakin. My friends and I were in The Okanogan Lodge and our counselors' names were Gail and Gayla.

We had an orientation, created our own lodge song and went to dinner. It was after dusk as we made our way back to the lodge. Each log cabin had two rows of ten bunk beds neatly spaced, with a small separate bunk room for the counselors. I lucked out and got a top bunk and climbed into bed. The day's excitement wore me out and I quickly fell fast asleep.

The next morning at dawn, the sound of a bugle playing reveille filled the air. The sky was gunmetal gray as we swiftly dressed and gathered in a big meadow. The cold, misty air was heavy on my skin, sending chills through me as we formed an enormous circle. We held hands and whispered excitedly to one another. My hands were being squeezed at rapid intervals and I squeezed back.

We quieted down when we heard the distinct low hum of an amplifier being turned on, followed by the scratchy sound of a needle being placed on vinyl.

As the first slivers of sunlight streamed over the mountain, Cat Stevens' "Morning Has Broken" began to play. His sonorous voice moved throughout the silence in concert with the sunrise, as filaments of light spread over us, making me feel holy. The inspirational, old Scottish hymn Cat Stevens put to his own music celebrated the dawn of a new day. It was an exquisite pairing of nature and music. Goosebumps cascaded up and down my spine.

Then, the needle lifted as another record was placed on the turntable. This time, the silence yielded to an African choir of children singing "Childsong" from Neil Diamond's *Tap Root Manuscript* album: "Weeping sky, we bring the sun, to make you glad and fill you with the day..."

The music had thunder and rain in the background blending with the sound of young children sweetly singing. Something ineffable stirred in me. Their innocent voices grabbed my heart.

I became still and stopped squeezing the hands of those on either side of me. Everything I looked upon became crisper and shimmered with life. The sun was gaining strength, illuminating the layer of dew that covered the plants, grass and trees.

The music filled me with longing. A beautiful sadness welled up in my eyes, producing huge tears that tumbled down my cheeks, soaking the collar of my sweatshirt.

I was in a state of oneness.

Little did I know, I was having a peak experience. My body was tingling from head to toe. I felt I was barely touching the ground. I was out of ordinary time, touching a piece of forever. I couldn't tell you how long it lasted, only that as the goosebumps and acuity began to subside, I told myself: *Whatever that was, remember this feeling.*

When the song ended, we all clapped and shouted with joy. Those precious moments of heightened awareness remained vivid in my mind as years passed and would heavily influence my choices as I got older.

That summer proved to be significant in unexpected ways. A new kind of sensuality emerged amid the playfulness of camp life and demanded my attention. Within days of arriving, I had crushes on both a female and male counselor.

Our counselors were recent high school graduates. Gail was what my grandpa would call a salt of the earth person, hale and hearty. Her personality radiated through her rosy-cheeked smile and caring manner. The animated way she expressed herself caused her long, golden brown hair to sway across her back and over her shoulders. She was warm and outgoing, with a touch of shyness.

I was utterly taken with her.

Whenever she passed by, the honeyed-scent of frangipani oil lingered behind her. The fragrance made me swoon as I subtly tried to take deep breaths without being noticed. I wanted to be like Gail in every way and felt impatient to grow up.

Few men were present during the girls' sessions. Two were prominent to me; Father O'Grady, Camp Field's director, and Dallas, an artistic, jack-of-all-trades handyman and stablehand who took us on horseback rides.

Dallas had presence, and not just because he was tall and beautiful, with curly, shoulder-length hair. He had a twinkle you couldn't put your finger on, something winsome and familiar. He announced himself with an earthy scent, no doubt from time spent in the stables. Along with Gail, he made my heart flutter like it had grown wings.

Camp was organized around inspections and awards. Each morning the lodges were rated on their cleanliness. We competed to win daily Honor Flags for the best job done.

Besides our three meals in the mess hall, if our parents allocated money for the Canteen, we could get snacks between meals. The food was good and we always had freckle cake (vanilla cake with sprinkles) for dessert.

The abundance of food and the option for a second helping was notable and not always the case at home. Providing for six children was a constant challenge for my parents. Generally speaking, we were served one plate of food and that was it. Perhaps because of this, while I was at camp, I ate more than I needed to on more than one occasion and felt sick afterwards.

Once we finished dinner we'd make a short trek to a campfire pit and climb the semi-circle of wooden bleachers surrounding it. In the pop and glow of the fire, we'd sing camp songs. The counselors took turns leading; some a cappella and some with their guitars. I loved being in the night air, looking up at the sea of stars amid the warmth of the campfire. I felt I belonged in this gathering of loving people.

This feeling of camaraderie was something I wanted to experience at home, but home was often hectic and always competitive. We were six kids vying for attention from parents worn thin from exertion.

After the campfire, when we were cozy in our bunks, Gail would tell horror stories designed to scare the crap out of us.

The best and absolute worst one was a story about a young nurse named Betsy who was working the evening shift at the local hospital in Leavenworth, many, many years ago. Her co-workers played a hideous prank on her, a prank that went terribly wrong. Gail masterfully told the story, modulating her voice for dramatic effect as she slowly began speaking to her riveted audience:

> "Betsy's co-workers had a severed arm from a fresh corpse, a woman who died in a car accident," she began,

already eliciting groans, "and they rigged it to hang from the pull-chain of the light in the medicine closet. Later that night, one of them asked Betsy to retrieve some medicine. The unsuspecting nurse went into the closet and grabbed the chain, giving it a yank."

"As the light came on, she realized it was a human hand that she had grabbed onto. Legend has it that the hand grabbed her back! Betsy shrieked in terror."

"Instantly, she went insane and her hair turned white at that precise moment, from pure shock. The poor nurse ran screaming from the hospital with the grotesque arm locked in the grip of her hand. In fact, the arm never let go of her."

"Betsy has lived in these mountains around Camp Field ever since that fateful, dreadful day. She's only been seen once or twice in all those years, as she sometimes scavenges for food in the area.

Who knows, maybe tonight will be the night we see Betsy once again..."

Gail's voice trailed off as she paused for dramatic effect. Invariably, at this point of the story, a sickening, perfectly planned, maniacal scream from outside our windows would jolt us out of our rapt attention as we all screamed in response, jumping out of our skin.

This made Gail and Gayla laugh and laugh, until Gail finished the story saying matter of factly, "Good night now, campers, sweet dreams!"

Notwithstanding the psychological damage of the ghost stories, it was the most spectacular place. I wished I could spend the entire summer there.

One night, when Gail and Gayla were at a meeting, a few of us sneaked off to the baseball field adjacent to the riding ring. A game of truth or dare was in progress and I had boldly (or stupidly) accepted a dare to run across the field in my underwear. There was no moon that night to light the way. The pitch black made it impossible to see what was in front of me.

A dare is a dare, I thought as I began to undress. First I took off my long-sleeved shirt and then unzipped my pants, letting them fall around my ankles. I was about to slip off my shoes when, without warning, a huge flood light came on. I was caught.

Instinctively, I crouched low, sitting on my heels to cover myself, when a man's voice yelled, "Hey! What the heck are you girls doing out this late at night?"

It was none other than Dallas.

Someone shouted, "We're playing truth or dare!" which made us all giggle nervously.

"What's the dare?" Dallas gamely inquired.

"Suzy has to run across the field in her underwear!" the gaggle of girls cried out.

There was a hefty delay as we all waited for Dallas to respond. Then he humorously exclaimed, "I've got news for you girls. Suzy will likely break her dang neck in the attempt! C'mon now, time to go back to your lodge."

Then he directed himself to me, "Suzy? Can you please put your clothes back on?"

He was far across the field, but the fact that Dallas was focused on me for that brief instant while I was half-dressed was incredibly thrilling. I did as I was told, secretly hoping he was watching me, and was thus spared a broken neck.

Back in bed, I was buzzing from our momentary interaction. This buzzing feeling continued to happen. Sometimes it was stirred up by Dallas and sometimes it was stirred up by Gail. I didn't question how I was feeling because it felt good and natural. At long last, what had previously been lavished onto a poster of David Cassidy above my bed (until his lips were gone and bare wall took their place) was now a real sensation.

Every evening when the lights went out, I could drift in the pleasure of when I'd be old enough to be kissed. Watching the flirtations between the counselors was also arousing, adding a new kind of sensual awareness I hadn't experienced before.

The glorious ten days of camp were going by way too fast. I wanted to put the brakes on to prolong my enjoyment with my friends. Flat out, I didn't want to go home. I loved being there by myself, not feeling lost in the shuffle of my siblings. It was also freeing to be out of the shadow of my older sister, Kris, who I felt was my father's favorite.

On the last day of camp, an award ceremony was held during the evening campfire. Incredibly, Okanogan won Best Lodge of the session. We went crazy realizing we had somehow beat the older girls. Then, to my astonishment, I heard Gail call my name when she announced the winner of the honor camper award for Okanogan. I tried to hold back my tears. Next, she called my name again as the winner of honor camper for the whole session.

On top of that, myself and the other lodge winners were inducted into something called The Order of the Cross, allowing us to enter a sacred labyrinth that led to a prayer circle. We were given lanyards with a CYO medallion backed by leather and trimmed with nylon braiding. Gail signed the back of mine.

Receiving this kind of attention was overwhelming and deeply moving. In an attempt to conceal my emotions, I covered my mouth with my right hand. As Gail presented the awards to me, she said they were given in recognition of my leadership

Receiving my award from Gail, my counselor at Camp Field in 1970. Leavenworth, Washington.

skills and for being an inspiration to my campmates. My left arm was around Gail, grasping her navy peacoat to steady myself. It was a momentous, unforgettable experience that made leaving so much harder to bear.

The next morning I moved slowly, packing with a heavy heart. When it came time to board, everyone was smiling and looking forward to going home except me. I was crying inconsolably. My friends asked why I was so upset. I told them, "I don't ever want to leave this place," knowing they didn't understand how I felt.

Gail did her best to console me.

It's fair to say my feelings were disproportionate to what was happening. I was embarrassed at the spectacle I was making, especially since it was obvious no one understood why I was so distraught. Honestly, I didn't really understand it myself, except that I knew camp had given me something I didn't want to lose. Buckets of sadness were pouring out of me.

Gail hugged me tight and suggested we become pen pals. She wrote her address in my Camp Field songbook which cheered me up a bit. At least I could stay connected to her until next summer.

Boarding last, I was morose and weepy as we made our way back to Richland. When we arrived, I saw Grandpa Doug waiting for me. I was happy to see him, but it didn't alter the huge loss I felt stepping away from the magic I had experienced at camp. Little did I know, my sadness was about to worsen exponentially.

Within days of being home, my parents gathered us kids in the living room and announced terrible news—we were leaving Richland to move back to Reno. The reason given was that my mother missed her friends. After three unhappy years, she convinced my father to return to Nevada. What's more, they told us cheerily, "as luck would have it" the people who purchased our old house were willing to sell it back to us. We were returning to the same home in the same neighborhood.

Of course, there were issues going on that weren't discussed, related to the fights my parents had and my father's awful temper. This offered explanation, however, placed the blame squarely on my mother's shoulders.

The soaring heights of my summer plummeted to the ground. My parents' decision destroyed the life I thought I was going to have in Richland. The unfairness of it all was a harsh pill to swallow. I angrily told my parents, "You are ruining everything! I will not leave here. I swear to god I will run away."

I could not fathom leaving Richland and Camp Field forever.

Though I was young, I was aware that our life in Richland was better than it had ever been. We moved to Richland in 1968, when my father was hired as the Regional Director for Evelyn

Wood's *Reading Dynamics*, a speed reading course.

After briefly living in a rental, my parents purchased our brand new four-bedroom, Spanish-style ranch house. They staggered their down payment based on upcoming bonuses promised to my father by his boss.

She reneged on every promise she had made.

As a result, my mother had to find work. She secured a job as a travel agent, while my father left Reading Dynamics and was hired as an agent with Northwestern Mutual Life Insurance. With both of them working full time, my maternal grandparents, Doug and Alice, left Milwaukee to live with us and help with child care.

The first time we saw our new home we went nuts, running through the house at full speed. Everything was brand-spanking new. Most of the house was carpeted in speckled avocado-green shag, except for the kitchen, which had patterned linoleum.

The master bedroom, living room and formal dining room were in the front of the house on either side of a spacious foyer, which led to an open kitchen with avocado-green appliances and a family room. Our bedrooms were on the far side of the family room, conveniently providing my parents a kid-zone buffer.

Kris got her own room, the one with bright, hot-pink shag carpet. The largest room went to the three boys, Mike, Tommy and Pete. The third room was for me and my younger sister Meg. The formal dining area became a makeshift bedroom to accommodate my grandparents, with a three-panel screen for privacy.

The property was not landscaped, which prompted my dad to purchase a rotor-tiller. We spent months following behind him, picking up all the big rocks he unearthed. This created "the rock pile" which grew to about fifteen feet long and three feet high. I always felt proud looking at it, knowing our little hands removed each and every one of those rocks. Dad landscaped the yard beautifully. We had a stunning home I was proud to live in.

Another indicator of our increased fortune was having four cars: a Volkswagen Beetle, a banana yellow Ford station wagon, an atomic blue '64 Plymouth Belvedere station wagon and a black '57 convertible Thunderbird we named *The Batmobile.*

Our home was adjacent to the Hanford Site, home of the nuclear reactors that produced plutonium for the Fat Man bomb dropped on Nagasaki during World War II. My father was enthusiastic about the wonders and uses of nuclear energy and had no concerns about living next to the site which still had one active reactor in use. Kris and I used to sneak onto their tennis courts to hit balls. We always wondered why there were signs that read PLAY AT YOUR OWN RISK.

The Columbia River was three blocks from our home. We swam in the strong currents and picked loads of asparagus along its banks. The annual hydroplane races provided dramatic entertainment while I collected autographs from the drivers.

My first close friend, Lisa, lived diagonally behind our home. Lisa's ancestors hailed from Norway. I'd never seen anyone with such thick, long, white-blond hair that blazed in the sun along with her pretty blue eyes. We spent hours listening to The Osmond Brothers, David Cassidy and Bobby Sherman and enjoyed adding to our stamp collections and doing jigsaw puzzles together. I was terribly sad to be saying goodbye to her.

Unfortunately, none of this mattered to my mom and dad. The impotence of being a child absolutely infuriated me.

I wrote to Gail, pouring my feelings onto the stationery, blurring what I wrote as my tears created wrinkles in the paper.

I had been dreaming of the day when I would be old enough to be a counselor at Camp Field and imagined myself spending many years there. Gail must've sensed how frantic I was to find a solution because she wrote back right away.

I couldn't open her letter fast enough. Gail commiserated with me but also voiced the unavoidable reality—I had to obey this course of action my parents had chosen. The words she wrote echoed in my mind, complete with Cecil B. DeMille's god-voice from *The Ten Commandments*—Honor Thy Mother and Father, citing the 5th commandment.

It was generous of her to respond. She was a young woman in college, yet still took the time to counsel and comfort me. Gail cautioned me against doing anything rash, suggesting I could, perhaps, still find a way to return to camp next year. "Focus on that," Gail wrote, "and time will fly by. You'll be back at camp in no time."

Her words worked like a miracle, calming me down. I began thinking of how to persuade my father to let me attend next year. Gail was right: the wretched fact was we were moving and I simply had no choice in the matter. With an aching heart, I said my tearful good-byes to Lisa, Gail, the Columbia River, my school and our beautiful home.

My grandparents decided to return to Milwaukee. Grandma Alice missed her family and wanted to go home. More sadness consumed me.

My father strategically packed the Plymouth to create a corridor in the back of the car which allowed one kid to lie down to sleep. In addition to us kids, we had our cockapoo, Samson; a mouse Kris dubbed Mrs. Mike; and a nameless horny toad, all in separate cages. Mom would drive the Plymouth, pulling a U-Haul trailer behind her, while dad drove a big U-Haul truck. He tied our battered aluminum garbage cans, stuffed full of small tools and hoses, onto the back of the truck. All last-minute items were crammed into every possible nook and cranny.

Long road trips were a staple in our family ever since we moved from Milwaukee to Reno. We usually couldn't afford to stay in motels, so customarily my father drove through the night, taking short naps when necessary.

I have wonderful sensory recollections of those cross-country journeys—especially waking in the middle of the night as my dad pulled into a gas station. While the filling station attendant pumped the gas, the fumes would fill the car and I'd take a deep breath, enjoying the smell of it. I loved the dreamy neon lights of the motels on the main street of nearly every town across America in the sixties and seventies. Brilliant lights and the pungent smell of gasoline mingled in my sleepy head, along with the exhilaration of being on the road, to forge the best kind of nomadic memories.

My father loved to make our drives educational, pointing out a herd of deer emerging from a thicket, or geological tidbits like sedimentary rock formations and fault lines or water lines from thousands of years ago. My mother was an excellent navigator, always in charge of the map and our next food stop.

It boggles my mind to think about how my folks managed to travel long distances with six kids on so little money. Occasionally, my mom would negotiate a motel room for as little as six or seven dollars, giving us the chance to take baths. Breakfast was typically eaten at a park on our way out of town. We wolfed down powdered sugar doughnuts and milk, or those individual boxed cereals that opened so you could pour your milk right into it.

Our favorite and biggest meal splurge, bar none, was dinner at an A&W drive-in. It was a rare indulgence to have a hamburger and fries with a root beer float in a frosty glass mug. This was road trip bliss.

Dad had a careless habit of running low on gas. It didn't help that the gas gauge on the Plymouth was broken. He either didn't pay attention or thought he could accurately guess when we needed to fill up. More than once we were stranded on the side of the road while dad hitched a ride to the nearest gas station. He seemed to love the gamble of it. On any hill descent, he'd put the car in neutral and holler, "We're coasting on fumes, kids!" It was a devil-may-care attitude for a father of six and it always made me a wreck.

When our dreadful last day in Richland arrived, I sat in my empty room wishing I could grab the reins of time and hold them still. As soon as the vehicles were loaded, dad announced that it was time to hit the road. I bawled my eyes out watching Lisa wave her goodbyes as we drove away in our ramshackle caravan.

Grandma and Grandpa loved to tell a story from that day when they stopped to get a bite at a burger stand, planning to catch up with us down the road. Another couple joined them at their picnic table. Before they even sat down, the woman exclaimed, "Holy smokes, did you see the poor family of vagabonds go by with the garbage cans and whatnot clanging off the back of the U-Haul truck? Goodness sakes alive, what a sight to see!"

"Yes, we did," my steely-eyed grandmother replied flatly. "That was my daughter and her family."

My grandparents followed us until the Jordan Valley in Oregon, before heading east for Milwaukee.

It was dark when we finally turned onto our old street, Everett Drive. My mother's face lit up when she spotted half a dozen neighbors outside waiting to greet us, waving and shouting their hellos. The men pitched in, unloading the truck, taking care to set up all our beds as a priority, while the women had dinner ready.

This was what my mother had missed: these people, in this

place. She was in heaven reuniting with her best friend, Lois. Even I had to admit, it was a warm and much appreciated welcome.

My parents were friendly with four families on Everett Drive; the Hansens, the Barelas, the Sourwines and the Brauns. There were seventeen kids among the families until the Brauns tragically lost their twelve-year-old son, Karl, in a dune buggy accident a year after we moved to Richland. We drove to Reno for a visit within weeks of Karl's death and grieved over the terrible loss.

Now that we were back, we took advantage of the little bit of summer that remained and gathered for barbecues, played tag in the street past dark, and went camping at Pyramid Lake on the Paiute Indian Reservation north of Reno. The Brauns, Barelas, and Sourwines all had speed boats which ran all day to give everyone a chance to water-ski or inner tube.

My father taught me to water-ski when I was seven by holding me and my skis on top of the water until Mr. Barela punched it and I jerked forward, somehow managing not to fall. I loved gliding over the water with the wind in my hair.

When summer ended, the adults began to have Saturday night cocktail parties. They rotated whose home the party convened at and gathered all their children at another house. The oldest child present, usually Kris, was put in charge. If we needed help, one of us would head to the party to find the appropriate parent. The house full of kids was a rowdy, hard to manage scene as there were far too many children for Kris, or anyone, to adequately watch.

Having gone several times, it was wild to witness our parents in various stages of drunkenness. In this setting, I rarely saw anyone dancing with their own spouse, except the Hansens. The others were entangled with light-hearted flirtations, draped over one another in the kind of permission that alcohol affords.

My 8th grade picture from St. Albert the Great Catholic School in Reno, Nevada.

2

forgetting

Most of my memories attending St. Albert the Great school were unpleasant. These experiences were on my mind as I returned for my first day of seventh grade. I said hello to a few old friends, including Colleen O'Gara, the person I most remembered from before. Her cute cousin, Sam, was in our class as well. Mike was also happily greeting old friends. We smiled at each other as the bell rang, as a way to say "Good Luck!"

Our teacher, Sister Rosario, was a short, plump woman with a face built for scrutiny. Her sharp eyes and pointy nose had an insistence about them that was unnerving, even behind the green-tinted glasses that never left her face. Heavy black robes and a long black veil added to her domineering presence. She wore a rosary with a huge wooden cross around her waist that dangled and swayed rhythmically as she walked.

During the year, I would be in trouble so frequently I became familiar with every broken capillary in her ruddy complexion.

The nuns at St. Albert's hailed from a Cuban order, The Sisters of St. Philip Neri. In the first grade, I remember seeing "The Singing Nun," starring Debbie Reynolds. She was joyful and kind, unlike the nuns at St. Albert's. Inspired by the film, I even thought I might become a nun one day.

As the year progressed, a battle was waged regarding the length of the girls' uniforms. When we kneeled, the hem of our dress had to graze the floor. The uniforms consisted of a sailor top over a sleeveless slip dress with a pleated sailcloth skirt. A red and white striped dickie snapped into the v-neck, resting behind a long red tie. Why we needed to look like sailors in the Nevada desert was beyond me. We devised ways to hike up our hemlines by folding the top of the slip a few times and fastening it with safety pins. One day, Sister Rosario shoved her hand under my sailor top, groping me as she felt for evidence.

"Hey, what the heck?" I exclaimed.

She ignored me, acting like it was the most natural thing in the world to fish around underneath my clothing. As my classmates watched, Sister Rosario smiled triumphantly, removing the pins on both sides of my uniform. While she manhandled me, I saw my classmates hastily removing their pins.

Then the punishment came. She announced in her Cuban accent, "Young lady, you will spend your weekend writing out *The Constitution of the United States.* I want it on my desk, first thing Monday morning."

The nuns were determined to squelch our natural sexuality and we were hell bent to defy them.

I had recently started babysitting. It was a great time to make phone calls because no one else needed to use the phone. I called Colleen and we got to talking about my crush on her cousin, Sam.

"I wish he wasn't so shy," I complained. "I don't even know if he likes me back."

"Well, you know, Dawn likes him too," she taunted.

"Really?" I said. "No, I didn't know."

"I'm sure he prefers you to her," Colleen volunteered. "You're way cuter."

"Really? Dawn is taller than me and has blond hair," I fretted.

"Really, Suzy," she said encouragingly, "it's no contest."

"Well," I said, thinking about it some more, "she does have a pretty big nose."

No sooner had I said it when Dawn's voice came on the other end. "You're so two-faced, Suzy!" she declared. "I hate you!" She'd been listening on the extension line all along.

I could hear the laughter of a number of girls in the background as they hung up the phone.

Dropping the receiver, I was momentarily paralyzed and equally thunderstruck at how easily Colleen was able to goad me into saying something unkind about Dawn. Even more upsetting was that this was a planned prank and I fell for it.

In the morning, I told my mother about the phone call and how I was tricked by someone I thought was my friend. I begged her to let me stay home.

"Oh no, you're going to school, that's final," she replied.

"But mom, *please, please,*" I pleaded, "this will be the worst day of my life!"

"This will be a tough lesson for you, honey," she said, "but gossip is never a good thing. Unfortunately, you're learning this the hard way."

It bummed me out to know she was disappointed in me. Then she uttered one of my parents' favorite refrains:

"You made your bed and now you have to lie in it."

When I told Mike what happened he comforted me, saying, "Don't worry about it, Suzy, you won't be alone. I'll be there."

Never had I been so grateful that we were in the same grade. It helped to know that at least I had Mike in my corner.

I spotted my enemies as soon as we walked onto the school grounds—all the girls in my class were whispering in a huddle with Colleen commandeering the platoon.

"Good luck, Suzy," Mike said, patting me on the back before joining his friends.

I walked near where they were gathered, but no one looked up or spoke to me. I turned away so they couldn't see me tearing up. I was angry and felt stupid that I didn't sense what they were up to. Their mean phone call and my lack of discretion had cost me all of my friends, making me an outcast.

One brave girl broke ranks, walking over to comfort me. Her name was Rita. She told me she thought what Colleen and Dawn did was wrong. She said she'd be happy to be my friend and I gratefully accepted.

In the meantime, Mike told all the boys what went down and they decided to confront Colleen and Dawn, telling them it was a rotten trick to play on someone. None of them spoke to me, but it felt incredible to have them rally on my side.

Rita became my best friend and the kerfuffle died down. I managed to survive the move and seventh grade—brutal as it was— and before I knew it, summer was nearly here.

Gail and I corresponded all year as I kept her up to date with my life in Reno. When I petitioned my parents to go back to camp, they said yes. I was ecstatic knowing I'd be back where I belonged. Everything would feel perfect again.

I floated along on that sentiment, but would soon discover my optimistic expectations were sadly naive. It was shocking what a difference one year had made. Before I even boarded the bus, it was apparent my old friends had no interest in me.

In fairness, I hadn't written a single letter to any of them during my year away. I'd only written to Gail. Why did I think they would all still feel close to me?

After a challenging year at St. Albert's, I was emotional about being back at camp and didn't realize how much I had riding on my ten days there. I desperately wanted to recapture the magic of the prior year. What originally stemmed from natural ebullience the year before was now forced and strained. I was performing and it did not land well with anyone.

Two once close friends were blunt, calling me a brown-noser who just wanted to win more awards. Their criticism landed hard because they were absolutely right.

Most upsetting, I didn't feel the same rapport with Gail either. My experience could not have been more dissimilar from what I had imagined. I would never go back to Camp Field. I even stopped writing to Gail. It was an awful, awful disappointment.

It took some time for me to realize there was a silver lining to this. The letdown of camp helped me finally stop pining for my life in Washington.

Back in Reno, summer ended, classes began, and my focus shifted away from the past.

I wanted to be a cheerleader. Kris had been head cheerleader the year before and was helping me choreograph a routine for tryouts. Tryouts were a straightforward popularity contest. Each girl performed her cheer for the seventh and eighth grade boys, who then voted to fill five positions. The girl who received the most votes became the head cheerleader.

When the day came, we all stood on the black pavement that was our recess area. Butterflies swirled in the pit of my stomach as I watched the boys gather to judge us. Luckily, I didn't have to go first and was able to gain some confidence watching others do their routines. Thanks to Kris, my cheer was better than average. Smiling broadly at the boys, I gave it my all. Within an hour, the winners were announced and to my delight, I made the squad.

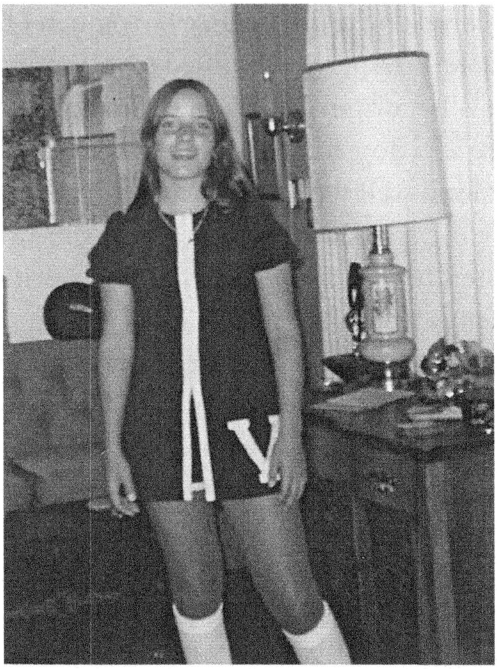

In my cheerleader uniform at Grandpa's home in 1972.

Later that day, I was stunned when Mike informed me I had received the most votes of all the girls. The nuns decided to give Colleen the title of head cheerleader. Mike overheard them say they couldn't possibly award me, when our parents were behind in their tuition payments.

I resented the nuns for their dishonesty and I resented that Colleen was riding high, thinking she had the most votes, but I didn't dare speak my mind. I didn't want to bring attention to my family's shortcomings.

This would be the first of numerous prejudices and slights my siblings and I suffered as parishioners in the Catholic diocese of Reno. This discriminatory pattern continued in high school as both priests and nuns shamed children for their parents' financial circumstances.

Eighth grade was the year pressure to go steady became a thing. At Christmas, Kris, Mike and I were singing in the church choir. I felt pretty in a new red velvet skirt and white button-down blouse, and my first pair of platform shoes with a two-inch heel. Even though I was young for my class, I was feeling quite grown up at twelve years old.

We filed onto the bleachers set up near the altar. I loved Christmas carols and memorized most of the words to the songs we were singing.

As soon as the program ended, Kris grabbed my hand, pulling me through the crowd into the school hallway. With a sense of urgency, she said, "Gordy is outside waiting for you. Didn't you know it's make-out week?"

"Wait, what?" I stammered, confused. "We've been going steady for two days! What is make-out week?"

"It means you have to make-out before the week is up. That means today," she enlightened me.

No one told me about this. I was trying to make sense of what she was saying, when she shoved a Chapstick in my hand and pulled me toward the double doors where Gordy was waiting. I smeared the balm on my lips as Kris pushed me out the door.

Shivering in the cold, I barely made out a figure wobbling in the dark, moving unsteadily toward me.

"Hey Gordy," I weakly managed to say. The smell of hard liquor preceded him as he moved closer, making me nauseous. He smelled like my parents' cocktail parties. Gordy was obviously drunk. I'd never seen anyone my age plastered. I didn't know what to do.

Gordy stumbled, then fell in the direction of my face. His lips collided with mine so hard, his front teeth broke the skin of my upper lip. His tongue rudely forced my lips apart. It was coated and slimy and tasted disgusting. Repulsed, I moved to get away from him, but his weight was pressing on me and my back was pinned to the door. I managed to swing my head to the side as his slobbery, open mouth slid over my cheeks and off my face, leaving a repulsive wake of saliva behind.

"See, that wasn't so bad, was it?" he moaned.

"Oh no," I said, lying through my teeth, "not bad at all."

Wanting to escape, I said, "Listen Gordy, I have to go, my parents are going to be wondering where I am."

I didn't wait for his reply. I spun around, wrestled the door open and ran like hell down the corridor back to the church. Fortunately, I wouldn't have to see Gordy again until after Christmas vacation. Wanting to avoid him altogether, I asked Mike to tell him it was over between us. Mike delivered my message and let me know Gordy was pissed off about it.

My first kiss was a disaster, and there were several more fiascos after that. Through it all, I only had eyes for skinny, freckled Sam with the bowl-cut who never paid any attention to me.

In the spring, our class began playing co-ed softball during our lunch recess. An ongoing topic of debate was who would win *The Battle of the Sexes* tennis match between Billie Jean King and Bobby Riggs. It became a way to flirt as we demonstrated our bravado about who would come out on top. Softball became an excuse for plenty of teasing and brief moments where we could get away with touching one another during the game. It got so we couldn't wait for the lunch bell to ring.

When it came time for graduation, our class of thirteen students had a short ceremony to receive our diplomas before we hurried into our casual clothes for an epic game of water-balloon chase.

That evening, Dawn Burkett's parents hosted a graduation party. My mother bought me the prettiest sunshine-yellow mini dress with big cream-colored puff sleeves. When Sam asked me to slow dance to Bread's "Make It With You" I was overjoyed. I rested my head on his chest, smelling Old Spice coming through his shirt. This tender dance, sadly, was the one time we ever made contact, but it was enough to send me soaring into summer.

Good news arrived in the form of my grandparents, who decided to move to Reno after a short time back in Milwaukee. It was lovely to have my grandpa back, though it was obvious my grandma was unhappy about the move.

That summer, Rita's home became a favorite hangout because it had a separate apartment in the basement where we didn't have to worry about her parents barging in on us.

One evening, Rita invited me and our friend, Joanne, over for pizza. She told us she had started her period and produced an enormous sanitary napkin her mother had given her. Her mama must've saved it from the fifties. We couldn't help but laugh at the monstrous thing.

"Why aren't you using tampons?" I asked her.

"My mother won't let me," she said, looking at the floor. Rita's mother was Honduran and her father was Puerto Rican. They were old-fashioned and a decade older than our parents.

"I have a tampon in my bag," Joanne offered. "Do you wanna give it a try?"

"Uh, I don't know," Rita said, "I'm not even sure how to do it."

Wanting to help, I put one leg on the coffee table to demonstrate the forty-five degree angle I'd learned from the instructions on the Tampax box. I confidently indicated how to glide the tampon in, aiming for the small of the back.

"It's not hard to do, promise," I assured her.

Reluctantly, and probably due to peer pressure, Rita went into the bathroom while we hovered outside the door.

We heard grunting from her efforts before she called out,

"Hey guys? I don't think I'm doing this correctly!"

"You can do it," we chanted.

"Use the forty-five degree angle!" I pitched in.

"Uhhh, ugh, I'm trying…" she replied.

We heard more grunting, followed by a big thud.

"Hey, Rita?" we shouted. "You okay?"

No reply.

"Rita?"

Nothing. Not a peep.

"I think maybe she fainted," I said to Joanne. "C'mon, help me get the door open."

The problem was Rita's body was blocking the door. Joanne and I body-slammed the door repeatedly until it was open enough for me to stick my head in to see what was going on.

There was poor Rita, passed out on the floor, her panties and pants around her ankles. The tampon was partly jammed in her butthole.

We nearly pissed ourselves laughing. When she came to, we screamed, "You put it in the wrong hole!"

We didn't bring up using tampons again.

Around this time, a new family moved into the neighborhood, the Carlsons. In no time at all, my mom developed a friendship with Mrs. Carlson, who was ten years her junior. They sat at our milk glass ice cream table for hours, smoking cigarettes, talking and drinking pink chablis. In no time at all, the Carlson's were added to the cocktail party mix.

My grandparents were often around when the weekend party was revving up. My grandma couldn't stomach it and freely expressed her disdain regarding the loose scene happening on Everett Drive. She rendered an astute observation, prophetically warning my mother: "Mark my words, Mary, this neighborhood will come to ruin."

"Adolescence is like having only enough light to see the step directly in front of you."

~ Sarah Addison Allen
The Girl Who Chased the Moon

3
riled up

Nothing in my childhood was as heavenly as the carefree, time-bending days of summer. In 1973, an innocence and charm seemed to sweeten the air I breathed as I enjoyed the precious in-between days before high school. My hopeless longing for Sam persisted as I dreamed of being kissed by him one fine day.

At last, I was content living in Reno. After months of playing softball at school, word spread about a non-profit softball league for girls called Miss Softball America. Kris and I and a bunch of our friends registered to play.

Our coach, Ron, was determined to have a winning team. We had long practices to sharpen our skills. Kris was assigned to play first base and I played second. We all got along well and achieved a great balance of fun and dedication at our practices and games.

The camaraderie was wonderful, it reminded me of camp. Kris and I were a dynamic duo and ended up having the most double plays in our league. At the end of the season, an all-star team would be chosen to attend the National Tournament in California. When our team won the title for Northwest Reno, we had high expectations that a number of us would make the all-stars.

There was a stand-out player I noticed from another team named Becky. Expecting we'd both be chosen, I wanted to meet her beforehand. Rita had a mutual friend and arranged for us to get together. We made plans to meet downtown to see *Live and Let Die*, the new James Bond movie with Roger Moore.

Rita and I rode our 10-speeds from her house. Once there, it wasn't long before we saw Becky approaching on her bike as well. She was a year younger than us and starting 8th grade at Clayton Junior High in the fall.

As we said our hellos, I couldn't help but notice Becky's provocative way of dressing. My father would have taken one look at her before labeling her promiscuous. Her faded bell-bottom jeans were deliberately torn along the outside seam, almost to her knees, and looped together with evenly spaced steel O-rings. She was inescapably braless, the shape of her luscious breasts on display through a nearly sheer, white halter top. An oval peace sign swung seductively between her breasts when she walked. When I complimented her pendant, she said it had once belonged to Janis Joplin. It was a gift from her wild Aunt Chelsea, a make-up artist, who she claimed worked with Janis in San Francisco.

At twelve, her body was more mature than mine. A twinge of envy ran through me, looking at her nipples beneath the thin polyester fabric. Her freewheeling attire was complemented by her coarse and wavy auburn hair. A constellation of freckles seemed to float on her pale skin. Everything about this girl was captivating.

After the movie, Rita had to get home. I felt guilty because I was glad she had to leave so I could have Becky to myself. I hugged her goodbye, thinking I was a pitiful friend, and Becky and I rode to 7-Eleven for cola Slurpees.

Sitting on a cinder block wall next to the 7-Eleven parking lot, we sucked on Slurpees and talked for hours as we watched the parade of customers come and go. Becky was fascinating because she was so different from me. It was past sunset when we reluctantly parted and rode home as the moon was rising.

After everyone went to bed, I was still stirred up from meeting Becky. I crept into the backyard to view the full moon. The backyard shimmered in the atmosphere of silvery light. I felt compelled to have that light on my bare skin. I undressed under our big apple tree and presented myself to the moon.

With my arms outstretched and my face lifted skyward, I sang songs from Camp Field and wept. I was thinking of my happy memories, but was also sad and filled with nostalgia. I was trying to capture the feeling I had in the meadow and though I didn't quite get there, I felt calm in the moonlight shedding my tears.

From that day forth, Becky and I saw one another every single day. Rita justifiably felt discarded and told me she wished she had never introduced us. I apologized and felt bad about it, but didn't know what else to say. I couldn't exactly tell her, "Sorry, I'm under Becky's spell right now," even though it was true. Becky and I lived a couple miles apart, and with our 10-speeds we could get around town easily.

Mrs. Carlson asked me to watch her two kids one afternoon and I invited Becky to join me. When she arrived, the kids were playing in their rooms.

We were hanging out in the living room, talking about softball and listening to my latest Carly Simon album, *Hotcakes*, on the fancy hifi stereo. My favorite song, "Forever my Love" was playing when Becky impulsively kissed me on the lips. Her brazen come-on made my stomach lurch. I was instantly nauseous.

I jerked away, exclaiming, "Hey, knock it off!"

Ignoring me, she kissed me again. Her body moved closer to mine. Again, I told her, "Knock it off," adding, "this is wrong!"

But Becky leaned in a third time, with a softer kiss.

"Argg," I complained, "I wish that you were Sam."

Hearing this, Becky scowled and punched me in the arm, "Well, fuck off then!"

"You fuck off," I shot back. "I *do* wish you were Sam."

"Anyway, this is wrong," I continued. "I feel sick to my stomach when you kiss me."

"That's because you're Catholic. You've been taught to think it's wrong," Becky replied. "It's not wrong, Suzy, it's love and there's nothing wrong with love."

I could only marvel at her keen response.

"Let me kiss you again," Becky asked.

I felt my body tense.

"No, I'm going to check on the kids," I stated. I needed to get away from her. I needed to think.

Other than the brief girlish crush I had on Gail at Camp Field, I hadn't felt any kind of attraction toward my own sex. Becky's attention frustrated me because I had liked Sam for such a long time and it had come to nothing.

When I returned, Becky was waiting patiently, but as soon as I sat down she pressed the issue again. She challenged me to think more openly about her desire to kiss me, saying it was her way of showing that she cared. She kept repeating the phrase, "It's just love, Suzy."

Eventually, she wore down my arguments until I succumbed and allowed her to kiss me again and again. I began to kiss her back and the feeling of nausea abated. This decision to surrender and return Becky's kisses ended my days of girlish innocence and defined everything about that summer.

When I got home, I went into the backyard to be alone. We had a clothing line on the side of the house, strung between two metal T-shaped poles. I jumped on one and began climbing to the top.

After moments on the pole, I stopped. An explosion of pleasure was happening between my legs. It was so intense, it took my breath away. *What in the name of God was that?* I wondered.

I had to know, so I asked Kris the next day if she'd ever had that kind of sensation and she said she did, when she laid down on a skateboard and rode downhill over our bumpy street.

Well, what a revelation that was. Neither one of us had a name for it, but I made damn sure to frequent the clothes-line pole and to my delight, explosions of pleasure happened whenever I did.

Our parents did not discuss anything with us about our bodies or sex. In fact, (I burn red to admit it) my mother told Kris and I our vaginal area was called our *second butt*, which, no doubt, you can imagine could fuck a girl up for life.

When I learned the proper way of referring to my genitalia, I was convinced my mother had done irrevocable damage to me. Then I babysat the girls down the street, who at five and seven years old, gleefully told me they called their vaginas their *Suzys*.

In July, an out-of-town weekend was planned between the neighborhood parents. They were going to Lake Tahoe to watch Englebert Humperdinck perform.

While mom was packing, Mrs. Carlson rummaged through her clothes, complaining she had nothing to wear. She took one of my mom's favorite dresses out of the closet: a vibrant blood-orange maxi dress with a plunging neckline.

"Oh, this is the one," she declared, not really asking if it was okay to borrow it. *Who the hell did she think she was?* I found her irritating and thought she was taking advantage of my mother.

Kris had plans that weekend, so fourteen-year-old Mike was put in charge of the kids' sleepover at the Barelas. Their house was especially fun because the garage had been converted into a huge recreation room with a pool table and they had TVs in more than one room. With no parents around, we raided the cupboards for munchies, while Mike invited some buddies over to raid their liquor cabinet. It was the perfect storm for pandemonium as we ran wild through the night. We cranked up the music and carried on until we dropped. It was a miracle that no one got hurt.

The next week, Becky and I both made the all-star team, along with Rita and Kris. Coach Ron designated Kris team captain. We met for three hours every day on the field at St. Albert's. I loved how demanding it was and I especially loved the feeling of improving.

Our newly formed team jelled well. Though rivals during the season, we now comprised the all-star team that would represent northern Nevada at the National Tournament.

I wasn't spending time with Rita anymore but was glad to see her at practices. She was decidedly not a fan of Becky's, for obvious reasons, but was gracious enough that we still got along.

After practice we usually went to Becky's house because her mom, Belvah, worked and it gave us time to be alone. We kissed for hours until our lips were bruised and kept on kissing, despite the pain. Whenever I spent the night, we stayed up late listening to Carole King's *Tapestry* and Helen Reddy's *I am Woman* while we talked, kissed, and caressed one another. Being held in Becky's intense gaze, I felt understood and loved.

One night, Becky wanted to take things further. When she

asked me to take off my shirt, I froze. I was shy about exposing my body. Becky coaxed me, telling me how beautiful I was as she pulled my shirt up over my head. I pulled her close, using her as a cover. Her hair against my bare shoulders felt good and her breathing accelerated as she kissed me some more. Overcoming my hesitancy and clumsiness with her reinforced our bond and my attachment to her grew deeper.

Becky's bed became our private world where secrets were shared, promises were made, and the landscapes of our bodies became familiar. We grew to love one another.

It was bewildering to me that, at twelve years old, Becky knew she had every right to be exactly who she was. No one would deter her from expressing herself. Because I was full of fears and insecurities, her strength inspired me.

Those first weeks we were inseparable. I enjoyed being with Becky, but knew no one could find out about us. For me, the fear of getting caught was almost always present. I didn't dare imagine how my parents, or the church, would respond if they knew what I was up to.

When we surfaced from cocooning at her house, Becky's mood sometimes changed. She was a jealous and possessive girl. The closer we became, the more she was threatened by our teammates. This was out of character with the confidence she exuded in other areas.

During practice, if I had any banter with another player, I'd get grilled by Becky about what was said. On more than one occasion, she pulled me aside to start an argument. Her behavior was starting to freak me out, as I did not want to draw any attention to the nature of our relationship. Becky, on the other hand, had no sense of propriety—she was reckless and unrestrained when it came to her emotions.

After a particularly agitating practice, I told her she needed to keep her jealousy in check or she would blow it for both of us, stressing that if my parents ever found out I'd probably never see her again. The thought of that kind of repercussion hit her hard and she apologized. A few days later Becky surprised me with a sterling silver cuff bracelet. She said it was a peace offering. It was a beautiful gift and I was touched by her sincerity. I loved it and wore it on my left wrist.

The National Tournament was held in Anaheim, California. My parents volunteered to chaperone, so when the day came, we piled in a rented van along with my siblings and a few teammates. Coach Ron drove his cab-over camper with the rest of the players.

It would take ten hours to get to Southern California, including breaks for lunch and gassing up. My hopes of enjoying the drive were short-lived, because Becky was a burgeoning firestorm of emotion. When I chatted with my teammates, Becky slumped in her seat, shooting angry looks at me. It seemed we could only get along if no one else was around. The talk we had about her jealousy was fruitless and I was at a loss for how to handle the situation.

At one gas stop, Becky pulled me aside and berated me for ignoring her, pleading with me to understand how she felt. I didn't understand and defended my right to interact with my teammates. Rita noticed Becky's behavior and found a moment to ask me if everything was all right. Embarrassed and afraid of exposure, I made excuses for her.

By the time we arrived at Chapman College, I wanted to be alone, but regrettably, we had decided beforehand to share a room.

The next morning we had breakfast in the cafeteria. Our team was assigned a noon slot for practice so we could get familiar with the playing field. Exerting ourselves in the oppressive humidity and hundred degree heat was miserable. Coming from the bone dry climate of Nevada, we were all negatively affected by the soggy, polluted air. After three hours of practice, a bunch of us were ill, either with headaches from the smog or heat stroke. Coach Ron ordered us to bed for the rest of the day. Despite feeling poorly, we trained hard for two days before the tournament began, hoping to acclimate to our surroundings.

Attending the welcoming ceremony was intimidating once we got a look at some of our competitors. The girls from the California and Arizona teams were physically much more mature than we were. They looked like women, not girls. With their deep tans, long blond hair and obvious confidence, I was worried we were going to be outmatched.

Our team lodged on the second floor of the dorms. Becky seized any opportunity to grab a moment alone with me. She'd pull me behind a door to kiss me when others were close by, or make-out with me in the restrooms until we heard someone coming. Her recklessness was unnerving. I wanted to have fun and to enjoy my friends and the competition, but Becky's unrelenting needs were starting to dominate everything.

On the morning of our first game, she and I were first to head out for breakfast. As we got to the stairwell, she suddenly climbed over the wall on the landing, dangerously hanging above the staircase below. I was terrified she was going to fall. She warned me, "I'm going to let go unless you say you love me!"

Thunderstruck, I replied, "Of course I love you. Climb back over, you're scaring me!"

My declaration wasn't enough. She accused me of loving Rita.

"Oh my god, Becky, you're being ridiculous!" I complained. "Please stop. You know I love you and we have to go to breakfast now." Thankfully, she clambered over the wall and back on her feet. I was shaken by her stunt and mad as hell at her antics.

My teammates felt the tension between us. Rita looked at me quizzically more than once. She asked why I wasn't hanging out with her and the other girls. I told her Becky was having a hard time. Rita rolled her eyes and walked away. I didn't blame her.

Needless to say, I didn't play well. We were up against the team from Scottsdale, Arizona—the tanned and buxom beauties who looked twenty years old. Before the game even began, I knew I was off. My attention was fractured from all the drama with Becky.

I played horribly. I missed three grounders in a row playing shortstop which cost us the game. Grounders were usually my specialty, but not on this day. Then came the embarrassment of being pulled before the game was over. My frustrations let loose in the dugout as I hung my head low and cursed, my angry tears hitting the ground. I could hear the other team laughing and making jeers about what a lousy player I was.

My excitement about being an all-star and my hopes for our team were dashed. In a few weeks I had gone from zero to ninety with Becky and was, in all respects, not equipped to deal with the situation.

Our proud Nevada State All-Star team got our asses handed to us. We were blown out of the competition in two games, losing to Arizona and California. They were superior to us in every way. In an effort to console us, Coach said they had longer training seasons because of their mild climates. Our one spot of sunshine was that we were going to Disneyland.

Becky and I were over the moon. Most of us had never been to Disneyland. It was exactly what we needed to take our minds off our piss-poor performance. The next morning we got ready in record time and lined up to buy our ticket books. My parents had my three younger siblings to contend with, so we made a plan to meet them in front of the park at closing time.

Initially, we stayed with the team, but then Becky and I took off to explore the park, running everywhere we went. Being in a new place, I felt bold and willing to take risks. The stakes weren't as high when surrounded by people you'd never see again. On any ride that had moments of darkness, Becky and I kissed. The shadowy Haunted House was our favorite ride due to the absence of lights.

The Disneyland stores were loaded with merchandise Becky and I wanted, so we decided to steal the items we liked. The park was jammed with people. We figured no one could possibly pay close attention to what was going on. We shoplifted trinkets, hats, t-shirts and I even got a Jiminy Cricket keychain.

Later that evening we heard security being paged over the loudspeaker. We held our breath, anticipating that maybe we were busted. We happened to run into Rita who told us one of our teammates was nabbed for shoplifting. Terrified of it happening to us, we stopped. In a bathroom stall, we tore off price tags and concealed most of our loot under our clothing.

From morning to night, we had run ourselves ragged. By the time we were back at Chapman College, I landed in bed with a hard thud and was out like a light.

When I woke up before Becky, I decided to slip off to enjoy breakfast with my teammates. As soon as Becky discovered I was gone, she hurried to the cafeteria, just in time to see me laughing with Rita and her friend, Luigi.

Afterward, Becky said I abandoned her and accused me of wanting to be with Luigi. Sick to death of the topic, I ignored her and packed my bag. I walked by myself to the van, relieved and happy to be heading home.

Mom put on the radio and I sang along, looking out the window while snubbing Becky in the seat beside me. As always, she made her displeasure clearly known, regardless of who was present. In more ways than one, she had ruined the trip for me.

Becky was letting out big heaving sighs, hoping to get a reaction out of me. When that didn't work, she swiftly jerked the cuff bracelet she had given me off my wrist. I tried to get it back from her, but she hurled it out the van window before I could get my hands on it.

"You bitch!" I screamed "I can't believe you!"

My dad heard me and tilted the rear view mirror to look at us, yelling, "Watch your mouth, young lady. What in god's name is going on back there?"

My temper got the better of me and I ignored my dad. I shoved Becky off the seat, jumped on top of her, and began punching her repeatedly. Now I was the one who was out of control. Her face was smeared with snot and tears as she landed her own blows. All my frustrations poured out as I screamed while Rita, Luigi and my siblings stared at us in disbelief.

No one made a sound except for my father, whose booming voice was shouting, "Goddammit, Suzanne and Becky, get back in your seats right now! Don't make me come back there!"

My father didn't make idle threats, so I got off Becky and returned to my seat, still fuming.

"What in the Sam Hill is the matter with you two?" my father asked. I was beginning to ask myself that same question.

Becky returned to her seat beside me. I was wiping away my tears with the sleeve of my shirt, trying to compose myself, when Becky reached from behind her back to reveal that she still had my cuff bracelet.

"Faked you out!" she said victoriously with a huge smile as she handed it back to me.

"Jesus, you are insane," I said, as I grabbed the bracelet and returned it to my wrist.

When we got home my parents sat me down to express their concerns about my friendship with Becky. They didn't feel she was a good influence on me. My father called her disturbed. I listened and nodded and then let Becky know she better not come over anymore.

Once softball season ended, Becky mellowed out and we had fun together again. We resumed our routine of hanging out alone at her house. We watched the game show, *Match Game '73* on TV after riding our bikes to the neighborhood store for snacks. Becky would go to the register to buy soda while I stuffed beef jerky and candy down my shorts.

During one of our petting sessions, Becky told me her mother had a stash of porn magazines in the house. She asked if I wanted to see them and I said no. Then she divulged that she'd already tried marijuana and had intercourse with a boy. This shook me up, especially when she added it had happened the year before. I thought it was awful that she was doing these things at such a young age. She scoffed at my reaction, saying it was no big deal.

Becky was my first sexual experience, so I had nothing to compare it to. I had slowly come around to letting her touch me and, of course, this led to more exploration. But I remained uncomfortable about her giving me oral sex and was reluctant to return the favor. Regardless, Becky was tenacious. Eventually I started to participate sexually the way she wanted me to.

I still didn't know the explosions of pleasure I felt when pole climbing were related to sexual arousal. When fooling around with Becky, I didn't have any sensations as good as that.

Being sensual, being close, felt good, but Becky could be unpredictable. Several times she scratched her nails down my back until I screamed in pain. This only made her laugh. I was often too uncomfortable to speak up about it and instead endured the discomfort.

When I finally gathered some courage, I asked her about the nail scratching. Becky told me things like that were normal in the throes of passion, which made me feel like a dummy. She asked if I'd ever read Xaviera Hollander's column in *Penthouse* magazine. The ludicrous nature of her question made me laugh. I replied sarcastically, "What the hell do you think?"

Becky and I spent endless hours in our love bubble. It never occurred to me that her mother had any idea what we were up to until one day when we returned from a bike ride to McDonald's for a Big Mac and fries.

We could hear Belvah snickering from the hallway as we headed toward Becky's room. Once we opened the door, we saw her handiwork: Belvah had plastered Becky's bedroom walls with pictures of nude men from her *Playgirl* magazines.

Until that day I had never seen an adult man naked, so the graphic, painfully real, large penises on the wall were gross and terrifying to me. Becky and I began ripping them off the walls as fast as we could while Belvah howled with laughter. If I'd had more pluck, I would've told her off. Belvah's behavior shocked me. I couldn't believe she chose to expose her daughter (and me) to X-rated pornography.

The last week before school we went to Idlewild Park to watch a women's softball game. A mutual friend introduced us to Terry, a star athlete and upcoming senior at Bishop Manogue High School. We got to chatting since I was about to start my freshman year there. Becky's mood turned and she interrupted me, making crappy comments to put me down. She laughed while telling Terry how horribly I had played at nationals. I was stunned and hurt by the meanness in her tone and leaned in to whisper, "Why are you being like this?" She blew me off and continued making me the butt of her jokes.

This was not how a loved one behaved, not by any stretch. It didn't just anger me, it altered my feelings for her.

Becky voiced her fears all summer that my going to Manogue while she was still in junior high would break us apart. After the way she treated me at the ballpark, when she wanted reassurance that we would stay together, I could not bring myself to say the words she wanted to hear.

In fact, I wanted to get off the roller-coaster. Becky and I went from being strangers to spending forty-three consecutive days together. During that time, I went from being an innocent girl to a sexually active teenager. I cared for Becky, but her jealousy and temperament had spoiled things. I was not about to start high school with an albatross around my neck. I broke up with Becky the night before school started.

A peaceful moment at the Truckee River.

4
ac/dc

Mounting the clothesline pole had become a glorious habit that provided bursts of happiness into my life. I sometimes made several visits a day for the little miracle contained in a shimmy. On the morning of my first day of high school, as soon as I opened my eyes, I felt the impulse to visit the pole. But a peculiar feeling came over me as I realized I was naked from the waist down.

As always, I'd gone to bed wearing my dad's hand-me-down pajamas. They were enormous on me, but I loved how soft they were from wear and washing. After looking in my room and the bathroom, I told my mom my bottoms were missing, but she was too busy making lunches to pay attention to me. The situation was so odd, I became weepy as I tore through the house looking for them. But they were nowhere to be found, so I gave up the search and got ready for school.

Kris, Mike and I had gotten up earlier than usual because we were picking up one of Kris' classmates on the way to Manogue. As we left the house, Mike shouted, "Hey, Suzy, I found your pajama bottoms!"

I couldn't believe my eyes. There they were, sopping wet, lying in the blackish muck of the gutter in front of our house. There was no explanation, no figuring it out, because how could they go from being on me to being outside in the street?

Pulling away from the curb, and my pajama bottoms, Kris said her friend lived near Clayton Junior High. As we poked along in the school zone, I rolled down the window to look for Becky. My expectations were low, so I was amazed when I spotted her.

She was slouched on top of the steps looking absolutely demolished. Oblivious to the throng of kids walking all around her, she was sobbing freely and rubbing her tears all over her face. It was gut-wrenching to see her in this distraught, open display of emotion. She was a blotchy, wet-mess of a girl. On the verge of crying myself, all I could do was look away. It was too painful to see her suffering so publicly.

The rest of the drive I tried to get my head in a better space. I was determined to put the fervent summer with Becky behind me. I wanted Manogue to be a new beginning.

It was a pleasant surprise when Terry recognized me as she passed by in the hall. She asked if I was trying out for the basketball team. Shrugging, I told her I wasn't sure.

Finding one's place in the social order of high school was a real and consequential pressure. Mike and I faced the same dilemma. Our affiliations would define us for the next four years.

I loved being a cheerleader, but it was much more competitive now. My experience with the dishonest nuns at St. Albert's, who disregarded my win as head cheerleader, lingered in my mind, especially because I suspected that my parents were still behind in tuition payments now that they had three children at Manogue. If I was right, I knew it would be held against me.

After much consideration, I chose to go for the jock track, partly because I didn't think I had any chance of making the cheerleading squad.

Mike decided to run for Student Council and was easily elected Vice President of the freshman class. He was popular and seemed to be doing really well, playing Junior Varsity baseball and acting in a school play, but at some point during the year, someone turned him on to dope. This set Mike on a path that would adversely affect the rest of his life. He changed dramatically in the span of a few months. Sadly, the close relationship we once had ended as a different brother emerged—one I scarcely recognized or could relate to. As a result, I detested marijuana and would have nothing to do with it.

The first week of school, a sophomore named Jim asked me to meet him for lunch on the school lawn. We ate in awkward silence and barely spoke before he kissed me. I was hoping for a soft kiss, but it turned aggressive when he thrust his tongue into my mouth, filling it with half-chewed potato chips.

"Arrrggghhh, so gross!" I groaned, recoiling from him. I leapt up and spit on the ground, trying to clear my mouth of his debris. That didn't do the trick, so I licked my napkin to wipe the potato chip particles off my tongue. Jim sat wordlessly like a dolt while I grabbed my books and split.

Kris and I both made the basketball team. In fact, anyone who tried out automatically made the team because hardly anyone showed up to play. While I excelled at softball and volleyball, I was a god-awful basketball player.

Basketball practice was merciless: we ran drills on the court until I was so winded I thought I might faint or hurl; when dribbling, the ball inevitably ricocheted off my foot into the bleachers; and free-throw practice showed my skill for air balls. I stunk. My ineptitude became a practice in humiliation. Terry got a huge kick out of my lack of skill, to the point where she was doubled-over laughing. She told me I played with a lot of heart.

Terry needed a helper to be responsible for shutting down the gym lights. I volunteered and she showed me where the fuse box was and which switches to flip. As we walked in the dark, Terry confidently slipped her hand in mine and gave it a warm squeeze. Her boldness startled me and I thought, *Oh wow, here we go again.*

No part of me was thinking about being with girls after Becky. For me, she was an anomaly—someone who aggressively pursued me and I adapted to her advances. I liked boys, without question, so why did Terry feel comfortable making a move on me? Then I remembered Becky's energy when we met Terry at Idlewild Park and figured it was probably obvious to her that we were a couple.

Terry was a popular, straight-A student with a buoyant personality. She had a driver's license and used her parents' silver station wagon on the weekends to pick me up. We'd spend the day in her bedroom, listening to Tower of Power and Rare Earth while playing board games and cuddling.

I spent less time at home. Staying away guaranteed that I wouldn't get roped into babysitting for the weekend parties. The partying annoyed me and I vowed to myself I would not drink, smoke, or carry on as my parents did.

For many months, my interaction with Terry was limited to kissing. Well, kissing isn't really an accurate description, because Terry was atrocious at it. When she kissed me, she opened her mouth really wide, placing her canines past my lips and onto my skin which was fairly painful. Her poor technique could be seen by looking at me; I often had a rash to prove it.

I don't know why I didn't tell her she was hurting me. I had done the same thing with Becky, who had been sexually aggressive in a way that did not feel good. Terry gnawed at my face for months, yet I couldn't find the words to say she was hurting me.

One weekend, Terry invited me to a double feature at the drive-in. Her friend, Pam, picked us up in her 1966 Mustang, along with Cindy, who had been crowned Miss Reno, and Gina, all seniors. Terry and I piled in the back seat with Gina.

Unbeknownst to me, Terry had been drinking and was pretty sloshed. When she offered me a beer, I declined. Shortly after the movie began, Terry put her arm around my shoulder to pull me close. Such careless behavior in front of her friends put my stomach in knots. I whispered in her ear, "Terry, no, this is way too risky." She heard me, but was indifferent to my discomfort. When I tried to say more, she stopped me with her mouth and proceeded to chew up my face.

Terry was unusually ravenous and I was so flustered I kept my eyes open, watching to see if Pam and Cindy were turning around to look at us. They were sitting upright with a larger than normal focus on the film, which suggested to me they knew what was what. My back was to Gina, but she could see us. I felt I had no choice but to go along with Terry. She was a senior, three years older than me and I didn't have the courage to say no. Terry's friends said nothing, so maybe they were cool with it, or maybe they were stunned into silence, like me.

After the movie, we went to a house party in progress. Terry led me into a bathroom where she promptly unzipped her baby-blue corduroy jeans, grabbed my hand and guided it inside her underwear. It was a tight fit. I could barely move my hand, but proceeded until I reached her pubic hair, which made me stop. Noticing my hesitancy, Terry whispered, "I cut my hair down there, I don't like it long."

Understanding why she felt different, I wiggled my fingers around in a pathetic attempt to stimulate her. Even though I'd been with Becky, I still had no idea what to do to please a partner.

By sheer luck, or my crap technique, Terry told me she wanted to lie down in the bathtub. I helped her in, just in time for her to vomit all over herself. Pam had been looking for us and knocked on the door—her timing was perfect. I let her in and she helped me clean Terry up so we could leave.

Once I'd made contact with Terry's pubes she wanted more time alone with me.

One afternoon, we arrived at her house and discovered no one else was there. Performance anxiety began to churn in my gut as she took me by the hand, pulling me toward her room. She said she wanted to feel me up, so I laid on the bed and eventually she pulled my pants down. Her efforts weren't doing much for me, but she got hot and repositioned herself, wrapping her legs around my left thigh. Rubbing her pelvis against me, she became more and more aroused. I seemed to be more of a prop than anything, so I laid still while she did her thing.

Without notice, the front door creaked open, followed by the sound of her father, cheerfully yelling, "Hey, is anybody home?"

I jumped off the bed in a panic, hopping toward the hallway to get into the bathroom. My one desperate hope was that Mr. Elsrode would make a right turn into the kitchen. He didn't. As I leapt across the hallway with my pants and undies still around my ankles, I looked to my right to see poor Mr. Elsrode looking as if he'd been hit with a two-by-four.

"Fuuuck!" I screamed, as I gave one more huge hop into the bathroom and locked the door. I was beyond mortified.

Luckily, her father was even more embarrassed than me. He went into the backyard and mowed the lawn. I hurriedly got dressed and Terry drove me home. I asked her if she was going to get grounded and she said she was pretty sure the situation would never be mentioned. She was right.

Getting caught half-naked by Mr. Elsrode sobered me up. From then on, I made excuses to avoid being alone with Terry. We never had any more sexual contact. There was too much at stake for me to be that careless, although being her girlfriend was nice. It afforded me more freedom and she had even given me her class ring. I knew kids whispered about me wearing a girl's ring, but I ignored it. I felt love and affection for her, but because of her poor kissing technique and my inability to speak about it, I kept more distance than I would have otherwise.

In November, an overnight bus trip was arranged so students could attend the varsity football match against Elko High School. Kris took the bus and I found a ride with a classmate. Although we managed to get to Elko, somehow, my sister and I fell through the cracks. Once there, we realized we had nowhere to sleep because no one made any lodging arrangements for us.

After the game, everyone descended upon a little motel on the main strip where a bunch of seniors had reserved rooms. It became party central, as no adults were around and there was an abundance of beer. Kids circulated freely between the rooms, drinking and fooling around. Kris and I passed one another a number of times and agreed that the best plan was to hope for a spot on the floor or a chair to sleep in. I spent the night roaming through the crowd, keeping mostly to myself as I had zero interest in getting drunk. The party didn't die down until after two o'clock in the morning.

Hunger and bitter cold woke me at dawn. I was in a tight fetal position, trying to take up as little space as possible at the bottom of an occupied bed. In a futile effort to keep warm, I'd placed a couple of pillows on top of me. I didn't remember having dinner the night before.

Stiff and chilled to the bone, I searched for Kris, who was a few doors down and in worse shape than me. We walked outside where a cheerless, dense fog hung low in the streets, trapping the smell of diesel fuel from the many eighteen-wheelers passing through and adding to the already inhospitable feeling I had about the place.

An ugly, desperate feeling ran riot through my body—we were like forgotten orphans with no one to care for us. Our neglect was on full display, which made it even worse. *No one gives a shit about you*, I heard in my head as I held back tears.

How was it that we had been offered transportation hundreds of miles from home, but no place to stay or food to eat? *No one gives a shit about you*, I heard again. Holding onto Kris, we slowly walked along main street, looking for a place to get some food.

Finally, lights began to come on in the buildings and we saw families from Manogue entering the local cafes for breakfast. Never had I felt like such an unwanted vagabond. We were on the outside of comfort, watching families eat a hearty meal, peering through the glass at what we could not have.

We had enough money to purchase some horrid black coffee and a box of brown sugar cinnamon Pop-Tarts at a gas station. The coffee was strictly for heat. We ate our allotted three Pop Tarts each before catching our rides back home. This experience in Elko solidified my feeling of being a have-not at my high school.

That winter we had another death in our neighborhood. The Barela family was leaving Pyramid Lake on the evening of February 19th, when Mrs. Barela lost control of their car and drove off the road. Mr. Barela didn't have his seatbelt on and was catapulted through the windshield. Mrs. Barela and their two daughters were not seriously hurt, but Mr. Barela was in a coma for a month and passed away on March 19th. He was thirty-four.

Grandma Alice received the terrible news as confirmation of the downfall she predicted for our neighborhood. Mrs. Barela was inconsolable in her grief and the whole neighborhood was shocked. This made it all the more stupefying when even his death did not slow down the weekend partying. Perhaps they had more reason to drink as they mourned the loss of their dear friend. What eventually became clear, though, was that his death foreshadowed a period of decline and disintegration on Everett Drive.

As the end of May approached, Terry prepared for graduation. She had achieved an impressive 4.0 GPA and mailed her college applications.

When summer came, we barely had time to see one another due to our schedules. Terry played softball for the Reno Royals, often traveling out of town for games, and I played for Miss Softball America. I made the all-stars again and went back to California for Nationals.

Terry received a notification letter saying she won a full four-year scholarship to the University of California at Los Angeles (UCLA). She was beaming with satisfaction and pride. I was full of congratulations, but hid my conflicted feelings about her news. Terry wanted to know what I thought she should do: should she accept the scholarship to UCLA?

"That's a heavy question," I replied, turning somber.

"It is," she almost whispered, taking my hands. "But, I need to know what you think. This affects us both."

I was wearing the charm necklace Terry gave me of St. Teresa of Avila, Jesus and Mary. Though I didn't consider myself Catholic or even religious anymore, I never took it off because it came from her. I played with the charms between my fingers as she asked me to weigh in on this important life decision.

Regrettably, the significance of her question was lost on me. I didn't know anything about college. My daily concerns were focused on getting my needs met. Being with Terry meant I could get away from the tensions at home between my parents. This self-serving motivation swelled in me and I told her, "I don't want you to go. I'd miss you too much."

Incredibly, that was all it took for Terry to give up on a dream she had pursued for years. She allowed an immature girl to make the decision for her, passing on her full scholarship to UCLA. Instead, she registered at the University of Nevada, Reno (UNR) for the 1974 fall semester.

Now that Kris, Mike and I were all teenagers, there was more conflict at home. My parents were fighting and Mike was getting into trouble. He had become moody, especially in the mornings when he was hung over and jonesing for some weed.

My father and I butted heads regularly. He got on my case for being on the phone too long and not keeping my room clean. I was messy and shoved piles of clothes under my bed or stuffed them in the closet, as opposed to Kris, who always put her belongings in their proper place.

My room with Kris was directly across the hall from my parents. One night, after we had gone to bed, my parents were arguing and I overheard my father complaining about me. He was sick of telling me to straighten up my room and asked, "Why can't Suzanne be more like Kristine?"

Subsequently, Kris heard me crying and whispered, "Sorry, Booze," her nickname for me.

It was painful but not surprising to hear him say it. Kris was logical and methodical like my dad, whereas I was emotional like my mother. For years, I had the impression my dad couldn't relate to me or didn't like me much.

We locked horns the previous summer because he wanted me to get rid of my cut-off jeans, saying they were too short and trashy looking. I ignored him because they were my favorites. I'd even sewn astrological patches on the back right pocket of Sagittarius and Aries, to represent me and Becky.

One day he blew up and yelled, "You look like a slut." He'd never spoken to me like that before. I turned red and ran to my room to hide. The next morning he threw them in the garbage while I was at school. I retrieved them and defiantly kept wearing them, making sure to hide them when they were not on me.

On another occasion, I came home to find he had dumped all of my dresser drawers, plus everything I had not put away, into our trash cans. They were in the street in front of the house for all to see. He had broken some of my knick-knacks and my clothing was soiled from the dirty bins.

He yelled from the window that the front door was locked and I better think hard before bringing anything inside, unless I was going to immediately put it in its proper place. I felt singled out as the rotten kid in our family.

When school began, the halls felt empty without Terry and her friends. What a mistake it was to solely focus on her my freshman year at the expense of my other friendships.

Terry found a way for me to be paid as a scorekeeper at UNR during her volleyball games. This was where I met Gena, a twenty-two-year-old grad student who also kept score for UNR. She was talkative and during the course of our first game scoring together told me she lived with her ex-lover, Kathy, who was twenty-eight. I was more than a little stunned at the casual manner in which Gena conveyed she was a lesbian. From the church to my parents to television, I'd only ever heard derogatory references to people who were queer.

After a couple of weekends scoring together, Gena took more interest in me. She asked for my number in case she needed someone to score a game last minute. A week later she called and invited me to take a drive around Lake Tahoe. I'd been to the north shore to visit the Ponderosa Ranch from the *Bonanza* television show and loved the idea of seeing the whole lake.

On a beautiful September day, as the aspens were beginning to turn, Gena picked me up in her brown Capri and we took a leisurely drive. As we headed up the serpentine road that defines Mount Rose highway, I confided in her about my relationship with Terry. Gena nodded knowingly, saying she'd picked up on our vibe when she saw us together. Lesbian love was apparently obvious to other lesbians. She listened attentively, taking my hand to squeeze it. She didn't let go.

It was a picture-postcard day, cool outside but warm in the sun. Gena was a photography buff and brought her 35mm camera to capture the day. We made lots of stops because she spontaneously pulled over whenever inspiration struck.

Initially, I was self-conscious about being photographed in such a studied way. I'd never been at the end of a camera lens like this, with her instructing me on how to stand or how to bring more light to my face. It was flattering, but also brought forth my insecurities.

I was wearing a yellow floral-patterned blouse with sailor pants and platform shoes. I had put on a few pounds and felt chunky. When I said this out loud, Gena heaped on praise, saying I was a beautiful girl, with incredible bone structure and a strong body.

Terry was out of town for a game the following weekend. Gena invited me over to her house to bake. I reminded her she'd have to provide transportation both ways. When I asked my mom if I could go, I told her Gena was also a scorekeeper at UNR and was glad she didn't ask her age before saying yes.

Gena and Kathy rented a brick bungalow built in the thirties and situated in an alley that flanked the south end of a park. The front door opened into an old-fashioned kitchen with a tiny Wedgewood stove. The living room had a pair of brown bean bag chairs and a bookcase made from cinder blocks and planks of plywood. It was crammed with plants, books and record albums proudly displayed next to the record player—without question, the most important item in the house.

We baked zucchini bread and Gena wrote down the recipe for me. She turned me on to Joni Mitchell's *Court and Spark* album, playing it over and over until I knew the lyrics. Kathy and I talked about our favorite books, discussing eastern philosophy and meditation.

Our conversation gave me the most wonderful sensation, like a waterfall was pouring in through the top of my head, washing out the old ways of thinking that had been handed down from my grandparents and their parents before them. The stimulation was intoxicating. I wanted to take it all in and make it mine. I wanted it to change me. I wanted knowledge to live as a beacon inside me, to shine the way forward as I lived in the world on my own.

Kathy and Gena's home became a place of refuge and my way of perceiving the world changed. I began to think of myself as a spiritual seeker and told my parents I was no longer going to attend mass. Incredibly, this declaration met with no resistance.

The neighborhood parties remained an unhealthy display of excess. I continued my strategy of leaving before I could get corralled to babysit. Now that some of us were teenagers, a house full of unruly, unsupervised kids was a different matter. Mike and his friends partied, drinking alcohol and getting high, while other kids were fooling around with matches and looking at porn magazines.

The next week, Gena and I were alone at the house. She put on David Gates' *Guitar Man* album and invited me to cuddle on the bed. She caressed my hands and arms while singing along to the music. Her touch was nurturing and calming. I became drowsy and drifted off to sleep. When I opened my eyes again, it was past sunset and the room was getting dark. Gena was sitting on the floor, looking at me and smiling. I smiled back. She got up and laid next to me on the bed, kissing me on the mouth.

Her kiss blew my bangs back. I had not been kissed like this. Stirred by my responsiveness, Gena's hands glided over my body, arousing me more. She moved closer, undoing her jeans, letting them fall to the floor.

Oh, wow, I thought, *she wants me to touch her down there.* Even in the privacy of my own thoughts, I was too prudish to use the word *vagina*.

Because Gena was much older than me, I felt immense pressure to be a good lover. My hand travelled between her legs, exploring around until Gena signaled her pleasure with moans and heavier breathing. Her passionate response was intense and I thought, *This is a woman.* My desire to perform well continued as I didn't want to embarrass myself or let her down. After all, she didn't have to know I didn't know what I was doing, unless of course, it was obvious.

I kept up a pulsing movement and she responded with increased animation. She wrapped her leg around me, pressing into me with her hips, which made it difficult to move my hand, as it was getting crushed. Her moans got deeper, becoming guttural like an animal, and her pelvic thrusts took on a life of their own.

The Gena train had left the station.

As it turned out, her intense sexual locomotion was too much for me to take. Overwhelmed, I felt myself swooning and was sure I was going to pass out. I squirmed until my arm was free and made the mistake of looking down.

There it was—a deposit in the palm of my hand. The abundant product of Gena's arousal.

The sight of it made me sick to my stomach. The room was spinning, my knees were buckling and I was going to vomit. I bolted to the bathroom, afraid I would otherwise puke on Gena's vagina.

"Oh my god, Gena, I'm sick, I don't feel well." I cried out as I retched in the bathroom.

I had to get out of there. I was way over my head.

"Oh man, I need to go home," I continued through the door. "Gena, can you take me home? I'm so sick."

"Of course, of course, we'll go right away," she replied, her voice shaky. No doubt she was disoriented from the jarring change of gears, or maybe she knew our interaction had made me ill.

Gena didn't talk once we got in the car, which I appreciated. Curling up on the seat, I kept my eyes closed until she pulled in front of my house. I thanked her for the ride and rushed in the front door. Like Dorothy in *The Wizard of Oz*, I was overjoyed to be back home, in my own room, and in my own bed.

The next day, I called Gena, fumbling my words as I told her I couldn't see her anymore. "You know I'm with Terry," I declared with false morality, "so this is wrong. Plus, I'm way too young to be hanging out with you."

She said she understood, but added emphatically, "You know you're an old soul, right? You are far beyond your years."

A part of me got off on the compliment, so I simply said thank you and goodbye, but in my head I was screaming, *No, I'm only fourteen-years-old.* As much as I enjoyed the perks of hanging out with adults, I was relieved to end it. Maybe it would be better to be the kid that I was.

My thoughts turned to Terry, but I put her out of my mind, not wanting to deal with the fact that I was a cheater. I had no idea how I was going to face her.

Volleyball season started and Manogue's first game was against Hug High, where Becky was a freshman. I was anxious about seeing her. As jealous as she had been, as much drama as she brought into my life, I still had feelings for her.

Game day arrived. As my teammates and I walked into the gym, we saw the Hug team in a huddle. I was looking for Becky and, wouldn't you know, Becky was looking for me. The second our eyes met, she scowled and stormed across the court, sneering at me, "We're gonna kick your ass today, Mueller."

Her out-of-the-blue hostility was startling. I clapped back with a lame response, unable to match her intensity. Becky sniped at me the whole game, making it clear she hated my guts.

Despite our best efforts, Hug beat us, Becky gloated, and we went home defeated.

Looking tougher. Lake Tahoe in the fall of 1974.

5

banished

Never mind her nasty temperament during the match, disregard the rude language she used to put me down, forget that she did everything in her power to humiliate me—after leaving the gym and her presence, Becky was all I could think about.

This perplexed me, but when it came right down to it, her unadulterated spirit was captivating. Becky had the chutzpah to be who she was, warts and all.

Seeing her brought back a flood of memories of our time together. I wanted to reach out, but the only phone we had was in the kitchen, the busiest room in the house. It hung between the cabinets and sliding glass door, a dingy mustard-yellow, rotary phone with the longest cord money could buy. I'd have to slip out the slider to the backyard to have any privacy.

After dinner, when everyone was watching TV, I tip-toed into the kitchen and dialed her number. Thankfully, Becky picked up, and we got into it right away. She let me have it, saying how much I hurt her when I abruptly ended our relationship. I apologized repeatedly, but she kept saying the same thing, over and over, until I was second-guessing my decision to call. Besides, I knew if we got back together it was going to be problematic. My parents were convinced Becky was a bad influence.

About an hour into our conversation, my father jerked the slider open, shouting, "Jesus H. Christ in a handbasket! You are not the only person in this household. Get off the goddamned phone, right now!" I hung up on Becky and received his usual lecture about my inconsiderate and selfish behavior.

Becky gave me another chance and I came up with a plan for us to be together with no parents around. I recently got a weekend job working in the cafeteria at The College Inn, a male dorm on UNR's campus. My boss was looking to hire another girl, and Becky filled the position. We made $1.75 an hour working the morning shift, making pancakes, bacon, and eggs. Best of all, there were no girls were around to provoke Becky's jealous nature.

I was excited about having my own money, but that notion was ruined as soon as my mother saw my paycheck. "Oh good," she said, "now you can buy your own bathroom products." When I complained to Becky, she insisted we open a joint savings account. I didn't know kids could do that on their own, but Becky always had a natural inclination to strategize about the future. She had a dream of us traveling cross-country one day on motorcycles.

Becky devised a way for us to meet during our school lunch break. Leaving campus was forbidden, but we got off on being rebellious. She sketched out a mid-point between Hug and Manogue that required each of us to travel about a mile, so we made plans to give it a try.

On the designated day, when the bell rang, I left the campus and ran most of the way to the intersection she instructed. Becky got there first. I was shocked to see a cast on her leg, as I didn't even know she had been injured. Incredibly, she had hopped the entire way. We were in an industrial district and found a place to tuck in where we could kiss without being seen.

The challenges we faced being together weren't easy. We wanted to be free to express ourselves, but society, religion, culture and family opposed us. Helen Reddy's song, "You and Me Against the World" became our anthem. Our bond was forged with passion and music. These love songs galvanized our belief that we were outsiders who only had one another.

Our brief rendezvous ended and I hustled back to school unnoticed, with barely enough time to beat the bell for fourth period English class. As I sat down at my desk, I heard snickering ripple throughout the room and thought it was because I was sweaty from running. It wasn't until I looked down that I knew the real reason. Someone carved a message into the desk:

Kris is a whore
Mike is a stoner
Suzy is a lezzie

I didn't dare look up because my face was burning hot. Who did this? Which hateful student thought this was funny? It wasn't something I could erase, it was carved into the wood with a knife.

I didn't dare look up. I wanted to smash someone in the face for hurting my family like this. What a joke this Catholic school was. From St. Albert's to Manogue, my family was treated unkindly by students and teachers alike. I covered the scrawl with my books, hating everything about Manogue from that day forward.

We were spending Thanksgiving in Saratoga, California, with my paternal grandparents, Norb and Lucille. My fifteenth birthday coincided with Thanksgiving that year, so I asked if Becky could come along and was pleased when my parents said yes. We spent my birthday at a flea market where I bought a wide-brimmed, leather hat and Becky bought me Cat Stevens' album, *Tea for the Tillerman*, because she knew how meaningful the song "Morning has Broken" was to me from my Camp Field days. Becky was lovely the whole trip and even managed to improve my parents' opinion of her. I was hopeful our year apart had done some good and we were a better fit now.

For months I had conducted myself as if my relationship with Terry was over without being considerate enough to let her know I was done. I sidestepped the situation until her nineteenth birthday arrived and I couldn't avoid it any longer.

When I heard her voice on the phone, I knew she was expecting happy birthday wishes, but my guilt for treating her so badly couldn't wait. I told her I was calling to break up. I didn't tell her about messing around with Gena, but when she asked if there was someone else, I admitted I was back with Becky.

Terry cried and fought for us to stay together, but I didn't feel anything. I'd been emotionally checked out of our relationship for some time and told her my mind was made up. When we got off the phone, I wrapped my charm necklace in tissue, put it in an envelope, and asked my mother to mail it for me. I'd returned her class ring a few months earlier because I was sick of being teased about it at school.

Becky's good behavior over Thanksgiving didn't last. Her resentment from the past kept flaring up. I was tired of apologizing to someone who seemed incapable of forgiveness.

We decided her house was the better place to hang out on the weekends. Belvah scoffed at me the first time she saw I was back in the picture and I did my best to ignore her. She referred to us as "you little faggots," mostly when she'd been drinking, which was more often since her divorce. She wasn't confrontational, it was something she muttered under her breath while walking away. This pejorative was always followed by one of her robust cackles. She was basically saying she knew what we were up to, while also making it clear she didn't want to discuss it.

In the weeks leading up to Christmas it was clear that something had shifted in our household. My parents weren't getting along and their fights had become more vicious. Dad often came home in a foul mood, ready to blow. We lived our lives at the mercy of his temper and knew if he had an audience when he was raging, he'd escalate faster and really put on a show.

Any number of things set him off; if the house was untidy with our toys and books lying about, dad would pick the items up and hurl them down the stairs into the basement, or he'd take his arm and sweep everything off the furniture onto the floor. If he couldn't find something he was looking for in a drawer, he'd dump out the contents and leave the mess for my mom to clean up. He became incensed at inanimate objects and circumstances beyond his control, losing his mind and cursing the wind in Nevada when planting trees, or beating a door frame with a hammer for being too narrow for a new washing machine to fit through.

In the throes of his anger he punched holes in the drywall and smashed things. When our Plymouth overheated on a weekend trip to the desert, he took a shovel out of the back and beat nearly every square inch of our car with the spade. We were all clenched with fear inside the car while this was going on, including his mother. He'd even struck Mike in anger on more than one occasion.

On Christmas Eve, deep-rooted hostilities and unresolved pain in my parents' marriage boiled to the surface in a way that changed our family irrevocably. It was the worst Christmas of my life.

I'd always found it painful to watch my mother become obsequious in the face of my father's temper. In an effort to placate him, she would apologize for whatever had set him off, like the house not being clean. He had zero appreciation for what it took for her to care for six children. It infuriated Kris and I to see her picking up after him as he raged through the house.

When my parents really got into it, they fought dirty. These were the times when my mother got so fed up she found her voice. They said terrible things to one another, hitting below the belt and exchanging rapid-fire barbs. From them, I learned how to eviscerate people verbally by the time I was a teenager.

This was the backdrop for what occurred on Christmas Eve. When dad got home I tentatively approached him with a poem I wrote about a friend of mine. It was my first effort at writing. As I got closer, I could see he was in a bad mood, but it was too late to retreat. I handed him the notebook paper, telling him what it was. He took the paper, read it, then shoved it at me, saying, "Too bad you can't write something like this for one of your family members."

I ran to my room crying, hurt by his nasty response. He left the house again, slamming the door with no explanation.

My mother served dinner and we ate mostly in silence. The night felt interminably long. We were all waiting for dad to come home so Christmas could begin.

It was our family tradition to open presents on Christmas Eve. Each year, our parents would send us to bed, where we would wait, eyes wide open, listening for sounds that Santa had come. Then a bluster of bells or footsteps on the roof would break the quiet and we'd hear, "Kids! Quick! Come downstairs!"

Sure enough, we'd scramble down the stairs to see Santa

had delivered our gifts. We opened all but one, which we saved for Christmas Day.

But, this year, dad still hadn't returned. We'd asked where he was but got no answer. Mom was frazzled, smoking cigarettes and drinking wine. We stayed up later than usual waiting for dad to come home.

Mike turned sixteen weeks before and had a driver's license, so mom suggested he drive to midnight mass at St. Albert's with Pete and Meg. Kris, Tommy and I were home when dad finally came through the door, drunk and surly. His speech was slurred when he told us kids to leave the room. We refused. I had the illogical notion that maybe I could help.

Dad verbally attacked my mother, falsely accusing her of betraying him. She retorted how rich that comment was considering he had been unfaithful to her most of their marriage.

Kris could not tolerate hearing this and ran out the front door. Tommy took off for St. Albert's to get Mike to come home.

Disturbed by what I was hearing, I slowly walked backward until I felt the wall behind me for support. My heart raced while I surveyed them both; drunk, angry, and hurt. I felt I had to intervene and to get him to stop.

I cried out, "Dad, why are you doing this? You're wrecking Christmas for everyone."

He turned on me, indignantly, "Oh, you think this is my fault? I'm not wrecking anything. This is *her* fault." he said, pointing at my mother. "She's a whore."

This was unbearable. I screamed at him at the top of my lungs, "You will not speak to my mother like that! What the hell is wrong with you?"

He reacted by spewing more insults at her, which dropped me to the floor. My mother was also on her knees, with her face in her hands, weeping. My dad looked at the two of us, walked out the door and drove away.

We had no Christmas that year. Things were falling apart. Kris, Mike and I whispered about the real possibility our parents would get a divorce.

"I hope they get a divorce before someone really gets hurt," Mike commented.

"...or ends up dead," Kris added solemnly. We all nodded in agreement because we felt the volatility between them. The aftermath of that horrible day lingered like a bad bruise.

Becky's parents recently split, but she was overjoyed when her father left. In fact, she didn't believe he was her real father. Through our family difficulties we leaned on one another more.

My mother confided more and more to Mrs. Carlson, who always seemed to be at our house, bitching about her own marriage. Meanwhile, my siblings and I spent more time away from home and one another. Other than Mrs. Carlson, I never saw my mother speak to anyone about her difficulties with my father. It was ingrained in her to protect him, not wanting his reputation to be harmed.

My grandmother mostly stayed at home since moving to Reno. She avoided our neighborhood and the chaos she saw there. While I sensed my grandparents had strong opinions about my father, they would never have spoken about him in front of us kids.

The new year arrived, but instead of feeling excited about 1975, I felt gloomy. During winter break, I asked if Becky could sleep over and neither of my parents objected. Belvah dropped her off after dinner and we watched TV until bedtime.

Mom dropped two sleeping bags on the living room floor, indicating where we would sleep. While everyone was upstairs,

Becky suggested we zip the bags together, saying we'd be warmer with one another's body heat. She was giggling and trying to be fresh with me. I told her to knock it off. We were not, in any way, in a private situation.

Knowing our living room was drafty, I grabbed some pillows and a wool blanket from my bedroom as extra guards against the cold. I changed into my flannel nightgown and climbed in the sleeping bag. Becky turned off the lamp and followed, looking adorable in old-fashioned cream-colored long johns.

We whispered in the dark, reaching for one another to snuggle close. It was illicit, it was dangerous, at least until I heard my mother close her bedroom door—then I sighed with relief. We were finally alone.

We began to kiss, lying side by side, moaning softly in our pleasure, enjoying some rare time to be physical with one another. Eventually, Becky rolled on top of me and we became more amorous. Her fragrant hair fell around my face like a shield of protection. I caressed her, gathering her hair to pull it back so I could look at her, but when I opened my eyes, I did not see Becky.

Someone in the dark was looming over us, looking down on me and Becky as we kissed.

It was my mother.

The jolt of her presence was cataclysmic. I jumped out of the sleeping bag like I'd been shot out of a cannon.

"Holy shit! Mom, what are you doing?"

"Never mind me, young lady, what are *you* doing," she hissed.

Becky immediately tried to talk to her, "Mrs. Mueller, please understand, I love Suzy..."

Nope. Mom wasn't having it. We had crossed a line and she was furious. I had never seen my mother hit anyone, but she swung hard at Becky, hitting her in the side of the head. She demanded, "You get out of my house this instant!"

"No! Mom! No! Stop, please!" I yelled, but Becky was already rushing to get her clothes on. Then, like a criminal, she went out the living room window because my mother was between her and the front door. I helplessly watched as Becky disappeared into the night, knowing it was below freezing outside.

"Mom," I whimpered, "how could you? How could you?"

I collapsed on the ground in disbelief, sickened with worry about Becky trying to get home, over two miles away, in the cold.

My mother spoke in a voice low and unfamiliar, "It's late, Suzanne. Go to bed. You'll talk with your father in the morning."

And then she was gone. Shutting my bedroom door, I sat in my bed weeping, in shock at how rapidly everything turned to shit.

In the morning, I wanted to call Becky to make sure she got home safely, but I was paralyzed with fear and didn't leave my bed. I stayed in my room, hoping to avoid the inevitable. Around eleven o'clock my mother came in to tell me, "Your father is ready to speak to you about last night."

I crossed the hall into my parents' bedroom to face the music and sat silently on the edge of my parents' bed. My father's face was heavy with consternation. In unfaltering tones, he reiterated my mother's account of the night before—that she caught Becky and I kissing and fondling one another.

Even uttering my crime caused him to pause and take a deep breath, the repugnancy of it clearly troubling him to no end. Standing with his left arm on his bureau, he rubbed his forehead with his right hand, like he was trying to massage his brain.

With his eyes fixed on the floor, he pronounced judgment: "There is something wrong with you, Suzanne. Your behavior is not normal, in fact, your behavior is deviant. I have concerns about the negative effect you could have on your siblings."

He paused, still unable to look at me and said, "It is unnatural to want to be with your own sex. This indicates that you don't have a desire to procreate. Do you understand what I am saying?"

The words *deviant* and *unnatural* seemed to hang in the air, suspended and vivid, like garish neon signs at a freak show. They took up residence in my psyche like poisoned seeds.

My thoughts turned to Becky and how I had reflected these same beliefs to her the first time she kissed me. I thought it was unnatural too, back then. But I had changed. I rejected my father's narrow-minded reasoning.

He stared at me, impatient for a response. No matter how much his words hurt me, I would defy him.

"That's a load of crap," I replied quietly.

"Oh, you think so?" he said angrily. "It is a basic and innate human instinct to procreate, which you seem to be lacking!" In his agitated state he paced back and forth in front of me.

"Well, I'm fifteen, dad," I began sarcastically, "so, no, I'm not thinking about procreating right now. Anyway, your thinking would condemn all priests and nuns as deviants too, because they obviously don't have any desire to procreate."

I couldn't wait to hear what he would say in response to that.

"Anyway," I continued, "I'm bisexual. There is nothing wrong with loving whomever I want to."

He offered no comeback, but my words enraged him. He swung to hit me. Leaning back on the bed, I kicked at him as hard as I could, my legs landing blows to his chest and midsection. The whole house probably heard me screaming how much I hated him.

In one motion, my dad scooped me off the bed, tightly squeezing me between his arms like an accordion.

"I've had just about enough out of you, young lady," he claimed while carrying me downstairs, out the front door, and to the car.

My mother was nowhere to be found. She left me alone with him and retreated. I didn't know if she was in agreement with what he was doing or not, but one thing was for sure, she got the ball rolling that led to this.

I had no idea where he was taking me.

Little did I know, prior arrangements had been made.

These are the only photos I have from when I was in Omega House, taken in a Woolworth's Photo Booth. Dorothy (top) and Teresa (bottom)

6
omega house

It was Wednesday morning, January 15th, 1975, when my father forced me into his Lincoln Continental. We were both breathing hard from our heated exchange. What I didn't know was that my father was taking me to a drug rehabilitation program called Omega House, which was modeled after a prominent rehab center in California called Synanon.

Mike had been forced to go to Omega House every day after school by his parole officer after he got caught in possession of marijuana. He told me it was a place for stoners and drop-outs.

Omega House was located in a dicey part of downtown Reno on the upper level of an oddly situated, L-shaped building with a side entry door that opened to a steep staircase. It had several offices, a group therapy room and a rec room that sported a foosball table, pool table and jukebox. The rooms were filled with faded, battered furniture more suited for a garbage bin than a treatment center.

The director of the program, John Tachihara, shook my hand introducing himself as "John T." before taking my father into his office. He was a wiry man of Japanese descent who wore crisply-pressed, navy Levis and fancy cowboy boots. His longish black hair behaved contrary to his tidy appearance, poking out randomly, here and there, beneath a white cowboy hat. His button-down shirt opened, Tom Jones-style, to reveal a thick gold chain and hairy chest. Despite his western attire, he had a distinctly militaristic air about him. I'd never seen such a tightly coiled cowboy before. He made a memorable first impression.

Two women named Denise and Allison greeted me, saying they were both counselors. I didn't expect them to be so nice. Denise had an effervescent personality and spoke in a strong, melodic Australian accent. Her expressive blue eyes complemented her wispy blond hair and the lively way in which she spoke. Her hands gesticulated accordingly, making her hair bounce around her face.

Where Denise exuded warmth and comfort, Allison was completely outta sight, and oh mama, was she sexy. She had a super-funky, cool vibe, a mellow voice, and thick, dull, brown hair so heavy it hung like a lead curtain around her face. Her hippie ensemble included azure-blue metallic sunglasses, a snug, white, cotton t-shirt that perfectly outlined her erect nipples and a wild print maxi skirt. I was more than a little caught off guard to find myself sexually aroused at that particular moment.

John T. interrupted my fixation on Allison, asking me to join the discussion in his office. It was a drab room that smelled like ashtrays, evidenced vividly by the nicotine-stained walls. A third counselor introduced himself to me, a stout man who looked better suited to life in a log cabin. His name was Jon Wallace.

"So, what's the problem here?" John T. asked succinctly. My father readily launched into a litany of my unacceptable behaviors while I sat hugging myself in a tight ball on the sofa with my nose between my knees. I listened as my father reported how I dressed lasciviously, didn't clean my room, and used the telephone with no regard for others. He summarized me as capricious, flighty and petulant. Additionally, he said this friend of mine, Becky, was trouble—a rebel who exerted a terrible influence on me. When he compared my personality and behavior to Kris's, his gold standard, I was fighting back tears.

When my father paused, Jon Wallace turned his attention toward me, "Are you taking any drugs, Suzy?"

"No."

"Do you have failing grades?"

"No."

"Do you drink alcohol?"

"No."

Mr. Wallace looked bewildered by my answers.

John T. leaned forward in his chair and asked, "Suzy, how do you feel about your father?"

"I hate his fucking guts."

John T. then directed the same question to my father, "Tom, how do you feel about your daughter?"

Without missing a beat he looked me straight in the eyes and said, "I hate her fucking guts."

My father turned to John T. and asked, "How much money would it take to get her out this afternoon?"

In order for my father to make the deal in private, I was taken into another office with Denise and Allison. They reassured me everything would be fine. Then, in hushed voices, they asked why I was brought in.

"My mom caught me kissing a girl." I replied.

"Far-fucking-out," cooed Allison.

Allison said she could already tell my father was the problem, not me, and, furthermore, being into women was a totally fine choice for me to make. Her unexpected assessment blew me away. I was pleased she was on my side.

Three-hundred bucks is what it cost to have me exterminated

from my home. I know because my prick father brandished the check in my face before handing it to Mr. Wallace. We went back home so I could pack my belongings.

Once there, I pleaded with my mother to change my father's mind. I was struggling to comprehend the fact that they considered me unfit to live at home anymore, and worse still, unfit to be in the company of my siblings. I protested there was nothing wrong with me, but there was neither sympathy nor any response to my pleas.

My mother receded to her bedroom with her guilt.

I put my clothing, records, my Happy and Sneezy Dwarfs that Terry brought me from Disneyland and everything else into six grocery bags.

When it was time to go, my siblings lined up at the front door so I could say goodbye to them. There was no containing my heartbreak as I held my little sister and told her I wasn't going to be living at home anymore. I hugged them all, especially the three youngest, Tommy, Peter and Meg, not wanting to let go. Sadness engulfed me as left my family home.

Memory is fascinating and bears mentioning here. One day, more than thirty years later as I pondered the significance of that day, I canvassed my brothers and sisters to hear their memories of the day I was removed from our home. It was a shock to discover that no one remembered much, other than Kris, who said she felt she better be on her best behavior or she might be next.

At first, this hurt me, but as I thought about it, I realized this day that was so sharply carved in my mind did not leave a heavy trace on them because it was my significant day, my wounding, not theirs. They had their own significant days to remember.

As we started the drive back to Omega House, I pushed into

the door on my side to gain every bit of space from my father that I could. I could not have hated him more.

Tears streamed down my face as I watched out the window. We were passing all the familiar sights of my childhood; past the church that was once an empty field where I made tumbleweed forts and prayed to Our Lady of Fatima; where I caught pollywogs and put them in my red wagon filled with water to sell in the neighborhood; past the public school where my siblings and I were tormented for being Catholic; and down the streets where I'd either roller skated or ridden my bike for years. Suddenly, everything around me was desperately more precious as I silently said my goodbyes.

Jon Wallace was waiting for me when we pulled up and carried my belongings inside. My father drove away without saying a word.

I sat in the rec room for hours waiting for whoever was supposed to drive me to the live-in facility, Omega House II, or The Residence, as it was more commonly known. A few kids came up to say hello, but I was unreceptive, mostly because I was in a state of shock.

Unfortunately, almost everyone was smoking and I detested the stench of cigarettes. Pink Floyd's "Money" and Lynyrd Skynyrd's "Free Bird" played on the jukebox as kids played foosball and visited with one another.

My eyelids were nearly swollen shut from crying and I was completely out of gas. I did my best to curl up on a couch, pulling my jacket over my head to protect me from the filthy fabric and to provide some semblance of privacy.

Becky was all I could think about, which was both comforting and worrisome. I had no way of contacting her, no way to tell her my life changed the instant we were caught. She would be wondering why I hadn't called. How would she even hear what had happened to me? What would she think? Was she okay? My mind ran in circles, chasing questions I had no answers for.

The glaring impotence of having no choice and no power to alter my circumstances in any way shook me to my core. Thankfully, exhaustion gained the upper hand and I fell asleep waiting for my ride. It was dark outside when a strange man woke me up by roughly shaking my shoulder, "Hey," he barked. "Are you Mueller?"

"My name is Suzy," I replied.

Ignoring my correction, he went on, "Well, Mueller, I'm Bill. We're heading out to The Residence now. Get your stuff."

With that terse introduction, I got up and loaded my brown paper bags into Bill's Celica.

It was half an hour drive to The Residence. Bill and I did not talk. I was numb anyway, and trying to muster some alertness, as I was going into an unknown situation. When we finally hit the dirt parking lot, I could make out a large rectangular building that looked like an old, derelict motel from a Spaghetti Western starring Clint Eastwood. The huge front porch, which ran the length of the building, was dimly lit.

It was pitch black out. The stars seemed almost close enough to touch. Bill parked next to a side entrance and grunted, "Okay, this is it." I stepped out into gusting cold air that hit my face with an unforgiving slap.

As we entered the building, Bill hit a light switch to reveal a spacious room that had obviously once been a saloon. Situated to the right was an enormous bar made of thick, careworn wood that had stories to tell. To my left, just like at Omega House in town, was a semi-circle of second-hand couches with scattered end-tables interspersed with ashtrays.

"The bedrooms are upstairs," Bill directed, taking four of my bags while I carried the other two. The room was empty, save for an army cot and two gray metal folding chairs. A candle, book of matches, and Carlos Castaneda's *Tales of Power* rested on one chair. The other chair was empty.

Bill told me to stay put and left. A few minutes later he was back with a flannel sleeping bag, ragtag pillow, glass of water and box of tissues, saying, "The bathroom is down the hall on the right, if you need to use it. I've got some things to check on, but I'll be back in a bit. I assume you can put yourself to bed?"

As soon as he was gone my emotions overflowed.

I couldn't believe I was there. I couldn't believe I no longer lived at home with my family. I couldn't believe I had no way to tell Becky what had taken place or where I was. She was a million miles away. Everything had changed so fast, my head was reeling.

I found my way to the bathroom down the hall, which was as dreary as I expected it to be. Back in the room, I threw the sleeping bag on the cot, struggled to get the zipper open, and then climbed in with my clothes on, burying my face in the pillow—sobbing so hard that every now and then an enormous yawn would overtake me, giving me a few seconds' reprieve from my sorrow.

In my mind, a tape-loop repeated, *I don't live at home anymore, I don't live at home anymore, I don't live at home anymore....*

This was how the night passed: heavy sobbing, which caused gulping-for-air yawning, until I was overtaken with sleep, only to jolt awake and remember where I was, which led to more sobbing and yawning, and so it repeated again and again.

Eventually, a somber thought emerged that took hold of me and would not let go: *If this is the price for being me, I won't be me.* Afterall, I wasn't fierce like Becky. I didn't want to live in a world where I was shamed and ridiculed for who I was.

At one point, I realized Bill was in the room, sitting close to me. I squinted to see, not wanting him to know I was looking. He was sitting on the folding chair, hunched forward with his forearms pressing into his thighs, holding his book, reading. He seemed engrossed, not noticing I was watching him. A single candlestick burned on the other metal chair, providing the sole light in the room. The building creaked and moaned as the wind howled outside and whistled through the cracks in the windows, causing wax to fly off of Bill's candle onto the metal seat.

What an alien sight, this man sitting so close to me, in the soft, dancing light. There was an unsettling intimacy about him being there while my heart broke open. He alone was witnessing the aftermath of my father's severe punishment. Fatigue swept through me and I decided it was better not to look, better to keep my eyes closed as another wave of sorrow engulfed me.

The wretched events of the day gave way, at last, to sleep. Maybe a couple of hours had passed until the sound of a girl screaming jerked me back to consciousness. I sat up, yelling out involuntarily, terrified and frozen on the cot. A tall girl of about sixteen had come into the room, wild-eyed and vibrating. She had a razor blade in one hand and was slashing it through the air, attempting to strike her wrist in the low light.

Bill was on his feet in a flash as he bear-hugged her from behind to restrain her arm movements. He ordered her to "drop the blade" in a steady voice, repeating himself until she acquiesced. Then, he carried her out of the room, still bear-hugging her like she was a toddler strapped to his chest.

What kind of fucking nuthouse had my parents put me in?

I slid low into the bag and pulled it over my head, curling

into a fetal position to get warm and finally fell asleep.

Judging by the sun's position out the window, I figured it was about ten o'clock when I woke up. I was alone. A tiny candle nub remained on the chair. The sunlight defined the room I had entered in the dark. It was plain, with an overburdened wood floor of uneven panels. An open door frame revealed a kind of a closet, with a little sink and a small vanity mirror. Next to the sink, wooden pegs ran along the wall to hang clothing on and a built-in bench provided a place to sit while dressing. I'd heard the place was a brothel a long time ago. The configuration of the room and closet seemed to confirm this.

Sitting up, my head was pounding at my temples and my vision was blurry. I was also hungry, as no one had thought much about feeding me the day before. Hearing footsteps in the hall, I heard Bill's voice as he opened the door.

"Mueller, come downstairs for breakfast," he said.

My shoes were under the cot. I put them on and got up. For some reason, I couldn't stand, I hit the floor like someone had shoved me.

"You okay?" Bill asked.

"I think so," I said, trying again to stand, but I could not keep my balance.

"What's wrong with you?" Bill asked.

"I don't know," I replied, "I can't seem to stand up."

A few more failed efforts confirmed that something was amiss. I had no equilibrium. My body had somehow forgotten how to stand and no matter the effort that I made, I kept hitting the floor. Bill put his arm around my waist to help me walk, grabbed my jacket and headed to the staircase. He carried me downstairs, across the big room to the tiny kitchen to grab a couple of danishes before carrying me to his car to take me to St. Mary's Hospital.

Someone must've called my mother because she was at the hospital when we arrived. I was comforted to see her, even though I was still upset about her betrayal. She filled out the admission forms as Bill told her what happened. In no time at all, I had my own room in a comfy hospital bed.

I hope this costs my father a fucking fortune, I thought happily.

That first day, I slept for hours, waking only if it was time for another test or to eat. Days went by and the doctors didn't know what was wrong with me. Eventually, I was given a spinal tap based on a working theory that I might have meningitis.

I was glad the doctors didn't know what was wrong with me because it forestalled going back to The Residence. My father never came to visit.

An official diagnosis never emerged, but on the fifth day I had recovered sufficiently enough to walk again. The speculation was that I probably had a brain infection, possibly from all the cigarette smoke I encountered at Omega House. But I had my own theory: The rug had been, metaphorically, pulled out from under me. Of course I had no equilibrium.

After checking out of the hospital, Bill took me to McDonald's before we drove back to The Residence. My room had been furnished while I was away. On the floor was a donated mattress and bedding from home, including the patchwork quilt my mother made for me when I was twelve. My record player and albums were there as well, along with a chest of drawers. Ironically, it was the first time in my life that I had my own bedroom, an odd bright spot, considering the circumstances.

Denise was the head of The Residence. She and Bill lived onsite looking after the eight children living there, including me.

Seeing Bill again, it occurred to me that he looked like a blond Adolph Hitler. His German features, small mouth and clipped mustache produced an uncanny resemblance to the Führer. At twenty-four years of age, Bill was a high school dropout with no formal training as a counselor. In the recent past, Bill had been heavily into drugs and claimed he had dropped acid "at least three hundred" times. Apparently because he survived all that, he was qualified to be in charge of minors at Omega House.

We gathered in the saloon, or what they called *The Game Room*, and Denise brought in a box of doughnuts. We went around the room and each one of us took a moment to introduce ourselves, for my benefit, since I was the newest addition.

The other kids were there because they got caught smoking weed. I met Dorothy, a nice-looking, hard-assed tomboy; Teresa, a skinny, shy brunette; Diana, the unhinged girl with the razor blade; and Jodi, a tall, willowy beauty from Malibu with a famous surfer deadbeat dad.

The boys were Tommy, a stocky, baby-faced, mouthy kid; Darren, a sensitive, pale, blond boy; and Les, an egotistical jock.

Denise went over the daily schedule and chores. A chart on the wall noted all chores, which rotated, so everyone participated in all aspects of maintaining the house. A fence needed to be built on the property as well, so we could look forward to early morning shifts digging post holes before school.

Winter break was almost over. I was the only one at The Residence who had not dropped out of high school.

Since I was still enrolled at Manogue, Denise informed me Bill would drive me to school each morning. I would be required to sit in his car until the bell rang, at which point I could leave to go to class. He would also be there when school let out. I was to walk directly to his car, without socializing with anyone.

What a kick in the teeth. The kids at school were going to see me confined with this weirdo, Hitler look-alike and his rocky mountain high, John Denver wire-rimmed glasses.

Next, the subject of *The Game* was discussed. Omega House was modeled after Synanon, which was founded by a one-time Alcoholics Anonymous acolyte named Charles Dederich.

Dederich developed a controversial therapeutic approach, simply called The Game. It was a brutal, tough-love approach, sometimes referred to as "attack therapy," wherein counselors (who were mostly ex-addicts) used whatever means necessary to get people to expose their innermost weaknesses.

The Game had two rules and they were strictly enforced:

1. No physical violence.
2. You are not allowed to leave The Game.

Omega House utilized The Game and it was "played" every night after dinner at The Residence, except Fridays when we went to town to the Omega House Day Program for their evening game. We usually finished about midnight, sometimes later.

What a misleading thing to call it, I thought. It should have been called *mind fuck*. It was an anything-goes free-for-all, a confrontational, battering ram technique designed to break down a person's barriers and defenses.

After dinner, we heard the call to assemble in the big room. Each of us chose our spot in the circle of couches. Cigarettes were lit by the smokers. Denise and Bill chose their seats last. The game commenced when Denise said, "Let's begin."

In the silence, Denise and Bill slowly surveyed us, looking back and forth around the room, ascertaining who seemed guilty, high, or nervous. Looking for weakness, they'd select their prey with an opening line, like, "So, Darren, why has your head been up your ass all day?"

If you were really in trouble, once singled out, you occupied *the hot seat*, a chair placed in the middle of the circle. Once in the hot seat, the intensity of questions increased and if you resisted answering, things could escalate quickly.

As weeks went on, I watched counselors, inches from a kid's face, yelling, "you're a loser, you're a piece of shit," etc. It was designed to cause a breakdown in the person leading to huge emotional release and catharsis. It was terrifying. Truly, we were being abused.

The Synanon game also promoted making commitments. For example, if a kid committed not to smoke weed, they also had to name their consequence if they broke their commitment. Often, the go-to consequence was a shaved head. Synanon believed the stoner persona was heavily linked to having long hair, so shaving it off was an effective way to free yourself from that identification.

Game nights stretched on forever. Four to five hours a night of being grilled and yelled at. Once you broke down, the energy shifted into making commitments and promising to do better. Finally, a dose of encouragement or praise was doled out, like a kind of adhesive to hold you together after being blown apart.

The kids got into it as well—anyone could talk to or yell at the person in the hot seat. Kids would narc on a friend if they knew they had smoked a joint or had weed in their bedroom. It was a good strategy, especially if you were guilty of something, because it would deflect attention away from you. I watched for weeks, struggling to stay awake for the duration and then had difficulty falling to sleep afterwards. Sleep deprivation became the norm.

My first day back at school was a nightmare. Most everyone knew I had been thrown out of my home. When Bill drove into the parking lot at Manogue, a small crowd assembled to witness my arrival. I slid as low as I could in the bucket seat. When I didn't get out, some kids walked up to try and talk to me, but Bill stuck his head out the window and told them to move along. Mortified and embarrassed, I was stuck like a captive zoo animal being stared at behind the glass.

And so it went, sitting with Bill until the bell rang, rushing to get to my first period class. A few friends spoke to me as we whispered about what had happened. Kris decided to avoid me altogether as our family dramas were a shameful embarrassment to her. Being snubbed by my sister was painful because I wanted to connect with my family in any way that I could.

Mike and I talked in the halls between classes. We could commiserate because he was attending the Omega House Day Program. The big buzz in the halls was that I must be using drugs to end up in a drug treatment program and no amount of saying otherwise changed anyone's mind.

The fact that Kris had given me the nickname Booze didn't help, even though her nickname for me had nothing to do with alcohol. It started out with her rhyming my name, calling me Suzy-Boozy, which, over time, was shortened to Booze.

In truth, my behavior prior to being put in Omega House had been frenetic. It was difficult to go from being a popular cheerleader at St. Albert's to being a nobody at Manogue. I joined the Pep Club, which sold candy bars, sodas and other goodies at all sports events.

During the game, I'd chow down on a couple of large Milky Way bars. Within twenty minutes or so, I was jacked on sugar. When my shift was over, I'd get in the bleachers and act up. I liked to entertain others for attention. My voice was loud and I did running commentaries that got the crowd laughing. This was when the rumors began that I was using drugs.

My freshman year, I had even imitated Becky's stunt and climbed over the wall from the second story staircase in dramatic fashion, acting like I was about to fall. When a crowd gathered, all of them pleading with me to climb back over, I'd relent to huge sighs of relief.

I began to cut forth period biology with Father Lahrs after he announced we would be dissecting a frog. I refused to do it. I was squeamish thinking about it. Instead, I'd go to the Mayfair Market and buy six donuts and a quart of milk for about a dollar. Then, at a nearby park, I'd eat until I was stuffed and pass out in a sugar coma. Sometimes I woke up in time for my next class, sometimes I was late, but I cut most of my biology classes.

With Bill as my assigned watchguard, I had become painfully conspicuous. I no longer held my head up when I walked. I stared at the ground and avoided eye contact.

My old friend from St. Albert's, Colleen, changed once we got to Manogue. She spent her time with other girls in her social class and largely ignored me and others she had been friendly with in grade school. Of course, she made the freshman cheerleading squad, further cementing the social chasm between us. Being brushed-off by her made me angry and added to my growing sense that high school was a hostile environment.

Another aspect of my plummeting esteem was how lousy I felt about my appearance. I'd gained weight from my sugar binges. I didn't feel well and was having headaches regularly. I no longer felt attractive and was convinced I was invisible to the boys in my class, mainly because none of the boys I liked ever liked me back.

Back at The Residence, whenever I wasn't doing my assigned tasks, I'd rush to my room to be alone and listen to music. Two albums in particular were played constantly. The first was Cat Stevens' *Tea for the Tillerman*. Even handling the vinyl was done with such care—dare I say reverence—because the music and lyrics were vitally important to me. Listening became a ritual, especially at night. I'd placed the record player on a crate next to my pillow so I could reach it while lying in bed.

The first song on side A was "Where Do the Children Play" and it always made me emotional. The whole album served as an outlet for my feelings. Cat Stevens' lyrics conveyed the quest he was on for deeper spiritual meaning, though sometimes I found them too mysterious to understand. I pored over the liner notes, pondering what he was trying to say.

The other album was side two of Loggins and Messina's *Full Sail*. Melancholy instrumentals helped me drift away from the realities of my life as a restricted, semi-incarcerated person.

Being isolated from my brothers and sisters, my grandpa and Becky was miserable. I was downcast and felt terribly lonely.

Who was I without them? Did I matter at all?

7
runaway

I was drifting peacefully into a nap on a Friday afternoon when I heard someone pounding on the side door that functioned as our main entrance. My curiosity got the better of me and I hustled down the stairs to see who was being so insistent.

It was some kind of a miracle. Standing on the stoop, breathless and grinning from ear to ear was Becky. I couldn't believe my eyes. "Becky!" I squeaked. "Oh my god, Becky! How the hell did you find me here?"

"Never mind that," she said. "Where's your room?"

Knowing her presence was against the rules, I grabbed her hand and raced up the stairs to my room. I closed the door quietly and locked it.

We dove for my bed, overcome with torrents of emotion, and smothered one another in kisses. She was here. She knew where I was. The worry of her not knowing was lifted.

Amid a profusion of "I love yous," Becky said she had a plan for us to run away. I lost my job when I was put in Omega House, but Becky reminded me we had our bank account. She said we could totally make it happen.

This was all so unexpected, it threw me for a loop. I didn't know what to say. The idea of the two of us striking out alone in the world was way too scary for me. Knowing we didn't have much time, I was content feeling her body against mine. I resumed kissing her and eagerly lifted her shirt over her head. There was that alabaster skin I had daydreamed about, so pale compared to my ruddy genetics. Wanting to still her, I lowered my head to kiss her nipples. She moaned and went silent as we held one another.

All my feelings of insignificance disappeared the moment Becky found me. I meant something to her. Her presence filled me with such a sense of belonging, I wanted it to last forever.

My romantic reverie was shattered by the angry sound of Bill's voice as he tried to open my door. He was furious to find it locked.

"Mueller, open this mother-fucking door right now!"

No, no, no, I thought, *not yet. Don't intrude. Go away.*

I rubbed my face against Becky's abdomen, wanting her scent to rub off on me so I could smell her later.

"Mueller!" he commanded. "Open the door!"

"Okay," I snarled, "give me a second!"

Becky was putting her shirt on and I was trying to shift from my state of sexual arousal to facing Bill's wrath, but his patience had run out.

"You've got three seconds, Mueller!" he threatened.

I yanked the door open and shouted, "What do you want?"

"You know goddamn well there are no extracurricular guests allowed here without clearance," he began, his eyes scanning Becky up and down as he spoke.

"Who are you?" he demanded.

"I'm Suzy's girlfriend, Becky. Who the fuck are you?"

"I the-fuck-am the guy telling you it's time for you to go," he said, as he reached for her to drag her out of my room.

"I love you, Suzy!" Becky cried. She dodged Bill's grip and

took off running. As fast as she had appeared, she was gone.

I smiled so big it hurt, thinking of what a stupendous and mighty person she was. Her courage was something to behold.

Bill caught me smiling, which made him angrier. He turned to face me saying, "You'll eat alone in your room tonight and then we're heading into town for The Game."

"Good! I love to eat alone," I shot back.

Decades later, I found out how Becky got to The Residence that day: Through Rita, she found out what had happened to me and where I was. She was at home that day, angry and upset about our forced separation when she noticed a man in a truck pulling up to the place next door. He left the truck idling and went inside the house. In an instant, Becky decided this was her chance to see me. She ran out in the snow, jumped in his truck and took off.

At fourteen years old, Becky drove that truck more than ten miles on the highway to get to me. After our visit, she drove home, leaving the truck a few blocks from her house with the keys in the ignition. No one was the wiser, and she got away with it. My girlfriend was one audacious babe.

After dinner we piled into the white van. Denise drove in her usual style, with her left foot on the bench seat, knee to chest, while her right foot worked the pedals. Bill sat beside her, still fuming about Becky's rogue visit.

Once at Omega House, we hung out in the game room where the radio was always blaring. I was starting to get to know the kids there, but chose to sit alone. I was thinking about how amazing it was to see Becky and to feel a connection to my former life.

My thoughts were interrupted by the booming voice of Wade Lieseke, a Vietnam veteran who served as a door gunner for the 282nd Assault Helicopter Company. During his time in Vietnam, he served in four major campaigns and was honored with multiple medals for his service, including the Purple Heart. He had seen it all. On rare occasions when he talked about Vietnam, we were riveted to our seats, horrified and sickened by his stories.

Wade (top photo) and Bill in high school.

Wade stood out distinctly from the hippie vibe of Omega House with his receding crew cut and conservative dress. He had a powerful, bulldozer build and a face hardened by war. His deep-set eyes seemed to squint with distrust from their hooded location. His tough-as-nails, don't-fuck-with-me attitude concealed a volatility that rumbled beneath the surface. You could feel it in the measured way he spoke or by the gulps of air he would suck in to steady himself. He seemed to teeter on the brink of violence, which made him the most terrifying counselor at Omega House. Wade was the only person I'd ever met who served in Vietnam.

"Let's go, we're starting!" Wade shouted and we all shuffled into the big room so The Game could begin.

It was a packed Friday night—there must have been forty people in attendance. Cigarette smoke choked the air. Denise introduced a new girl named Jackie and said that she'd be joining us to live at The Residence.

Kids were hustling to get the spot they wanted and pretty soon, the couches were full. A few of the guys were sitting on the backs of the sofa, behind friends. Mike was there as well. It was good to see someone from home. We smiled at each other across the room.

Lighters were passed around as more kids lit their cigarettes.

When we settled, the counselors filed in to take their seats. Wade grabbed an old hardwood chair, marched into the center of the room and deliberately set it down with a heavy thunk, as if to say, *The shit is about to go down.* Wade jerked his head in my direction and gave me a look that made me shudder.

Bill stood up and surveyed the room, looking for the weak link to kick things off. This was the excruciating beginning of every game. The scan. When you know you're being scrutinized, it's almost impossible to try and look relaxed. Ironically, that trying rapidly gets you noticed.

I was surveying too. It had become something of a habit of mine to see if I could guess who they would pick. They all knew I didn't do drugs, so I was pretty much exempt. Bill was turning his body in a slow circle to catch the eye of any anxious kid in the room. Finally he made his choice, but his back was to me so I couldn't see where he was looking.

"Mueller. In the hot seat, now," he commanded.

No! I cringed, *Please, not my brother, leave him the fuck alone!*

I was looking across the room to where Mike was sitting. He

hated Bill. Mike was shaking his head in disbelief and started to get up.

"No. Not you, Mike," Bill interjected.

"You."

A megavolt went through me as Bill swung around, pointing directly at me. His eyes were fixed, his jaw set and determined. He was gunning for me. I didn't move. I had never been called to the hot seat before, not once.

Here? Now? In town? I didn't know at least half of the kids in the room.

"You're up to bat, Mueller," he chided. "Take your seat."

Self-consciousness overtook me. I was on crutches from a recent basketball injury that tore the ligaments in my right ankle. My armpits were tender from hefting myself around. I let out a huge groan and made my way over to the chair.

Denise wasn't at The Residence when Becky arrived or left, so she leaned in, curious to hear what Bill was going to say.

You can't leave and no physical violence is allowed, those are the only two rules right now, I reminded myself.

Bill launched his attack as soon as my butt hit the chair. "Mueller here broke the house rules today at The Residence by sneaking in a friend," he began.

"Somehow she managed to make plans for her friend, Becky, to drive out for a visit. What I want to know is how the fuck you made that happen."

"I didn't make anything happen, Bill. I had no idea she was going to show up," I replied.

"Bullshit!" exclaimed Wade. "You're shining us on."

"No, I'm not!" I defended.

"I don't believe you either," barked Bill. "Tell us how you did it, Mueller. You are in my car before and after school and there is a lock on the phone at The Residence, so you have some explaining to do."

Clenching my teeth, I set my jaw and stared at the dirty carpet. There was no way I was going to cop to something I did not do.

Bill saw my resolve and so did everyone else.

Cat-calling started from kids who didn't even know me. They were yelling, "You're a fucking liar!" "Tell the truth, bitch!" And so on. Bill hammered me for a good thirty minutes with threats and insults, assuring me he would "get to the bottom of this."

But Bill wasn't getting anywhere, so Denise chimed in, "This can be a short night or a long one, Suzy. You might as well tell the truth." This pissed me off because it seemed she believed Bill over me when she wasn't even there. I snapped at her, "I am telling the truth, Denise, but none of you are listening to me. I had no idea Becky would show up at The Residence today."

On and on it went, being shouted at and called names. I thought of Becky's bravery and kept staring at the floor.

Fuck this place, I thought. I don't deserve this and I didn't do anything wrong.

Bill was worked up. He moved closer and Wade followed, both of them chastising me to tell the truth. They were so certain that I had schemed for Becky to visit me, they felt entitled to insult me over and over, calling me names and accusing me of concealing something.

Having Wade virtually on top of me was too menacing to take, so I jumped out of my chair, forcing Wade and Bill to step back. "Get off my back! I refuse to own up to something I didn't do! Fucking leave me alone!"

I sat back down, trying to keep it together, but I was

beginning to crumble. Bill was pacing in front of me and he was pissed. He'd been ineffective and he wanted to get his result.

He squared off in front of me, his arms folded tightly across his chest. I swear to god, I saw the lightbulb pop over his head as he thought of what to say. A disturbing, sardonic smile came across his face as he relished the moment.

I braced for impact, and he hit me with it, "Hey Mueller, why don't you tell everyone how you were sucking on your girlfriend Becky's tits in your room today?"

Dead silence. No one expected that. Throwing myself forward, I put my head between my knees, holding my head with my hands. It was too much.

At that moment, all I could think of was that my brother was in the room. *What will Mike think of me now?* The ruthless joy Bill derived from outing me was hard to take.

No one said a word. They were all waiting on me.

My mind was blank. I couldn't think of anything to say. I felt like I was falling into a deep hole that I would never emerge from again. This forced exposure was devastating. My sexuality was private. I was terrified Mike would judge me and I'd lose the one person in my family I still had contact with.

Why was Bill such an asshole? Why did he do that?

Finally I spoke, "What do you want me to say, Bill, that I'm a lesbian?"

"Thank you!" Bill declared, feeling victorious.

Denise intervened at this point, saying, "I think that's enough for her, Bill, let's move on."

I had to get out of there, so I said to Denise, "I have to pee."

Denise gave me permission to leave the room.

As I approached the door, Mike was coming toward me. I tensed up, but there was no need. He surrounded me with a warm bear hug and whispered in my ear, "Don't worry about anything, Suzy, I don't care about that at all."

I left my crutches and hopped to the bathroom. I had to get away. I needed a moment to myself to think.

Bill's vulgarity and perverse delight in exposing my relationship with Becky was sickening. How could Omega House endorse this kind of abuse? How could I go back in the room? Thinking about it made my heart race. My teeth were chattering from the severity of it all.

I knew I didn't deserve to be treated like this. No one did. This place was bullshit. The Game was bullshit. It was used as an excuse to justify berating and harming children. My heart ached thinking of how my parents threw me away like trash.

I was angry and fed up. I decided to run away.

Unbolting the bathroom door, I opened it slowly to see if anyone else was around. I could already hear the next victim being reamed. I made my way down the hall, then hopped down the stairs to the heavy metal door that would bring me my freedom, making sure it didn't bang as it closed.

Once outside, I wished I had grabbed my crutches. It was dark and raining. Not wanting to get caught, I was hopping as fast as I could, which quickly left me out of breath. I had to put some weight on my cast to keep moving at a good pace. After about a block and a half, I saw a phone booth in front of a motel. Luckily, I had change in my pocket. Despite breaking up with Gena, she was an adult, so I called her for help.

"Oh my god, Gena!" I shouted when she answered the phone. I was so damn grateful she was home. Talking fast I continued, "I'm so glad you picked up. It's Suzy. Can you come and get me? I've run away."

I was starting to panic about someone coming to look for

me. "Hey Gena? Please hurry, I'm all alone on Fourth Street."

Even Gena and Kathy had heard what happened to me. I heard Gena yell, "Kathy, come here, quick!"

Getting back to me, she asked, "What's your cross street?

"Hang on," I replied, hopping out of the phone booth to look, "I'm at the corner of Center and Fourth Street."

"Hang tight, Suzy, we're on our way," she assured me.

"Thank you!" I yelled back. The feeling of support I had in that moment was profound.

The motel I was hiding at had been built in the fifties with a typical neon sign out front that reminded me of happier times—the road trips with my family when I was little. I crouched behind some bushes in case anyone from Omega House discovered I was missing.

Gena and Kathy arrived in no time at all. I was relieved when I saw her Capri pull up at the curb. Stepping out from the bushes, they saw I was wearing a cast. Kathy jumped out of the car to help.

"You're soaked!" she exclaimed.

"Well, it *is* raining..." I replied.

"Come on, get in the car. Let's get you warm."

I filled Gena and Kathy in on what had taken place during The Game, which was a hard thing to explain to people, but they got the gist and were pissed.

"How dare he expose you like that," Gena fumed. "This doesn't sound like a good place for you to be at all."

"They're absolute assholes," I concurred.

When we got to their house, Gena got me a dry shirt and a towel to blot my hair. They brought me some food and a cup of chamomile tea. Gena and Kathy said all the things that I wanted to hear, "You are safe now, we'll take care of you, they won't find you here, it's all going to be okay."

The relief I felt was immense. For the first time in three months, I let my guard down. I wasn't being watched or scrutinized. I felt like my shoulders dropped four inches, but I was incredibly fatigued. Between the adrenaline of running away and the emotional ordeal of The Game, I was spent. I wanted to call Becky, but they cautioned against it, saying we couldn't guarantee she'd be the one to pick up the phone.

Gena took me to her bedroom and I undressed down to my undies and got in bed. She laid next to me, softly singing while stroking my back. Her kindness was a revelation. Life had become so jarring.

If it wasn't so late at night, I would have called my grandpa. It pained me that I never got to see him before I was taken away and I wondered what he thought of what my parents had done. I was lost in my thoughts when Kathy came into the room.

"Hey, Suzy," Kathy began, "if you are gone too long, I think you'll be considered a runaway."

"What do you mean?" I asked.

"Well, it's a legal situation. We should make a phone call."

Gena found a 24-hour runaway hotline number in the phone book and told me to call and explain what had happened.

The person I spoke to was knowledgeable and asked if I was a ward of the court, meaning was I sentenced to be in Omega House by a judge or did my parents voluntarily put me there.

"The latter," I said.

"That's good," she replied. "Now, if you are gone more than twenty-four hours, you'll legally be considered a runaway. In that circumstance, you could find yourself a ward of the court and they could sentence you to Omega House for an extended period of time." I thanked her for the information and hung up the phone.

"We need to get you home in time so you won't be a runaway," Kathy stated. "Are you willing to call your mom in the morning?"

"Yeah, for sure, " I said, and meant it. The thought of being sentenced to Omega House was dreadful. We all went to bed and I slept soundly next to Gena's warm body on her futon.

In the morning, Gena made me breakfast. Then she and Kathy coached me on what to say to my mother; that I was fine and with friends and I'd come home if she promised I never had to go back to Omega House again.

I made the call. When my mother heard my voice, she cried, "Suzy, oh my god, you're okay, you're okay." She sounded like a total wreck. "Mike and I have been up all night driving the streets looking for you."

"I'm okay, mom," I reassured her. "I had to get out of there. Omega House is an awful place. I want to come home, mom."

She was silent so I kept talking.

"Is it okay if I come home?" I asked. "I mean, can I come home to stay? I want to come home now."

She hesitated and then said, "Yes, honey. Come home."

"But, what about dad?" I asked. "Will he let me come home? Can you talk to him?"

"Yes, I'll talk to him," she assured me.

"So, for sure then?" I asked again, wanting to be certain. "You're saying that I can come home today and stay?"

"Yes, honey, come home."

I was so thankful she said yes. I was done with Bill and his crude comments about me and Becky. I could finish my

Gena and Kathy's tiny brick house.

sophomore year like a normal person.

When we got to Everett Drive, Gena dropped me off a few houses down the block so as not to attract attention to herself.

It was a peculiar sensation though, standing at the front door of my own home like an outsider, getting ready to ring the bell.

I paused, taking a breath before I rang.

My mother opened the door and said my name with the oddest sound in her voice.

My smile disappeared before I could even respond. To my horror, Bill Dansie stepped out from behind the door.

"Let's go, Mueller, in the car."

I had been so absorbed in my happiness at returning home that I didn't notice his Celica parked across the street.

I glared at my mother, who wore a pained expression.

"What kind of mother does this?" I shrieked, shaken to the core. "You tricked me? You fucking lied to me?"

Her betrayal collapsed the floor beneath me.

Up until that moment, I thought my father was the main reason I was put in Omega House, but now my mother had deceived me and set me up. I felt like I had no parents anymore. They had washed their hands of me, and clearly, I was not welcomed in their home. My father was at work, making her involvement obvious. It was too terrible to take in. I turned on her with all my fury.

"My god, mom, I cannot believe you lied to me and tricked me. You are such a bitch! I fucking hate you," I yelled through my tears.

I wasn't going home. I was following Bill to his car.

8

crash & burn

Running away had consequences. Every fuck-up at Omega House did. I lost favor with Denise, who distanced herself from me, and I no longer had a room to myself. Jackie, the new girl, became my roommate. She was miffed about it and complained in front of me, saying, "Why do I have to sleep next to the lezzie? What if she feels me up when I'm asleep?"

Teresa and Dorothy snickered. At that moment, I realized my friendships with them would be different now, thanks to Bill. Jackie was asked by Denise why she thought she had any say in the matter, so Jackie reluctantly brought her belongings to my room. The first chance I got, I made sure to let her know I didn't find her attractive in the least, so she had nothing to worry about.

Bill changed the door knob, removing the lock. Also, when we were in town for The Game on Friday nights, I had to have a counselor or a junior counselor with me at all times, including when I went to use the bathroom.

Junior counselors were older teenagers with trustworthy reputations who had been in the program awhile. I had a crush on one of them, a handsome seventeen-year-old old named Clint Stanley. He had a long mullet of soft, brown curls and a chiseled face. Clint was a little taller than me, with a sinewy build and the beginnings of a good tan he would cultivate all summer. He was a cool kid, hip in all the right ways, and to his credit, intent on helping younger kids clean up their acts.

As luck would have it, Clint was instructed to keep a watchful eye on me when I was in town. He had a pretty girlfriend my age, Annette, who was all that I was not: blond and thin with ivory skin and an ultra-feminine personality. I liked Annette, even though I felt sorely inadequate around her.

While my parents hoped Omega House would set me straight, both literally and figuratively, instead it had a rather bad influence on me. The new kids I was hanging out with had been in much more trouble than I ever was.

Over the Memorial holiday weekend, a Native American jewelry show was being held at the Nevada State Fairgrounds. John T. was a big fan of turquoise and invited the kids from The Residence to come along for the day. I got to go because no one wanted to stay behind to watch me.

Several tribes were represented as artists displayed their crafts amid the many booths set up in the arena. The jewelry was spectacular. I had an instant appreciation for it. There were endless pieces of turquoise and sterling silver jewelry: cuff bracelets, rope necklaces, squash blossom necklaces, and inlaid rings. It was a feast for the eyes.

Traveling from booth to booth, it felt impossible to choose one piece of jewelry to purchase. The artistry before me was stunning and I coveted all of it. I imagined how beautiful I would feel lavished in turquoise and silver. I decided to steal because the fifty dollars I took out of my savings account wouldn't get me enough of what I wanted and felt I deserved.

One might think that my appreciation of Native people and their incredible art would deter me from stealing, but it did not.

Instead I convoluted my thinking, telling myself *because* I had such appreciation for the culture, I *had* to have some jewelry to make myself feel better.

I canvassed different tables, noticing who was paying attention and who was not, made conversation with the silversmiths, and told them how much I admired their craftsmanship. Then I left for a bit and when I came back around, they had an easy sense of me as I reexamined the pieces I liked. I spent a little money at each place I stole from, opening my purse wide to dispel any suspicions. The stolen jewelry was under my clothing.

I have no idea why stealing came easily to me or why I was good at it. Coming up with clever ways to lift a ring unnoticed from a display came naturally.

A couple of hours into the show, I had multiple pieces of jewelry in my bra and my shoes. I went to the bathroom to put some in my underwear. I wore the jewelry that I paid cash for and had the handwritten receipts ready to show if asked.

My emotions ran the gamut from excitement and satisfaction to disappointment and regret. I tried to push away the guilt but it sat in the pit of my stomach. When Denise saw me in passing, I told her I was getting incredible deals—building the case for why I would be wearing more jewelry when she saw me later.

Heading back to The Residence, I was thinking about what I had done. My sense of right and wrong were battling because I knew damn well stealing was wrong. And yet, my need to have lovely items to wear, items that might make me feel a little better about my situation and myself, took precedence. My emotional needs eclipsed all other considerations. As it turned out, the jewelry did make me feel beautiful, but I also felt ugly inside.

The closet was a good hiding place for the jewelry, which I stuffed in my shoes. The next day I smuggled it to school.

Once I was free of Bill, I put it on for everyone to see. In my careless desire to show off and get attention, it didn't occur to me that I would arouse suspicions.

When my classmate, Cathy, complimented my jewelry, I couldn't resist the urge to boast and told her I had stolen nearly all of it.

That night it was my turn to cook and I was having a good time making spaghetti and meatballs. The radio was playing the Eagles "Best of my Love" and Captain and Tennille's "Muskrat Love" which I was partial to because the lyrics were about "Suzy and Sam," my unrequited crush.

After dinner, we assembled for The Game. I sat comfortably, waiting to see who would be the night's victim, when I heard Denise talking and slowly realized she was addressing me, "So, Suzy, what do you have to tell us tonight?"

"I'm sorry, what?" I asked.

"Oh, have I got your attention now? Good. What would you like to tell us about last weekend at the Indian Show?"

"What do you mean? I've got nothing to tell," I lied.

Denise continued, "You know, we were all mystified when you came to Omega House. Sweet Suzy, our little 'Rebecca from Sunnybrook Farm' who never did any drugs. We all wondered why you were here."

I sat motionless, becoming more paranoid by the second. All I could think was *What does she know?*

"Who was with Suzy at the fairgrounds?" Denise asked the others. "Who was shopping with her?"

Teresa piped up, "None of us were, really. She kinda went off on her own."

"Off on her own, eh?" Denise replied. "You were all told to stay in pairs. Who was Suzy's pair?"

"I was," Dorothy admitted. "But we got separated early on and after that, I couldn't find her."

"Well, isn't that interesting…" Denise trailed off.

Then Bill spoke up, loud and threatening, "We can be here all night, Mueller, so why don't you fess up!"

"Fuck you, Dansie," I shot back.

"Fuck me?" Once again, he was inches from my face, using the technique that brought most of us to tears.

"You know what you did, and this time you are going to own it. Not so sweet after all, are you, Mueller? Just a common criminal. Oh, did we mention the police may be involved? Did we mention you might be going to Wittenberg Hall? Looks like you and your stoner brother will both have parole officers."

Now he had my attention. Wittenberg Hall was the juvenile detention center in Reno and while my brother had been several times, I never had. This threat was terrifying. Cathy must have ratted on me. I was busted.

Bill was still in my face, chiding me, "This is your chance to come clean, so what did you do, Mueller?"

"I stole some jewelry. That's it," I admitted, seeing no way out.

"Let's see it." Bill demanded.

"That fucking bitch, Cathy," I muttered under my breath. What an idiotic mistake it was to be boastful.

"Let's see it." Bill repeated.

"Fine. I don't have it on me. It's in my room."

"Go get it, and get every bit of it."

I did as I was told, carrying it all in a bandana; three necklaces, seven rings and two cuff bracelets.

"Holy shit, Mueller," Bill exclaimed when he saw it. "How did you manage to steal this much jewelry? Did you do this alone?"

"Yes."

"How?"

"I don't know, I smiled at people and they trusted me, I guess. They were busy with other customers."

"Bloody hell, this is a game-changer," Denise said. "I gotta say, I'm blown away, Suzy, and incredibly disappointed in you."

It was easy to see everyone was looking at me differently. After all, as Denise said, I had seemed like a sweet, wholesome girl. No one could understand what I was doing in a place like this.

Denise was crestfallen. I had shattered her view of me. It was awful to feel the coldness that took the place of our once mutual affection.

I was confined to The Residence for two weeks: no in-town privileges, no trips to the market, no nothing. When Denise loaded everyone in the van to do errands or day trips, I was left with Bill.

As the days went on, I began to crave company. Bill's room was down the hall from mine. I'd wander by and see him lying on his bed reading. My curiosity and loneliness got the better of me and I began to pass by his door more frequently, until one day he invited me in.

"What are you reading?" I asked.

"*Tales of Power* by Carlos Castaneda," he replied. "Are you familiar with it?"

"Only in that it was on the chair the first night I was here," I replied.

Bill loaned me Castaneda's first book, *The Teachings of Don Juan*, which I found fascinating. Discussing the books we were reading became a regular reason to spend time together.

Mind you, I was in a drug treatment program, discussing the psychedelic trips of an anthropology student from UCLA with a drug counselor. Nonetheless, there was a romance about the story that enthralled me. I loved the idea of journeying to another land to find a teacher that would unlock the secrets of life.

I eagerly read the pages, glad to inhabit the world Castaneda described. It was amazing escapism and filled my imagination with new concepts and ways of thinking. Carlos and his teacher, Don Juan Matus, frequently had discussions about death, a subject that tormented me since I was a child.

Way back in first grade, the rote questions and answers during catechism didn't bring me any comfort. When Sister Mary asked, "Who is God?" we were to reply, "God always was, always has been and always will be." For me, this answer was wholly confusing. Adding to that, the terrifying biblical depictions of God as angry, vengeful and prone to raging tantrums—just like my father—were even more unsettling. Why would a loving God turn people into pillars of salt when they displeased him?

Every Easter, Cecile B. DeMille's film *The Ten Commandments* aired on television. While I loved the movie, the portrayal of God as scary and intimidating made no sense to me.

As a little girl, I'd lie in my bed and try not to think about death, so naturally, it was all I could think about. In my head I'd hear, *You're going to die someday and so are your parents* and anguish would overtake me. The impossible task of trying to understand the nature of time and eternity would bring me to tears. No amount of thinking helped, because my mind couldn't work it out. It only churned up more questions:

What will happen when I die? I won't have my body anymore, so what will I be? What is eternity and how does forever work?

I'd work myself up until I was in tears. Most of the time I'd eventually drift off to sleep and wake in the morning feeling fine. However, there were several occasions when I was distraught enough to get out of bed and seek comfort from my father.

After a long day, my father loved nothing more than to relax in front of the TV with a cold mug of Schlitz Bock beer. Back then, his favorite programs were *Laugh-In* and *Star Trek*. My father would rave about the stellar imagination of Gene Roddenberry. This ritual of *Star Trek* and Bock beer was interrupted one night when I came down the stairs, troubled and upset.

I walked up to my father and stood before him in my floral print flannel nightgown, blocking his view of the show and cried, "Daddy, you're going to die someday, and mom, and grandma and grandpa too!"

My father leaned to the right, looking past me to continue watching the program while reaching for his Bock beer. He handed it to me and said, "Here honey, have a few guzzles of this, it will help you sleep."

I did as I was told. My first guzzles of cold beer burned my throat like Coca-Cola. It was delicious. I drank probably close to three ounces before he took it away from me.

"That's enough," he said. "Now go back to bed and you'll fall fast asleep."

Dad was correct, I passed out instantly.

This death obsession came and went from my life. Years would go by and I'd sleep fine until, out of nowhere, I'd get in bed one night and the word *death* would boom in my mind, setting off another phase of anguish.

The more I read Castaneda, the more his forthright way of discussing death appealed to me. Bill had the whole series and I was reading them as fast as I could. This sparked more curiosity about how others viewed death, especially other religions.

As I spent more time with Bill, I hated him less. He told me more about his drug history, especially dropping acid. He said it made him a more fluid thinker. His trip descriptions were outlandish and didn't seem real, cementing my fear of taking LSD. I knew I would never touch it.

Before coming to Omega House, I'd watched an after-school program called *Go Ask Alice*, about a girl my age who got addicted to drugs and died. It scared the bejeezus out of me, which was the whole point of the movie. At Omega House, an overdose story circulated about a man on LSD who died trying to fly off a rock outcropping that loomed over the Truckee River.

I didn't get it. Being out of control on drugs did not appeal to me in the slightest. On the contrary, I felt like I needed to gain control. And yet, when I read Castaneda, the context was different. He had a guide, someone to make sure he was safe, someone to share his experience with when he came down. Paradoxically, I was attracted to the idea of mind expansion in spite of my aversion to being out of control.

One afternoon as I was walking past Bill's door, he motioned for me to come in. I sat on the metal folding chair from my first night there. Bill stared at me for a long time and then smiled slightly as he extended his arm toward me. With his index finger, he reached into the opening of my blouse to lightly stroke the inside of my breasts. He then returned to his book, saying nothing. I got up and left, also in silence, stunned at his bold gesture. This marked a shift in our relationship. I was summoned more and more to Bill's room and our conversations deepened as time went on, though he didn't touch me like that again.

As I spent more time with him my view of him slowly began to change. Over the course of several months, the drama of our heated interactions in The Game faded. My loneliness didn't have high standards and Bill was paying attention to me, so I welcomed the comfort of his company. To my surprise, he even started to look attractive to me, especially as his fine blond hair had gotten longer. His gold wire-rimmed glasses made him look smart and approachable. When something tickled him, he had the shiest smile that would gradually emerge across his face.

I enjoyed his endless curiosity about the nature of the universe. Bill turned me on to *The Urantia Book*, *Seth Speaks* by Jane Roberts and *Zen and the Art of Motorcycle Maintenance* by Robert M. Pirsig. He became an unexpected mentor, introducing me to new thoughts and ideas. His input, combined with Cat Stevens' lyrics, were my preferred field of study.

It took awhile for things to calm down after my fall from grace. Inspired by Clint, I asked Denise what I could do to become a junior counselor. She said I was too young, but made suggestions that would improve my standing in the house. I volunteered for more duties and chores. Denise warmed up to me eventually and things felt more or less back to normal.

On Friday we went to town for game night. The Omega House director, John T., and his wife had been away on vacation and decided to stop by unexpectedly. When they came into the rec room to say hello, my eyes bugged out of my head: both of them were wearing the Native American jewelry I had stolen. I was outraged.

I was told the stolen jewelry would be returned to the artists that made it.

What a great lesson in hypocrisy, I thought resentfully. *They punish me for stealing and keep the goods for themselves.* I lost all respect for John T. after that. No one else took notice of their unscrupulous behavior and I was way too intimidated to try and take on John Tachihara. Bill also did nothing.

Beyond that transgression, something remarkable was taking place: I started to like living at The Residence. We had become a family. Playing The Game, despite its aggressive methods, peeled back our armor, allowing intimacy to develop between us.

Jodi, Jackie and I loved hanging out. We were demonstrative in our affections and cuddled together often. Perhaps we were mothering one another in the absence of our families.

One day, Denise told us girls to get in the van because she had a surprise for us. We were to attend a Women's Consciousness Raising Group led by local psychologist, Rebecca Jankovich. Each of us received a copy of *"Our Bodies, Ourselves,"* a trusted compilation on women's health and quite an eye-opener.

We discussed female sexuality in the frankest terms I had ever heard. We were provided with mirrors and took turns going into the bathroom so we could become familiar with what we looked like *down there.* Whenever we used the term "down there" we were encouraged to use correct anatomical names like "vulva" or "vagina" which made us all giggle. Personally, I was overjoyed to call it anything other than my "second butt" or my "Suzy."

Next Dr. Jankovich made the outrageous suggestion that we learn how we tasted. This freaked out a number of girls who thought it would mean they were queer. I had tasted Becky, so it wasn't a big deal to me. She encouraged us to let go of being self-conscious so that we could instead become empowered.

At the end of our time together, she proudly showed us a stunning, woven tapestry she had brought back from a trip to Africa. As we ooh'ed and aww'ed over it, she told us it was completely made out of pubic hair, which totally grossed us out since we had been running our hands over it.

When we got back, the boys were keen to hear about our experience and Tommy even got a boner when we told them we were asked to taste ourselves. We all laughed our asses off as he ran from the room.

Occasionally, a few of us would sneak out onto the roof after Bill went to bed, since he stayed up later than Denise. We could easily access one another's rooms from the sloped roof outside our second-story windows. More than once, I caught people smoking weed, but mostly we'd sit and talk about family and our hopes for the future.

Finals were a week away and I was studying hard. My current grade in biology was a D because I had cut class to avoid the frog dissection. So far, nothing about my absences had gotten back to Omega House.

That week during English class, a secretary came in and whispered something to the teacher, Sister Maura. Looking flustered, she told me to gather my things and come with her. We went to the office, where I was stunned to see Teresa and Dorothy, who were acting really weird.

"These girls were sent from Omega House to collect you," Sister Maura began, "because...I'm afraid...well, I'm afraid I have the most terrible news. I'm sorry to inform you that your mother has passed away. You have permission to leave school now, to be with your family."

Of course, this was utter bullshit.

Their faces gave them away, but Sister Maura bought it, hook, line, and sinker. As I walked down the hall toward the exit with two girls who were trying to hold it together, I was chuckling over Manogue's massive oversight. No one put together that Kris and Mike should be notified of this "death in the family" as well.

Once outside, we howled with laughter. Dorothy and Teresa had been given some free time while Denise tended to a personal matter in town and were told to be back at Omega House in a couple of hours. That's when they hatched their plan to bust me out of school. We were in the parking lot when Dorothy noticed

A yearbook photo for the "Sodality" group at Manogue. I wasn't in the group, but sneaked in to be in the picture. I'm 2nd from the left in the front row, along with Sister Maura, 5th from the left.

all the girls down on the football field.

"What are they doing?" she asked.

"Track and field practice," I said. "Do you want to see the locker room?"

"Sure!" they replied.

"Oh, I almost forgot," Dorothy said, "I brought you some clothes so you could get out of that hideous uniform."

"Thanks, that's so cool!" I gushed.

She loaned me one of her cutest tops, a white embroidered top from India with mirrored circles all over it. While changing my clothes, Teresa called out, "Hey, Suzy, why are all their belongings on the benches instead of in their lockers?"

She was picking up a purse as she asked the question.

"Beats me," I said. "Hey, what are you doing?"

"Just snooping a little," she smiled. Removing a wallet from one of the bags, she looked inside and exclaimed, "Oh my god, there's a hundred bucks in here!"

She pulled the money out and stuffed it in her bra.

"Oh wow, really?" I asked.

"Yeah! Fuck yeah!" Dorothy chimed in.

"Suzy, you be the lookout!" Teresa ordered.

Dorothy and Teresa began rifling through the purses. They took more than two hundred dollars in total. My old friend Colleen and her cousin Julie had more money than anyone else in their bags.

High on adrenaline, we skipped down the road, laughing and boasting about our coup. Eventually we made our way downtown to the Import Trading Post. Shopping there was like taking a trip around the world. It had a bohemian vibe and was stuffed with one of a kind items: textiles and clothing from India, hippie jewelry, lava lamps, patchouli incense, and essential oils.

We divvied up the money and spent it. I got some cool items for my room: a fisherman's net to hang from the ceiling, a couple of inspirational posters, a gorgeous purple and orange mandala bedspread, and some frangipani essential oil that I put on as soon as we walked out the door. It instantly brought me back to Gail and Camp Field. Then we headed over to Woolworths to get our pictures taken in the photo booth to commemorate the day.

The weekend passed uneventfully, but on Monday, all hell broke loose. Apparently, we had been seen whooping it up in the parking lot. Sister Maura was brought up to speed, surely annoyed to learn she'd been duped by two hooligans from "that druggie place." John T. was contacted by Father Wolf, the principal of Manogue, who explained what transpired and what had been stolen from my locker room.

With this occurring on the heels of my theft at the fairgrounds, Manogue swiftly lowered the boom. I was expelled three days before finals. Jon Wallace tried to intervene on my behalf, asking if they would allow me to take my tests. He was told that while the teachers certainly *could* allow me to take my finals, they flat out refused to do so. As a result, my teachers gave me a failing grade for all my courses for the final semester of my sophomore year. I could not advance to my junior year.

Some boys from the senior class called Omega House claiming they would beat the crap out of me if I ever set foot at Manogue again. My dirty secret, that I was a thief, was now common knowledge from Omega House to Manogue.

Getting kicked out of Manogue didn't bother me, though it was an unexpected way to exit high school. I hated it there and was glad to be done with it. However, I did care about passing my classes and making it to my junior year.

Another Game ensued as Bill and Denise ripped into me, but this time Teresa and Dorothy were in the hot seat as well. They stepped up big-time, insisting the whole thing was their idea. They also relayed that they stole the money, not me. I was amazed at their loyalty. They suffered the consequences and no one caught on that I purchased goods from my cut at Import Trading Post.

For once I was glad I wasn't at home. My father would have been far harder on me. Regarding my expulsion, he communicated with Denise within days, informing her that he expected me to take all the classes I failed via correspondence courses over the summer. That was good news to me as I was relieved to find there was a way to graduate my sophomore year. My parents ordered the courses I needed and I completed them with lightning speed. When fall arrived, I would attend Proctor Hug High School.

The abrupt and scandalous end of my education at Manogue

meant I didn't get to say any goodbyes. Mostly I would've liked to say goodbye to Rita, who was always loyal, and a better friend to me than I ever was to her.

I thought of Kris and how embarrassed she would be when she learned of my disgraceful behavior. For myself, shame and embarrassment were becoming a familiar part of life. Ironically, since my arrival at Omega House, I was getting into more trouble than ever before, and thought of myself as a bad girl—the black sheep of the family. Now, everyone knew I was a thief. I knew I would never show my face at any class reunions with the people I had known since the first grade.

There was one lovely, bright side: I would never have to spend another second at Catholic School.

9

before the breathing air is gone

Being expelled had another silver lining, it gave me a jump start on summer vacation. Though it pained me that I wouldn't be water-skiing or camping at Pyramid Lake with my family, I was hoping for some lazy days with my friends at The Residence.

None of us expected much in the way of fun, which made it all the more spectacular when, out of the blue, Denise told us that Jon Wallace and his girlfriend, Barbara, were going to take us on a backpacking trek through Yosemite National Park. We were bouncing off the walls with excitement as we headed into town to meet with Jon, who wanted to discuss the details of the trip and what we would need to bring. He told us we'd be hiking four to five miles each day and stressed that we only had a few weeks to train for the physical demands of the journey.

A local business generously donated camping supplies, so we were set up nicely with new tents, backpacks and sleeping bags. Jon was a big fan of dehydrated food and tried to excite us about the menu for the trip, though most of us groaned when he waxed on about the tastiness of dehydrated cheesecake.

When Denise told me my parents sent money so I could buy hiking boots, I was at a loss for words at their unexpected show of support. At the shoe store, the salesman recommended a rugged pair of Vasque boots that weighed a ton and were stiff as can be. Luckily, we could hike right out the back door of The Residence, as it was situated at the eastern base of Peavine Mountain. We took long hikes to condition ourselves. They helped to break in our boots and gave us time to recover from our blisters.

There was yet more news—before our trip to Yosemite, Denise said we'd be taking part in an event called a Marathon. This was not a running event. It was called a marathon because we would be deprived of sleep for thirty-six hours while participating in a variety of sensory awareness and trust building exercises sourced, in part, from a book called *Sense Relaxation: Below Your Mind* by Bernard Gunther. He was a teacher at The Esalen Institute in Big Sur, California. Esalen was famous for its counter-culture approach to self-actualization and the development of the Human Potential Movement. The Marathon would commence on Saturday morning at 8:00 a.m. and finish at 8:00 p.m. on Sunday.

When Friday came, Denise treated us to Straw Hat pizza for dinner before we headed into The Game. Thankfully, I was not picked on or called out in any way. Tommy got busted for smoking weed on the roof and was asked to make a commitment to shave his head if he smoked weed again. Tommy loved his long hair. Bill was at him for more than an hour until he acquiesced. We finished around midnight and went straight to bed.

We were awakened at sunrise to shower and dress. After breakfast, the Marathon began. Denise and Bill guided us step-by-step through a variety of exercises from the book throughout the day.

We participated in several trust-building activities, including a group exercise where we took turns carrying one another around the room and another where we practiced falling backward into a partner's arms. We also did one-on-one eye-gazing exercises, which transitioned from sharing what we found beautiful about each other to more challenging reflections on what we found frightening. That caused some ruffled feathers, so Denise helped us process through the difficult emotions that arose as a result. And so it went all day long, moving from one exercise to the next.

We had a late dinner and Denise checked in with all of us to see how we were feeling. Around midnight we were given Coca-Cola to pep us up. Bill brought in a turntable and we had a lengthy dance session where we chose music from Bill's considerable album collection. We were told to keep one another on our feet and moving so we'd stay awake through the night.

I loved dancing and was feeling wired and flirtatious. I had a crush on Tommy, but also felt attracted to Jodi, though I made sure to keep my feelings for Jodi private. Telling her how I felt wasn't worth the risk of losing her as a friend. Plus, I already enjoyed how affectionate we were with one another and didn't want to lose that.

After dancing, we were told to lie on the floor in such a way that each of us had our head on someone's belly. Then we were told to begin to belly laugh. It was forced at first, but our laughter became infectious until we were howling at how our heads were bobbing up and down from each person's laughter.

Then Denise asked us to form a circle to share what had brought us to Omega House as well as what we missed, and what we hoped for ourselves when we got out.

We all came from difficult home lives. It was heartbreaking to learn one another's histories, a depth of connection that was missing in our usual Game nights. I was accustomed to the focus being on us as the source of our problems, but in truth, our parents were as responsible for our placement there. We were children who had been neglected and abused on a number of levels.

This session was the deepest we had ever gone with one another. I felt tremendous love and empathy for everyone. It was getting close to sunrise when Denise told us to go upstairs for a short break while she and Bill prepared the room for our next exercise. When we returned, the floor of the main room was covered in white sheets. On top of the sheets were trays filled with fresh fruit, cheese and pastries.

"This is a love feast," Denise began, "but not a feast where you feed yourself. Think of the food as a representation of the love you have to offer. You can only offer love (food) to one another, and you cannot refuse someone's love (food) when offered to you."

We all sat near a tray of food until Denise shouted, "Begin!"

At first, some people were offered more food than others, but we caught on, making sure no one was left out. We began to take our time, savoring the moment of bringing a strawberry to a boy's lips, knowing he had to receive it from you (which was pretty exciting) and then seeing who wanted to offer you food.

It wasn't intended, but it became a sexually charged endeavor. The control the giver had in not being able to be refused created undeniable chemistry we were all aware of. I was as turned-on by the girls feeding me as I was the boys. Eventually, we got full and began moaning when someone presented more food to eat. Looking back, not being able to say "no" was a poor boundary to be teaching. Many of us were uncomfortably stuffed when Denise finally said we could stop.

Breaking from the rules, Denise gave us permission to climb

out on the roof to watch the sunrise. My head was buzzing from lack of sleep, but I felt pretty good, all things considered. We were feeling close as we sat on the roof with our arms around one another to greet the new day. I rested my head on Jodi's shoulder, and she rested her head on Darren's. It was a special moment after months of rough Game playing.

Summer made us even more isolated. I had no trips into town for school and we didn't go to the day program as often either. The phone in the downstairs office had a lock on it and Denise and Bill had the only keys. I had thought about breaking it more than once to call Becky or Grandpa: Becky because I felt lonely and Grandpa because I was sure if I could reach him, he'd bring me home.

Becky and I had not had any contact since she stole the truck to visit me. If she had written me letters, I hadn't received them. As time went on, I was growing and changing in such a way that the pull of her lessened.

Up on the roof, my thoughts turned to family. I wondered when I would be allowed to leave The Residence. *What were things like at home? Did anyone miss me?* That was hard to think about. I was missing out on all the fun at the lake and I missed riding my bike and going to movies. Most of all, I missed being able to move about freely in the world. Such a simple thing I had always taken for granted. Pangs of sadness and anger rose in me as I thought about my confinement. I'd been away from home for six months.

My thoughts were interrupted by Bill's voice yelling for us to come downstairs. He added that we passed the twenty-four hour mark and we gave a big cheer to celebrate.

Coming down the stairs, you could hear a succession of gasps as we saw what awaited us:

A plain, pinewood coffin was resting on a wooden stand in the center of the room. Candles and incense were burning around it and mournful dirges were playing on the record player. We gathered around the coffin holding hands as Denise solemnly said, "Each one of you is going to die today." We tightened our grip on one another as she continued. "One by one, each of you will take your turn in the coffin. Today, you will have the unique opportunity to hear what would be said about you and the life you have lived so far, if you died."

Our jubilant mood plummeted as we listened. A familiar anguish washed over me, intensified by the coffin in the room and the thought of getting into it. My dread around the subject of death was stronger than ever.

This death process took hours to complete. Our fatigue had perfectly lowered any resistance we might have had about doing the exercise. Our emotions were raw and at the ready.

All the built-up pain I had since my parents put me in Omega House came pouring out of me. Each person's turn produced a deluge of feelings. Everything about the exercise looked and felt real. Once someone got inside and closed their eyes, imagining them dead was not hard at all.

When Jodi laid motionless in the coffin, my head was pounding with such ferocity I could barely speak. To lose her would be unimaginable. I told her what she meant to me and how sorry I was that she was abandoned by her father.

For over six hours we witnessed one another's deaths. Through it all we expressed regrets for things we'd done and for things we wished we did. We were shaken to the bone by the uncertainty and vulnerability of life.

When it was my turn, my insides were churning. I thought of our neighbors who died, people I once knew who were gone.

The finality of death was crushing. However, I was not prepared for the beauty and tenderness that my comrades showed. It was incredibly moving. They wept as they told me how they felt about me. What a stunning thing it was to discover that I mattered deeply to these people. These rag-tag Omega House hooligans cared for me, loved me, and saw things in me I had not yet recognized. To our astonishment, this death experience was life affirming.

Then Denise took her turn in the coffin. This was simply too much to bear. We all lost it. She was our mama bear and we adored her. By the time we finished, we were exhausted.

As lonely as I had been, the coffin exercise made it clear we were a family; we loved one another and were invested in one another. The exercise didn't remove my fear of death, but it did confirm that living and loving fully was vitally important. I would keep reading Castaneda's books to see what Don Juan would teach him, and me, about death.

Looking us over, Denise said we could take showers and assigned each of us a buddy to make sure we didn't fall asleep. She and Bill were looking tired too.

When we reconvened downstairs we had peanut butter and jelly sandwiches on the sofas where we played The Game.

"Not to worry," Denise assured us, "we are not here to play The Game." As we all sighed with relief, she added, "We are going to share what we learned in the coffin."

As much as we tried to share, we were too rummy with fatigue. Our sincere efforts gave way to hilarious attempts to speak, as we tripped over our words and erupted into huge bouts of laughter, endlessly making jokes that had us holding our sides as tears streamed down our faces. It was nearing seven o'clock. Denise took pity on us and said, "This marathon is complete!"

With that, we took off running for our rooms and the sublime comfort of a face-forward fall into bed. I slept fourteen hours straight and woke up feeling noticeably different about where I was and who I was.

The love and connection we felt during the Marathon made us a much tighter group. We were riding high on amazing energy that carried us right into our Yosemite adventure.

It was a three-hour drive to Yosemite Valley where we would begin our trek. Our goal was to hike from the Valley to Tuolumne Meadows. Jon was the father figure of Omega House, our papa bear. He even looked the part of a mountain man, a regular Grizzly Adams. Barbara was always fun to be around. She was a good storyteller and had a real exuberance for life. Her long dark hair was usually tied in a ponytail at the nape of her neck beneath a cowboy hat.

On the drive they coached us on the finer points of hiking in the wilderness, explaining how we would reconstitute our dehydrated meals using water, and how to suspend our food bags between trees to thwart bears scrounging for a meal. They recommended having a planned cut-off time for drinking fluids to avoid having to go outside in the dark to pee.

I'd always fancied the idea of being a hiker and a camper. Listening to "Be Free" by Loggins and Messina nurtured a desire to move to the country. It was the clarion cry of the seventies. Cities were vilified as smog-choked prisons of humanity that we should escape whenever possible. John Denver really drove home the point in his song, "Rocky Mountain High." I was excited to have a chance to get out in nature and see what it was all about.

We pulled into Yosemite National Park in the early afternoon. Jon and Barbara gave us permission to walk about within close range while they dealt with the permits, unloaded gear, and checked our provisions.

The view, even from the parking lot, was stupendous. Nothing could have prepared me for the awe I felt viewing Half Dome. I headed over to a large log beside a small creek and straddled it. The sun was warm and lulling on my bare skin. I laid down, falling forward onto the log in a big embrace. With each breath I inhaled the aroma of the woods, water and earth. Every part of me was vibrating with gratitude. My body grew heavier and heavier until I fell asleep.

I had been napping for a short while when a bird's cry woke me. The sound was coming from my right. I decided to follow it, boulder-hopping over a creek and exploring until I came to a small meadow. Overcome with an urge to be naked, I took a look around and surmised that I could get away with it. I undressed and sat down on a small slab of granite among the tall grasses and flowers. Emotion flooded me and I began to sing.

Remembering my experience at Camp Field four years earlier, a tingling began to rise up my spine and then cascades of goosebumps rushed over my body.

It's happening again! I thought buoyantly as I sang the words to "Morning has Broken." The joy I felt revisiting this incredible feeling of oneness meant so much to me. It made me feel I was not lost after all. Despite the grief of being away from my family, the hardships of living at Omega House and my loneliness, I was able to feel this awakening once again.

As I finished singing, I opened my eyes in amazement to see a mature buck with impressive antlers standing in front of me, not more than five feet away. I calmly took in the magnificence of this animal, who seemed unafraid of me. We looked at one another for what felt like a long time and then it slowly went on its way.

I had been transfixed by the deer, but as soon as it departed, I became aware of the many mosquitos that were landing on my naked body. With a yelp, I jumped up and shooed them off while dressing as fast as I could. I ended up with at least a dozen bites that vexed me for days.

No one had missed me while I was in the meadow. Around five o'clock we were ready to go. With the long summer days, Jon figured we had a couple of hours of hiking time before we would need to make camp. Dinner would be served late, so we each got a silver foil packet of brown sugar cinnamon Pop-Tarts to munch as we hiked to help keep our energy up. And so, the first steps of my virgin hiking trek began.

Jon set a fast pace. Determined not to be in last, though Jon's stride was easily double my own, I pushed hard and found a rhythm that worked for me. The lush beauty and dramatic panoramic views of Yosemite were like nothing I'd ever seen, especially coming from the desert landscapes of Nevada.

We climbed in elevation and eventually Jon called out that he was looking for a place to make camp. We were in steep terrain, which was challenging, when he spotted a chunk of level land in the middle of the river. Balance came into play as we had to boulder-hop to get to it. Not accustomed to having forty pounds on my back, I was shaky at the prospect. Jon shouted encouragement over the sound of the rushing water and we all made it over, with Barbara bringing up the rear. She looked nervous, but gamely leapt, landed badly and wiped out, belly-up, on her backpack in the chilly creek water. She looked like a turtle flailing about while the cold water soaked her and her pack. Her denim jeans looked stiff and heavy as she struggled to roll over. Jon and the guys got to her rapidly while Barbara cussed up a blue streak. Together they dragged her onto the ground.

Making camp and getting a fire going was elevated to the highest priority so Barbara could get dry and warm. The sun was already behind the mountain and temperatures were falling fast. Her teeth were chattering as she changed into dry clothing. Jon wrapped a foil blanket around her as she sat close to the fire to get warm. Jodi, Jackie and I set up our tent.

We finished our reconstituted dinner, which failed to impress, when I noticed a man setting up camp near to us. He was alone. I asked Jon if I could invite him to sit with us around the campfire. Jon had no objection, so I approached him.

"Hello there," I began. "I'm Suzy. We're camping next to you and want to invite you to come by for some dessert in a little bit."

I didn't mention it would come from a dehydrated packet, so as not to dissuade him. He smiled and said, "Thanks, I'd love to. I'll play you a tune on my banjo."

He had that gypsy look of someone who'd lived on the road a long time. His shaggy mix of brown and gray hair was in a ponytail that was almost as long as his unruly beard. He wore a beat-up cowboy hat that had seen better days and a gray wool sweater. His Levis were covered in flower patches that managed to hold the pants in one piece.

He came into our camp grinning and said, "Hello all, my name is Billy Faier."

"Welcome," said Jon, "Please join us by the fire."

"What kind of music do you play?" I asked.

"I play music of the wilderness," he said mysteriously as he sat down. He swung the banjo from behind his back, adjusted his glasses and said, "This song is two hundred years old. It's called 'The Darby Ram.'"

Little did we know, this man Billy Faier was something of a legend, and part of the Greenwich Village folk scene in the late 1940s. He'd even played on Broadway. But right now, as far as we knew, he was just a wanderer who was probably used to playing for his supper.

His musical gifts were apparent from the first note, as he sang to us under the breathtaking Yosemite sky. His music even made dinner taste better, when reconsidered. He reminded me of Woody Guthrie. He told stories about each song he sang; where he learned it, who taught it to him, how he'd changed it a little bit here and there; and how that was okay because folk music found its way through generations, person by person, and each musician left their mark on a song.

"Where are you headed?" I asked

"The Grand Canyon," he replied.

"Wow, that's a long journey on foot!" I replied.

"It is, but I only have to take it one step at a time, isn't that right?" He teased me.

We had the immense pleasure of his company for a couple of hours as he entertained us. I went to sleep that night basking in the warmth of his songs.

Physically, our time in Yosemite was enormously challenging. None of us had hiked before and though I prided myself on being athletic, the rigors of backpacking earned my respect.

We all looked forward to nighttime by the campfire, where Jon boiled water to make our meals as we shared about the day. The best part of all was that we never played The Game once. We continued to grow closer to one another, letting down our defenses while basking in nature's stunning beauty. It was the trip of a lifetime and I was sad when it was time to leave.

As soon as we got back to The Residence, I found myself buzzing with restlessness. The time away gave me a big taste of freedom and ignited a strong urge to return to a normal life.

As much as I was feeling connected to everyone there, I missed my family more.

A few weeks later when I broached the subject with Denise, I got immediate resistance. She didn't feel I was ready to go home.

"Remember," she said, "your father blamed you for the problems in his marriage and your parents are still having marital issues. It's an unhealthy environment for you to be in."

Her response angered me. Honestly, whether she thought I was ready to go home or not was beside the point. I'd had enough. I was done with The Game and the constant rules and restrictions we had to follow.

Summer was coming to a close. I would soon be starting at Hug High. First impressions were important. The last thing I wanted was to be known as the new girl sitting in the parking lot with weirdo Bill, waiting for the bell to ring. I'd been in the program for nearly eight months already. I had to get out before school began.

My desperation to leave was fueled by Teresa and Dorothy. One day they told me they were running away.

"How is that possible?" I asked.

As it happened, they were outside weeding in the front lot and three guys on Harley-Davidson motorcycles stopped to talk with them. Amazingly, Denise and Bill hadn't seen them. At any rate, the men asked them if they'd like to run away and they said yes. Since there were three of them, they invited me as well.

While I had no intention of joining them, I did think of a way that I could use the invitation to work to my advantage.

That night I had an upsetting dream that my Grandma Alice was going to die. The dream was so real, my face was wet with tears when I woke. Once again, I went to Denise. I told her of my premonition that my grandmother was going to die soon and that I had to go home so I could be with her before it happened. Once again, Denise said no. She dismissed me, saying, "It's a dream. It doesn't mean anything."

Her refusal to take me seriously sucked, but I said nothing. My determination to leave Omega House deepened even more.

The Residence phone was in a small office on the main floor. I'd been trying to figure out a way to break the lock when a few days later, I got my chance.

Denise and Bill went into town to buy supplies with several kids, so no one was downstairs when I went to the kitchen to get some juice. To my delight, someone neglected to lock the office door. As soon as I discovered this error, I ran outside to pick out a big rock. Placing the phone on its side, I hit the cylinder lock hard, then I hit it again, and on the third try the lock broke.

Before I could chicken out, I dialed home. It was hard to breathe with my heart pumping like crazy in my throat.

My father answered the phone.

"Tom Mueller," came his customary greeting.

"Dad," I declared, "It's me, Suzy."

"Hello Suzanne," he replied in his stern voice. "Are you supposed to be using the house phone there?"

"No dad, I'm not." I replied. "In fact, I broke the lock off the phone to call you."

Before he could interrupt me, I continued, "I called to tell you that if you or mom ever want to see me again, you'd better come get me, *right now.* Otherwise, I am running away tonight with a guy on a Harley."

I hung up.

Of course, I was lying, but I decided it was called for. Drama was needed to get a strong reaction out of my father. Plus, I knew he would try to reach Bill or Denise to warn them and they would be gone for hours. When he failed to reach them, I hoped he'd get concerned.

Within half an hour, I watched from my window as my father's Lincoln Continental pulled into the parking lot.

I was ready to go, gambling that he would come. My clothes, record player and albums were packed. I left everything else for my roommate, Jackie. It was opportune that no one was around. I didn't have to say any goodbyes or catch flack from Denise or Bill.

I wasn't a ward of the court, so Omega House had no say in the matter. My parents had all the power. The only thing that could mess this up was if my parents betrayed me. This time, for some reason, my gut told me they wouldn't do that.

My father greeted me cheerlessly, "Hello, Suzanne."

"Hello, dad," I returned.

It was a relief that he was quiet on the drive home. I was excited to see my brothers and sisters and couldn't wait to see Grandpa. My body was surging with a feeling of liberation.

I did it. I was going home.

Douglas James Ryan 1905-1993

Alice Marian Ryan 1908-1975

10

the return

My father spoke as we pulled into the driveway, "Well, Suzanne, I hope it did you some good, being out there and that you can turn your life around now."

"Thanks, dad, I think it did," I said cheerfully, like a good little Stepford-child. It was a manufactured response. I wasn't about to say what I really felt because I didn't want to fight with him, or worse, have him turn the car around.

"Explain to your mother that you've come home," he continued as he got my things from the trunk.

"Aren't you coming in?" I asked.

"No, Suzanne, I'm going back to work," he said.

Crossing the threshold, a wave of melancholy washed over me. I felt weirdly unfamiliar, a stranger in my own home. Without a doubt, Omega House had changed me. I wasn't the same girl who left eight months before.

My mother was in the kitchen as I came through the door, the same door Bill was hiding behind when she lied to me, saying I could come home to stay. I hadn't forgotten her deception, but when she rushed toward me, my edginess vanished and we hugged one another.

I could forgive her because I knew she was incapable of acting against my father in any way. For better or worse, my mother was a product of her generation. Where I felt she had faltered, due to her loyalty to my father, she made up for in her warmth and love.

My siblings looked different. Eight months away was plainly evident in how much they had grown, especially the three youngest. It was incredible to see them again and their excitement to see me felt good, like I had been missed.

Perhaps in a mea culpa effort to rebuild our relationship, my mom took me shopping for school clothes the next day at Park Lane Mall. She had recently gotten her first credit cards, one at Weinstocks and another at Joseph Magnin. She helped me pick out two maxi skirts and a Gunne Sax prairie dress in a gorgeous brown and lavender calico print with lace trim.

We also went to Shim's, a popular army surplus store on Sierra Street. They carried the pants all the kids were wearing: sailor-style bell bottoms in dark or pale-blue chambray with decorative anchor buttons in front. Mom let me buy three pairs of pants and three cotton henley shirts. In the dressing room, I stared at my reflection in the mirror. I hoped I was going to have a fresh start.

While I was in Omega House mom had gotten closer to our neighbor, Mrs. Carlson. They still smoked cigarettes and drank Ernest and Julio Gallo Pink Chablis at our bistro ice cream table, forging their bonds as confidants through the smoky air.

Mr. and Mrs. Carlson were ten years younger than most of the neighborhood. Mrs. Carlson had a big personality. She was loud, liked to laugh, and seemed ditzy at times. She was easy to talk to, and we chatted from time to time when I babysat for her.

Seeing the two of them engrossed in conversation reminded me of Becky. Although I was overjoyed to see her at The Residence, I was not inclined to contact her. With all that I had been through, I didn't think we'd fit together anymore because I couldn't tolerate the limitations imposed by her jealous nature. I would inevitably see her when school started.

I reconnected with Gena's ex-girlfriend, Kathy. She and Gena still lived in the brick house I had run away to months before.

Kathy informed me that Gena and Terry were now an item. Not long after that, I saw them at Idlewild Park while I was sunbathing at the pool. It was an Eliza Doolittle moment. I was flabbergasted at the transformational impact Gena had on Terry. Once modest and prudish, she was now looking confident and sexy in a bikini. She had come out of her shell.

Terry overtly caressed Gena when they came over to say hello, in an effort to make me jealous. I couldn't help but grin—there was nothing about them that appealed to me anymore.

Kathy and I spent a few weekends together, going on hikes, baking, and listening to music. She took up the role Bill once occupied, referring new reading material to me. Through her, I was introduced to *Be Here Now,* by Ram Dass, Ayn Rand's books, *The Fountainhead* and *Atlas Shrugged*, and the writings of Lao Tsu. She also taught me how to throw the I Ching using pennies. My curiosity about other cultures continued to expand.

Kathy was sexually attracted to me, but unlike Gena, she was conflicted about her feelings. Our large age difference didn't sit well with her. At the time, I was fifteen and she was twenty-nine.

My involvement with Terry and subsequent involvement with Gena and Kathy were heady experiences. Being spoken of as *precocious* by older women whom I admired was flattering and made me feel special. It never occurred to me that their sexual interest was inappropriate. I liked and wanted their attention.

When Bill brashly reached into my blouse to stroke my breast at Omega House, I had that same feeling. For whatever reason, I garnered attention from older adults and in my need for validation, I felt complimented by it. It wasn't until I turned the ages they were when they pursued me that I felt repulsed by their actions.

When I was with Kathy we lightly kissed and caressed one another at length, but she couldn't let things progress too far. As soon as Kathy became more aroused, she'd abruptly pull away and leave the room. I found it frustrating and annoying. Eventually, I lost interest and the sexual tension between us lessened, allowing us to become friends.

As I was anticipating my junior year at a new school, an internal shift was taking place. It stemmed from the thought that implanted in my brain my first night in Omega House:

If this is the price for being me, I won't be me.

This produced a resolve—I did not want to be with girls anymore. I didn't want to have to hide or skulk around. Perhaps shame had a vice grip on me that was influencing my decision, but the stress of being with a girl was unappealing. Once upon a time, I wanted a boyfriend and I hoped I would meet a nice boy at school.

Junior year started. My first day was going well, despite the fact that I was scared and intimidated. Hug had three times the student body of Manogue, but I managed to find my way around campus.

When I arrived at my fourth period class I saw Becky and froze. I suddenly realized that not contacting her beforehand was a huge mistake. Clutching my books, I chose a desk in the back row, but Becky turned her head just in time to spot me.

Becky was antagonistic from the get-go, clearly hurt that I had not been in touch. She walked up to me to let me know she had a new girlfriend, Karen, and bragged that she was more attractive and sexier than me. Her belligerence was off-putting and became the norm anytime we crossed paths. Being harassed by Becky was so unpleasant it caused me to regret going to Hug. I was excited to play sports again, however, and made the volleyball team. Unfortunately, so did Becky.

The newness of everything fit in with my desire for a fresh start. My reputation had been ruined beyond repair at Manogue, but here I was completely unknown, save for Becky.

Manogue was a college preparatory school, but Hug offered unusual classes like Native American literature and amorology (The study of love). I signed up for both.

My Native American literature class was taught by a local journalist, Sandy Macias. On the first day of class she told us we would be required to keep a journal. She said it was a place where we could write poetry, our feelings, or how our day was—much like a diary. I took to the habit of writing easily. I still have my journal pages from that class in 1975.

A month after school began, Grandma Alice became ill with pneumonia. When her symptoms worsened she was hospitalized. My mother's two brothers came to town and we all went to see her. As I walked into St. Mary's Hospital, the foreshadowing of my dream was powerfully on my mind.

I wasn't prepared for the frightening sight of my grandma hooked up to machines with tubes coming out of her arms. I immediately became emotional, though my mother encouraged me to be brave. This was her mother, after all, and I could see she was making a tremendous effort not to fall apart.

Grandma looked forlorn and afraid. Her wide eyes moved from side to side like an owl, looking at our faces as we stood around her hospital bed. It occurred to me that she would know she was in bad shape seeing that her sons had flown in to be with her.

As a distraction, mom suggested I feed her some Jello. I took a spoonful and tried to put it in her mouth, but her head was shaking as she tried to take it off the spoon and I was shaking too. The Jello slipped off the spoon and plopped onto her chest. Being Jello, it wiggled and jiggled there for a moment.

Inexplicably, this made me roar with laughter. I was laughing as hard as I had been crying. The tsunami of emotion bursting out of me could not be contained. I rushed into the hall so Grandma wouldn't see me. I didn't want her to think I pitied her, though that was exactly how I felt.

When I regained my composure, I went back in and leaned over her, kissing her forehead as she had done to me hundreds of times throughout my life.

Because of the dream I had, when I left Omega House I made sure to visit her often. She'd share stories about life in Milwaukee, mostly in a wistful way, because she never wanted to move when Grandpa decided to follow my mom to Washington. She was profoundly sad and resentful about having to sell her home and her belongings and grieved the distance from her family. It never occurred to me that Grandma didn't want to move or that as a woman she'd had no choice in the matter.

Sometimes when her back was hurting she'd lie on the sofa and I would massage her. She loved it when I rubbed her back. She'd hold up my hands and say, "You have magic fingers, Suzy. You should be a nurse with hands like that."

Prior to spending time with her, I often judged my grandma, thinking she was a mean and bitter person. As I heard her stories, compassion replaced judgment.

My heart was full as I stood on my tiptoes to whisper, "I love you" in her ear. She managed to squeeze my arm, her eyes brimming with tears. My head was pounding from the effort I was making to hold back my feelings.

The realization that eight months in Omega House robbed me of precious time with her hit me like a freight train. When the nurse came to tell us visiting hours were over, I didn't want to leave her side. It would be the last time I ever saw her.

Grandma Alice died Wednesday, October 8, 1975.

It was both inexplicable and marvelous that my dream accurately foretold her death. I was grateful that I listened to its directive, getting out of Omega House to spend time with her.

At her funeral it was unbearable to see my Grandpa Doug grieving. In my whole life I had never seen him cry. Not once. Grandma Alice was the first loss of a family member for my siblings and me. This wasn't a rented coffin at The Residence. This was real and there was no climbing out of it. The finality of it all, that I would never see her again, was hard to comprehend.

So many feelings were set free in the permission that grief affords that I found myself weeping over all the events of the last year, not only for being alienated from my grandparents and siblings, but also because things had taken a turn for the worse with my parents. Coming home was not a return to the family we once were. Everything was different.

At one point, I got a gusher of a bloody nose from how hard I was crying and was taken from the church by a family friend to try and stop the bleeding.

After my grandmother's passing, my old fear of death emerged again and held me in its grips. Lying in bed at night, I wondered where she had gone. Could she still see me or had she vanished into nothingness?

But then, fortuitously, I had the most incredible dream.

In my dream, Alice was young and full of vitality; we seemed to be almost the same age. The dream presented a montage of us engaging in fun activities; we were swimming, running, playing, and enjoying life. Our joy was evident on our beaming faces.

Then the dream shifted and we were on bicycles, riding side by side down a beautiful lane, flanked by glorious tall trees swaying rhythmically in the breeze. I could feel the wind on my face. I was surrounded by beauty. We turned to look at one another, smiling at our pleasure.

Then, Grandma spoke to me, her eyes lit with aliveness.

She said, "Isn't this great, Suzy? We could never do these things together when I was alive."

Her eyes looked deep into me, penetrating my heart. I could feel her. *It was her.*

Her words were a thunderbolt of truth and I became lucid in that moment, fully aware that I was dreaming. Through the intensity of my grandma's gaze I understood that she wanted me to know I was connecting to her spirit through the dream. She was showing me how alive she was. She was also placing a balm on the grief I had that her life wasn't lived more fully. I woke from the dream, filled with wonder and peace.

My grief abated after having this dream. The magnitude of the experience caused a shift in my perspective, broadening my understanding of death. Now I could feel connected to her in a meaningful way. Grandma Alice let me know she was okay.

My dream life continued to be vivid during this time. I was practicing a dream technique Bill taught me using the power of suggestion. Each night before I went to sleep, I would repeat over and over, *I will fly in my dreams tonight.* After a few tries, it worked. I began to fly in my dreams at will. It was exhilarating. Amazingly, I was also lucid in these dreams. I loved the feeling of soaring through the air, knowing I was dreaming, though it felt completely real.

After Grandma's death I made a focused effort to spend more time with Grandpa Doug. I was concerned about him after his loss. Because he drove me to volleyball practice, I was able to visit with him five mornings a week. Our team was good and easily won our first match. I looked forward to playing and beating Manogue, but unfortunately, I never got that chance.

My mother received a letter notifying her that someone had reported me to the school board as a player who transferred from Manogue to Hug for the sole purpose of benefiting the volleyball team there. The letter said I was immediately suspended from the team until a scheduled hearing in Carson City to plead my case. I couldn't believe it. I was forbidden to play in our upcoming match.

Naive as I was, it did not occur to me that Mrs. Casci, my coach at Manogue, was the person behind it. We discovered this at the hearing which was brief and cruel. They weren't interested in anything that my mother had to say in my defense. The board had already concluded that I would not be permitted to play *any* sports at Hug, period.

Apparently, expulsion wasn't enough punishment. This was retribution from Manogue. Mrs. Casci found a way to hurt me for stealing. Playing sports was a huge part of my identity. The loss was tremendous.

I had started forming friendships with my teammates, and because so much time was spent at practice and games, I knew I wouldn't see them anymore. In the wake of this development, I became a loner at my new school. I reached out to Kathy and started spending weekends with her.

In an attempt to cheer myself up, I treated myself to a new hairstyle. I went to The House of David, Reno's trendy downtown hair salon. The summer before, I had tried to make my hair blond using Sun In. It looked so easy in the commercials: girls sprayed their hair and were transformed into gorgeous blondes. My hair turned an ugly, brassy orange instead and the product damaged my hair, leaving it dry and full of split ends. I had a wide strip of grown-out brown hair, which looked awful against the orange hair. I wanted the bleached hair to be cut off.

The foot-tapping stylist listened impatiently as I explained what had happened, saying, "Got it," as he turned the chair around so that my back was to the mirror. I guessed he wanted to surprise me. Feeling anxious, I closed my eyes and listened to the radio. Twenty minutes later the stylist declared, "All done!"

He swung the chair around so I could see. I stared in disbelief at the outcome. He cut so much more than the bleached hair. I looked like a boy.

"Oh my god," I muttered. "Oh my god."

"Oh yay, you like it!" The clueless stylist-from-hell exclaimed.

"Oh my god. Uh, thanks," I stammered, heading straight to the bathroom to hide.

He thought I liked it? Was he out of his mind?

The bathroom had a tiny porcelain sink in the corner. I jammed my head in it and turned on the faucet. I'm not sure why, since water doesn't miraculously grow hair, but I hated how it was styled and thought maybe it would somehow look better, plus the sounds of my upset would be less audible with the water running.

People will really think I'm a lesbian now, I thought, ignoring whoever was knocking on the door to pee. My head stayed in the sink while I tried to think. Thinking led to submission. There was nothing to be done.

Ten minutes into my retreat, the salon manager pounded on the door, reminding me I had not paid my bill. Regardless of my soaked appearance and sad eyes, the manager took no pity on me. I handed over my babysitting money and left.

At a pep rally later that week, Becky and Karen sat directly in front of me in the bleachers. At one point, Becky turned around to shove a Polaroid in my hands. It was Karen, naked on a bed with her legs spread wide. "Look who I'm with now," she boasted, "she's so much better than you."

Karen had an annoying smirk on her face, pleased that I was taking a gander at her goods. Their vulgarity was repulsive. "Who the fuck cares, Becky?" I replied. "Not me."

Shoving the photo back in her hand, I told her to go fuck herself. She was an insufferable girl who did her best to make my time at Hug miserable. I missed my friends at Omega House and the depth of connection we had. As hard as Omega House had been, at least it had been real. The contrast from that to the shallow idiocy of high school was depressing. I wanted to be done with it.

As the year progressed, I had crushes on two boys, but neither liked me back. Beginning with Sam in eighth grade to boys I liked at Manogue, the rejection was the same. I didn't understand why.

Ultimately, the conclusions I came to always landed hard on my shoulders. It must be my shortcomings, especially my looks and my weight. My haircut wasn't helping my esteem either. When I looked in the mirror, I felt boyish and unattractive.

I decided to reach out to some Omega House friends. Through Jodi, I learned that Teresa and Dorothy never ran away with the guys they met on the highway. I also learned that Denise and Bill were perturbed at my abrupt departure and were upset that I hadn't communicated with them before leaving.

Jon Wallace invited me to attend the Friday Game night at Omega House when Residence members attended, but there was no chance in hell that I'd ever voluntarily play The Game again. I did go a couple of times on the weekend to see everyone.

Ever since returning home, I desperately wanted to regain some sense of normalcy and stability. My grandma's death was a tear in the fabric of the family I had always known. Kris was nearly eighteen and while I was away, she got a job at McDonald's and purchased a lime green Volkswagen bug. I rarely saw her. Mike was still getting high, getting into trouble and stealing money to buy weed. I was trying to get my footing based on who our family used to be. It wasn't working.

My mom liked to entertain, and had recently purchased a fondue set. She planned a dinner party so she could use it. For some reason, using long forks to dip bread in melted cheese was all the rage. It was an adult party, so my siblings and I were farmed out to various locations.

Later that night when I went upstairs, I was startled and irritated to find Mrs. Carlson sitting in the bedroom I shared with Kris. She was slumped on my bed in the dark, three sheets to the wind. She stunk up our room, reeking of cigarettes and hard liquor.

Disgusted, I hit the light switch and demanded, "What are you doing in my bedroom?"

"Oh Suzy," she cried, "I'm in love with your father."

My face turned to stone. "Get the fuck out of my bedroom," I demanded, slamming the door behind her.

Her abrupt declaration upset me, especially because she was one of my mother's closest friends, but I didn't say anything to anyone about it, hoping it would blow over.

In no time at all, I discovered I was dead wrong. My father left my mother for Mrs. Carlson shortly after my grandma's death, filing for divorce after eighteen years of marriage and twenty-three years together. It was a shock to the whole neighborhood.

As soon as my dad left, my brother Tommy stepped up. He was fourteen years old but fibbed about his age to get a job bagging groceries at Warehouse Market. He worked weekends and after school until nine o'clock. Tommy often provided groceries for us through his job. His manager would let him fill a cart of groceries now and then because he felt bad about how little he was paid.

It's an understatement to say that my mother was devastated by my father's betrayal. Despite his womanizing for most of their marriage, she would never have considered divorcing him. It was forbidden in the Catholic faith. She did not believe in divorce, and in fact, my mother did not recognize a governmental divorce as valid, since her covenant of marriage was taken before God. Being stabbed in the back by both my father and someone she considered a friend made everything exponentially worse.

My mother started drinking alone at night. I became much more attentive to her, putting her to bed, consoling her, and stroking her hair until she dozed off. She had lost her bearings and was floundering in a sea of grief.

During this time (and under the influence of alcohol) she began to share details of her history with my father. The stories of my father's many infidelities and his mistreatment of my mother lit a bonfire of hatred in me toward him. His unapologetic selfishness was appalling. He clearly operated in life with no integrity, making the rules up as he went. He hadn't just left my mother either, he had left all of us. He was off with his new younger girlfriend: the perfect cliché of a man in a midlife crisis.

Christmas was a sad affair that year. My mother stopped going to Sunday mass because it was too painful for her to sit and watch the other families come in together. The stigma of divorce in a Catholic parish was a harsh sentence.

On top of all this, the turbulent vibes intensified when, in the dead of winter, Reno was rocked by a shocking tragedy. A former Manogue classmate of Kris's who was attending UNR was murdered near the campus. An elderly couple found her lying in their garage with her throat slit. Her name was Michelle Mitchell. Her car had broken down. Sometime after she called her parents for help from a phone booth, she was murdered.

This news tore at the heart of our small town. We never locked our homes or cars, feeling there was no need. When Michelle was killed, my sense of safety completely vanished. I became gripped with fear about predators hiding in the shadows. My mom would sometimes loan me her car to go out at night. When I'd return home, I'd sit in my locked car trying to get up the courage to walk from the car to our front door. I'd break out in a cold sweat, terrified that someone was lurking somewhere, waiting to get me.

It didn't help that many nights when I got home, no one was there, except for our cockapoo, Sam. He was seven years old and a great comfort. Without him, I don't know if I would've gone in the house at all.

There was such a heavy, burdensome energy during this time. I began having recurring nightmares of my father trying to kill me. Sometimes in my dreams he succeeded. He would shoot me with a gun and I would witness myself dying. The terror of these dreams left me waking with sorrow and tears. My once enchanted dream life was now polluted with violence.

The sobering truths of life outside the bubble of childhood were troubling and I continued to sleep more and more to escape reality. That urge grew even stronger when my parents' divorce was finalized in March of 1976.

My father would marry Mrs. Carlson in December that year.

"There can be no keener revelation of a society's soul than the way in which it treats its children."

~ Nelson Mandela

11

acidhead predator

What a shock it was when, out of the blue, I had a phone call from Bill late one Friday evening in May. "Hey Mueller, how are you? It's Bill," he announced after my mother called me to the phone. I couldn't imagine why he would be calling.

"Uh, hello. What's up?" I responded.

"You know, I wanted to see how you've been doing since you left," he said. "We like to check in and see how kids are doing once they are back at home."

"Really?" I said, not believing him. "Well, I left nine months ago and this is the first time anyone has called me. But, yeah, I'm doing good."

"Who's still at The Residence?" I asked. After a brief rundown of who was where, Bill got more to the point.

"Actually, Mueller, I'm calling to see if you'd like to catch a movie tonight."

"Tonight?" I responded, "Isn't it a little late for that?"

"No, there's a movie playing at The Keystone Theater," he countered. "Can you ask your mom if you can go?"

I was tired, but intrigued to hear from him. Curiosity prevailed so I asked my mom if I could go.

"It's okay with me," she said. "But only because he was your counselor."

"Yeah, well, that term should be applied loosely," I whispered sarcastically, not wanting Bill to hear. I told Bill she said yes, and he said he'd be over in fifteen minutes. I had enough time to wash my face and change my clothes.

The Keystone Theater was a short drive from my home. When we pulled up, the lights were dimmed. The marquee said *The Story of O* which was not a movie I had heard of.

"What is this movie about?" I asked, but instead of answering, Bill said, "Let me see if we can still get in."

The girl at the ticket window said we missed the last showing.

"I've never heard of this movie, what's it about?" I repeated.

"I'm not sure," he said. "Hey, you wanna go for a drive?"

"Where to?" I asked. I was never out this late.

"Why don't we take a drive up Peavine Mountain to look at the stars? Have you ever done that?"

"No, I haven't," I replied. "Okay."

My feelings toward Bill were conflicted. He had been my rule-maker and enforcer in Omega House, the embarrassing person who drove me to and from school, making me stay in his car while my classmates stared. He had outed me as a lesbian in the most humiliating way, and was hiding behind my front door to take me back to The Residence after I ran away.

On the flip side, Bill had also opened my mind by sharing the books he was reading. He ignited an appetite within me to learn about how others saw the world, which led to my fascination with studying other cultures.

The Human Book Store had recently opened in town, and it was stuffed with books on yoga and eastern thought, meditation pillows, candles, tapestries and all manner of items that would soon fall under the banner "New Age." I went as often as I could, always leaving with at least one book.

I told Bill about *Be Here Now,* Ram Dass' masterpiece on being in the present; *Autobiography of a Yogi,* by Yogananda; and Paavo Airola's *Are You Confused?* which turned me on to the benefits of dry brush massage and cold showers.

Between my reading material and new way of dressing, there was a divide between myself and most kids my age. At Hug, my classmates called me a hippie. My self-image was getting more rooted in being unconventional, something that did not escape my parents'notice. My mother called me a free spirit, while my father shook his head disapprovingly.

As we headed up the mountain, Bill asked me what happened the day I left The Residence. He said he was stunned I'd left without any explanation, adding my housemates were, too. When I told him the dream I had about my grandmother dying, he nodded in support and said it was good that I trusted the dream, as it turned out to be accurate. In my fever drive to get out of there, I never considered how it affected those I left behind. I was sorry to think I'd hurt any of them. Bill told me Tommy had left, as well as Diane and Darren, and new kids had taken their place.

He asked what I was up to now. I told him about school, and not playing sports, but didn't mention Becky also went to Hug. It was none of his business.

It took an hour to climb the switchback road up Peavine Mountain. Though it was May, nights were cold and even colder still as we rose in elevation.

Bill found a spot near the top that was wide enough to turn around. He maneuvered the truck bed to face the city lights. His truck had a camper shell, so he dropped the hatch and lifted the window, opening the back fully. The stars were brilliant against the pitch black sky.

As I climbed in back, I saw pillows and a blanket to cover us while we took in the view. I clenched my jaw to stop my teeth from chattering as we continued our conversation.

Bill often used the phrase "fuck the bees" which he made up on one of his countless acid trips. For him, *Fuck the bees* meant fuck the establishment. He likened society to a beehive that was trying to control and take over the sovereignty of individuals. He began a rant about the bees and the rules of man and how we all needed to be who we were without being polluted by society, which I found rich, since he had no problem slamming my individuality while I was under his care at The Residence.

While he was talking, a bizarre thing happened. My right leg flew up in the air, like a lightning bolt had hit it. Then my left leg did the same thing. "What the heck?" I stammered, confused and mortified by my body's behavior.

"What's going on there, Mueller?" Bill chuckled.

"No idea," I said. "Maybe it's cuz I'm so cold."

Then it happened again. I was embarrassed and didn't know how to make it stop.

"It's just energy," Bill stated matter-of-factly.

"Energy?" I asked. "What do you mean?"

"Well," he ventured with a cunning smile, "I think it's safe to say you know what's going on here, right? You can feel the energy that is building."

I didn't know what he was talking about. But, there was something in his smile that betrayed what he wasn't saying. As I paused to think about it, his implication hit me like a linebacker: *Oh my god, Bill brought me here to have sex with me.*

I was silent, thunderstruck by the realization. That ex-plained why we took this long-ass drive up the mountain. How could I have been so dumb, not catching on until now?

"Why don't you lie down," Bill urged.

I didn't respond. Time felt dense and heavy, like it was pressing in on me. Bill's intention was clear, this was his plan.

Bill was twenty-six years old, I was sixteen. Other than the time he briefly touched my breast at The Residence, he'd never expressed any sexual interest in me, so I was taken aback by his reappearance in my life and now obvious intentions. My mind was trying to catch up with what my body already knew.

At least Bill doesn't feel unsafe to me, I told myself. Maybe having sex with an older guy would be better than a boy my own age. Anyway, no boys my age were interested in me, that was sadly evident. It felt like I didn't move for a long time, rolling all this around in my head.

While my thoughts were spinning, Bill remained quiet while patiently holding up an old quilt. He moved closer to me and I felt his presence, his heat, and his desire fully. I felt my body succumb in agreement and without a word, I slid down under the blanket.

He asked me if I was a virgin and I said yes. I didn't think what I had done with Becky qualified as sex in the same way intercourse did. From what I had learned from Dr. Jankovich, I was sure my hymen was intact.

"I'll be gentle," Bill assured me.

"It's going to hurt though, right?" I asked.

"Yes," Bill said. "It will hurt."

He didn't kiss me. He didn't say anything. He removed my pants and underwear and got on top of me. My teeth banged against each other the whole time. I was nervous and freezing cold. The energy bolts of lightning continued flashing through my legs.

I winced with pain when he entered me. He moaned loudly and said how tight I was. After several minutes, he said he better stop as we had no protection and he didn't want to get me pregnant. As he zipped up his pants he said, "You'll need to get on the pill."

We made small talk as he drove me home. My underwear was wet with blood and whatever else. I was exhausted. It was after one a.m. when he dropped me off.

Climbing into bed, I had one thought and a noticeable absence of feeling: *I'm not a virgin anymore.*

This was how Bill became my boyfriend. I decided to ask Mrs. Carlson to take me to Planned Parenthood so I could get on the pill. Though I felt guilty asking her and not my mother, I was pretty sure my mother would say no.

The first week after we had sex, several people told me I looked different, glowy even, and asked me what had changed. When I looked in the mirror I felt the same, but the notion that some people could perceive that I had gone through a rite of passage fascinated me.

Bill no longer worked at The Residence, though he never told me why. He lived with his parents. Meeting them was awkward. Bill introduced me, but they said nothing, filling the room with their disapproving silence. My age mattered to them: it was the galavanting pink elephant in the room.

When Bill suggested I spend the night, I balked, especially after the icy reception I received. He showed me his bedroom and his little twin bed. He looked ridiculous: a grown man occupying the room of his youth. It struck me as more than a little pathetic and I declined, saying I'd have to ask my mother first. In order to do that, I'd have to tell her I was on the pill.

Bill was working at Omega House in town, and whatever money he made covered his expenses for gas, food, movies and books and not much else. He lived in T-shirts, a couple of pairs of slouchy shorts, and hiking boots.

I told my mother Bill and I were having sex and confessed that Mrs. Carlson helped me get on the pill. On the heels of being betrayed by Mrs. Carlson, this news hit her hard. She burst into tears, terribly hurt that I didn't come to her. She said she wanted us to be able to talk about anything with one another. I told her I'd like that as well and apologized for hurting her feelings.

She gave me permission to sleep at Bill's parents' house on the weekend. I was amazed and could even say disappointed. More and more I felt myself free-falling with no adult supervision. I would have benefitted from stronger boundaries and guidance. Honestly, some push-back about the fact that he was ten years older than me and my former counselor would have been appropriate. But during that time, my mother was overcome with sorrow over her divorce and had little to give.

The first night at Bill's parents was uncomfortable and cramped. Having sex was a muffled affair of going through the motions. The one unavoidable noise was the creaking metal springs of his ancient mattress. All I could think about was his parents listening to us. It was unpleasant and felt perverse that our sex was being witnessed through the walls. I told Bill I didn't want to stay there again. His solution was for us to have sex in the back of his truck on the street in front of his parents' house. We got caught by the police one night because the windows were steamed up. They let us off with a warning.

My mother even allowed Bill to spend the night at our house

one weekend. Kris had moved out so I had our room to myself. My three younger siblings were home and I felt it was giving them a terrible message. It felt wrong, so I policed myself and never had him over again. From then on we went out in the boonies to have sex.

Bill rarely kissed me, which bummed me out, and I noticed he preferred to have sex the same way every time. My only comparisons were the sexual experiences I had with Becky, since my interactions with Terry were negligible. Nothing about sex with Becky felt like intercourse with a man.

It is puzzling to think about now, but I still made no connection between my pole-climbing pleasures and sex. Nothing Bill was doing felt similar to the sensations I had when I climbed, so I did not associate the two. I wasn't visiting the pole as often because I had been caught in the act by Mike several times when he went out back to get high. Thankfully, he didn't really know what I was up to when he scared the crap out of me, coming around the back corner of the house. On the fly, I made up a story, saying I was doing stomach exercises, but it was more than bizarre to be interrupted on the pole by my brother. We were the only ones who went back there other than my mom, when she was hanging laundry.

Initially, I was reluctant to tell anyone I was having sex with Bill but, as time went on that feeling faded until, weirdly, being with him became something to brag about. It was the familiar feeling of being singled out as special in the same way I had been with Gena and Kathy.

Another feeling I had was vindication. I knew it was a slap in the face to my father for putting me in Omega House to begin with. When my mother told him I was having sex with Bill, she said he was livid and threatened to file statutory rape charges against Bill. Ultimately, it was an empty threat, because filing a lawsuit would have required far more attention in my direction than my father was willing to give.

My father didn't do anything. In fact, no one did anything—not John T., the director of Omega House, who employed Bill, and not any of the women counselors, several of whom had also had sex with Bill. I learned later on there was plenty of rapprochement and discourse among themselves, but no one spoke up on my behalf to say this is wrong.

I became defiant in my role as Bill's underaged girlfriend. When we went to Omega House for an evening dance program where an ex-lover of Bill's was performing, I showed up in a cotton sundress with no bra, feeling sexual and brazen, enjoying the shocked faces of my former counselors as I walked in.

Fuck them all, I thought, *no one is going to tell me what to do.*

My junior year at Hug ended in an unremarkable way. I had long since checked out of the social aspects of high school, so I had no one to say good-bye to. Mostly, I was overjoyed I wouldn't have to deal with Becky's nastiness anymore.

Wasting no time, I signed up for all my senior classes via correspondence courses. Once completed, I would enroll in the work-study program which would give me credits for having a job. I would spend my entire senior year off campus.

Unfortunately, my mother wasn't doing well. Most of the kids in the neighborhood witnessed our parents in various stages of drunkenness at the cocktail parties, but this was different. She was drinking alone and often. I became her caretaker, putting her to bed at night as she cried, sitting with her until she fell asleep.

She shared more stories of her godawful past with my father. In 1954, they became pregnant at seventeen-years-old. She was sent to New Orleans to a Catholic home for unwed mothers to avoid shaming her family in Milwaukee. New Orleans was chosen because it was closer to where my father was stationed at the Biloxi Air Force base.

My mother wanted to keep the baby and at one point our dad's mother sent my father a wedding band. It looked like they were going to keep the baby and get married. But my father received a telegram from his mother at the last minute stating that she had changed her mind and could not give her consent. My father told my mother to choose between him and the baby. She chose my father and the baby boy was put up for adoption.

Discovering that I had a full sibling somewhere in the world was deeply upsetting. As I learned of my mother's history with my father, my opinion of him plummeted further and I became entangled in their relationship in unhealthy ways. I had no skills to manage the feelings I had about what my mother was sharing.

Summer arrived so I had loads of free time to spend with Bill. We took day trips rockhounding near Reno and spent hours looking for chrysocolla, turquoise, opals, rubies and garnets. Bill made me a rustic silver ring out of a sapphire chunk he found.

Unpleasant news about my father showed up in the paper when he was arrested for both drunk and reckless driving in July and September. According to my mother, his September arrest occurred after he called her when he was drunk to falsely accuse her of infidelity. He took his grandfather's pistol (though he had no bullets for it) and went downtown in a rage to shoot the man in question. He was intercepted by a family friend and police officer who took dad to the Nevada Mental Health facility for an overnight evaluation. Mom seemed to think he was considering suicide by cop as a way of ending his life.

It was all too much to process. I stayed away more and more, finding relief with Bill and our rather odd relationship.

Before summer ended, I had to find a job to qualify for the work-study program. A new restaurant called The Good Earth was hiring waitresses. My mom bought me a gorgeous denim dress to wear for my interview. When I met the manager, Keith Burns, his puppy dog eyes immediately put me at ease. He had shaggy dark hair, the palest skin I'd ever seen and a huge infectious smile. His manner was kind and welcoming. As he looked over my application, he saw I had almost no work experience. I was keen to get the job and did my best to persuade him that I could handle it. He had reservations because I was sixteen.

"I'll be seventeen in three months," I pleaded. "Please give me a chance."

Keith paused to consider my request while I held my breath. Finally he said, "Okay, let's give it a try. You'll have to prove yourself though, so don't let me down."

For my new job, once again, I relied on my grandpa to take me to and from work. He was always willing to help and I let him know I was going to save up to get my first car as soon as I could. It didn't take long before I'd saved nine hundred dollars to put down on a brand new, brown, 1976 Honda Civic. My monthly payment was one hundred and thirteen dollars a month.

The Good Earth was a new concept restaurant built on a healthier way of eating. Keith took me under his wing, training me himself on how to waitress and do meal prep, as well as stocking supplies and cleaning. I loved it and was excited to learn new things.

Within weeks of being hired I met a man who delivered our fresh-squeezed orange juice. He was lean and handsome with wide-set, dark eyes.

He greeted me one day while putting a few gallons of orange juice in the walk-in, saying his name was Didar Singh. He and his wife recently opened a cafe on Fourth Street called Earthen Joy. He invited me to stop by for a meal to check out their menu.

Wearing all white and a turban, I asked him what his manner of dress represented. Didar said he was a Sikh, a practitioner of a religion from India. As such, he did not cut his hair and wore a turban. His clothes were casual: a white t-shirt over narrow-fitting pants called churidars. I thought they looked like upscale long underwear. Honestly, the man was a walking advertisement for the comforts of cotton fabric.

He said he was part of the Healthy, Happy, Holy Organization founded by his spiritual teacher Yogi Bhajan. It was a brief interaction, but I found myself curious about the lifestyle he lived.

While other kids my age were talking about college, I was looking ahead to my job and my boyfriend. Maybe even Bill and I would marry one day. Whenever the Fifth Dimension song "Bill" came on the radio I'd sing along, "Won't you marry me Bill?"

Sadly, Mike was partying heavily and was difficult to be around. He often woke up hungover and in a foul mood, which he would take out on his siblings. He stole from me more than once to buy weed. I put a lock on my door, but he easily broke it off. Addiction took over the trajectory of his life, while we all watched, powerless to make him change.

That fall, he and two friends burgled a house around the corner from where we lived. They thought they got away with it, but then one of the boys called the police and turned in the other two.

Although there was no proof linking them to the crime, it so happened they broke into the house of a prominent judge. When Mike went for sentencing he pleaded for permission to join the armed services rather than be incarcerated. Since he was almost eighteen, the judge consented. However, because he was still a minor, he needed my parents' consent as well, and while my mother wholeheartedly supported Mike, my father did not. He refused to allow it. Acting as judge and jury, he declared Mike unfit for the military. This condemnation was a devastating blow to Mike in many ways.

Mike would have done well in the military. Boundaries and rules would have benefitted him. My father's pig-headed determination to thwart his request was cruel and punishing. It solidified the mutual dislike that simmered for years between my brother and father.

Consequently, the judge sentenced Mike to the Nevada Youth Training Center in Elko—a prison for wayward boys. On a bleak winter day, he boarded a bus for Elko to serve his term. I was sad for Mike and hoped his time there would turn his life around.

As Thanksgiving approached, Bill proposed we take a road trip to Montana to visit his brother who lived in Dillon. There were opal and ruby mines to visit along the way.

Under the influence of my new work environment, I became a vegetarian and was on my first juice fast, so I brought a cooler full of juices. Fasting was challenging in the frigid temperatures, especially because I was ingesting mostly cold beverages. Nonetheless, I held to my conviction and toughed it out.

On the way we stopped in Boise because Bill had a favorite rock shop there. They had a large selection of star sapphires, Bill's favorite stone. He dabbled as a jewelry maker though his pieces were crudely rendered.

We stayed with Bill's friend, Linda, who was in Omega House before my time. She moved to Boise six months prior and worked as a taxi driver. Bill crashed early, while Linda and I stayed up talking.

We arrived in Dillon the next day. I took a long, hot shower at Bill's brother's house, trying to melt the chill out of my bones. His family seemed like good people. Sitting with my bottle of papaya juice, I looked at the Thanksgiving feast on the table. Golden mashed potatoes with gobs of melted butter floating on top, stuffing and gravy, fresh cranberry sauce and turkey and venison Bob hunted locally.

My resolve to continue fasting was at a low point.

"Mueller," Bill said, "Have you ever had venison?

"God no," I replied. "I'd never eat Bambi."

The whole table erupted in laughter.

"You've got to try it," Bill insisted. "At least once in your life, really. You never have to eat it again. C'mon, whaddya say?"

"All right," I conceded. "But give me a super small piece."

This was a bad choice as I was on the ninth day of my juice fast. Bill proffered his fork with a small chunk of meat on it and I bit half. I chewed it like a person who didn't want to taste what I was eating, with a few half-hearted chomps before I swallowed.

The venison hit my stomach and my body said *Oh, fuck no!* as it shot like a missile, up my esophagus and out of my mouth, hitting the facing wall with impressive velocity. Then I fainted.

Looking up at Bill's relatives as I opened my eyes, I saw a sea of startled faces. They'd never heard of juice fasting and they'd never seen someone pass out from a nibble of fresh meat. Their expressions made me chuckle because they looked at me the way I would look at an alien if one showed up in my living room.

Bill helped me to my feet as I apologized, grabbed my papaya juice and went to bed.

The next morning, I couldn't wait to eat food. We went to a pancake house and I ordered a huge stack. With each bite, I felt my energy returning. Fasting in the winter was a lousy idea.

Not long after I got back to work, Keith hired a new cook, a boy my age. We flirted when we worked together. He was an attractive, arrogant, combative guy. We had sex a couple of times before I discovered he had a girlfriend. She showed up at the Good Earth to cuss me out, which was a highly embarrassing but effective way to put me off her boyfriend.

Feeling ashamed of my behavior, I decided to take a literal guilt-trip to Boise to buy Bill a sapphire ring. My mother booked my round-trip, same-day ticket and I contacted Linda to help me make it happen. I was filled with a sense of daring when she picked me up at the airport and could hardly contain myself. We went to Bill's favorite rock shop where I found a breathtaking, translucent star-sapphire ring set in gold with a price tag of three hundred dollars. This was the mea culpa I was looking for, so I proudly plopped the cash down on the counter, feeling like a big spender. I flew home, high as a kite, pleased with my adventure and the outcome.

The next day, February first, was Bill's twenty-seventh birthday. When I presented the ring to him, Bill stumbled over his words, he was so caught off guard. I was smiling from ear to ear at the success of my grand gesture. He loved the ring, in part because he had taught me how to recognize clarity and brilliance in sapphires. It was a spectacular gift that helped alleviate my guilt about being unfaithful.

Right around this time, an attractive woman named Debbie came to work at The Good Earth. I liked her immediately. She looked like she stepped out of a Botticelli painting with her long, honey-colored hair and small, perky breasts. We quickly became friends. However, within weeks of Debbie's arrival, I was fired because I called the new manager, Gloria, a bitch during an argument we were having. She and I were a bad match from the start. She was bossy and rigid, the opposite of Keith.

When I begged him to give me a second chance, Keith admonished me, saying, "If only you had said she was *bitchy*, it would not be a fireable offense, but you used a noun, and that doesn't fly."

I took my lumps, dismayed that my temper got the better of me. I'd let Keith down as well, and was sorry to lose my job and my friends at The Good Earth.

12

synanon

Bill invited me on an overnight trip to San Francisco. Arrangements had been made to transfer a boy from Omega House to the Synanon residential drug treatment program in downtown Oakland. Since Synanon was the main influence behind Omega House and where *The Game* originated, I was curious to see it for myself.

Omega House operated out of a ramshackle building in a dodgy part of Reno. It was unimpressive in every way, so as we pulled up to the Synanon building on Clay Street, I was blown away. The enormous size of the place was intimidating. The art deco building covered two city blocks in Oakland. The place was packed with teenagers and young adults, many of them bald. Head-shaving, which started as a consequence of relapse, now seemed like a requirement to join the community.

Bill took his ward and went to find the person he was turning him over to. I stayed in the lobby, seated at a table by myself.

People approached me right away, asking why I was there, wanting to know if I'd been interviewed yet to join the family. They were friendly, though a bit aggressive in their questioning. Several people offered their testimonies of how life-changing Synanon was and how they willingly embraced shaving their heads. It was obvious that they considered their time there as an ongoing commitment—part of a lifetime plan. One person even assured me it wasn't a cult. Beneath the barrage of information coming at me, I felt sincerity in the invitation they were offering.

Witnessing this unorthodox community with their uniform appearance and unsolicited testimonials was somewhat unsettling, but there was something appealing about it as well. Their unfiltered sense of belonging and conviction was seductive. They were more like a religion than a drug treatment program in the solidarity they so openly shared. It touched a longing in me that wanted to belong and be a part of something bigger.

By the time Bill came back to say it was time to go, I was ready to get outside and breathe some fresh air. Synanon felt like a web that I could easily get caught in.

We left and ate dinner at an inexpensive diner. It was getting late, but instead of finding a motel for the night, Bill asked if I'd like to go to a club. I reminded him I couldn't go to a club where alcohol was served. He chuckled and said the place he had in mind wouldn't card me.

The club Bill had in mind was a dingy strip club on Market Street with neon lights that blinked irregularly like a weak call for help. A short, square-shaped man with a rough complexion in a tattered overcoat advanced toward us before we reached the door. He looked like he stepped right out of a film noir detective caper with Edward G. Robinson and Humphrey Bogart. Bill told me to stay put and met the man for a whispered conversation. I saw the man nod as Bill slipped him some money and then motioned to me to come forward.

"See how easy that was?" He grinned, pleased with himself. "Have you ever been to a strip club?" he asked, as he yanked the heavy door open. My body tensed as I walked through the door.

"Gee, Bill, what the hell do you think?" I snapped, instantly irritated by his stupid question. I was also irritated he thought it was a good idea to bring me to a strip club in the first place.

Bill took my hand and pulled me down a dark, narrow aisle toward the front of the stage.

Melancholic music with a slow beat crackled through a blown amp. The air was choked with cigarette smoke accented by blue lights scattered randomly around the stage. It created an eerie effect—that sickly blue-gray smoke stretching out like moody, dying clouds after a storm. There wasn't a single window in the place. I imagined no fresh air had traveled through there in decades. That thought made it harder for me to breathe.

A young woman was performing alone on a raised platform on the stage. She was tripping on something strong, something that turned her eyelids to lead, making it impossible to open her eyes beyond mere slits. Similarly, her dance movements were lethargic, awkward and heavy, like someone who was about to pass out cold.

Bill took my elbow and guided me to the second row where we sat down. The front row was fully occupied with what looked like business men from the forties. They wore trenchcoats and Fedora hats, pulled down low to obscure their faces. Each man had a newspaper over his lap, serving as a tent to conceal the fact that they were masturbating. Their activity was given away by the rhythmic movement of the newspapers. The friction of it created its own percussive contribution to the music. Tension began to build in me. I was uncomfortable and disgusted with what I was seeing. Bill leaned toward me to whisper in my ear, "Don't watch them, Suzy, watch her."

The woman was on all fours, trying to remove her panties as a part of her strip tease. They were stuck halfway down her right thigh. Her left leg was raised and she had somehow hooked her left stiletto heel through the leg opening.

It was an impossible task because she was on her knees, so there was no way to pull the underwear off. The fabric was being stretched to the point of discomfort, but would not budge a bit. Because she was wasted, she moved mechanically—bending her knee as her stiletto moved toward butt, and then extending her leg to try and pull her panties off. Her motions had no effect on the panties other than stretching it each time she extended her leg.

She had a look of frustration on her face but didn't have any other ideas of how to remove them. Thus, the monotonous motion continued, in time to the music, until her leg reminded me of a parking garage lever that lifts and lowers so you can exit.

The sight of her was disturbing. I wanted to laugh and cry. For me, there was nothing sexual about her—I thought she was desperately sad. I couldn't imagine what had happened in her life that she ended up in a depressing shithole like this.

Thinking about her life upset me, and then the sound of fluttering newspapers pulled my attention toward the disgusting men that were jerking-off to her bizarre performance. My anger finally rose. I was furious at Bill for subjecting me to this tawdry place and shouted at him, "I am getting out of here!" He was closest to the aisle so I roughly climbed over him to split. He followed me out the door.

Once we got in his car, I let him have it. Bill apologized, but I felt he was insincere. We found a cheap motel and I wanted to sleep, but Bill climbed on top of me to have sex. I guess the girl on the stage made him hot. When we got home the next day I couldn't wait to get away from him.

Meanwhile, after six months in Elko, Mike was released for good behavior. My father picked him up, insisting that Mike live with him because he believed mom was too permissive. Within weeks of being back, Mike was arrested for drunk driving and spent the night in jail. Mike's addictions ruled his life thereafter. For years, I braced myself, dreading a call that would tell me he was dead. Because of Mike, my resolve to stay away from drugs and alcohol grew ever stronger.

Within weeks of being fired, I found work as a cashier at the Pay-n-Pak hardware store. I also went to Earthen Joy to see what kind of food they offered. Didar recognized me right away and introduced me to his wife, Didar Kaur. Seeing my confusion, he explained their names were Didar Singh and Didar Kaur.

He said they needed help handling their lunch rush and asked if I'd like to work there on my days off. I'd get a free meal each shift I took. "Absolutely," I said. "I'd love to."

To make up for his poor judgement in San Francisco, Bill planned a four-day campout to one of his favorite places, the Black Rock Desert, located 100 miles north of Reno. It featured a massive, prehistoric dry lake bed that seemed to go on forever. We brought summer and winter clothes to accommodate the huge temperature differential from day to night. We seemed to have the place completely to ourselves. I had recently become a vegetarian, but it slipped my mind as we got ready to leave. I wasn't used to having to plan special foods for myself. Bill thought it would be a good idea to bring a tub of Kentucky Fried Chicken, some apples, and cheese.

By the second day, I was hungry and irritated that if I wanted to eat, I had to break from my new diet. More than a diet, it had become important to me, philosophically, to not eat animals. Right around the time I finished eating all the apples and cheese, we got a flat tire and Bill had no spare. We sat on the side of the road for most of the day before a single soul drove by. A rancher helped us out, and we headed home a day early so I could get some food.

Later that week, Bill joined me for a run in the evening at Idlewild park. We went a mile before he was too winded to continue. He motioned for me to sit with him on a park bench while he caught his breath.

All of a sudden, he whispered, "Suzy, can you feel that?"

"Can I feel what?" I asked.

He tried again, "There's a sinister energy here. Can you feel its presence?"

"No, Bill, I don't sense anything. But you're scaring the shit out of me," I complained.

Then, Bill tilted his head like he was a radio antenna making adjustments to get better reception. He found a spot he liked and closed his eyes. I felt anxious watching him. He opened his eyes and hissed, "We gotta get out of here, this is not a friendly being. We gotta go, NOW!"

Bill leapt up and raced down the path toward his car.

"Wait for me!" I screamed, completely spooked as I chased after him.

Bill had been fascinated with aliens for years. He had a subscription to *Probe the Unknown*, a UFO magazine full of stories of human encounters with alien species and a copy of Jim Moseley's "Book of Saucer News." When we got together, I was initially willing to hear what he had to say about UFOs , but then Bill frightened me with what he said were actual accounts of alien interactions. They were mostly gruesome stories, detailing human experiments that didn't end well, so I told him I didn't want to hear about aliens anymore.

But, when I began to have some unusual experiences at night, Bill seemed like the person to talk to about it. The first thing that happened was I woke up several times in the middle of the night to find a small bird flying around in my room. I never got a good look at it because as soon as I threw the light switch on, the bird flew out my large open window.

When I relayed this to Bill, he said, "Well, I hate to be the one to tell you this, but birds in your bedroom at night are a sure sign of an alien presence."

The second thing I told him was how I sometimes woke up from a feeling of immense pressure on my body, especially my chest. It felt like I had a board on top of me with a hundred pounds of rocks on top of it.

Hearing this he exclaimed, "That is another sure sign of an alien presence!"

"Really?" I asked. "Are you sure?"

"Oh yes, I'm sure," he confirmed. "I would say that you are definitely on their radar."

His response freaked me out.

After giving it some thought, Bill concluded that the remedy to the situation was for me to spend the night alone in the Black Rock Desert.

"You are going to have to offer yourself up to the aliens. There is no other way to deal with this situation," he said matter-of-factly.

"Are you insane?" I replied. "There is no way in hell...."

Bill jumped in before I could finish, "Listen to me, Suzy, if they take you, they take you... but, *if they don't*, they will 100 percent leave you alone after that."

"If they *take* me?" I squeaked in disbelief. This was the most outlandish and disturbing conversation of my life. How I wished

I had never said a word to him.

His tone was somber and convincing when he added, "I'm dead serious right now. Otherwise, these phenomena will keep on happening to you."

I had to make a decision.

The following Saturday, my mom was at a party, so I drove there to ask her if I could go to Black Rock by myself. Bill and I had just camped there, so at least I was familiar with the location. When I asked her about going, I duplicated Bill's somber tone, hoping to convey the seriousness of the situation.

Most importantly, I emphasized that I'd be going *totally alone, to a remote area.*

"Sure honey," she said, like I asked for money for the ice cream truck. "That's fine. You know I never worry about you."

This was not what I wanted to hear.

Bill was pressuring me to go, but if my mother said no, then the subject would be closed and I'd be off the hook.

So, I tried again, "Mom, please listen. Black Rock is over three hours away. I'd be spending the night, by myself, completely alone in the desert…."

"Okay honey, you have fun!" she responded enthusiastically.

What? I was dumbstruck. My mother was giving me permission to pursue this cockeyed plan? Not knowing what else to say, I gave up and drove home thinking, *I guess I'm doing this.*

Checking the time, I realized I needed to hustle. Grabbing my sleeping bag, bivy sack, pillow, and down jacket, along with some fruit, nuts and water, I quickly loaded up my Honda and hit the road. I didn't even call Bill to tell him I was going through with it. My mom was the only person who would know where I was—if she was able to recall our conversation.

Now that I had committed to going, I took on a fatalistic

attitude because the truth was, I was afraid either way. Staying meant I might have more alien experiences and going meant I might be taken or I might die. Something about Bill saying that they would leave me alone afterward was compelling, so I leaned toward that resolution. I expected to arrive at Black Rock pretty close to sunset.

All of my Cat Stevens 8-tracks went with me. He'd be my comfort and companion. As long as I was absorbed in his music, I didn't feel afraid about what I was doing. At least that worked for the first half of the trip, but as I got closer to Black Rock, my emotions started to percolate.

It bothered me that I felt compelled to do what Bill told me to do, even though I desperately wanted to stay home. My plan to ask my mother, hoping she would say no, completely backfired. The big question was: *Why couldn't I refuse on my own?*

In the summer, the high-to-low temperature range in northern Nevada could easily cover fifty degrees or more. It would get cold quickly once the sun went down. I passed through the largely forgotten town of Gerlach without seeing a soul and made my way up the road on the western side of Black Rock Desert looking for a good place to pull over for the night. I didn't want to be close to the road, but I didn't want to be too far from it either.

The sun was setting when I spotted an area that looked like it could work and pulled off the road. I began to panic and rushed to put on my coat before grabbing my water and gear. I ran about fifty yards to a spot that called to me. Just like Carlos Castaneda had rolled around on a wooden floor all night to find his power spot, I hoped I had found the right place for me.

My legs felt like rubber as I got into my sleeping bag. The vast space around me mocked my puny existence as the air turned cold. I laid on my back, shivering and moaning into the vast and empty darkness.

My fears skulked in the shadows, taunting me. I was afraid of animals finding me in the dark. A hungry pack of coyotes or a rattlesnake might kill me while I slept. *What if someone menacing spotted my car? What if they decided to investigate?*

My mind played out worst-case scenarios: *Maybe I'd be murdered, like poor Michelle Mitchell. Who would even know I had been killed? Would my mom remember where I said I was going?* I was most afraid of animals and strangers, the aliens were too abstract for me to catastrophize about. It was a big mistake not to tell anyone else where I was going.

Mercifully, my state of hypervigilance gave way to exhaustion. Lying on my back, I looked to the heavens where stars were rapidly popping into the darkening sky and thought *I might die tonight*. The thought made me want to cry, but I was too tired for that. I conked out despite my fears and slept straight through the night.

The unmistakable dry heat of Nevada's morning sun woke me. It took a couple of beats for me to remember where I was. When I did remember, I was amazed I survived.

I shouted to the new day, "I'm alive! I'm alive!"

I couldn't load the car quick enough to head for home.

The weird things going on in my bedroom stopped after that. Perhaps it was a placebo effect, or maybe I simply closed my window at night, but I attributed the change to Bill and his assessment of my situation.

13 strangers

Compared to the lively, stimulating atmosphere at The Good Earth, working as a cashier at the Pay-n-Pak hardware store was a tedious bore. My creepy boss and the assistant manager liked to duck below the register counter when I was checking someone out to run their hands up and down my legs. I needed a new job.

It was another monotonous day when a young man breezed into the store. He was a stone cold fox with an enormous blond afro and oceanic blue eyes. He reminded me of Willam Katt from the horror film, *Carrie*. As soon as I saw him get into my line, I became flustered.

"Hello, Suzanne," he purred, reading my name tag in a voice nearly as pleasing as his looks, "How are you today?"

"I'm good, thanks," I managed back.

"May I ask you a personal question? he asked, not waiting for a reply. "Are you a Christian, Suzanne?"

"I was raised Catholic," I replied, "so, yeah, I guess so."

"Well, I'd like to invite you to meet me for mass this Sunday in Truckee. My name is Pat, by the way."

I was speechless. That was the last thing I would have expected him to say.

"How about this," he pressed on, "if you'll give me your phone number, I can call you with the address."

"Sure, I can give you my number," I said, reaching for paper and pen to write on.

"Great. Thank you, Suzanne," he said, placing my number in his pocket. "I'll be in touch this week." And then, I'm pretty sure he floated out the door on a magic carpet.

As soon as I got home, I told my mom about him and she commented how she'd be happy for me to date a boy my age. I was just meeting Pat at church, so I didn't think I needed to say anything about it to Bill.

I fasted on juice all week to drop a few pounds and my mom took me shopping for my church outfit. I found a gorgeous Gunne Sax prairie dress in a lovely, blueberry calico with white lace trim. My leather Earth sandals from San Francisco looked awesome with the dress.

Pat called on Thursday and we had a short conversation. He gave me the address and directions to his church, and I found out he was twenty years old. The church was off Highway 267 in Truckee.

Though I was no longer religious, I thought maybe it would bode well for me to go out with someone who was. Maybe it would mean he'd be a good guy. I headed out Sunday morning to meet him for the eleven o'clock service with a map and a handful of dimes for a phone booth in case of an emergency.

I was glad to have on a pretty new dress when I saw him smartly dressed in a suit. I felt flattered by his interest in me. The mass was pretty ordinary, but different from Catholic mass. I didn't notice what denomination the church was. Afterward we said hello to a couple of his friends before Pat suggested we take a short drive to Kings Beach.

"Leave your car here. I'll bring you back later," he said.

"Okay," I responded. I hadn't expected to do anything more

than mass but liked the idea of spending more time with him.

On the way to Kings Beach, Pat told me about growing up at Lake Tahoe. I couldn't imagine waking up in such a spectacularly beautiful place. The small towns on the lake felt like they were frozen in time, quaint villages of a bygone era.

I was daydreaming about living at the lake when he said he was house-sitting for his neighbors and needed to stop by the house to feed their cats.

"Oh, okay, that's cool," I responded.

The cats lived in a home nestled in the pine trees, half a mile or so from the lake. Pat led me to the living room, telling me to wait there. I plunked myself down on a cushy sofa and took in the luxe furnishings of the room. Envy crept in as I tried to imagine what it would be like to be wealthy, living each day with ease and security.

When Pat returned I was hoping he would take me into town to show me around. He sat next to me on the sofa and immediately began kissing me. Flushed by his passion, I kissed him back.

After a minute or so, he took me by the shoulders and moved me onto my back. His moans of excitement increased as he laid on top of me, kissing me intensely. Then he reached under my dress, found my panties, and pulled at them until they slid off my hips. Things were moving fast, but I didn't object. He unzipped his pants and had sex with me for a good forty-five seconds. As he pulled his pants back on, he said, "I should get you back to your car before it gets too late."

Well, that's that, I thought. It's time to go.

"Oh, okay," I replied, hiding my misery at the economical way he achieved his objective. The drive back to the church was quite different from the drive to Kings Beach, which held the prospect of sex for Pat. He thanked me for going to mass with him, which I found ridiculous and hypocritical, considering he invited me there for sex. By the time we reached the parking lot, I was bent.

I drove down the mountain screaming and cussing until my ears rang from the volume of my voice. How utterly stupid was I to think he sincerely liked me? The sex was lame and my new dress was all wrinkled.

The phrase "you used me" was a common refrain during the seventies to characterize a guy that used women for sex. My scrawled journal entry reflects my feelings about Pat:

Hurt Used Fucked Over. I'm sick of it!

When I got home I told my mom how disappointing my day was without telling her I'd had sex. Being on the pill allowed me to have sexual experiences free from the worry of an unwanted pregnancy, but this wasn't a good feeling at all. The whole unpleasant incident really shined a light on how unhappy I was with Bill. I'd cheated on him again and this time there would be no grand gesture to assuage my guilt. I wasn't even sure if I felt any guilt at all.

Pat unexpectedly called midweek to ask if I could meet him for mass again on Sunday. This was confusing, as I had already brushed him off as a lesson to be learned. Despite saying no, he was persuasive and convinced me that he "really wanted to see me again."

"But," I insisted, "this time is for church only."

"Yes," Pat agreed. "Church only."

Sunday came and I was back at Pat's church at eleven. He was waiting for me and got in my car as I parked.

"Hey, nice to see you again," he said nervously, continuing, "um, well… I wanted to let you know that my girlfriend and I got back together so, uh… I can't see you anymore."

"What?" I asked, stunned. "You have a girlfriend?"

"Well, yeah… I mean… we broke up for a couple of weeks and got back together last night," he revealed.

I saw red.

"Then why am I even here, Pat? Why didn't you tell me all of this on the phone?" I snapped.

"Well," he muttered, "I couldn't call you last night cuz I was with her and so that's why I'm here to tell you now. Uhhm, sorry… but I kinda need to go in, my girlfriend's waiting for me."

With that, he opened the car door and walked away. I yelled at the top of my lungs, hoping the churchgoers, and especially his girlfriend, could hear me, "You're a real asshole, Pat. I hope you know that. Thanks for wasting my time."

Off he went with his head hanging down, Pat the Ass, to his girlfriend in the church. I was so angry and hurt, but mostly, I felt stupid that he duped me twice.

Having just arrived, I wasn't ready to go home yet. I decided to drive to Lake Tahoe to take a walk and clear my head. When I got to Kings Beach, I parked on the side of the road, opting to walk on the sidewalk rather than the beach. It was a perfectly beautiful day, but I was too downhearted to enjoy it.

It figures, I thought. From the moment I met Pat, I believed he was too good for me. He had such a confident way about him and I assumed he came from money, which intimidated me. Being rejected by him hurt all the more because I expected it.

About fifteen minutes into my walk, a pale-blue Mustang drove by, slowed down, and then backed up until it was beside me.

A man of about twenty-five leaned over to roll down the passenger side window as he yelled my way, "Hey lovely lady, how are you? I'm Jason."

"Hey Jason," I said, apathetically, "What's up? Are you lost?"

"No," he replied. "What's your name? Do you live up here?"

" I'm Suzy," I told him. "I wish I lived here. I'm from Reno."

"Well, you're awfully pretty to be walking alone on a beautiful day like today," he said cheerfully.

"Such is life," came my deadpan reply.

"So, hey, would you ever wanna work up here?" he asked.

"Why?" I replied. "Do you have a job for me?"

"I might!" he declared.

"Really?" I responded, "Doing what?"

"Well, my brother has offices at the Hyatt in Incline Village," he explained. "He's looking for a receptionist and we haven't been able to find the right person for the job."

"And you think I'm the right person?" I said with some snark.

"Yeah, why not? You could be!" Jason persisted. "Plus, it pays really well, a thousand dollars a week!"

"That's a shit-ton of money, Jason."

"Well, it's a demanding job, answering phones, making schedules, you know. It's not super-hard, but it is demanding. Why don't I take you over there right now to meet my brother and he could interview you?"

"Really?" I said, feeling skeptical and curious. He was so earnest, maybe I was in the right place at the right time.

"Sure, I promise," he said encouragingly. "Come on, get in the car. You can fill out an application and I'll bring you back in no time. It's ten minutes from here."

He pushed open the passenger door, and waited.

Like most girls my age, I had been told my whole life, *never get in a car with a stranger*. As I stood on the side of the road looking at him, he seemed like a nice guy. The possibility of a silver lining after my shitty interaction with Pat sounded appealing. After all, I deserved to have something good happen to me. Maybe he was sincere. Maybe I would move to the lake and have a new life and a good job.

I wanted to believe he was sincere, so I got in the car.

On our way, Jason told me he was from Los Angeles but came to Lake Tahoe to help his brother with the business.

The ground level of the Hyatt Hotel was a complex of retail businesses and office space. Jason parked and we walked to the space his brother rented. As we went in, I noticed a bar adjacent to the offices with a few people drinking and sitting outside.

Jason motioned to the front desk saying, "That's where you'll work, answering phones and booking appointments."

It felt good that he was speaking as if I already had the job. As we moved past the desk, I saw a showroom with floor to ceiling windows and a series of bed displays: king-sized beds with fancy linens and lighting set up all around.

"What exactly does your brother do?" I asked.

"He, uh, well, the beds are…he'll tell you all about that."

Jason went looking for his brother while I walked around the showroom trying to figure out what the business was. Did they sell mattresses or fine linens? When Jason reemerged he said his brother was in the bar and we would meet him there.

We made our way to a standing table inside the bar. My first jolt happened when he pointed out his brother because he had an uncanny resemblance to my father.

Jason introduced us and told him I was interested in applying for the receptionist job. His brother asked me a few questions about my work experience and I told him I was working as a cashier at the Pay-n-Pak hardware store in Reno.

While I was talking, I was aware that he was looking me up and down. I was mid-sentence when he abruptly snatched the bottom of my dress with both hands and lifted it over my head.

"Let's have a look at the goods!" he said laughing.

Horrified, I pulled my dress down and slapped him across the face, "How dare you!" I exclaimed, outraged at his gall.

I got my second jolt when he slapped me much harder than I had slapped him. My ears were ringing from the impact.

"How dare I?" he sneered. "Do you know what happened to the last chick that hit me? She's at the bottom of the fucking lake!"

My hand rose to cover the place where his hand had landed in an attempt to soothe the heat rising there. Try as I may, I couldn't think properly. I was dumbfounded by the severe change in direction that had taken place. My whole body was shaking. I couldn't feel my legs beneath me. I looked to Jason, who was looking at the floor and taking a few steps back from his brother. Alarms were going off in my head as my mind screamed, *What the fuck is happening here?*

I knew I was in danger.

The people around us in the bar saw what he had done, yet not one single person responded or said a word.

Jason finally spoke, saying, "Hey, Suzy, let's get a drink." This was the out I needed as I rushed to Jason's side. We sat at a table across the room.

"I'm so sorry about that," he whispered, "my brother can be hot-headed." I didn't respond. My mind was racing a million miles an hour. I was in trouble and I didn't know how to get out of it.

Jason ordered drinks. I had lemonade and sipped it slowly, holding the cold glass up to my face to numb the pain and also to hide behind it. Jason's brother was talking to a balding, fat, disheveled man with slouched posture. It was obvious they were talking about me. The man made vulgar gestures, grabbing his crotch while he looked at me. My stomach convulsed.

Then I heard him say, "We are going to get lucky tonight."

Hearing this, I grabbed Jason's arm, saying, "Hey Jason, I'm ready to go home. Can you take me back to my car now please?"

"No," he said gravely, "I'm sorry. I can't do that."

"Why not?" I demanded. "I'm not the person for this job."

"I can't," he replied. "My brother wants me around. I need to run an errand for him later."

"But, Jason, you said you'd take me right back to my car," I complained.

Jason changed the subject by saying how beautiful I was. He asked me questions about myself and I answered politely. At one point, I managed to briefly get the bartender's attention and mouthed the words "help me" when he was looking at me, but he looked down and shook his head, saying no.

The fat slouch was yucking it up, most likely at my expense. I couldn't even look in the direction of his brother. His resemblance to my father made me sick. In an effort to prepare for the worst, I began to tell myself I will likely be raped this night and perhaps by more than one of them. My mind began strategizing my options.

I decided to flirt with Jason—maybe I could make him an ally. Scooching my chair closer to him, I began asking him about his life. We talked for about an hour and I realized that as we were engaged in conversation, it kept the other two at bay. That gave me some ease. Then the two men left and Jason informed me that we had to wait there. Hours went by until the fat man reappeared and told Jason, "It's time to go."

He handed Jason a black briefcase and whispered something in his ear. Jason took my hand saying, "We're taking a drive."

"Where are we going?" I asked, but he declined to answer.

Walking to his Jeep, Jason pulled back his denim jacket to reveal a gun. "Don't get any ideas," he barked.

My confidence that he was becoming an ally vanished. Jason waited for me to buckle up and locked the car doors before opening the briefcase. It was full of neatly bundled stacks of hundred dollar bills. My teeth started chattering uncontrollably.

I didn't have a sweater, and even in summer, it's cold at the lake when the sun goes down. My hand tightly gripped the door handle. I was thinking maybe I should jump from the car, but Jason was driving fast and I didn't want to die, get run over, or plummet down a sheer drop-off trying to escape.

We drove for about twenty minutes until Jason pulled into a long driveway. When he got to the house, he flashed his beams and a man came out to get the briefcase. I had hoped he would leave me in the car so I could make a run for it.

They whispered briefly before we headed back to Incline.

"Jason, please take me back to my car now," I pleaded with him. "I *really* need to get home. My mom is going to be worried sick about me."

"No," he said again. "I'm sorry, I can't do that."

So I asked him outright, "Am I going to get raped by your brother and that guy?"

"No," he replied, "I won't let that happen to you."

His answer terrified me, since his reply confirmed my suspicions. I couldn't believe he wouldn't take me to my car. I hoped my mom would call the police, but I knew she wouldn't. She told me she never worried about me. Even if she did, she'd have no idea where I was or who I was with.

I kept up my plan to stay close to Jason when we got back to the offices. It was getting close to midnight. The front reception area was dark, but the bed set-ups were all softly lit.

Jason's brother and the fat guy came into the showroom drunk. The fat guy took a swipe at me, trying to grab my ass, but Jason stopped him, saying, "Take it easy man. She's with me."

The fat guy smacked his lips and snickered, but it had the desired effect as they soon left us there alone.

"Is this where we are sleeping, in this showroom?" I asked.

"Sleeping?" Jason smiled. "Yeah, eventually."

He led me to a bed in the spacious showroom and told me to undress. I obeyed, thankful it was him and not the other men.

As he climbed on top of me, a continuous tape-loop played in my head. It may as well have been my father's voice, repeating his favorite reprimand: *You made your bed, Suzanne, now lie in it.*

This was my fault.

Over and over I heard the indictment playing in my head: *You got in the car. You got in the car. You got in the car.*

It was oddly soothing, a kind of distorted mantra I could focus on while Jason fucked me. At least he didn't take too long.

When he was finished, I rolled into a fetal position with my back to him and closed my eyes, my tears flowing onto the pillow. I was spent from the ordeal and so the gift of immediate sleep kindly embraced me.

It was after sunrise when I woke up. I gave Jason a shake.

"Jason, wake up, I have to go home right now."

"Okay," he mumbled, to my great relief.

Thankfully, my car hadn't been towed. As I stepped out of his car, I could hear Jason saying he'd call me. I had the dreadful realization he had my phone number and home address from the job application I filled out. I nodded in response, because if I tried to talk I would explode. I hurried into my car and locked the doors.

I waved goodbye as he drove away. As soon as he was out of sight I took off. Emotion poured out of me. My own cries didn't feel like my own. I sounded like an injured animal, making raspy, unfamiliar noises.

I don't remember the drive to Reno. No one was home when I got there so I went to bed, wishing it had all been a bad dream.

When my mom came home, I told her what happened and she called Maury, a policeman friend of Grandpa's. We didn't hear back from him for a few days. During that time, Jason called the house asking for me. My mother told him never to call our house again. When we heard from Maury, he said a man from the FBI was going to come and talk with me. He said the people I met ran a pornographic ring out of Incline Village. The FBI was involved with at least one missing-girl case. This made my blood run cold as I wondered if that was the "chick" Jason's brother referred to as being "at the bottom of the lake."

A man from the FBI came to our house and questioned me for hours. I kept telling him I didn't know anything, but he seemed to think I was trying to protect someone. I assured him that wasn't the case. I didn't know whose house we drove to that night or the name of the man who came out to the car. For that matter, I didn't even know Jason's brother's or the fat man's name.

Then he asked me about being raped by Jason. I said I didn't feel I was raped, but he insisted I was. The amount of detail the agent wanted in this department was uncomfortable for me and really, what did it matter? Then I noticed his upper lip getting sweaty as he asked where Jason put his hands on me and what kind of intercourse we had.

At the end of our interview he told me I should move out of my house as soon as possible. Incredulous, I asked why this was necessary. He replied, "These are bad people, really bad people."

The following week, Jason called again and I happened to answer the phone. He was rattled when he heard my voice and said he was sorry for how things had gone and he wanted to see me again, because he was in love with me. He wanted me to go to Los Angeles with him. I told him to stop calling me and that I never wanted to see him again.

The following week, a woman my mom worked with at the travel agency in Richland came to visit with her two kids, Mark and Sandy, both close in age to me. Sleeping arrangements were made for her son to sleep in my room while I bunked with her daughter in the room next door.

Their first night staying with us, Mark woke up in the middle of the night, hearing noises. He was shocked to see a man coming in through the second-story window. Grabbing the baseball bat next to my bed, Mark yelled and swung at the man and discovered he was standing on another man's shoulders. Based on Mark's description, it was Jason, who fell to the ground before the two men took off running. I never heard from him again after that.

For decades, I convinced myself I wasn't raped because I got in Jason's car. To my mind, that choice made me a participant in what took place—not a victim. It was my fault. Perhaps this was a coping mechanism, but faulty rationales colored my perception for years.

Throughout the ordeal, my focus was to survive it. I cozied up to Jason to inspire him to want to protect me from the other two men. I feel incredibly lucky that my strategy worked.

The man from the FBI told me I was probably filmed while Jason raped me. Hearing this, I shrugged my shoulders—what could I do about that? Honestly, I felt grateful to be alive. We both knew it could have been much, much worse.

Bill was oddly subdued when I told him what had happened. He wanted to see where Jason had taken me, so about a month later, we drove to Incline Village. What a shock it was to discover the offices and showroom were empty. They had vanished. I felt sick thinking my report may have been the catalyst and hoped I would be safe from any kind of retaliation.

It took many years and a good therapist for me to understand I was victimized. Forgiving myself would take even longer. After this happened, my sense of self was shaken. I felt lost and terribly far away from the girl in the grassy meadow at Camp Field.

Where was that amazing feeling of oneness? How could I ever find my way back to that experience when I had no idea how it had happened in the first place?

Only one thing was certain—I would never, ever, get in a car with a stranger again.

14
chemical combustion

Not long after the Tahoe ordeal, Bill and I drove to Boise to fetch Linda, who was moving back to Reno. We took Bill's truck so we could load up Linda's belongings. Bill and I had an unusually nice connection on the drive, primarily because he was being loving toward me, demonstrative even, which was rare.

Linda greeted us warmly and we had a relaxing evening at her place. The next day, Bill wanted to visit some rock shops before we hit the road. We left Boise late that afternoon.

On the drive back, Linda and Bill both revealed they had drugs on them. Bill had speed to keep alert, because he would not let anyone else drive, and Linda had weed. We pulled over somewhere in Oregon, next to a sloping hillside. Linda got high and went into the darkness to pee. I could hear her clear as a bell as she walked further and further away. She was silent but then yelled out she was going to attempt Don Juan's "gait of power" from the Carlos Castaneda books.

This was a technique Don Juan taught Carlos for how to safely move over varied terrain. The technique involved cupping one's hands and a specific kind of running gait.

Linda was running back toward the car whooping it up, yelling that she was doing the gait of power, until we heard her wipe-out with many grunts and groans. Silence again. More silence. Then her voice crackled through the air as she wailed to the night sky, "Don Juan lied!" We all busted up laughing.

As we sat in the dark, I could feel sexual tension coursing between us all. Linda whispered to me that she was in love with Bill. In her altered state, her feelings for him were palpable. Linda began tenderly stroking the length of my arm. It felt nice, but I didn't respond in kind.

My cryptic journal entry from July 31, 1977, says:

> *Strange feelings coming down...so much love. Went to Boise to get Linda. Speed Columbia. What a trip we went on. loving Linda. exciting—Touching—smiling is nice.*
>
> *Considering staying in Reno, but moving out of Everett. Not too safe at Tahoe—too much going on [in] my head to leave.*
>
> *Linda & Bill. Heavy trip-strangely beautiful and simple though no head trips. No games. feel good.*

Nothing had happened, but the potential of what might have happened was laden between us. Linda's return had perfect timing for me.

A week later, heeding the FBI agent's advice, I moved out of my family home for the second time. Linda invited me to be her housemate in the one-bedroom duplex she rented in Sparks, east of Reno. Her furnishings included a sofa, rocking chair, kitchen table set and a double bed, which we would share.

My job at Pay 'n' Pak was intolerable, especially after what happened at the lake, so I quit. I also stopped working at Earthen Joy because they couldn't afford to offer me many shifts.

Through Bill, I got a job interview for a manager position

at a new frozen yogurt shop in town. The owner, Kent, was a former Omega House counselor. He was a little on the square side, but was kind and willing to hire me even though I had no managerial experience. My shifts were 7:00 a.m. to 3:00 p.m.

The Good Earth closed and then reopened as The Arbor with a similar menu. Keith was managing a second location (The Arbor South) which was close to the yogurt shop. Keith hired me to waitress the swing-shift a few days a week. Debbie was working there as well.

Surprisingly, my intense work schedule made me more efficient. In addition to my fourteen-hour workday, each morning I got up early to run along the Truckee River at Idlewild Park. Being busy suited me as it took my mind off of other things like my waning relationship with Bill who I barely saw anymore.

Linda and I were getting used to sharing a bed. Her mattress was on the floor, so I draped myself partly on the bed with one leg hanging over, to give Linda more room. There was intense chemistry between us, but I said nothing. Life had taught me to suppress my urges; they were too risky to explore, especially because I didn't want to jeopardize my living arrangement. It helped that I was exhausted when I got home. I didn't have the energy for anything but sleep.

My dream life continued to be spectacular, though I was no longer sleeping excessively as a means of escape. One particular morning, right before waking, I had a fantastic dream in which a series of vignettes told the story of my life as a medieval noblewoman. As I became lucid, I took a moment to get my bearings—I was levitating above a small European village, unseen, as I observed this alternative version of me.

It was a brisk autumn day, my favorite kind. I saw myself dressed in a sumptuous, golden velvet gown with long, flowing sleeves. To my amazement, I could feel the weight of the fabric swaying with each step as I walked along the cobblestone street, the autumn leaves swishing up from the ground as I passed.

My hair was covered with a tall steeple-shaped headpiece decorated with a veil that emerged from the top and fell past my shoulders. The veil floated through the air in a most pleasing way as I moved. These scenes didn't seem to have any particular purpose, though they were nonetheless captivating to witness.

The regality of my appearance was enhanced by haunting yet familiar music, which was steadily growing louder. I could hear the rhythmic strumming of a lute and the lilt of a recorder coming from the forest. Transfixed, I tilted my head to listen and identify what I was hearing.

It was the song "Your Move" by the British rock band, Yes. The imaginative melody and lyrics reverberated through me, evoking something ineffable and timeless:

"Take a straight and stronger course
To the corner of your life
Make the white queen run so fast
She hasn't got time to make you a wife..."

Jon Anderson's ethereal voice intensified the already magical essence of the dream. Exquisite harmonies filled the air. The music expanded my awareness until I found I had rejoined a stream of consciousness that contained all of my lifetimes. This music was surging through me like life-force energy itself. I was ecstatically and momentarily suspended in the experience until the powerful chords of a church organ crescendoed and returned me to my body.

Slowly, I began to wake up, feeling the mattress solid beneath me. It was then that I realized the song was coming from the radio in the kitchen. I was amazed that the song had penetrated my dream, becoming a part of it. During this brief experience I converged with something eternal, something I could not put into words. The depth of it has remained with me.

A few nights later, I had another lucid dream. This one was mystical and felt like it might be a glimpse into the future. In the dream I was high in the stratosphere at a kind of way station between worlds. Soft, radiant light and wispy clouds surrounded me. Someone was approaching through the mist. A wizened, thin, old man in a flowing white robe came into view. His white beard reached past his navel and his white hair cascaded down the length of his body. Kindness and love emanated from him. I was spellbound. He floated, weightless, until he stood beside me.

Without saying a word he gently picked me up and lovingly cradled me in his arms. I felt peaceful and safe. He carried me to an endless pile of the most fluffy, pillowy clouds I had ever seen. They descended for miles toward the Earth. Extending his arms, he tenderly laid me down on top of the bed of clouds and whispered:

You are going to be meeting your benefactor very soon.

I was gazing into his limitless eyes as he released me to the clouds. Slowly and gently I descended through the puffs. The sensation was tranquil and mesmeric—down, down, down I went. The deeper I went into the bed of clouds, the deeper I went into my consciousness. A sensation of dropping through millennia overtook me. I closed my eyes and surrendered to the bliss.

At last. I'd been longing to feel this again, like I did at Camp Field. Tremendous hope swelled in me. Maybe I wasn't lost after all. Without question, I believed his words were a prophecy. Something significant was coming.

As soon as I woke, I wrote in my journal:

I had a dream that was an omen. My benefactor should cross paths with me soon...Prepare.

My perspective at that time was heavily influenced by Carlos Castaneda who used the word *benefactor* to describe his Yaqui teacher, Don Juan Matus. Castaneda's books were the sole place I had ever encountered that word in that context.

My dreams were fantastic and thrilling, but they also scared me. I didn't know anyone who was having similar experiences that I could share with. I hoped the message of the benefactor dream would become evident at some point.

During this time, even though I was earning a decent living, I began to steal again. There were many things I wanted and money only went so far.

It was important to me how I appeared to other people. In my mind I had cultivated a specific persona I wanted to portray. Observing the many Californians who came into the Good Earth restaurant had influenced me greatly.

In the seventies, hippie culture was commodified to the point that department stores had racks of bohemian clothing. This was a look I adored. I wanted to wear colorful cotton prints, maxi skirts and paisley dresses from India to make a statement to the world about who I was, or more accurately, who I wanted to be.

Paradoxically, it never crossed my mind that the real statement my wardrobe would make was that I was a thief. I didn't stop to consider that no amount of lush apparel could cover the emptiness I felt inside. Instead, I opted for a hasty, temporary fix to bolster my anemic self-esteem.

A boutique called Norfolk opened in town in a charming colonial revival mansion built in 1905. Everything about the place celebrated the romance of a bygone era.

The owners were a lovely couple who painstakingly restored the wood floors, windows, trimmings and stairway banister. It was a labor of love for them. Their credo was to fill the shop with the "unique and unusual" from both local artisans and imported items from all over the world. From batik fabrics to hand-woven textiles, metal sculptures to needlepoint, soaps to incense, they were a precursor to the big-box import shops that would follow. All was done with impeccable style. They created a stimulating shopping experience, blending old world charm, stunning artistry, and a feeling of far away lands you could take home with your purchase.

One day I came across a dress from India that looked like something a monk would wear. It was a floor-length gown that opened in the front, with round wooden buttons made from coconut that went all the way to the floor. The rustic, white cotton fabric had a weighty, crisp feel to it. The collar was thick from rolled fabric and it featured dramatic, billowing three-quarter length sleeves. The dress had two large poppies hand-painted down the front, long and slender. It was austere and beautifully made. The price was higher than I thought it would be, but after all, it had been imported from India.

I wanted this dress.

An itchy urge crept up inside of me, saying, *Steal it. Just take it and it's yours.*

The urge was so strong, I left the store, but my desire continued to gnaw at me. The next day, my first thought was of the dress. Arguing in my head, I told myself the dress mattered—it would help me show people who I was. That was all it took for me to return to Norfolk to steal it.

My behavior was the same as always, chatting with the owners, being friendly. I had found a way to separate how much

On Everett Drive with the unfinished walls dad would never get to. Seventeen years old.

I liked them from the fact that I was ripping them off. My body, however, registered my crime as a hollow sinking feeling in the pit of my stomach as I left the store. It was an ugly feeling—the bottom dropping out of my morals. My body made sure to register what my mind fought to ignore.

Usually, the bad feeling would fade eventually and then I could enjoy the spoils. My appearance wearing the dress, Earth sandals and a headscarf was plain and minimalistic. I felt monastic and holy wearing it.

But a journal entry during that time reflects the internal battle I was fighting:

I've always said I have no guilty conscious [conscience] about stealing—but now I know I do. Most times when I am feeling really good, I feel I deserve it and most times when I'm around my friends I feel they are better people than I. Stealing puts me in debt.

How can I honestly enjoy myself and feel happy and good when I cause others heartache. How can I feel respect for myself when I don't respect others? Stealing puts me in an awful circle. I never have stolen out of necessity—whenever I steal it's for something that will make me look good.

A prime example is the Indian Show. I surround myself with beautiful clothes, jewelry, friends because they should be a reflection of what is inside but I'd feel so cheap and so ugly.

Dying fast. And I wonder why my self-image is so awful.

This was a rare moment of honesty. For the most part, I didn't allow myself to have those thoughts. Instead, I functioned compulsively, looking for a temporary fix to feel better, like any junkie would. I continued to steal, especially clothing. Everyone around me knew how much I was working, so no one questioned how I got my amazing wardrobe.

There was a boutique in the yogurt shop complex where I worked. It was an expensive store, and harrowing to steal from because it was small and the owner was watchful. It posed a challenge and I wanted to prove I could do it.

There was a chemical rush I got from stealing that became addictive because it made me feel more alive. In time, I wanted the adrenaline rush as much as I wanted the clothing. I managed to steal a London Fog raincoat and a luxurious pink and blue woven knee-length cardigan. The things I stole were my favorite clothing because of the effort and skill it took to acquire them.

At the yogurt shop, some old friends from Omega House were coming in to give their support to Kent's enterprise. Jon and Denise came by one day, and Bill stopped by in the first few weeks as well. It was noticeable that Bill and Kent had a strained, borderline unfriendly relationship. I didn't know their history, but Kent was naturally fatherly toward me. He strongly disapproved of the age difference between Bill and I.

"Suzy, why aren't you dating a guy your own age?" Kent inquired after Bill left.

"I don't know, I guess because guys my age have never seemed interested in me," I said with a shrug.

"How did you and Bill get together anyway?" he probed.

It was near closing time, so I thought it would be okay to tell him. We were emptying the yogurt machines and wiping the equipment down, so I didn't have to look at him as I shared. When I finished the story of Bill's attempt to take me to an X-rated movie and the drive up Peavine mountain, Kent's normally pale complexion was flushed red with anger.

"This guy's a jerk, Suzy! He took such advantage of you. By all rights, he should be in jail."

"Shit, I'm sorry, Kent. I shouldn't have told you. It's not like that," I stammered defensively.

"No, Suzy, it's *exactly* like that," Kent declared, "and I don't want to see that guy in here again."

Even though I defended Bill, I secretly loved what Kent said to me. He was the only man I knew who ever said anything that addressed the inappropriate nature of my relationship with Bill. Regardless of my involvement or feelings for Bill, Kent's outrage meant the world to me.

Adding to that was my ongoing dissatisfaction with Bill. After going out for nearly a year, he'd never once said "I love you" or given any indication how he felt about me. There was no romance between us. It was a cold union.

Another journal entry references this and Omega House:

Is it so terrible to say
I love you
Why must you feel a threat
can't you accept a loving cord
and let it flow
let it feel good
instead of being uptight
you can give so much to O. H.
but where do I come in...

One day, Kent's college friend, Brent, came in with his younger brother, Michael. Brent had been a junior counselor at Omega House before counseling at another drug program called Gemini Ranch. Kent and Brent began to chat, leaving me with Michael, so I asked him if he'd like some frozen yogurt. He smiled and looked at the floor, saying, "Sure, Suzy, I've never had the stuff, but I'll give it a go." His shyness was sincere and sweet. He was sexy in a subtle way and I loved hearing the sound of him saying my name.

Without wasting any time, Michael said, "I heard from Brent that you're going out with Bill Dansie."

"Oh, yeah, I am," I replied, a bit taken aback. "Why? Do you know Bill?"

"Yeah, I know him from Omega House," he said, his tone changing. "He's a real piece of shit, I mean, sorry to say that about your boyfriend, but I hate that guy."

"Yikes." Was all I managed to say, looking at the floor. I was cringing inside.

Michael left it there. I served him a bowl of chocolate-vanilla swirl. Brent got a cone and they sat at one of our bistro tables to eat. This allowed me to look at Michael, while acting like I was doing other things. Kent walked by and leaned close to me to whisper, "What do you think of Michael? At least he's closer to your age." He chuckled in a satisfied way as he went in the back, clearly enjoying his matchmaking attempt.

I was intrigued. Michael was the same age as my older sister, which instantly made him more relatable. Conversations with Bill about his acid trips and aliens had become tedious.

Michael had lived at the Gemini Ranch drug treatment program due to his struggles with alcohol. Kent relayed that Michael got married at sixteen, but was already divorced (he wasn't divorced but I wouldn't know that for some time). He and his wife, Mary, had a two-year-old son. Michael saw him on the weekends. It was a lot to take in and I wasn't sure if it mattered to me or not.

Bill and I were circling the drain, not only because I cheated, but because Bill had no ambition for his life. He was content living with his parents, having sex with me in his twin bed or in his truck, and venturing to rock piles around Nevada to look for gems. My biggest issue was his lack of emotionality. He could not express any love for me, and was crude when he wanted to have sex. My last journal entry about Bill records my dilemma:

Bill
William
I'm so afraid
I'm deeply in love with you
dear Bill
so far—so distant

please love me
please!
alone:lonely
have you ever heard of
making love
I'm sick of "fuck"
I just want you
I feel so bad
bummer.

Kent said Brent was married to Bill's younger sister, Phyllis. They lived south of Reno, on the edge of town. I wanted to figure out a reason to visit them, hoping that I might see Michael again.

Unbeknownst to me, Kent had the same line of thinking. A week later, he asked me to bring an order of frozen yogurt to Brent's house. This was a first, as we didn't offer any kind of delivery service. On the drive over, I hoped Michael would be there, and I hoped he wanted a reason to see me again as well.

Tingling with anticipation, I walked up the stairs to ring the bell. I could hear great music playing, symphonic rock music I'd never heard before. Taking a breath, I knocked on the front door.

A tremendous thrill erupted inside of me when I saw Michael to my right as I came in the door. I couldn't help but smile, realizing Kent had set the whole thing up.

God in heaven, Michael made me swoon. I loved that, despite being quiet and reserved, he oozed magnetism. He smiled and his eyes widened when he saw me, which felt incredible. This was something new. I hadn't had this kind of chemical response to a person before—the blizzard of sensations swirling in my body caused goosebumps to ripple over my skin. He had an impish quality, a playfulness conveyed between his shyness, haphazardly cut hair, and chocolate brown eyes. Something about him was simply irresistible.

I met Bill's sister, Phyllis, once before, in passing, so we said our hellos. When Brent greeted me, I asked him what music he was playing. He said we were listening to the album *Scheherazade* by Renaissance. I bought the album the next day.

I sat on the living room carpet across from Michael as we all chatted. Brent and Phyllis told me they were moving to Oregon and Michael was taking over the rent at the house we were in. I was nodding but not really hearing much of what was being said. The pull I felt toward Michael overtook my senses. At one point, I asked where the bathroom was to get a moment to myself.

When I exited the bathroom, I walked into the kitchen to get a glass of water. As I entered, Michael was coming in from the living room. We looked at one another, smiled, and walked straight into one another's arms and kissed. It was a kiss that instantly shifted my perspective, and in that moment I realized how much I lacked chemistry with Bill.

We kissed for a long while and then hugged one another close, as if to say, *this is us now.* No words needed. The familiarity of our embrace was both soothing and peculiar.

Rejoining the others, we talked late into the evening. Phyllis served a tasty dinner. When Brent and Phyllis said they were going to bed, I said my goodbyes, expecting to leave. It was getting late.

As I picked up my purse, Michael walked over to me, took my purse and set it back down on the table. Then he kissed me again. Being alone, he was more passionate than before and his sounds of pleasure lit me up. We ended up making love on the living room floor. Michael was a far superior lover to Bill. Who knew I had been languishing in mediocrity? Having a new experience of what sex could be was thrilling.

There was one hitch: I didn't know Michael smoked cigarettes. The taste was there, unmistakable and putrid. The bumper sticker "Kissing a Smoker is like Licking an Ashtray" came to mind. I tried to convince myself to get past it, since my knee-jerk response to cigarettes was overwhelmingly negative. I didn't want anything to get in the way of us happening.

The next day, I felt shy when Phyllis and Brent got up and I was still there. Phyllis didn't pull any punches when she greeted me enthusiastically, "Well, my dear, you certainly got ravaged last night!"

Her directness was embarrassing and awkward, since I was with her brother. "I'm going to tell Bill today, don't worry," I said, serving up my guilt front and center.

"Hey," Phyllis replied, "none of my business."

As soon as I got home, I called Bill to tell him I was coming by. His mother let me in before disappearing down the hallway. Bill was at the kitchen table, reading the newspaper. I delivered the news, "I can't be with you anymore, I'm sorry..."

"Why? Did you meet someone?" he asked.

"I did, yes. I'm so sorry, Bill, it just happened."

"Who is it?" he demanded.

"Michael Schon."

"Michael Schon? You've got to be kidding me! Everything that guy touches turns to shit!" he yelled.

"I'm sorry. Goodbye, Bill," I flatly responded and left.

Driving away, a sadness came over me, mainly because Bill had given so little to our relationship. It wasn't until I broke up with him that I could see how lackluster our time together was. Bill had always had the upperhand and I accepted whatever he offered. It didn't occur to me I could have something more. My thoughts turned to Michael, which improved my mood. I smiled, imagining what was to come.

Within a few weeks of meeting Michael, I stopped taking the pill. I'd been on it for a year and was having chronic headaches. My gynecologist said it might be an indication that my body was forming blot clots from the pill, which could lead to a stroke.

I had recently subscribed to both Ms. magazine and *Psychology Today* and eagerly read them cover to cover when they arrived in the mail. An ad in *Ms.* highlighted a new birth control method called Encare Oval. It was a vaginal suppository loaded with spermicidal. The ad persuaded me to give it a try.

Michael invited me to move in with him at Brent and Phyllis's former house, so I gave Linda notice and took the leap, placing all my proverbial eggs in his basket.

I quickly discovered that Michael was a heavy smoker of both cigarettes and weed. He also liked to drink, which I learned as he was telling me of his father's struggles with alcoholism. The red flags of his objectionable habits were flapping in the breeze, but I steadfastly suppressed my concerns because of how handsome he was, because I liked having sex with him, and because he was offering me a place to live.

Fortunately for us, Brent and Phyllis left behind a good deal of furniture and household items. After a year of sex in the back of a truck, sharing a home with Mike felt grown-up and exciting. Buying my first vacuum cleaner was a rite of passage and I relished eating celery with peanut butter while sitting on the kitchen counter at midnight that first night in the house.

Michael worked for his father who had a janitorial business. They cleaned commercial buildings late into the night. Our schedules prevented us from seeing one another much, so I quit both of my jobs and found work at The Golden Temple

Restaurant, Didar Singh and Kaur's latest enterprise that opened earlier that year. The shifts there were more flexible which gave us more time to be together.

Michael's family job afforded him certain dubious liberties: He could smoke and drink on the job. As he cleaned the Truckee River Bar and Grill each night, he poured himself a few drinks. I noticed the smell of liquor on him when he came home each night.

Hard liquor always reminded me of the cocktail parties on Everett Drive when I was a kid: I had an instant revulsion to the smell. Michael's drinking worried me, but I knew he wouldn't respond well if I brought it up. I'd learned from my brother Mike not to bring up addiction to an addict.

A few months into our relationship, Michael's moodiness was becoming more apparent. I began to feel apprehensive when he came through the door, trying to anticipate what headspace he was in. We barely had a honeymoon phase before things became much more intense.

One night, Michael came home stinking drunk. I woke up when he climbed on top of me to have sex. Because he consumed so much alcohol, he struggled to orgasm but would stay the course until he was satisfied, sweating profusely all the while. I was half-asleep and didn't get up to use the Encare Oval suppository that night. Six weeks later my gynecologist confirmed my suspicion that I was pregnant.

A teenage pregnancy at eighteen, just like my mother and father. I was repeating history. *How could I have been so careless and stupid?*

I went to see my father to have the difficult conversation that I was pregnant, hoping he would financially help me with abortion costs. Being devoid of empathy, he chastised me instead, saying though he was not at all surprised to find out this news, he was, nonetheless, extremely disappointed in me.

His judgmental attitude enraged me. One of the more horrific skeletons my mother had released from her marital closet was how my father convinced her to allow him to induce an abortion when they got pregnant a year after my brother, Peter, was born. Another pregnancy was unwelcome news to my father, who was already struggling to provide for five children.

A woman he was having an affair with at work advised him to buy surgical tubing and insert it into my mother. She told him it would cause her uterus to cramp and she would miscarry. When he came home from work he explained his plan to my distraught mother. He hammered at her, insisting they simply could not afford another child, until she reluctantly agreed.

That evening he inserted the tubing, telling her she would cramp and lose the baby. In the morning, he went back to work, leaving her alone to miscarry by herself while caring for five children. When he returned he found her on the floor, ash-white from substantial blood loss. She came close to dying at the hospital that day.

Thinking of what he put my mother through, my rage boiled over. I screamed at him, "You've got some fucking nerve, dad, judging me when you performed an abortion on your own wife!"

It was as if I punched him in the face. My words rendered him speechless. He had no idea I knew this detail of his indefensible past and there was nothing he could say. My father refused to help me and Michael managed to come up with the money.

The abortion was physically and emotionally painful. I threw up afterward. I felt like a failure for getting pregnant when I had birth control on the nightstand.

We never discussed keeping the baby. Michael made it clear

he was already overwhelmed trying to be a father to his infant son and I knew I didn't want to be a mother at eighteen. I was raised to believe that abortion was wrong, and though I no longer believed in the Catholic Church, lingering vestiges of guilt and shame stayed with me for a long time.

Michael's family owned two memberships at the Canvasback Gun Club outside of Fallon, Nevada, about eighty-five miles from Reno. It was a hunting membership that originated with Michael's paternal grandpa, who built a modest home there. Michael loved getting out of the city and had spent years going to Canvasback on the weekends.

Located on the Stillwater marshland, Canvasback hosts many species of waterfowl. Canals were built between the natural ponds so hunters and fishermen could navigate the waterways. It was a peaceful place off-season. In the summer, I loved going out in the boat among the tall cattails and grasses in the marsh.

However, once the weather turned cold, our routines at the club quickly became unhealthy. I'd been running twenty-five miles a week all summer and fall, but as the temperatures dropped, I didn't keep it up. Michael watched football and pounded beers, becoming more remote as he drank. Feeling alone and bored, I moved into my default behavior of binge eating, planning big meals and heavy desserts as my form of entertainment. Winter trips to Canvasback were not good for us.

For the most part, Michael was not around at night. He went drinking after work, coming home after I had already gone to bed. I loved Michael, but was coming to the sad conclusion that he wasn't good for me.

One night I was violently awakened by the unmistakable sound of gunshot. I sat up screaming in fear and saw Michael sitting on the edge of our waterbed frame with a pistol in his hand, shaking uncontrollably.

"What the hell!" I screamed. "What are you doing?"

He tried to respond, but his words were slurred and incomprehensible. His head hung low in such a pathetic way, I moved toward him with more care in my voice.

"Hey, are you okay?"

I put my arm around him.

"What happened, babe? Did your gun go off by accident?"

Michael slumped into me, groaning. His hair was wet from sweat, and his skin was ice cold. A chill ran down my spine as the realization hit me. I didn't dare say what I was thinking—that Michael was contemplating ending his life.

My journal entry that morning reveals that I couldn't face the truth of what I had realized; instead, I framed it as an accident:

March 07, 1978 Tuesday

My dear Michael!

How can I help him in this life? If I had the money I would get him out of debt, buy him a car and care for him until he felt strong... But would that matter? Spiritually, I know he is lacking something. He needs nourishment for his spirit so things in Reno don't become so important and overbearing. I don't even know if I can give him what he needs. Loving him and feeling this frustration is difficult to deal with...tonight I will meditate on it.

This morning at 4 am Michael was fooling around with his gun and it went off, shooting a hole in the dresser. I had a premonition it would happen...

I'm scared for myself, but even more so scared

for Michael—He has been robbed of his right to be happy and loving. I don't know how, but that seems to be lost within him. What do I do, give him strength and hope he wants his life to be beautiful, enough to battle this despair...

And this entry from later the same day:

Shall I throw you a lifeline and hope you grab hold?

To need to lean on me is what a friend is for; but the desire to fight off opposition and live to your fullest must originate in your soul.

I love you.

And addressing myself:

You had better come to terms with the thoughts in your head before you can't salvage anything good of your feelings for each other.

Letting go isn't always bad.

I want to talk to Denise.

From that point forward, Michael's volatility weighed heavily upon me. My focus shifted as I tried to help him change, hoping he could find his way to a joyful life. I would discover Michael didn't want to change and he resented my attempts to fix him. My efforts were, of course, futile.

Michael and I on a rafting trip heading out of Tahoe City, California in 1978. We would have a huge fight down river that ruined the day.

15
ch-ch-ch-ch-changes

Michael told me we needed to find a housemate to help with expenses. As luck would have it, Debbie was looking for a place to live. She came by to check out our place, loved it, and moved in immediately. Shortly after moving in, Debbie quit the restaurant and was hired as a highway construction worker. Her shifts began at 6:00 o'clock. I'd sometimes crawl out of bed when I'd hear her in the bathroom to say good morning. I'd watch her braid her thick hair and clip the braids on top of her head to fit under her wool knit hat. I loved having her at the house. She eased the loneliness of being in a relationship with someone who seemed to love alcohol more than me.

Eventually, Debbie and I got in the habit of having our tea together each morning in the kitchen. We grew closer, learning about one another's pasts and sharing our dreams for the future.

Michael procured a new account at a nightclub called Lips. Lips opened soon after *Saturday Night Fever* catapulted disco music into the stratosphere. When I lamented not being old enough to go to the club, Debbie told me she had a fake ID and could get me one as well.

Within a week, she came through and we started going to Lips on Friday and Saturday nights. It was mystifying to get in with an ID that looked nothing like me. Michael was working, so Debbie and I assured him we would dance with one another, giving him no cause for worry. We went most weekends that summer, always inviting Michael to come by after work, but he always said no. I ordered cranberry juice or water. We danced for hours, singing the words to every song and moaning along with Donna Summer on "Love to Love You Baby."

My mom let me borrow her purple-striped halter dress and I bought a pair of platform sandals that made me three inches taller. I felt sexy and powerful walking into the disco. Although we called Debbie my "safe bet" to assure Michael that I wouldn't dance with any men, the more we danced together, the more my attraction to her grew.

After weeks of trying, I finally convinced Michael to join us, telling him how much I wanted to dance with him.

"I don't really dance," he grumbled, but agreed to go anyway.

It didn't occur to me that he would feel uncomfortable about his position as the custodian at Lips or that he might be worried to see the club owner. But something was up, because his tension level rose as we walked up the ramp to where the bouncers were.

Wrapping my arm around him, I gave him a squeeze. No response. We got cleared to go in and Michael made a beeline for the bar. Debbie and I hit the dance floor. I was excited for Michael to see me dance and hoped he would like my moves. I saw him watching us from the bar and went to him, playfully pulling him to join me on the dance floor.

"No, babe, I'm not a dancer, I told you," he said, clearly irritated with me. Feeling frustrated, I kept tugging on his arm.

"Come on, Michael, please!" I begged. "I really want to dance with you."

My persistence wore him down enough that he relented. We

made our way to the dance floor. Still holding his beer, he began to dance. To my great delight, he moved really well, though he was painfully self-conscious. He mostly looked at the floor until a guy approached us, wanting to cut in.

"Hey pretty lady," he began, "finally I see you dancing with a man. I'd sure like a turn."

"I'm with my boyfriend, sorry," I said, but he was undeterred and asked again. Michael escalated right away, aggressively coming at the guy.

"Back off, mother fucker," he threatened, "like she said, she's with me."

Michael's intensity was so disproportionate to the circumstance that the guy took off.

"I'm outta here," he stated flatly.

"Michael, please, no! Please don't go. This is so fun." I pleaded.

"Not for me, Suzy, it's not fun at all. Debbie can bring you home," he said, shaking his head. He turned and left without another word.

Earlier that evening, Debbie asked me if I had ever tried speed. I said no and she said she had some, suggesting we take it before heading out. She said it would give us great energy for dancing. We popped it in our mouths on the way to the club.

I hadn't told Michael I took speed, but there was no way I wanted to leave the club so early. Debbie saw Michael split and rushed to my side, seeing how upset I was.

"He got pissed and took off," I told her, then asked, "Why can't he be like a normal boyfriend?"

Debbie hugged me and whispered in my ear, "Come on lady, let's dance. That's what we came here for, right?"

Debbie took my hand and away we went, dancing until the bar closed and we were soaked with sweat. The pounding beat and shimmering lights of the disco ball were exhilarating. Dancing had become my favorite way to express myself and let off steam.

We drove home shivering in our wet clothes. When we pulled up, Michael's car wasn't there. This bothered me, but it was too late to call anyone, so Debbie and I went in and made tea. Our hair smelled like cigarette smoke, so we each got in the shower to get the smell off of us before curling up on the sofa together.

"Why do you stay with him, Suzy?" Debbie asked.

"I keep thinking I can help him. He seems so lost," I ventured.

"Your boyfriend shouldn't be a project," she stated.

I knew she was right, but I loved him. He had such a sweet side and I thought if I kept loving him, he'd get better.

Debbie scooched closer to me, leaned in, and kissed me. This was not surprising, as we had been building sexual tension for weeks on the dance floor. She tasted good. I took her hand and led her to the bedroom I shared with Michael.

Debbie had never been with a woman before but her novice status didn't show. We fell asleep wrapped in each other's arms on the warm waterbed. I crashed hard and slept soundly until many hours later when the roar of Michael's voice jerked me out of my slumber.

"You have *got* to be fucking kidding me!"

He was home. Debbie hadn't moved from our naked, entwined embrace.

"Oh shit! Deb, wake up!" I said, giving her a hard shove.

He stormed out of our room and began breaking and throwing things in the living room—his rage unleashed. Debbie and I huddled in the bed, shaking with fear. When he was through thrashing our home I heard him yell, "Fuck this, and fuck you, Suzy. I'm outta here." He peeled out of the driveway and down the road to who knows where.

Debbie and I waited a few minutes to make sure he wasn't going to come back before emerging from the bedroom to witness the aftermath of his rage.

"He kicked in my Panasonic speakers!" Debbie screamed. "That mother-fucking asshole."

He'd destroyed so much of our beautiful little home. He smashed our teacups, broke record albums in half, ripped the tonearm off of the turntable, ruined Debbie's speakers and punched a hole in the wall.

Memories of my father's temper flooded me. I don't think we ever lived in a home that didn't have at least one punched hole in the drywall. A familiar feeling of impotence came over me, that feeling that there was no way to anticipate or stop this kind of rage once it was uncorked.

Of course, I admonished myself for having sex with Debbie. What a sight for him to come home to. Debbie was quick to point out that he had been out all night and probably cheated on me, but we all know two wrongs don't make a right.

The truth was, I made a choice that blew everything up, maybe that was the only way I could figure out how to end it. Debbie called her boyfriend, Dave, and moved out that day.

"You're insane to stay here, Suzy," she warned. "He'll end up hurting you."

I hoped her words would never come true. It was upsetting to me that Michael and I had soured so quickly. In our first months together I had high hopes and could not have foreseen the demons he was fighting privately. Debbie had become one of my closest friends and now she was gone and our house was in a state of ruin.

Michael didn't come home all weekend. I did my best to clean up the mess, in the exact same way my mother always cleaned up the wake of my father's destruction. It was sickening to realize the parallels to my parents' relationship.

On Sunday night I heard Michael's car pull up and froze, not knowing what to expect. As he came through the door, I could see how downhearted he was. He looked spent. I didn't speak to him or approach him-I was too afraid. He saw that I had cleaned up, walked silently past me into our bedroom and went to bed.

When I went to bed, Michael had been asleep for hours. As I quietly crept under the covers, he was immediately on top of me, kissing me, fucking me, squeezing my flesh hard as if he wanted to pull my body inside of his. I mistook his desire for forgiveness and thought maybe things would be okay.

We never talked about what happened. When I woke up the next morning, Michael was gone. He left a note on the kitchen counter saying our rent was paid through the end of the month, which gave me a couple of weeks to move out. He wrote nothing more and didn't sign his name. Who could blame him? He was justified to leave. I had destroyed his trust.

I went back to bed and cried myself to sleep. Sadness and relief competed for my attention. The high hopes I had for us came to nothing. We were a bad match, a flaming torch that burned out quickly. I didn't mourn our break-up for long because not being around Michael, I was more relaxed and light-hearted. The emotional weight of him was felt most in his absence.

Luckily, I was able to move back into Everett Drive and had my own room, which I painted bright yellow.

When summer finally came, Debbie turned me on to Chimney Beach at Lake Tahoe, which was harder to get to and less frequented than other beaches at the lake. Most people at

Chimney dispensed with swimsuits and the vibe was chill. I found it invigorating to sunbathe in the nude. Everyone I met at the beach was friendly and likeable. We went whenever we could, making the trip several times a week.

My friends from The Golden Temple also knew about Chimney Beach, so we started going together as well. Our shifts didn't start until the afternoon, so we'd head up to the lake in the morning and hike in, carrying an assortment of mangoes, watermelon, bongo drums, some finger pianos, and a guitar. During the course of the day, we had musical jams and took turns until everyone had received a group massage. It was exactly what I needed to unwind and feel like myself again.

Even though we were at a beach on the Nevada side of the lake, we met a fair number of Californians, and just like at The Good Earth, I found myself attracted to the open-minded attitudes they expressed. They were more laid back and curious about life, as far as I could tell.

One such Californian, Bob, a man in his early twenties, approached us on the beach one day and asked if either of us would like a free massage. He had completed massage training and wanted to practice his techniques.

"Right here? On the beach? I asked.

"Yep," he replied.

Knowing Debbie would be right there with me, I said yes.

He asked me to lie on my stomach as he wanted to start with my back. Using a fragrant lavender oil, I heard him rubbing his hands together before he firmly glided up my spine. I knew instantly he was going to be amazing.

As the sand from my towel got mixed up with the oil, he encouraged me to think of it as an exfoliant, like a loofa sponge that would soften my skin. He massaged me for well over an hour. More than once Debbie exclaimed, "Why didn't I say yes?" as she heard me moaning in bliss.

When he finished, I wanted to give him a tip but he declined, saying he wanted his offering to be "purely a gift." As he walked away I realized we'd probably never see one another again. This made it all the more special.

We were two human beings interacting for the briefest of moments. I felt young and free and euphoric. I wanted to make sure to enjoy this moment in time.

Debbie was making good money in construction so she rented a two-bedroom A-frame house at the lake, south of Tahoe City. She and I had an easy friendship that sometimes became sexual. Neither one of us felt like restricting the other.

On a whim, we decided to take a weekend trip to San Francisco and we both fell in love with the city. We discovered an amazing vegetarian restaurant called Shandygaff on Polk Street and began to head to the bay area frequently so we could dine there. They had non-alcoholic fruit wines that were delicious and made us feel like adults. My bohemian wardrobe grew as I stole from the many boutiques in Haight-Ashbury. Taking cash from the till at work covered our motel room on Saturday nights.

What we loved the most about San Francisco was the freedom to hold hands and kiss in public. It was an incredible feeling after so many years of hiding in shame. This was the first time I felt like I could be wholly myself without fear of persecution or reprimand.

Looking back, it's a miracle we survived those trips. We drove in the dead of winter one night, heading to Shandygaffs for dinner, like it was down the street. After our meal, we got back on the road at 10 pm, as a blizzard was starting over Donner Summit.

As if that wasn't perilous enough, we were drinking Boone's

Farm Strawberry Hill wine that we had panhandled in the city.

As we crested the summit, I was falling asleep at the wheel, so Debbie pounded on my thighs to keep me awake. Then the wipers on her Volkswagon bug froze and I had my head out the window trying to see the road. Somehow we made it home, guided by angels or pure luck.

Debbie invited me to stay at her cabin one weekend, saying she wanted us to have a ménage à trois with her Italian-American boyfriend, Dave. We all had a good time, save for the moment when Dave cried out in his Brooklyn accent, "Hey, what about me?" when Deb and I were more into one another than him.

The next morning, Deb was up early for work and woke me with a less than friendly shake.

"Wake up! You have to get up now too, Suzy," she said. "I'm not leaving you two alone here."

"What's the problem?" I asked, as if I didn't know.

"Obviously, I don't want you two fucking without me," she said testily.

"Deb, honey, I'm exhausted and want to sleep. Go to work."

Dave and I had sex as soon as she left. She never asked, so I never told.

We also discovered there was a gay bar in Sparks, called The Forum. Debbie and I made up a disco routine to an Earth, Wind and Fire song, and like in the movie, *Saturday Night Fever*, people would clear the floor to watch us perform.

Many old friends were there as well. I saw Terry and her new girlfriend, and other girls I had played softball with years ago. One evening as I was chatting with them, I was heavily criticised for saying I was bisexual. The lesbians said it was nothing but a cop-out and a sign of being unable to commit in one direction. The vibe turned ugly. They said I came to the bar to be a tease. I couldn't believe I was being attacked by the community where I had finally felt safe. It was devastating. I stopped going to The Forum after that.

It had been a summer of fresh experiences, rousing freedoms and blurred boundaries. I discovered that I liked living on the fringe of convention and I liked defying the rules of my Catholic upbringing. It made me feel wild and free, though there were times when that unfettered feeling teetered way too close to being out of control—a sensation I did not enjoy in the least.

At some point, I went to live with my father, though I can't recall why. It was an awkward situation. I wasn't around much, and was repulsed by Mrs. Carlson, watching her fawn over my father. He assigned me chores, making sure I was contributing to the household, with a formality that was more suited to a boarding house than what one might expect from their own dad.

One weekend, while he and his wife were out of town, Debbie came over to spend the night. We were having sex in the master bedroom when something new happened. I had an orgasm that made me sit up straight and scream, "What the hell was that?"

Debbie laughed and said, "You just came, silly."

I was thunderstruck. This had never happened with Becky or Terry or Bill or Michael. Up until that moment, I thought I was experiencing everything that sex was and I know you're probably thinking—what about all the pole climbing?—but I never put together climbing the pole and sex. Never. It seems like a blatant oversight in retrospect, but since that feeling had never occurred with my partners, I thought it was something special and separate.

This realization hurt. It hurt because I didn't know I should have wanted more from sex. Moreover, the fact that it happened with a woman caused me tremendous shame. My face burned hot with it.

Years later, a therapist would say I had internalized the shame and judgments of my parents, but in that moment, I felt repulsed.

"Of course it would be with a woman," I muttered softly, mostly to myself, before bursting into tears.

Debbie was understandably confused. Why wasn't I happy? As I wept, an avalanche of thoughts and feelings were descending upon me. I was completely overwhelmed. Even more, I didn't know if I would want to have that experience again with Debbie.

Something else was gnawing at me.

I was eighteen and the reality of adulthood was looming. As the clock ticked, I was all too aware that I didn't feel prepared to be a grown-up. This was something I admitted in the dead of night when, alone in my bed, I told myself the truth. I had a hard time picturing what my life would be like as an adult, which made me deeply insecure about the future. I wrote in my journal:

Why have I felt so sad—
Even now I want to cry.

Every time I get close to really loving myself

I kill all my efforts
God! I want so much to be stable.

In the midst of this anxiety, I missed Michael terribly. I decided to go to Lips that night to see if he would be there. When I walked in, I couldn't believe it. He was there. We both rushed to one another and embraced. Seeing one another again stirred up so much emotion for both of us that we left the club and drove to The River Inn, a hot spring and motel just west of Reno. We had a passionate evening together and decided to get back together.

When I told Debbie the news, she expressed her disgust and disapproval and we stopped seeing one another.

It didn't take long before things deteriorated with my father and after having a yelling match one day, I split. Michael was living with his mother at her apartment across the street from Idlewild Park. She invited me to stay there, but made a point to say it had to be "short-term" as it was a small one-bedroom place and we'd be sleeping in her living room.

The weather turned cold and we stopped going to Canvasback. One weekend, we went to the movies and saw *Comes a Horseman* with Jane Fonda, Jason Robards and James Caan. Filmed in the Coconino National Forest in Arizona, it was a visually stunning film about a female rancher (Fonda) trying to make it against all odds.

The movie cast a spell on Michael. It epitomized what he dreamed of: the open-sky life of a rugged rancher. For weeks after seeing the film it was all he talked about. He wanted to live far from the city and thought that doing so would solve a lot of his problems. That movie lit a fire in him and I could see his resolve to make it happen.

For weeks, he scanned the classified ads until he found an opening for a caretaker position at a ranch in Dixie Valley, Nevada. Michael had a phone interview with the ranch owner, Pete Uccelli. It went well enough that they arranged to meet the following weekend in Redwood City, California for lunch. We left early in the morning to make the drive.

I was good at reading maps and navigated us through the California traffic, which was enough to put Michael into culture shock. The congested six-lane freeways were intimidating. We pulled up at the restaurant in Pete's Harbor (named after Mr.

Uccelli) exactly at the appointed time and had no sooner told the hostess who we were when a voice boomed in our direction.

"There you are!" he exclaimed, coming toward us with his hand extended.

"Glad you made it. How was the drive?"

This was where Michael really excelled. He had charm in abundance when he wanted to and he really wanted this job.

"The drive was easy, Mr. Uccelli. Thanks for having us here." Michael smiled his best smile and my heart melted for him. I so hoped he'd get the job.

"Call me Pete, please," Mr. Uccelli requested, though we never called him Pete. He seemed like a man from another era and was always "Mr. Uccelli" to us.

Pete Uccelli looked every bit like a rancher. He was short with a stocky body and a sun-baked, leathery face. His tanned skin was set off by an ample head of bright white hair.

I sat back while he told Michael about the job duties and responsibilities. He owned a beefalo ranch on his land in Dixie Valley and had thirty-six head of the cattle-buffalo hybrid that needed tending.

While Mr. Uccelli detailed the job duties that went with the position, Michael nodded attentively and assured him he was up to the task. It became more than a little uncomfortable for me as the interview progressed because Michael was fabricating experience he simply did not have. He had never operated farm equipment, or run a generator or dug postholes, yet claimed he had. I made a mental note that I could teach him about posthole digging from my time at Omega House. It was clear to me he wanted this opportunity so fervently, he'd planned to get it by any means.

Moreover, as Mr. Uccelli described the ranch, I began to recoil. The reality of Michael's dream now had real-world possibilities and I had to decide if that dream was something I wanted to be a part of.

After the interview Michael was more animated than I'd ever seen him. He was fired up at the idea of having a new life and talked hopefully about how good it would be. Pursuing this dream had great meaning to him and I was concerned how he would take it if he didn't get the job.

There was no need for concern as we soon discovered. Within days we heard from Mr. Uccelli; Michael was hired. The rapidity with which he'd made this happen was amazing and disconcerting. I'd never witnessed this side of him. Although our assumption all along was that we were in this together, I was struggling to catch up with the suddenness of it all. This would be an enormous change in direction.

I was thinking about all my good friends in Reno and the routine of my life, which suited me well. I loved the great conversations and camaraderie I felt at the Golden Temple. Without a doubt, I was thriving in that environment. As a vegetarian, the restaurant provided delicious food, which supported my new way of eating.

Something else was tugging at me. I'd had a secret crush on a gorgeous man who often came for lunch. His name was Brian. He was handsome to the point that I found it hard to look him in the eyes. I was attracted to him and enjoyed that he subtly flirted with me. He even seemed normal-in the best possible way-but I never made my feelings known to him because I was too intimidated. I didn't feel good enough about myself to think that I could deserve a man like that.

Brian had sent me a letter at the restaurant the year before. He remembered my birthday while working in Gerlach. He made a beautiful card for me that said:

"Happy Birthday Suzi, from a beautiful sky."

He drew a lovely image of the sun setting in the mountains with colored pencils and wrote his message to me in big block letters against the sky. I was moved Brian remembered my birthday and wished I could feel deserving of him, but he was out of my league. I didn't even mind that he spelled *Suzy* wrong.

Brian's letter is still in my keepsakes to this day. It is a fond remembrance of a sweet flirtation as well as a somewhat bittersweet memento of a road not taken.

At the Stillwater Gun Club in Fallon the year before we moved to Dixie Valley.

16

whistling dixie

For days, I was in a funk about what to do. I loved Michael and it was thrilling the way he had pulled this off. I talked to Didar Singh about it. He had known me for a couple of years and I looked up to him. After hearing my concerns he cautioned me, saying I always seemed pulled in multiple directions. He added, "Suzanne, right now you have your feet on several paths but the real joy comes when you pick one path and commit to it."

His view of me was hard to hear, especially given the fact that my father's go-to unflattering adjectives for me were *flighty* and *capricious.*

"If I go, can you recommend some books for me to take that will keep me on a good path?" I asked.

"Only this one," he said, handing me a book called Peace Lagoon by Sardarni Premka Kaur (aka Pamela Saharah Dyson). It was a book of translated writings from the Sikh Gurus.

"This is all you need," he emphasized, as if he was telling me a secret.

The juxtaposition between my reluctance to move and Michael's excitement weighed on me. He was so clear about the life he wanted on a ranch, while I was full of doubts about what life would have in store for me. Ultimately though, I didn't want us to break up over it, and so I went with his trajectory since I didn't have one of my own.

I called Didar Singh to let him know I was moving and quit my job. He kindly told me, "The door is always open for you here."

Since I wouldn't have an income in Dixie Valley to make my car payment, I sold my Honda Civic.

My dad loaned me our old family car, the '67 Plymouth station wagon and Michael went to find a proper truck for ranch life. Michael wanted to have dogs at the ranch, so we went to the pound and got two Labrador puppies, Jesse, a male golden lab, and Boobie, a female black lab.

Dixie Valley was 134 miles from Reno. As we entered the valley, its haunting beauty captivated me. It was thirty miles wide and a hundred miles long with twelve ranches in the area.

Mr. Uccelli mailed Michael directions to his property along with a key to the home we'd be living in. He included detailed instructions of his expectations and said he'd be flying to the ranch a week after we arrived to see how we had gotten settled.

As we turned onto the property, my heart sank. The pretty ranch house I had envisioned turned out to be a brown, run down, single-wide mobile home. A few cottonwood trees flanked the trailer and to the right was a huge steel barn that held the hay and farming equipment.

As my expectations crashed, Michael pointed out the Mercedes Benz diesel engine that was our electric generator. Mr. Uccelli's instructions were emphatic—when the sun went down, the generator was turned off. Our evenings would be spent in the glow of candlelight.

We got busy unloading the car. The trailer was small and filled with thrift store furniture. A dark-green tattered sofa from the fifties, a stained coffee table and a stiff upholstered chair was all the living room could accommodate. The kitchen was tiny, with almost no counter space for cooking. A drop-leaf table with four chairs filled the nook. There were four cupboards, two up and two down. I put our dishes and groceries away as efficiently as possible.

I purchased a vegetarian cookbook, *Laurel's Kitchen,* to help me with meal ideas. Michael was a carnivore, so I would prepare our meals separately. While I was busy inside, the dogs raced around the property, sniffing at everything. Michael went to the barn to check out the farm equipment and feed the cattle for the first time.

Later on, Michael got a fire going in the wood burning stove in the living room. We were both amazed at the instant chill that gripped the trailer as soon as the sun went down. As we ate leftover pizza and kept warm by the stove, I thought to myself, *I've gone back in time. I'm a pioneer woman.*

Fortunately, Michael's body temperature ran hot or I don't think that first night would have been bearable. The stove in the living room provided heat for the living room and kitchen, but it didn't make it down the narrow hallway to the bedrooms or bathroom.

The bedrooms were freezing. We piled on blankets but it was Michael's body heat that got me through the night. He was quickly out like a light, but I was awake with worry about our new living situation.

In the morning I went for a run and did some hatha yoga. It felt important to me to establish healthy routines that would keep me strong and feeling good. Michael laughed when he saw me cooking his breakfast steaks while wearing Playtex gloves. Being a vegetarian had turned me off to meat and I didn't want to touch the steaks.

After breakfast I followed him around to see if I could help in any way. He said he had it under control. I'd hear him during the day, out in the barn starting the backhoe to drive it around. He was teaching himself how to use it. All in all, Michael was genuinely happy and I complimented him on making his dream come true.

When feeding time came, I liked to sit on the fence and watch the cattle come in. One cow in particular grabbed my attention because she had a comical way of chewing her cud. Her jaw was loose; in fact, it almost looked unhinged when she ate, which made her look like a cartoon cow. Her winter coat was a pretty gold color, so I named her Goldie. The cows slowly munched the hay and then moseyed off.

It was odd not having a job. At first, I was stoked about it until I felt the absence of my own money. Mr. Uccelli popped in as promised, and seemed satisfied with how things were going. When Michael got his paychecks, we'd drive ninety minutes to Fallon to load up on groceries and sundry items. We went to town about twice a month, which made it difficult to keep fresh produce on hand.

Once Michael had his chore routine down, he began to take off for little jaunts. He never said where he was going and I was content occupying my time with things I liked to do. It didn't escape me, though, when he'd return with a case of beer or when I'd see him getting high. I had no idea how he managed to buy weed. Michael had all the money and power to decide where it was allocated.

I loved Michael. He had a tender quality residing beneath his edgy exterior. On those rare occasions when he'd let his guard down, he was lovely to be with. He could be playful and expressive, or passionate and funny, but I didn't experience those aspects of Michael nearly as much as I would have liked. Though I tried, I could never orchestrate an alchemy that made him open and loving. Instead I did my best to convince myself that the brief encounters with his gentler side were enough for me.

Our new doggies loved playing and exploring around the ranch. But tragically, within a month of arriving in Dixie Valley both Jesse and Boobie had distemper of the brain.

We woke up one morning hearing a rapid thumping noise and rushed into the kitchen where we found Jesse in a full-blown seizure: He was foaming at the mouth and vomiting, his breathing was labored, and he'd lost control of his body. His legs were thumping the ground involuntarily, causing the noise we'd heard. The sight of him suffering in this way upset me terribly. I was bawling and didn't know what to do.

We were an hour and a half from Fallon and the nearest vet. Jesse was in a desperate and acute state. Michael was spewing expletives as he stormed outside, kicking things as he went. I clung to Jesse holding him tight, trying to quell the seizure.

Michael came back inside ten minutes later and said, "I think we need to end his suffering, Suz."

"What do you mean, end his suffering?" I asked.

I hadn't even finished asking when Michael pulled the gun out from behind his back.

"Oh my god, Michael, no."

"Listen to me, babe," he said calmly. "Jesse has distemper. He's not going to recover. Now, we can load him in the car and have him in agony for another two hours driving to a vet to put him down…or we can handle it now and end his suffering."

"No, oh my god, no, please!" I begged.

"Either way, babe…Jesse's life is over."

I couldn't think straight. Our beautiful puppy wasn't even a year old. How did this happen?

Michael went outside again to give me time to wrap my head around what he was suggesting.

I laid on the floor and pulled Jesse to me. His body flopped around as I told him over and over that I loved him and I was so sorry. But while I wanted to console him, it was obvious he was already gone. His brain was in the grips of distemper. I knew then Michael was right about what had to be done.

When Michael returned, I nodded. He came over and kissed me on the forehead and then picked up Jesse and kissed him too. Holding him tight, Michael began to cry as he whispered, "Man, this sucks so bad, Jesse. I'm so, so sorry."

He carried him out the door and told me to stay inside. I couldn't have gone with him anyway. I watched him walk toward the barn and set Jesse on the ground. Michael was kicking the ground, yelling and wiping tears on his sleeve. When I saw him raise the gun, I dropped to the floor, covering my ears. The gunfire ripped into my heart, leaving me despondent.

We'd lost our beautiful Jesse. Michael dug a grave and buried him behind the trailer next to the tall cottonwood trees.

Early the next morning, I hit the road for Reno to get Boobie checked out at the vet. It was a two and a half hour drive and Boobie seemed fine until we were about thirty miles from Reno. I pulled over to pee and when I looked in the back seat, Boobie was foaming at the mouth and had lost all motor function. She was put down an hour later and I drove back to Dixie Valley with two huge holes in my heart.

Michael and I took the loss of our dogs badly. Michael got drunk every night for a week after the dogs died. Their deaths seemed to instigate a backslide into his city way of being.

His mood went dark when he drank. It was frightening.

Anything could set him off and he was a mean, mean drunk. Maybe the glamour of ranch life had already worn off. Maybe he thought he could escape himself by relocating to the outdoors, but it was like the adage says *new pot, same plant.* Whatever Michael's demons were, they'd most certainly accompanied him to Dixie Valley.

At sunset, it was a relief to shut down the generator for the night. Having electricity meant dealing with constant noise and fumes—an unpleasant necessity that destroyed what would have been tranquil silence. When the generator was off, we had several hurricane lamps that we lit in the living room. I liked to read *Peace Lagoon* in the evenings, but Michael liked to play a French card game called *Mille Bornes* (A Thousand Milestones).

The gist of the game was each player was a car trying to go the most miles. You could place hazard cards on other players such as flat tires, accidents, or running out of gas. For whatever reason, every single time we played, I'd win the game. It was uncanny how lucky I was. Michael didn't like losing and the more that I won, the more pissed off he got. His fury about losing got so bad, I dreaded playing the game with him.

It was clear to me that something was off with Michael.

Mr. Uccelli flew to the ranch twice a month to check on the herd and to check on Michael. He would let us know by mail what day and time to expect him. This worked well for Michael, as he had taken to frittering away his days doing god knows what. I was never privy to their interactions nor did I know if Michael was doing a good job. The visit was typically an hour or so and then Pete would fly back to Redwood City.

Michael and I began fighting more because I disliked how much he was smoking and drinking. The writing was on the wall, but I didn't want to admit our lifestyle choices were incompatible.

What had started as a genuine desire to help Michael morphed into me wanting to fix him so he would be more like me. Then, I reasoned, we would be compatible. I believed the way I was trying to live my life was better than the choices Michael was making, and I'm sure he didn't appreciate my judgment. He began to leave more often.

Michael took off one morning without a word about where he was going, which was typical. Hours went by as I busied myself with running, cleaning, and attempting to make an adzuki bean stew that turned out awful. I had begun watching Michael make the fires each night, because it dawned on me I might need that skill in case I was on my own. That concern came true that evening when after sunset, Michael was nowhere to be found. I sat by the fire with one lamp lit for hours, worrying about what had happened to him.

When the front door opened at last, I jumped out of my skin because I was expecting to hear the sound of his truck coming down the road.

"Oh man, Michael, you scared me! I didn't even hear you pull up," I explained. Michael looked irritated that I had jumped at the sight of him.

"You didn't hear my truck because I walked home," he disclosed. I wasn't sure I wanted to hear more.

"What happened?" I asked anyway.

He said he had gone up in the hills, off-roading to check out the area. He freely admitted he was drinking and smoking weed. At one point he stopped to take a piss. As he was peeing, with his pants around his ankles, his truck began to roll away from him.

He hadn't set the emergency brake.

Panicked at the sight of his runaway truck, Michael began running as fast as he could, while also pulling up his pants, trying to catch the truck. He managed to get to the door, reached out for the handle and at that crucial moment tripped over a huge boulder, falling flat on his face. He lifted his head, watching the truck gain momentum as it disappeared from sight, plummeting to the bottom of a ravine.

He had been walking for hours to get home.

I stared past him at the wall, not wanting to look at his face, thinking to myself, *What an idiotic fuck-up! What am I doing out in the boonies with this guy?*

"I'm going to bed," Michael said, not waiting for me to form a sentence.

Mr. Ucelli flew in that weekend and Michael told him the sad and fateful tale of his truck. Michael omitted the weed and alcohol in this version. The conversation happened in my presence and Pete's face grew deeper shades of red as Michael relayed the details. Pete made a phone call, presumably to get help to pull Michael's truck from the ravine. They were gone all day because Michael had a hard time finding his way back to the location where it all had gone awry. Pete left as soon as the truck was deposited by the barn, gritting his teeth and shaking his head as he left.

Not surprisingly, the truck was toast. The Friendly Motors dealership in Reno where Michael bought the truck ceased being friendly when he stopped paying the loan.

Silencing Michael's contempt for himself required a lot of beer. He was drinking heavily the weekend after the truck fiasco. Once again, he insisted we play Mille Bornes. Once again, I was winning. When I won the game, Michael became incensed. He picked up the cards and threw them in my face.

My temper rose to match his, "What is wrong with you? It's a stupid game." I chastised him, "Grow the fuck up."

He flew across the table at me, pushing me into the wall. I scrambled to get away, heading for the hallway, but he grabbed me by my flannel nightgown, swinging me around so fast that I lost my balance and crashed to the floor. The sleeve of my gown tore along the seam, leaving a gaping hole.

"You mother fucker!" I screamed.

He dragged me into the living room. He was breathing hard and raspy as he leapt on top of me, his hands closing around my neck. He was choking me and banging my head into the floor repeatedly. Gasping for air and realizing he might kill me, I fought back hard, thrusting my hips in the air while I dug into his rib cage as hard as I could with my nails.

Michael moaned in pain and toppled off me, but grabbed me by my nightgown once again. I was screaming, trying to crawl away from him. My nightgown continued ripping into pieces until it was on the floor. I escaped out the front door.

Not caring I was naked, I ran as fast as I could, not feeling my legs beneath me. I contemplated running to the next ranch but knew it was twelve miles away. I stopped after a couple of minutes because I was so out of breath and folded on the ground.

In yoga, it's called child's pose. My forehead pressed into the earth beneath me, calming and grounding me. I was breathing hard, sweating from my exertion. My body felt heavy, like I weighed a thousand pounds—like I could sink into the earth and disappear.

I had never been choked or hit by a boyfriend and I knew I never would be again.

This was the end of my life with Michael.

The stillness of the Nevada desert surrounded me like a soothing blanket. I didn't move for a long time. I wailed into the night, knowing no one would hear me. Tears surged from my eyes like heavy rain and were absorbed into the land that steadied me.

When I finally opened my eyes and lifted my head, I was greeted by the intimacy of a new moon sky. Thick with brilliant stars twinkling their light, I said a prayer. I felt lost. I wanted to belong to a family. I wanted to feel safe and connected to something more. I prayed with all of my being, with the stars as witnesses.

The neighboring ranch was too far to reach, especially since I had no clothing on and it was below forty degrees outside. At that time of night, there was no chance anyone would be on the roads either. I had no choice but to go back to the trailer.

I ran back and quietly let myself in, thankful Michael hadn't locked me out. Cold from exposure, I crept into the spare bedroom. The frigid cold took up residence in my legs and wouldn't leave. For hours, I tried rubbing them together with bundles of blankets tight around me, but nothing alleviated the chill in my bones. I barely slept, but didn't dare get up in case I'd wake Michael. Time moved slowly as I stared into the dark, making plans to leave.

To my relief, Michael was in the barn when I woke up. We avoided one another for several days, neither wanting to talk. I was afraid to tell him I wanted to leave. I was afraid he would hurt me if he saw me packing my things. My biggest priority was keeping him from escalating in any way. He had a gun in the house, after all. I was not safe there. Keeping my distance, I went to bed early in the spare room, making excuses that I was coming down with something. I knew he felt terrible about what he had done because he left me alone.

Mr. Uccelli came again that weekend. I suspected he had lost faith in Michael. But this time when he landed the plane, I could hear him yelling as he jumped from the cockpit. His head count of the cattle was one short.

Somehow, we had lost a cow.

Michael was supposed to do a headcount every morning and night, which he did not do. For Mr. Uccelli, it was a costly loss: one cow represented upwards of three thousand dollars at the time of slaughter.

Mr. Uccelli and Michael flew over the property and a calf was discovered, drowned in a small, swampy pond. It had gone in to drink or cool off but got stuck in the muddy bottom.

When they came back to the barn to get the backhoe, Mr. Uccelli was beside himself with anger and told Michael he would be the one to drag the dead calf out and bury it.

I kept my distance, mostly tucked behind the trailer out of sight. It was agonizing to watch Michael trying to maneuver the backhoe out of the barn—his lack of experience on full display while being scrutinized by Mr. Uccelli.

It was now crystal clear that the skill set he had claimed during his job interview was completely fictitious.

Michael had a slow ride to the site, so I went with Mr. Uccelli in the truck he kept at the ranch. It was tense and uncomfortable. Mr. Uccelli didn't direct any hostility at me, but his rage level was similar to my father's, so I had a knee-jerk fear response and kept quiet so I would not be noticed.

Seeing the dead calf in the water was memorable. It was grotesquely bloated with a gigantic swarm of gnats around it. Mr. Uccelli estimated it had been dead for more than a week, which highlighted Michael's neglect even more.

Michael was angry, muttering to himself in disgust about the task at hand. He put his waders on and trudged into the rank water to rope the dead cow.

Crouching low behind a large bush of sagebrush I grimaced at the sight. Because I was highly squeamish, I could barely watch the scene as it devolved into a gruesome travesty.

I knew this would be our last night at the ranch. The lost cow was an unexpected answer to my prayer to get out of Dixie Valley and away from Michael.

Michael was waist-deep in the water now, swatting at the gnats and cussing as he slung a rope around the cow's neck, tied it, and hooked it to the backhoe. Then he slowly applied pressure to the gas pedal in order to drag it out of the pond.

This didn't go as planned.

Instead, a sickening sound cracked the air as the dead cow's head was ripped almost entirely from its body. Mr. Uccelli thundered a yell so loud that Michael stopped the backhoe abruptly. The resulting slack in the rope caused the partially severed cow's head to plop into the water.

Cussing profusely, Mr. Uccelli told Michael to get back in the pond and to rope the cow around its midsection. Michael must've also realized his employment was over and cussed back at Mr. Uccelli freely. We were past any niceties or attempts at civility. I ducked lower behind the sagebrush.

Once again Michael ventured into the murky stench of the pond. This time, the only way to get the rope around the swollen calf's body was to go under the foul water. Whether he wanted to or not, he had no choice but to submerge.

Michael took a deep breath and plunged into the water—my stomach churned thinking about it. He successfully got the rope around and then burst out of the water cursing and spitting. With the cow properly secured, he was able to slowly drag it onto a clearing in the desert landscape.

It took him almost an hour to dig the cow's grave while Mr. Uccelli and I watched. Michael's backhoe driving was downright ridiculous—he had no idea what he was doing. I nearly burst out laughing several times, out of nervousness.

To make matters worse, he brazenly cracked open a beer he had brought along. He seemed to want to provoke Mr. Uccelli. When he finished the beer, he threw the empty can into the grave he was digging and cracked open another one. Mr. Uccelli's jaw was clenched tight and the veins on his forehead were bulging as he endured Michael's outrageous behavior, waiting for this task to be completed.

Finally Michael decided the hole was deep enough. After several tries he managed to scoop the cow into the bucket. Then he rolled the backhoe forward to the edge of the grave and dropped the cow in. The cow landed on its back. Using the backhoe bucket and then a shovel, he pushed the dislodged earth into the hole to fill it.

When he finished, I stared dumbfounded at the absurd display of his incompetence—Michael hadn't dug the grave deep enough. Even with all the earth patted down, the cow's four hooves were unceremoniously protruding above ground.

"Isn't that goddamn perfect," Mr. Uccelli sneered at Michael. "You're fired. I want you out of here tomorrow morning."

"Fine by me," Michael snapped back.

Despite the hostility between them, I felt a huge relief in the words Mr. Uccelli spoke. In fact, I felt bad for him. He seemed like a decent and hard-working man. Michael had misled him with his lies.

Mr. Uccelli assured us he'd be back in the morning and I didn't blame him; he wanted to make sure we cleared out. Michael kept drinking that night while I packed our stuff into the Plymouth. He planned to abandon his wrecked truck there. If Friendly Motors wanted it, he said they could come and get it. We had less to take home than when we'd arrived six months earlier.

Mr. Uccelli, solemn and motionless as a sentry, stood at the front gate as we departed. No goodbyes were said. Michael was badly hungover and slumped across the backseat. Our brief and colorful time in Dixie Valley was over.

We didn't speak at all on the drive back to Reno. What was there to say, after all? Michael's pipe dream had gone south. In less than three months, his addictions had ruined everything. When I dropped him at his mother's house, I simply said "bye" and drove away.

We never said we were breaking up. The space around us said it for us. I didn't feel sad; in fact, I didn't feel much of anything at all. His violence toward me killed any desire I once had for him.

In truth, I was exhausted from the onslaught of the past four years. On top of that, since my ordeal at the lake, I didn't feel like I could trust myself. My decision to get back with Michael when there were ample reasons to walk away increased that feeling. Anxiety about the future weighed heavily on me.

Although my father attended college for nine years, he never spoke to me or my siblings about continuing our education. My own view of college was that it was impossible. How could I work full time to pay my bills and manage that as well?

Maybe if I wasn't running on empty the thought of school would have been manageable, but as it was, anything taxing being added to my life was more than I could handle. Conversely, working as a waitress was certainly not going to secure the future I hoped to have. I was in a quandary.

At nineteen, there was nothing about my internal state that made me feel like I was properly approaching adulthood. Fears of what I might choose going forward worried me. It's not that I thought I would become promiscuous or take drugs, it was more insidious than that. I feared putting myself in harm's way again because of my poor choices, especially when it came to men.

As for Michael, he taught me not to fall in love with someone's potential. He taught me that I couldn't heal someone simply through my fervent desire for them to get well.

More than anything, I wanted to find solid ground, but moving back to my bedroom on Everett Drive was no longer an option.

17
ashram daze

It all started with a phone call between my parents. My mother mentioned that she was feeling overwhelmed with the upkeep of the house. In lieu of support, financial or otherwise, my father concocted a plan to move my mother and siblings out of our home so that he, Mrs. Carlson and her two kids, could move in.

Within weeks, he told my mom he had purchased a mobile home for her in Sun Valley, a large trailer park community a few miles north of Reno. Sun Valley attracted low-income families as well as society's less-desirables; felons, life-long criminals and sex offenders because it was situated outside city limits—an unregulated no-man's land. This barren area was also where people went to dump their trash.

Did my father think this was a good place for my mother to reside? It's more accurate to say that he wanted to live on Everett Drive and this was what he could pull off. His nonstop sales pitch on how this was the best solution possible compelled my mother to surrender our home to him. When the day came to vacate, he had the nerve to show up with his new family and a moving truck, telling my mother, "You go out the front door and we'll come in the back door."

His insensitivity was legendary. My sister Meg was asked to help Mrs. Carlson's daughter set up her new bedroom in what had been Meg's room.

More and more I thought of him as a scumbag and this furthered my conviction. My mother and younger siblings moved into the trailer only to discover some weeks later that she did not own it. Someone else had proof of purchase and they were evicted. This resulted in Tom and Pete moving back to Everett Drive with dad, while my mom and Meg moved in with my mother's boyfriend.

It sickened me to hear about it. Meg was the most uprooted, leaving her childhood friends and neighborhood. I felt guilty for not being around, for not being available to my mother when all this was going down.

This displaced us all. Kris was living at my grandpa's because she had recently discovered her roommate was selling drugs. Mike shared an apartment with some friends. I moved out the year before, but for the three youngest, Tom, Pete and Meg, it was a massive change. Returning from Dixie Valley, I was sad that I couldn't go home.

After dropping Michael off, I drove straight to my grandpa's to see if I could stay with him while I got back on my feet. Kris was already staying in his second bedroom. He said he could offer me the living room sofa.

Grandpa was well aware I didn't have anywhere else to go. This magnificent man spent decades making up for the ample deficits of my father. The three of us were cramped in his tiny single-wide trailer and Kris didn't hold back her complaints and objections to my presence.

The next day I called Didar Singh at The Golden Temple to let him know I was home again. He made good on his promise and gave me back my job.

My urge to write returned with this journal entry:

April 4th, 1979

Back home again!

Absence does make the heart grow fonder as I am truly enjoying being back in the city. Friends and family are stimulating and I find the things I am doing most fulfilling. Baking bread, running, yoga, work, people are all fresh and alive.

I do feel my time with Michael has passed. It's probably even good to write it down so I can see it in black and white. No matter how much love we feel for each other, we can't change what we are and I feel that I'm growing now, whereas before I felt stagnant.

The Bible and Peace Lagoon are sources of strength to me and I feel a closeness to god that is unexplainable.

I try each day to be open to the love-consciousness of the universe and to let it flow with me, through me. I am so appreciative of what I have, may I forever rejoice in my blessings. I just feel so good, even without the physical surroundings. I feel as though I have "come home" to a contentment and peace that strengthens my every fiber.

My father heard I was back from Dixie Valley and promptly let me know he wanted the Plymouth station wagon returned. The Golden Temple was a couple of miles from Grandpa's, so I walked to work.

Didar Singh warmly welcomed me and said he'd hired a restaurant manager since I was last there. He introduced me to Stephen, a twenty-two-year-old man from Connecticut and a music major at UNR. He had recently received a spiritual name from Yogi Bhajan and was transitioning to the name *Kirtan Singh*. Didar said he lived at the ashram and had recently learned how to tie a turban.

At the restaurant, Didar Singh mainly played music produced by followers of Yogi Bhajan. This music was unlike anything I had ever heard. Talented musicians with folk music in their veins created melodies paired with mesmeric mantras and lyrics about a different kind of life—one centered around community and loving God. It was out of this world to listen to as well as instructive about living on a spiritual path. Going to work was a pleasure simply for the chance to spend eight hours bathing in those enchanting sounds.

Kris's inhospitable attitude toward me made it imperative that I find another place to live. An idea came to me while listening to the music at the Golden Temple. After discussing it with Didar Singh, I decided to move into the ashram.

Considering I'd been back from Dixie Valley for five days, it was a bit desperate. But, the ashram felt like a solid choice where I would learn to meditate and practice kundalini yoga. Like me, they adhered to a lacto-vegetarian diet. The prospect of living in a wholesome environment with like-minded people that supported one another felt nothing short of revolutionary after what I had been through.

Years before, Didar Singh told me the ashram had an open invitation to anyone who would like to experience a forty-day sadhana. Sadhana meant daily discipline.

According to Didar Singh, Yogi Bhajan said it took forty days to create a new habit. If I committed to the time period, I would learn firsthand what living the teachings of Yogi Bhajan was all about while also learning about their Sikh religious practices. At the end of forty days it was my choice whether to leave or stay. Staying meant I was committing to this way of life.

The practicality of a tryout appealed to me, though I had concerns about making a significant commitment after such a short period of time. Nonetheless, I wanted to give it a try.

This is my brief journal entry from that day, April 9, 1979:

> *...Talked with Didar Singh today and I've decided to move into the ashram May 1st. I feel euphoric!*

Prior to moving in, Didar invited me to spend the night at the ashram so I could have my first experience of sadhana which was the cornerstone of their lifestyle. Thinking it would be smart to dip a toe in to begin with, I agreed. I was getting used to being greeted with the words *Sat Nam*, a versatile salutation commonly used in 3HO. Sat Nam means God's name is truth.

On the appointed night I was nervous about what was in store for me. There were six people living at the ashram; the owners of the house and ashram heads, Didar Singh and Didar Kaur, their son and daughter, Kirtan Singh, and a woman named Asha, who was visiting from Arizona. I would sleep in her room, dubbed the single-ladies' room, which was a small room with french doors off the kitchen. She had a bunk bed and offered me the top bunk.

Everyone got ready for bed shortly after dinner and were tucked in for the night by nine o'clock. I hadn't gone to bed that early since I was a kid. Being far more accustomed to disco hours rather than ashram hours, it took a long time for me to nod off.

I was in a deep-wrinkle sleep when I heard the pleasant sound of guitar strumming as Didar Singh sang us into wakefulness with varying degrees of success at three-thirty in the morning. Asha took me to the bathroom to introduce me to the rituals performed in preparation for sadhana. They were as follows:

First, brush your teeth with a mixture of alum and salt. Alum is aluminum potassium sulfate and is commonly used for pickling and leather tanning. Nasty stuff. It puckers the inside of your mouth until you feel there is no moisture in it. According to Yogi Bhajan, this was a way to pull toxins out of your body. As if that wasn't unpleasant enough, you also gagged yourself three times by sticking your toothbrush down your throat to activate the vomit reflex to "clean out your monkey glands."

What the fuck is a monkey gland? I mused as I nearly puked in the sink. It's not the monkey gland cocktail invented in the 1920s with gin, orange juice, grenadine and absinthe, and it definitely wasn't referring to monkey testicles either. Yogi Bhajan was referring to the lymph nodes in the back of the throat.

Next, apply cold-pressed almond oil to your naked body and jump into a cold shower. *Cold* as in well-water that was essentially snow run-off from the Sierra Nevadas. *Cold* as in my body instantly had an ice cream headache. *Cold* as in the water hit my body and I hit the back shower wall trying to escape it.

In an effort to be helpful, Asha told me if I chanted wahe guru over and over it would help. She lied. It didn't help at all. It was a freezing misery to endure.

The last step was how to poop. When one had to defecate,

one should squat with their feet on the toilet seat in a crouched position (crow pose) so that one's alimentary canal was in proper alignment to fully release the bowels. As I looked at the seat with distinct dirty footprints indicating layers of crud from various ashram members, I determined not to use that toilet, not ever.

Thus far, their morning routine thoroughly grossed me out.

As I came into the living room, which they called the sadhana room, I saw Kirtan Singh tying his turban. His hair was centered in a bun at his hairline. Asha called the bun a *rishi-knot* (a Hindu term). Women tied their rishi-knots at the crown of their heads and then covered them with a lace doily secured with an elastic band.

Didar Singh handed me a large sheepskin to sit on, which seemed weird, considering they were vegetarians. Sadhana began with Didar Singh reciting *Japji Sahib*, a prayer by the first Sikh guru, Guru Nanak.

A strenuous set of kundalini yoga and an hour of meditation followed. Once the chanting began, I was overcome with fatigue and tipped forward, my face landing on the inviting, soft, wool pile of the sheepskin. I passed out instantly.

Didar Singh gave me a strong shake to wake me for the last portion of sadhana, which was more prayers, concluding with a song that seemed like their anthem and a small handful of gorp.

What a fiasco, I thought as I gathered my things to leave. Afterward, I felt awful. I was nauseous and couldn't think straight—my body rhythms were out of whack. It was a challenge to stay awake long enough to make the drive to Grandpa's so I could get some sleep.

Sadhana was not for me. It felt unnatural and I did not want to force myself into a rhythm that my body detested. I knew I would fail at this early morning requirement.

Despite this, there was a strong pull motivating me to commit to a forty-day sadhana; I had a mammoth crush on Kirtan Singh. His spiritual nature and artistic talents were different from any man I'd ever met, save Didar Singh. People loved his warmth and humor. Best of all, he had a more than decent resemblance to Cat Stevens, who I adored.

Both of Kirtan Singh's parents had Italian ancestry so his Mediterranean skin looked especially good against the soft, white cotton *kurta* tunic and drawstring yoga pants he wore as his daily uniform. He was naturally lean and limber with a body built for yoga.

It was easy to imagine myself with him, feeling safe and secure at the ashram. This took precedence over any other concerns or difficulties that might present themselves. I resolved my course of action and stuck to it.

Before moving into the ashram, I called a couple of friends to let them know how my life was changing and to pre-warn them of my suspicions that 3HO might be a cult. I asked them to check in on me from time to time saying, "If I get a glassy-eyed or a vacant look, please, kidnap me and get me out."

I wasn't joking. It was a preemptive move, but I didn't realize that if you do join a cult, your friends are no longer around. They would have no idea if I had been brainwashed or even how to get ahold of me. My wariness was rooted in the national news.

The decision to get involved with 3HO fell in the considerable wake of the tragic Jonestown Massacre at The People's Temple in Guyana.

Six months earlier on November 18, 1978, Jim Jones, a deranged, drug-addled, cult leader, led more than nine hundred followers—including hundreds of children—to subject themselves to what he called "revolutionary suicide."

They drank a poisoned, non-carbonated soft drink similar to a more popular brand, which inspired the now ubiquitous anti-cult admonition: "Don't drink the Kool-Aid."

The watershed of the sixties created the perfect climate for the so-called enlightened ones to come to America. The credo of Tim Leary (Turn on, Tune in, Drop out) seemingly had run its course. The once enticing prospect of expanding one's consciousness that initially surrounded the use of psychedelic drugs changed, especially once cocaine had infiltrated America. People were overdosing and dying, and no matter how many times you tripped, it wasn't solving any world problems. "Better living through chemistry" (a hippie slogan co-opted from a Dupont ad campaign) failed to live up to its promise.

Some teachers from India, like Jiddu Krishnamurti and Paramahansa Yogananda, had been in America for decades. Even so, the current craze to find a spiritual teacher was arguably sparked when the Beatles went to Rishikesh to study with Maharishi Mahesh Yogi in 1968. Not long after that, the floodgates opened. Having a guru or teacher became a new pursuit and created a mystique around a number of charismatic teachers from India: Swami Prabhupada, Sai Baba, Swami Satchidananda, and Sri Chinmoy, to name a few.

Spiritual life was portrayed in an atmosphere of etheric romanticism that was attractive to many disillusioned young Americans who clamored for a different kind of life in the post-psychedelic years. It offered an alternative utopia, one of their own choosing.

My thinking was influenced greatly when I read *Siddhartha*, Herman Hesse's 1922 novel that chronicled the numinous endeavors of a young man seeking enlightenment. When friends from the restaurant, Rick and Susie, took spiritual names and moved to California to study with Baba Hari Dass, it solidified the option of adopting a spiritual path. It felt like a legitimate and safe way forward.

This was tempered by experiences I had as a girl. When my father traveled for business, we all went to the airport to see him off. On one occasion, we encountered dancing, chanting Hare Krishna devotees. A pretty lady approached and handed me a copy of the Bhagavad Gita, but my father saw what she was doing and intervened, taking it out of my hands and returning it to the woman. I was eight years old. He sternly told me not to speak to cult members. That was the first time I ever heard the word *cult.*

On another occasion, we saw Moonies at the airport. Once again I saw my father's negative reaction, and once again he admonished me not to speak to cult members. Their leader, Sun Myung Moon, believed he was the second coming of Christ. When Reverend Moon performed mass weddings in California, it made the headlines. Some former Moonie members claimed brainwashing techniques were used to recruit and keep followers.

Despite these fears and the looming requirement of sadhana, I moved in. Initially, living at the ashram was a wonderfully nurturing experience. The calm environment was a stark contrast from how frazzled I'd been feeling for a long time.

Maybe this could be my new family. Simple things like having our meals together and bonding over conversations and laughter meant so much to me. Communal life was familiar to me from Omega House, but instead of the brutality of The Game, we prayed together and forged an alignment through our shared daily practices. Also, we had an extended community that the restaurant provided. Slowly and steadily, I began to feel more whole.

Kirtan Singh and I were getting to know one another as well.

He'd moved to Reno from Connecticut to attend university. His uncle lived in Reno and took him in while he pursued his B.A. degree in music.

He confided in me that his Italian, Roman Catholic mother strongly disapproved of his new way of life. He was her only son, the only one who could carry on their family name. She bitterly blamed his uncle because he had introduced her son to marijuana. She believed this was the turning point that led her son to abandon his Catholic upbringing.

When she learned her son had changed his name to Kirtan Singh, she declared, "You have finally made a decision so that you'll never have to make another decision again."

It was a heavy pronouncement for a mother to make, which I understood as her saying that deciding to follow Yogi Bhajan was the ultimate capitulation—Yogi Bhajan was now the authority in Kirtan Singh's life.

"Whoa," I said. "Do you think that's true?"

"No, of course not," he replied.

My family was fairly easygoing when I told them I was moving to the ashram. A few rolled eyes, perhaps, but honestly, it didn't seem like anyone was all that surprised, except for Grandpa. He couldn't understand what I was doing or why.

Kirtan Singh's girlfriend Wendy also waitressed at the restaurant. She was a blond jock who, unbeknownst to him, fancied girls. I remember the day she returned from a tantric course in San Francisco where she met Yogi Bhajan and received a spiritual name: Ek Ong Kar Kaur. Wendy hated the name so much that she soon broke it off with Kirtan Singh and quit her job, removing herself completely from the community.

Though I judged her as shallow, her response made me chuckle because I understood her reaction. I was thinking about getting a spiritual name too, but had reservations. I wanted a name that wasn't difficult to pronounce, and more importantly, I did not want a name that began with "Guru." In America, I'd spend my life explaining the name and didn't want the hassle.

With Wendy gone, I hoped to win Kirtan Singh's heart. I was young, immature and falling in love with the *idea* of this new kind of life, but not necessarily the *reality* of it.

Kirtan Singh instructed me on my duties at the restaurant and in the ways of the 3HO lifestyle. When it came to discussing what he broadly called "the teachings" he was always earnest and I did my best to pay attention to everything he said. It was obvious that Kirtan Singh held himself to the highest standard. When he wasn't giving directives to those of us at work, he was melodically chanting to Guru Ram Das with every breath: Guru Guru Wahe Guru, Guru Ram Das Guru.

Each morning we would peel fifty pounds of carrots for juicing, and all the while, Kirtan Singh chanted. When I felt confident enough to sing along, I joined in. One day he commented that it was nice to hear me chant. This was all I needed to hear to emulate his example.

My work schedule at The Golden Temple increased, thus, my time with him increased. He was hurting over Wendy's departure, and told me his past relationships were a source of discomfort for him. He said his tendency was to throw himself so unabashedly into love, demonstrating his love so fervently, he would inevitably overwhelm the object of his desire to such a degree they would break up with him. Ashamed of his past behavior, he told me he intended never to repeat it.

Yogi Bhajan was teaching a White Tantric yoga course in Eugene, Oregon in May. Kirtan Singh wanted to go but didn't have a car. One day, he casually proposed we buy a car together.

I gave absolutely no consideration as to how this might be a complicated arrangement. Neither did I consider, for one second, saying no. We both had a little money saved and bought a 1969 Volkswagen Beetle we found in the classified ads for nine hundred dollars.

A week or so later, we were having lunch together at the park. Out of nowhere, he declared, "So, Suzanne, we seem to have an attraction for one another."

I was embarrassed by his blunt, out-of-the-blue statement. I had seen no indication he was interested in me, but he continued, "As far as I'm concerned, our options are simple: We can relate to one another as a brother-sister relationship or we can be married. We should go to Eugene for the Tantric course and ask Yogi Bhajan for his permission to marry."

"Why would you need his permission?" I immediately replied, bristling.

"Because he is my spiritual teacher," he answered sternly, adding, "your spiritual teacher knows more about you than you know yourself."

This extraordinary claim did not sit well with me, but I kept quiet, deciding not to contradict or challenge him.

"I will not get married without his permission," he reiterated.

His mother's declaration came to mind and my jaw muscles tightened as I heard his literal rules of engagement.

Then with great conviction he made this pronouncement, "Suzanne, I want you to know that the only thing I will ever love in any woman is God... and since God is in all women... you could be any woman."

With that, Kirtan Singh managed to drain all the color out of what had been a beautiful day.

Wow, I thought, *how utterly unromantic.*

He certainly was direct. Obviously, this was Kirtan Singh choosing to be the opposite of how he behaved in the past with other women. Lucky me.

I paused to consider what he said. Nothing about who I was as an individual mattered to him. His intention was sterile, not infected by emotion or personality or desire. It didn't match any daydream I ever had about being proposed to, but there it was, cut and dried.

Perhaps at that moment I had all the information I needed to step away. But my desire to land *somewhere* and to be more stable was paramount. When I asked myself what else I had going for me, the answer that boomed in my mind was *nothing.*

After a brief pause, I simply said, "Okay."

Even though I didn't like the way Kirtan Singh spoke of our proposal, I was excited and hopeful that I would soon be engaged. Once Kirtan Singh established his interest in me and how we would proceed, he lightened up considerably and we began to have some fun together. We went swimming out at Pyramid Lake, did Tai Chi together and had long talks at the ashram. I was falling more in love with him and the devotional life we would share together.

We had a few sexual interactions that were problematic, mainly because Kirtan Singh felt we should abstain until we were married, but he had a hard time sticking to his conviction. Because of this, he wasn't able to enjoy himself when we fooled around. Instead he became riddled with guilt while doing it. He rushed every interaction and heavily recriminated himself afterward. It was confusing because I definitely thought we should have sex before marrying to make sure we clicked in that department. As it happened, we never had a normal love-making session, just quick, stilted escapades that serviced him.

What was obvious was that Kirtan Singh was a man at odds with his sexuality. He was deeply passionate, but seemed to despise his passion. One day he made an off-the-cuff comment that he might be better suited living as a monk.

Oh dear, I thought, *many a truth said in jest.*

This was my first time wearing a 3HO turban.

18
tantric trickery

Kirtan Singh unilaterally decided that in order to prepare for the tantric course, we should begin a forty-day diet of cucumbers and celery. Yogi Bhajan prolifically dispensed dietary advice and was known for prescribing a variety of mono-diets (dietary regimes that focused exclusively on certain foods) to his students to address physical, emotional, and mental issues. I had completed juice fasts before so the idea wasn't unfamiliar to me. On this particular mono-diet we were allowed to ingest raw cucumber, raw or steamed celery, and cucumber-celery juice.

It was a pretty spring day when we departed for Eugene in our cream-colored bug. Neither one of us owned a suitcase, so we improvised, throwing our white clothing, turban material, sheepskins, and sundry items into a couple of laundry baskets which we stuck on the back seat.

We were on our tenth day of what was proving to be an intensely challenging fast. It is no exaggeration to say we were the living cliché of a space-cadet, new-age couple. Personally, I was weak from hunger and desperately wanted to quit. It was much harder than juice fasting. The steamed celery we had prepared in advance for the trip tasted like soap, but I forged on, not wanting to look weak or to disappoint Kirtan Singh. The gorgeous drive up through Mt. Shasta took my mind off my hunger for a while.

Upon arriving at the Eugene ashram, I was introduced to a swarm of women who were tickled to learn that I was a newbie to ashram life. After answering a barrage of questions about myself, they enthusiastically offered their services to tie a turban on me for the first time. Not wanting to be impolite, I said okay.

Looking back, I am struck by the carelessness of that offer. I had only been in the ashram for a month. I had no context or understanding of the meaning and reverence that was embedded in the choice to wear a turban—or *dastar*, as it is more accurately called.

The early female followers of Yogi Bhajan had devised their own unique style of head covering. The 3HO women's turban looked more like an homage to ancient Egypt not India.

Because of this, I had strong reservations about this change. Altering my outward appearance so dramatically felt confronting, an experience exacerbated by my lack of understanding regarding its significance. At the time, I had only been told that wearing white represented purity. Consequently, I secretly hoped to delay wearing a turban for as long as possible.

My concession kicked off a frenzy of activity. One woman was brushing my hair to gather it in a rishi knot, using her own doily to secure the bun. Other women were folding five yards of F16—a gauzy cotton fabric from India—fresh from the dryer. They circled my head, going round and round, as the height of the turban rose ever higher. Finally, they tucked the copious fabric around my bun while someone went to find a mirror.

An eager young woman rushed into the room with a floor length mirror and held it in front of me so I could see the finished product. When I saw myself I was completely overwhelmed at my altered appearance. I began to cry and ran out the door to the park across the street. I had to get away from everyone at the ashram. I hated how I looked. It didn't feel like me.

For Christ's sake, I thought, *not that long ago, I was getting dolled-up to dance at the disco.* Yet here I was, with this over-the-top, stovepipe, American-made Nefertiti-wannabe turban.

How could I marry Kirtan Singh if I was uncomfortable in the 3HO garb? I was mortified. The women fetched Kirtan Singh to tell him I had a turban on. He rushed to the park and when he spotted me, the delight on his face was unmistakable. He was overjoyed seeing me in a turban and insisted on taking my picture, oblivious to the tears streaming down my face. We could not have been further apart in our perspectives.

That moment became frozen in time. I wiped my eyes and managed a half-hearted smile as Kirtan Singh took the picture.

Returning to the ashram, I asked if there was somewhere that I could nap and was taken to the single-ladies'room, which smelled like sandalwood and patchouli. I pulled the tightly wound fabric off my throbbing head. It felt good to lie down and pull the covers over my head in an effort to create some space for myself.

No one disturbed me until it was time to get ready for the yoga course that evening. Sleeping did me a world of good, but it was short-lived. Once I got up, I was bombarded with what I'm sure was well-meaning advice from nearly everyone around me.

Quoting Yogi Bhajan, I quickly learned, was a hallmark of ashram life. Many sentences began with the words, "The Siri Singh Sahib says…." *Siri Singh Sahib* was a title Yogi Bhajan claimed was bestowed upon him in India. This lengthened his formal designation to Siri Singh Sahib Bhai Sahib Harbhajan Singh Khalsa Yogiji. It was a mouthful to say.

In particular, I was being told what to expect at the course and how tantric yoga worked according to Yogi Bhajan. People were making fantastical claims that would be hard to prove. It sounded nothing like the Hatha yoga classes I had taken. Kirtan Singh tried to explain it to me on the drive up but said, ultimately, I would have to experience it for myself.

When we arrived at the auditorium, I was struck by the sight of so many people in white and how at ease everyone seemed to be in their garb. Over their churidars (leggings) men wore knee-length button-down kurtas and women wore beautiful cotton or silk dresses. I tried to imagine myself fitting in there, becoming comfortable with the dress requirements.

Important-looking people were attending to the logistical details before the course could begin. Men and women sat in separate rows, facing one another. Alignment was crucial: attendants held long ropes the length of each line and instructed us to scooch around in order to get our heads and spines centered right underneath the rope. The rope holders were strict about getting us shipshape. Once they determined our angles were aligned, then Yogi Bhajan would arrive to instruct us.

The excitement was palpable as the buzz of conversation filled the room. We would be asked to hold positions with our arms and/or legs while doing breathing exercises called pranayama for long periods of time, from fifteen minutes up to an hour. We were to maintain the position no matter what.

"Even if we are in excruciating pain," Kirtan Singh made sure to emphasize.

Yogi Bhajan claimed this form of yoga purged your karma. Indeed, we were told that while we struggled to hold the yoga positions, intense feelings of negativity, anger, rage, etc. would be generated inside of us. This energy would then swoosh up our spines and down the straight tantric lines to Yogi Bhajan, who would magically take it all on and burn our karma for us. He called himself a Mahan Tantric and, as such, he claimed he had the power to accomplish this feat. He also claimed he was the only person alive who was endowed with this power.

Just like Jesus took on our sins, I thought wryly.

Truly, it sounded far-fetched, but there I was, in Eugene, barely subsisting on cucumbers and celery, and hoping to get engaged to my own version of Cat Stevens.

Kirtan Singh on the other hand was already heavily imbued with the dogma, believing fervently in the mystical magic of it all.

A murmur of whispers accompanied Yogi Bhajan as he entered the room. This was my first time seeing him. He was not at all what I expected—I had Don Juan Matus from Carlos Castaneda's books in my mind. Don Juan was a small, thin man whereas Yogi Bhajan was tall, thick, and large. He didn't look like a yogi at all.

Yogi Bhajan bellowed commands into the mic. He told us to lock eyes with our partners and raise our arms above our heads at a forty-five degree angle while doing breath of fire.

Breath of fire is a rhythmic, diaphragmatic pumping of the navel while breathing rapidly through the nostrils. If you make the rookie mistake of breathing shallowly into your chest, you will hyperventilate and faint. Luckily, I was good at this technique, so we were off and running. We were expected to keep this up for half an hour. Because this was my first tantric course, I wanted to do well, but it didn't take long before my arms were burning with pain.

"Keep up!" Kirtan Singh hissed at me when my arms started to lower toward the floor. "Don't break our gaze!"

Ugh. I tried to get back into it. But re-establishing my gaze with Kirtan Singh was deeply unsettling.

He was doing breath of fire with feverish intensity. His nostrils were flared and one nostril was full of snot. When he exhaled, the snot blew out of his nose onto his upper lip for a mere millisecond until his inhale sucked it back up his nose. It was nauseating. In and out, in and out it went. I wanted to hurl.

Cat Stevens would never look like this.

Additionally, the anger on his face because I was not keeping up was concerning. Kirtan Singh was displeased with my poor performance. This was so much harder than chanting together while peeling carrots.

After completing the first exercise he lectured me, emphasizing the whole point of tantric yoga was to keep up and push past our weakness and negativity.

Keep Up was a 3HO mantra that was the go-to answer for resistance of any kind to anything. If we kept up, our negativity flowed toward Yogi Bhajan and he burned away lifetimes of karma. Kirtan Singh warned me if I didn't keep up, it wouldn't work and we would have wasted our time and money. Worse than that, our karma would not be transcended. It occurred to me that nothing in his explanation was provable. Clearly, tantric yoga was an exercise in blind faith.

My hesitancy was bolstered when I looked at the stage during the exercise to see Yogi Bhajan munching on what looked like a bag of Doritos while talking to one of his secretaries. He wasn't doing anything at all. Was I the only person in the room seeing this?

I kept these thoughts to myself because I didn't want Kirtan Singh to be disappointed in me. Offering a sincere apology, I promised to do better.

Then I politely asked him to please blow his nose.

The next exercise was a forward stretch. We sat with our legs out in front of us. Grabbing our big toes, we took a powerful inhale up and exhaled while stretching forward so our heads lowered toward our legs.

Once again, Kirtan Singh fervidly obeyed Yogi Bhajan's instructions. He was breathing like a locomotive. As flexible as he was, the might of his effort caused his forehead to hit his shin bones on each exhale into the forward bend. As he found his rhythm, the speed with which he performed the exercise caused his turban to fly off. His rishi knot came undone leaving his long hair flying through the air as he head-banged his way through the exercise. I'd never seen anything like it and didn't know if I should be impressed or frightened by his approach to yoga.

Twelve minutes into the exercise Kirtan Singh passed out. *Well,* I thought, *at least I don't have to do the exercise anymore.* I let him lie there, figuring he'd come around in a jiffy.

A short break was given and Kirtan Singh said it was time to ask for an audience with Yogi Bhajan. I asked him what would happen if he said no to us being engaged and Kirtan Singh replied, "Then we won't be getting married."

Even though he said that before, it irked me. I didn't see why we needed Yogi Bhajan's permission and resented having to ask. After all, I wasn't even asking my parents for their permission.

I followed Kirtan Singh to the stage where he spoke to one of Yogi Bhajan's staff to ask if we could be fit into his schedule.

Prior to our arrival in Eugene, Kirtan Singh briefed me on a 3HO ritual I would undoubtedly observe. Yogi Bhajan's followers touched his feet when encountering him, then placed their hand at their third eye, between their eyebrows.

This gesture, he said, symbolized humility and reverence for one's spiritual teacher. He further explained that we did this to "touch the dust of the feet of a saint" and then placed that "dust" at our third eye as a blessing.

This was the first time I heard Yogi Bhajan referred to as a saint, which alarmed me. This touching of the feet was an ostentatious ritual. Shouldn't a spiritual teacher also be humble?

While we waited, I observed Yogi Bhajan interacting with other followers who wanted his attention. He had a booming voice that came even more to life through his gesticulations. Sad to say, my overall first impression of him was that he was arrogant and bombastic. He did not look like a yogi. He didn't act like one either. I knew I had to keep my newly forming opinions to myself if I ever wanted to marry Kirtan Singh. After waiting for fifteen minutes we were motioned to come forward.

"Sat Nam, Siri Singh Sahibji," Kirtan Singh respectfully began, as he bent down to touch Yogi Bhajan's feet and then raised his hand to touch his third eye, "We would humbly like to ask for your blessing and permission to be married."

"How old are you?" Yogi Bhajan asked.

"I'm twenty-two, but I'll be twenty-three in October," Kirtan Singh answered earnestly.

Turning to me, Yogi Bhajan asked, "How old are you?"

"Nineteen," I replied.

"Perfect!" he bellowed, as if addressing the entire auditorium. Then he flicked his wrist, waving for us to go away, like we were a couple of pesky mosquitoes that had landed on his sleeve.

I mustered up the courage to address him, "Excuse me, sir, but I'd also like to get a spiritual name."

"What is your name?" he asked Kirtan Singh.

"Kirtan Singh," came the reply.

"Then, Kirtan Kaur, of course!" He declared.

"Thank you!" we said in unison as we hurried away.

I was engaged and had received a name that I loved, Kirtan

Kaur Khalsa. Kirtan Kaur meant "The princess who devotedly sings God's praises." In 3HO, all Yogi Bhajan devotees took the surname Khalsa, which meant "the pure ones."

When the course was completed that day, I wanted to celebrate. Filled with excitement about our engagement, I told Kirtan Singh we should go out to have carrot cake and tea. There was a popular restaurant in town called Lithia's that I'd been told was fabulous. Kirtan Singh did not like my suggestion. He wanted to continue on the cucumber-celery diet, but I pushed and pushed until he finally agreed. We went to a juice bar and picked up some fresh squeezed juices first, cucumber, celery, and beet, and then headed to Lithia's.

We never made it.

Red beet juice was flying through our spinning Volkswagen after we were broadsided by a truck. After several rotations we came to a stop. Our car was inside a little triangle of space, flanked by an electrical pole, a cement wall, and a light post. We weren't hurt, but to the people that ran up to check on us, we looked like we were bleeding profusely. The bright red beet juice all over our white clothing gave them a shock.

Kirtan Singh was fuming and angrily pointed out that if we hadn't been on our way to break our diet, we wouldn't have gotten hit. His words were like body blows, heavy with condemnation, "*You* were the one who didn't keep up, you were the one who wanted to quit our fast."

The blame was clearly and squarely mine.

Calling from a nearby phone booth, we found someone from the ashram to come pick us up. We finished the tantric course Sunday night and on Monday morning, I felt like a hobo, ashamed and conspicuous as we loaded our laundry baskets of red and white clothes onto a Greyhound bus for home.

Our bug, which we had owned for a mere nine days, was totaled. While I was embarrassed by our lack of luggage, I couldn't help but notice my fiancé took pride in our lowly circumstances. This difference in our perspectives would accelerate over time.

Unexpectedly, the trip to Eugene revealed new aspects of Kirtan Singh's personality—*strident and judgmental* were not words I would have used to describe him prior to going. He was much more intense and serious about fulfilling all the prescribed teachings of Yogi Bhajan than I was.

Still, now that we were engaged, I was determined to do sadhana consistently. Though I wanted to meet his level of commitment, my best efforts proved to be erratic. I was painfully aware of Kirtan Singh's persistent expectations.

Upon returning home, he wanted me to wear a turban every day, but I resisted. Wearing bana in public was a big deal, a change I wasn't ready for. *Bana* is the identifying appearance of a Sikh, and 3HO had its own specific dress code. I wore my hair in a rishi-knot, telling myself it was a step closer to the end goal.

When I completed forty days in June, Didar Singh met with me to ask if I was ready to commit to the lifestyle. It was a formality, since everyone knew I was tethered through my engagement to Kirtan Singh to continue on at the ashram. It was an emotional day when I gave away all of my gorgeous bohemian clothing to friends, sealing my decision even more.

What I didn't foresee was the shift in expectations that occurred after the forty days were concluded. It was subtle at first, but the pressure to fully enroll with the program was clear. This meant dressing in bana, getting up for sadhana, and presenting oneself as a Sikh. What had been an elective was now a mandate.

We hosted a get-together with the friends from the restaurant, a summer picnic on the large lawn, playing scrabble, volleyball, and even doing sensitivity exercises I had learned at Omega House. I was now a part of something bigger than myself.

One night Didar Singh put on a Shakti album featuring John Laughlin, the great British jazz guitarist. Side B was a song with what has to be the longest title in history—"What Need Have I for This-What Need Have I For That-I'm Dancing At The Feet Of My Lord-All Is Bliss-All Is Bliss". Well into the nearly thirty-minute song, we all began dancing as the rhythm of the tablas picked up. It was ecstatic dance, free and expressive as we all moved through the ashram dancing happily.

Out of the corner of my eye, I caught Didar Kaur watching me with a disapproving expression. I danced over to her smiling, hoping to loosen her up, but instead she hissed at me, "Red tantric yoga!" as a condemnation of some sort.

"What does that mean?" I asked her.

"Red tantric is the energy of sexuality and the devil," she said. "It's lower chakra vibration energy."

"I'm dancing," I replied. "We're having fun." She shook her head and walked away.

This initiated a tense dynamic between the two of us. She had the same kind of strident energy that I witnessed in Kirtan Singh in Eugene. Over time she weighed in with her criticisms of me more and more. Didar Singh, on the other hand, was super chill and easygoing. I preferred interacting with him, avoiding Didar Kaur when possible.

Kirtan Singh monitored my lack of progress when it came to sadhana and we were beginning to fight about it. I did not respond well to the new level of scrutiny I was under. If anything, it made me want to rebel against it. My internal dilemma of wanting to belong and have family was at odds with urges to flee. I did my best to squelch those urges because I believed I had found a good place to settle and survive. Being on my own was far too terrifying to consider.

Anyway, these pressures and criticisms were not unfamiliar to me. This was the way my father related to me, this was the way Omega House related to me. To an outside observer, it would probably seem unreasonable that I stayed connected to the group, but for me, this was a known pattern that I did not yet know I could question.

With Eugene behind us, the next event was coming up. Each summer, Yogi Bhajan and his followers convened in the mountains outside of Española, New Mexico, for a summer solstice celebration that lasted ten days. Two summer camps followed that event; the Khalsa Women's Training Camp, informally referred to as Ladies Camp, and the Khalsa Children's Camp.

In an effort to get me more up to speed with the lifestyle, Kirtan Singh was sending me to Ladies Camp for six weeks. Yogi Bhajan encouraged attendance, claiming it was healthy for a husband and wife to be apart each year. This was common in India, he said, as during the monsoon season women went home to their families for several months. He said this contributed to the longevity of marriages. I was happy to have a long vacation and curious to see what it was all about.

Asha was also attending Ladies Camp and she helped me compile a list of what to bring. Kirtan Singh and I went to an army surplus store to purchase a cot, large flashlight with batteries, and a regulation green trunk. I already had a sleeping bag and bivy sack from my trip to Yosemite.

We needed another car after our accident in Eugene. Kirtan Singh found a Dodge Dart Swinger in the classified ads. It was beautiful, a deep blue color complemented by a white roof. It had a huge trunk that fit all of our belongings.

Debbie and I had taken a few trips to the Bay Area, but I'd never taken a drive that covered more than a thousand miles. I was psyched for the adventure. We'd head south to Las Vegas and stay overnight at the ashram there, finishing the journey the next day.

"I have never been one to ignore the signs. Unless, of course, it works in my favor."

~ Jaida Jones, *Dragon Soul*

19
ominous beginnings

A few people warned me about the drive from Reno to Las Vegas, saying it was ugly and tedious. I found the wide-open desert landscape inspiring. The sculptural shapes and shadows as they moved across the mountain ranges were spectacular.

We did have some tense moments when we stopped for food at a roadside cafe. Asha wore a turban which got us noticed immediately, while I was wearing white yoga pants and a white shirt. Being stared at or ridiculed openly was uncomfortable and I disliked the way people responded to the garb. Grandma would've said, "Kill them with kindness" so I compensated for my discomfort by being extra friendly.

When I asked for two veggie burgers, the waitress snickered. She served us Wonder bread buns with one piece of lettuce, one slice of American cheese, and one slice of tomato. In the late seventies in the Nevada boondocks, that was a veggie burger. We ate quickly, leaving the narrow-minded locals behind as we got back on the road.

To my dismay, Asha didn't want to help with the driving and instead slept on the roomy backseat for most of the day. To stay alert, I blasted the radio and kept the windows down.

We found our way to the Las Vegas ashram and were warmly

greeted with smiles and a hot mug of yogi tea. They had a guest room with twin beds and a pitcher of water on the nightstand. After dinner and I was more than ready for sleep.

The ashram head told us we'd be roused for sadhana, and I nodded, knowing I had no intention of getting up at 3:30 a.m. It was far more important that I sleep and be rested for the drive. Asha got up for sadhana but I slept in, not caring what anyone thought of me.

The hospitality at the ashram was top-notch. We had a yummy breakfast of homemade yogurt with fruit and nuts and freshly baked bread. We lingered over our meal for far too long, not leaving until noon. With a ten-hour drive to Española ahead of us, I was concerned about being the sole driver for the haul.

Hoover Dam was impressive to cross, but after that it was pretty boring terrain. As the temperature rose, I quickly became drowsy. I took to pounding on my legs (like Debbie did when we crossed Donner Summit) and sucking on ice in an effort to keep cool and stay alert.

As we pulled into Flagstaff the temperature was pleasantly cooler. I told Asha I had to sleep and found a public park to rest at. We crashed for two hours, longer than I had planned, which guaranteed that I'd be driving late into the night. My frustration turned to anger at having to shoulder the driving alone. I called my mom, asking her to book a motel room in Albuquerque. We'd be pretty close to Española, but I wanted to have accommodations arranged in case I couldn't push through.

There were many eighteen-wheelers on the road that day and I remembered as a kid how we used to make a pumping gesture out our windows, signalling the drivers to blow their air horns. To keep amused, I began doing this with all the trucks going by. Most of them were friendly and honked their horns, smiling and waving as they passed. Unfortunately, one driver was a real nuisance.

For hours, this forty-something driver repeatedly pulled up beside me and gestured for me to pull over, with his tongue flicking in and out of his mouth. Ignoring him, I slowed down, hoping he would drive by, but instead he stayed behind me, honking and gesturing.

We'd stop to gas up, or he would, but inevitably we'd pass one another again on the road and he would ride up on my bumper again beeping.

"What a disgusting pig," I said to the sleeping blob in the backseat, "How do we get rid of this guy?"

This was twelve years before the film *Thelma and Louise*, but the truck driver in that movie was remarkably similar to the one I encountered that day.

Near midnight I passed a sign saying we were forty miles from Albuquerque. The eighteen-wheeler was still on my tail. All of a sudden, a coyote ran onto the highway.

"Ohhh shit!" I screamed, swerving to miss it. It worked, but I lost control of the car because I over-corrected. Then the coyote turned around to run back to where it had come from. This time, I hit and killed it. The car was fishtailing like crazy.

I continued screaming, "Ohhh shit, Ohhh shit!" while trying to regain control. Asha woke up from the lurching of the car and began chanting, "Wahe Guru, Wahe Guru!"

Looking in my rearview mirror, the semi's lights were rapidly crawling up my backside. I knew he was going to hit us because he was following so close. I cranked the wheel hard to the right, veering us onto the shoulder. The truck driver laid on his horn, barely missing us as he flew by. The huge gust of slipstream from the truck whizzing by pushed the car further off the shoulder. I hit the brakes hard and we skidded, kicking up a massive cloud of dirt before we came to a hard stop.

"What happened?" asked Asha.

"I hit a coyote, Asha, that's what happened, and that semi nearly mowed us down!" I was pulsing with adrenaline and tried to breathe more slowly.

Asha piped up saying, "We have to chant for the coyote's soul to help it cross over, we do it three times." She began to chant akal, which meant "undying."

I tried to join in, but was overcome with emotion from killing the coyote. Plus, I was livid at that jackass driver. I wanted this day to be over. I wanted to be in a cozy bed under the covers.

Asha urged me to get back on the road. Telling her she had to stay awake with me, I gathered myself for the last push.

We rolled into Albuquerque after midnight. I found the motel, only to discover the lights in the office were out. We banged on the door to wake the manager, who finally came and gave us the keys to our room.

Even at midnight it was hot outside and I was sticky with sweat from the long drive. Seeing a swimming pool, I thought a quick dip would be refreshing. After we finished unloading, we went to the pool wearing *kacheras* and t-shirts. Kacheras are a type of undergarment and one of five articles of faith worn by Sikhs. Only a few months ago, I would've been wearing my itsy, bitsy, teeny, weenie, yellow polka dot bikini.

The water felt good and reviving until I heard noises and hushed Asha to listen. A few men were approaching us from the far end of the property. I didn't speak Spanish, but their whistling and yelling gave me the impression they were catcalling.

Feeling fearful, I grabbed her arm, whispering, "We have to go, now!" After my ordeal at Lake Tahoe, I was quick to respond to any signs of danger. We made haste, running up the stairs to our room. They tried to catch up to us, but we made it inside and locked the door. For greater security, we pushed the desk in front of the door. The sleep I needed so badly would have to wait. I was afraid to close my eyes.

Eventually I dozed off and felt cheerful when I awoke, knowing we would arrive at Ladies Camp in a couple of hours. We ate the motel offerings of doughnuts and coffee and went to the car.

Before driving, we always did a particular chant three times. We were told it provided protection, but I had my doubts considering how things were going.

After chanting, I started the car and backed out of my parking space, but something was wrong. When I got out to look, I discovered all the tires had been slashed. We weren't going anywhere.

Trying to hold it together, I called my mom from a phone booth. When I heard her voice, I lost it. She couldn't understand a word I said because my voice was pinched with emotion.

Were these unfolding events heralding a gloomy future for me? The menacing truck driver; hitting the coyote; being harassed when we arrived at our motel; and now this. My mother's voice seemed impossibly far away—I wanted someone to come and take care of me.

Eventually I calmed down enough to relay what had transpired. My mom said she'd hang up so she could call a local garage to replace my tires. I was amazed at how efficiently she took care of all the details. Within several hours we were on our way.

All my tuition money for Ladies Camp was used to purchase new tires. How was I going to attend? I hadn't called Kirtan Singh—somehow I knew I wouldn't get much empathy from him.

Camp started the week before. As we pulled in, we could see Yogi Bhajan giving a lecture under a big yellow-and-white striped circus tent. I could see a little booth where people were checking in and parked near it.

The woman in the booth was patient as I explained all of our mishaps en route to Española. She arranged a payment plan for me to pay my tuition. We were given a brief orientation and told where to pitch our tent.

Ladies Camp was situated on a large spread of land dotted with several mobile homes. Old cottonwood trees were scattered throughout the property, reminding me of my runs along the Truckee River.

As we finished up, I walked slowly around the tent. Yogi Bhajan lectured from an elevated platform on what looked like a throne. The lecture had ended and most people had dispersed. I watched as he stepped down to make his way to a Jeep that was waiting for him.

As he walked toward the car, a woman in the distance caught his eye. "Sangita, come here!" he bellowed.

A petite woman approached. He berated her in his thick East Indian accent, "Your husband tells me you are not behaving as Khalsa woman with all this kind of bitching bullshit nagging you do!" I was stunned by his demeanor and language. I moved closer, glad he was taking no notice of me.

Yogi Bhajan was aggressively moving toward the woman, yelling in broken, staccato sentences, "Why you are neurotic, bitching female? Tell me, Sangita Kaur, why you are continuing to behave in this way?"

To my amazement, he then punched her in the face. The power of his blow knocked her to the ground. I froze, looking around to see who else might have witnessed this. A few women were in the tent and a security guard stood nearby. There was no response from anyone. Yogi Bhajan concluded his tirade, saying in a threatening tone that he did not want to hear any more complaints about her from her husband. The woman remained crouched on the ground with her head bowed in supplication.

I instantly thought of Michael's violence toward me in Dixie Valley. Yogi Bhajan's behavior was shocking—how could this possibly be considered acceptable behavior from him?

When he was through yelling, he simply walked away. I rushed to her side, taking her arm to steady her as she slowly stood up.

Holding back tears, I asked her, "Oh my god, are you okay?"

With her hand holding her already bruising jaw, she quietly said, "Something in my aura must have needed adjusting."

I could not believe my ears. Hearing this, my mind was screaming, *Oh my god, this is a cult.*

Why on earth was she offering up a lame justification for Yogi Bhajan striking her? She thanked me for helping her up. I stood speechless as she slowly walked toward her tent. Witnessing this firsthand cinched my negative perception of Yogi Bhajan. I seriously had to think about this and what it meant for my future.

Asha yelled from the car that we needed to get our tent up. The place was already crowded with green canvas Coleman tents. We scoped out what we thought was a good place in the area we were assigned and got to work. We had rudimentary but adequate provisions. Asha then informed me she was going to tent with a friend from Arizona, so I would have our tent to myself.

The rest of that day and into the night I thought about what I had seen. It altered everything. How could I go forward with my marriage to Kirtan Singh?

I was up for hours, trying to find a way.

I tried to focus on the beneficial aspects of 3HO because I wanted to make it work with Kirtan Singh. I loved the sense of community and belonging, and wanted to learn more about Sikhism. Of course, the other strong influence was that I no longer had a family home to return to. This sad reality made finding a solution imperative.

Well, I reasoned, *why couldn't I still pursue those things I loved?* It's not like Yogi Bhajan was going to be a big part of my life. I'd see him once a year if I came to Solstice or Ladies Camp.

This line of thinking made me feel better, so I resolved to focus on my upcoming marriage and learning about Sikhism while moving Yogi Bhajan into the background. That way, I told myself, *I wouldn't be in a cult.* I'd be participating in my own chosen way. If I could compartmentalize, I could stay.

The next day we had an orientation on the camp schedule: *Gurmukhi* lessons (the scriptural language of the Sikh holy book); *Gatka* (a traditional Sikh martial art); military marching; vegetarian cooking; protocol regarding *Gurdwara* (a Sikh place of worship); and daily lectures or yoga classes by Yogi Bhajan.

Yogi Bhajan's lectures were challenging because I had a hard time understanding his accent. He often lapsed into long stories from Hindu mythology, interspersed with him speaking in Urdu. I found myself dozing off more than once.

A few lectures stood out due to the presence of Yogi Bhajan's secretary, Hari Har. She would come to the lectures late and when Yogi Bhajan spotted her on the periphery of the tent, the lecture stopped so he could banter with her.

Being nineteen and used to the energy of boys my age, I was blown away at how blatantly Yogi Bhajan was flirting with her. He would giggle and get flustered and laugh at her replies.

I was dead sure he was having sex with this woman and looked around at all the other women who were witnessing his horny display of lust to see if anyone else was clocking his behavior. All I saw were the devoted faces of his followers.

Hari Har's presence was another factor in my disillusionment with Yogi Bhajan. Especially since I was told the purpose of Ladies Camp was to provide training on how to be graceful Khalsa women. As members of 3HO, we all took the surname Khalsa, which means "the pure ones"—a name that is rarely used within mainstream Sikhism. My perception at the time was that the teachings I was learning came directly from India.

Coming from an American Catholic upbringing, the cultural richness and novelty of what I was learning was exciting. Meditating with and keeping the company of women was a unique experience. I'd never lived with no men around. The environment inspired me.

The first wave of women who had followed Yogi Bhajan were ten to fifteen years older than me. Somehow, they managed to camp and they look impeccable at the same time. Many had been to India and purchased traditional tailor-made clothing that fit them perfectly. They looked so authentic in their accoutrements from India, I envied them.

New Mexico reminded me of home. The sudden, heavy downpours of rain were the same summer storms we had in Nevada. They came in quick and vanished just as quickly.

The assigned area for our tent was located in a depressed area of camp, geographically speaking. When the rains came, my tent flooded with water. The long-timers were all tenting in a small elevated area of the camp. They obviously had first dibs on the optimal land.

One day I was invited to meet the Gurmukhi teacher, Ram

Das Kaur. She was the Secretary of Religion for Sikh Dharma, the religious branch of 3HO. She was hanging out in a tent with a long-timer from Virginia. My eyes bulged out of my head as I entered her tent.

The woman from Virginia had a huge asian carpet covering the floor, along with access to electricity that provided ambient light, a fan, an ironing board set-up, and a boom box. There was no electricity available in the swamp zone. Lovely music played in the background. She was reclining on a full-size mattress with cozy bedding and fluffy pillows. Her tent was bone dry. The lush accommodations she was living in gave me quite a shock.

"Oh my god," I gushed, emerald green with envy. "I had no idea people could live like this in tents!"

The woman laughed, saying, "Well, I've been at this awhile, and some of us have figured out how to make it bearable."

By coincidence, or maybe *because* I saw how paltry my situation was, that night was my worst night there. As I laid on the stiff cot, freezing cold and uncomfortable, I felt angry, angry that some had it so good at the camp while people like me were in the swamp zone. The disparity between my experience and the woman from Virginia really got me down.

A friend of mine from The Good Earth happened to be visiting her family in Española. She stopped by to see me at camp. I told her about Yogi Bhajan's violence and my conclusion that 3HO was a cult. She agreed. I explained the rationale I had come up with so I could stay. She shook her head gently saying, "I don't know, Suzy, maybe...if you think you can pull it off, it might work."

I was grateful to have someone to talk to and I was glad she knew what had happened.

Regardless of the pressure around me, I still wasn't ready to wear a turban. I rarely made it to sadhana and was reprimanded for it. Fortunately, they didn't throw you out of camp for these transgressions, they just shamed you. I enjoyed camp in the way that worked for me, getting to know others in our community while being served delicious food and learning more about Sikhism. Six weeks went by quickly.

Yogi Bhajan's declaration of spousal benefits by being separated did not account for how difficult it was to return home. I didn't expect it to be so jarring to leave the company of women and rejoin the men. By comparison, they were a rough lot.

On the return drive I already knew Asha would be no help at all. We left Española heading toward Las Vegas. We would find a motel rather than stay at the ashram. We left after lunch and rolled into Vegas near midnight.

Asha's slothful nature continued to annoy me. Whenever we were in the car, she was asleep. When we got to Vegas, I was fed up and wanted to get home. I drank three cups of coffee at a diner and told her we were going to keep going. We were heading north on Highway 95 and would be in Reno around eight o'clock in the morning.

There was no moon that evening. The black night wrapped around us. We were alone on the road. After hours of driving, I was drowsy, despite the caffeine. I pulled over to look at the map because I thought I may be lost. Jumping up and down in the cool air, I hammered my legs with my fists to get my blood moving. We had to keep going—there weren't any motels for miles.

Soon after getting back on the road the engine's hum and the rhythm of the road lulled me again, making me sleepy...that is until I flew past a sign that read:

WELCOME TO ARIZONA

I snapped to, suddenly wide awake and stunned to find myself in the wrong state. *What in the name of God was going on?* Hitting the brakes, I threw the car in reverse, whizzing backwards toward that goddamn sign.

"Oh my god!" I yelled. "We are in goddamned Arizona!"

I had no idea what I had done wrong. It should have been a straight shot to Reno. How could I have driven for two hours and be in Arizona, when the state line ran through the Hoover Dam? It made no sense at all. My brain was in a knot.

"Whaaaaa?" came a sound from the rear.

"You know, Asha, if you helped out *at all* on this trip, we might not be here!" I complained, taking my my rapidly mounting frustrations out on her.

There was nothing to do but drive.

On a positive note, getting angry woke me up. Since we were alone in the boonies, I put the pedal to the metal and headed back to Vegas. At four o'clock in the morning, I gassed up, coffee'd up and got on 95 North, for sure this time. We arrived in Reno at noon. I'd been up for more than twenty-four hours. When I finally fell on my bed, I slept like the dead.

Somehow Becky heard of my engagement and showed up without warning at my dad's house one day when I was there. She had a tricked-out van to show me. When I got in, she turned on the engine and pushed in an 8-track cassette of Nilsson Schmilsson to play "Without You," one of our love songs. As the plaintive voice of Harry Nilsson filled the van singing, "I can't live, if living is without you," Becky pleaded with me not to move into the ashram, insisting that I was making a terrible mistake and that it was a cult.

She was leaving the next day for college, a new life in Pocatello, Idaho and wanted me to come with her, right then and there.

"We'll get married," she stated. "We'll be together."

Tears filled her eyes. A feeling of nostalgia clutched at my heart and I became emotional as well. We began to kiss. Instantly, the days of Becky and I at thirteen flooded my mind with memories; good memories of how I had found belonging with her. I still was searching for a place to belong, but felt a million miles away from those days. So much had happened since then. I was a harder, more calloused version of that young girl.

Becky still wanted to be with me after all we'd gone through. I was flattered and moved by her love for me, but I couldn't go to Idaho. Not wanting to hurt her, I did my best to explain why the ashram felt like the right place for me, but as soon as she realized I was rejecting her offer, she became angry.

"Get out of the van now, I'm leaving," she commanded.

As I shut the car door, Becky sped down the street and out of my life. It would be more than over thirty years before I'd see her again.

Kirtan Singh's hope in sending me to camp (that I would learn more about the 3HO lifestyle) worked, but it had unexpected consequences as well. I didn't tell him that I witnessed Yogi Bhajan strike one of his followers. That would be my secret because I didn't think he would respond well to the news. I also didn't want to have to explain the convoluted rationales I had devised in order for me to stay, as I was pretty sure they'd sound stupid if I heard them spoken out loud.

Additionally, the discrepancy between the experiences of the elite members of the *sangat* (community) and someone like me was bothersome. It was counter to what I thought communal living was supposed to be about. Their posh circumstances put a spotlight on my own feelings of insignificance, and I wondered how I could gain status in the larger community.

Shortly after returning home I got the puffed-up notion that it would be cool for Kirtan Singh and I to be married by Yogi Bhajan. A truly bizarre contradiction, I know, considering that I strongly disliked what I had seen of him thus far. In hindsight, it reveals how my motives were less about him and more about wanting to feel significant in the community.

Determined to make my far-fetched idea happen, I called the headquarters in Los Angeles and boldly stated my desire to the secretary on the line. I went so far as to propose that Yogi Bhajan could teach a tantric course in Reno the weekend after our wedding, which was set for October 18, 1979.

The next day the secretary called saying Yogi Bhajan would teach a one-night lecture on the seventeenth. They didn't think Reno would pull in enough people to sustain a tantric course. She said she'd be in touch with Didar Singh to get him up to speed on the required preparations for the arrival of someone of Yogi Bhajan's stature. I couldn't believe they said yes. We all got a jolt of nerves which we put to immediate use in cleaning, organizing, and planning for his arrival.

For me, procuring our wedding clothes was on the top of my list. I called fabric stores in town to locate white, 100 percent cotton fabric. Incredibly, there was none to be found anywhere in Reno. Fortunately, my mom's best friend, Lois, was an excellent seamstress. She suggested a solution: buy Wamsutta cotton sheets, and that is precisely what I did.

Lois made the cheerleading uniforms for my squad in 8th grade and, once again, generously offered to help me with our wedding outfits. I chose a Butterick dress pattern. Needing churidars as well, Kirtan Singh supplied a pair of his in lieu of a pattern. Thanks to Lois's considerable skills, our handmade clothing was absolutely beautiful.

Didar Kaur offered to bake a carob wedding cake with cream cheese frosting. Like most health food sweets in the 1970s, the thing was a brick bomb. It weighed a ton and you could've killed someone with it, but it was delicious.

The day of Yogi Bhajan's lecture was a frenzy of activity.

The lecture was at UNR before a relatively small turnout of about three dozen people. Perhaps because of this, Yogi Bhajan seemed to be in a nasty mood when he walked in the room. The lecture itself was challenging because many of us had difficulty understanding his accent. At the end, he said we could ask questions. Our good friend from the restaurant, Gary, who had recently gotten the name Guru Amrit Singh, asked a question.

Yogi Bhajan became angry and yelled at him, "In all my years of teaching, this is the stupidest question ever asked by a student!"

Yogi Bhajan continued to put him down and I thought about the woman he hit at Ladies Camp. It was upsetting to watch our friend being treated this way as he recoiled from the unwarranted assault.

Yogi Bhajan's behavior showed his blatant contempt for the audience, speaking to us like we were beneath him. His attitude and treatment of Guru Amrit Singh created a hostile vibe in the room. The lecture ended abruptly with those of us who had hosted the event feeling unsettled and embarrassed.

Some members of the San Francisco sangat came for the lecture, including Sat Santokh Singh who prior to becoming a Sikh was The Grateful Dead's road manager. Two secretaries, Krishna Kaur and Sat Simran Kaur had accompanied Yogi Bhajan from Los Angeles. We cleaned tirelessly in preparation for their arrival. Didar Kaur, in particular, put tremendous effort into making sure everything was right.

Kirtan Singh's mother and grandmother came to the wedding, though it was obvious how uncomfortable they were with his choices. My interactions with them were strained. I had no way of making them feel better about what they were witnessing or how it would affect their family's lineage.

As soon as we got back to the ashram we got busy: Didar Kaur was baking our wedding cake; we used the leftover Wamsutta sheets to cut triangular scarves for people to use as head coverings; and Didar Singh was trying to find accommodations for the visitors. It was close to midnight when Didar Singh came into the kitchen to tell us that Sat Santokh Singh, Yogi Bhajan, and his staff were going out.

"Apparently, Yogiji wants to go to some strip joints," he said.

"What?" I replied, incredulous at this news. Sat Santokh Singh chimed in, with a chuckle in his voice, "Yogiji says it's a good test of his celibacy, watching naked women dance."

I was seething. Something was off, *really* off about this. This certainly wasn't behavior that fit my ideas of how a holy man should conduct himself. Didar Singh was also disturbed by the news and was called a prude by Krishna Kaur. Sat Santokh Singh stated that this was something Yogi Bhajan did all the time. I couldn't contain my anger, "This is messed up. My wedding is tomorrow morning."

"Don't be such a prude, Kirtan Kaur," Sat Santokh replied. "He's a spiritual master. This is fun for him."

When I told Kirtan Singh, he also dismissed me, claiming, "He's our spiritual teacher. He can do what he wants."

Didar Kaur and I finished up in the kitchen. There were no beds left to sleep in, so I grabbed a blanket and pillow and put my sheepskin on the kitchen floor. As I laid down, I began to cry. I was disturbed by what was said and the way the men

Our wedding day. October 18th, 1979. Washoe Valley, Nevada.

discounted my feelings, making fun of me.

I left the Catholic Church because of hypocrisy, feeling betrayed by clergy and nuns who did not emulate any kind of Christ-like love in their treatment of children. Yogi Bhajan seemed like a hypocrite as well. This was not at all how I wanted to feel on the eve of my wedding. I didn't understand so much about what having a spiritual teacher meant. Feeling troubled by all of it, I finally drifted off to sleep.

Morning came quickly. The weather turned and I woke up to a blustery day. The sun poked out here and there through stormy clouds, but it was a chilly day for an outdoor wedding.

My throat was tight and sore, signalling that I was coming down with a cold.

Our families had been prepped on what to expect on our wedding day. They would remove their shoes and be given a white head covering before entering the ceremony area. My family was good natured about it, and even had a laugh because the head coverings we had cut barely fit around the circumference of most people's heads. They looked pretty ridiculous.

Despite all the arrangements and planning, Yogi Bhajan didn't marry us. Sat Santokh Singh stepped in to officiate our wedding. Yogi Bhajan never spoke to me or even came outside. He lounged in bed while the ceremony took place. My father was livid at this rude dismissal of his agreement and complained, "Your yogi can't be bothered to participate."

Even worse, Yogi Bhajan and his secretaries took off while the ceremony was happening. They sneaked out the side door like thieves, driving past us down the long driveway. He could not have made a more ugly impression on my family.

I was glad when Yogi Bhajan left. The only thing he and his secretaries brought to Reno was tension and trouble. I regretted asking for him to marry us and wanted to put it behind me.

On the plus side, I was now a married woman and that made me happy. I had found a place which gave me a great sense of comfort and security, as long as Yogi Bhajan wasn't around.

Our honeymoon was spent at the fantastic Shakespeare Festival in Ashland, Oregon. Kirtan Singh was able to relax and I could see how much he loved the creative atmosphere of the theatrical world. I found myself fantasizing about a life with him as an actor because he was so impassioned about each performance we saw. I had never seen him so high-spirited and playful as he was amid the Renaissance setting. We discussed the themes of the plays we saw while enjoying scrumptious vegetarian food at local cafes.

Our week together was wonderful and I couldn't help but notice part of what made it special was because we were detached from any 3HO influences. A wave of melancholy washed over me as I realized this was the first, and probably last time, we would simply be two young people enjoying one another in a carefree way. Our lives would always be in an ashram, bound by the teachings of Yogi Bhajan. I found myself contemplating who we would be if we struck out on our own. Kirtan Singh's light, affectionate, and fun demeanor during our honeymoon was something to behold. I loved being with him in this way.

It wasn't a sexy honeymoon, however, because besides my head cold, my period started the day we arrived and I had painful cramps for days. Sex during menstruation didn't appeal to me because I disliked how messy it was. As a result, we had sex one time in Ashland. Regardless, it was a memorable trip that brought us closer together.

When we got home we found out that our couple's room at the ashram was to be in a separate structure about one hundred feet from the house, in the side yard. The layout consisted of a large main room with a sizable attached closet, but no bathroom. We didn't want to have to schlep into the main house in the middle of the night in a snowstorm, so we opted for a large bucket in the closet for peeing. Any other business would have to be done in the house. We had a space heater for warmth, but as we were heading into winter, it was a cold room to live in.

Our wedding gift from my mother and Kirtan Singh's parents was a gorgeous, oak bedroom set with a massive four-pillar bed frame, large bureau, and two nightstands. It was delivered right after we got home. We managed to fit it all in the room by stacking the two night stands so we could accommodate Kirtan Singh's upright piano. I ignored him when he complained about the gift, saying yogis should sleep on the floor. I knew my mother was making payments on the set and wished he would show some appreciation for her generosity.

When he wasn't practicing Debussy or Bartok compositions, Kirtan Singh liked to improvise blues tunes. He could make up hilarious, overwrought lyrics on the spot. I was amazed at his creativity as he made up hilarious, overwrought lyrics on the spot. I loved how fluid he was at the keyboard.

After our wedding, Kirtan Singh intensified his pressure on me to wear a turban, saying, "You are a Khalsa woman now. You have to do sadhana and you have to wear bana." Understandably, Kirtan Singh felt that our marriage also represented my commitment to the lifestyle and he expected me to live up to those requirements. Living the teachings of Yogi Bhajan was part and parcel of our marriage, so I began to wear a turban in public. I still disliked being so conspicuous and really hated the attention it garnered, especially the ridicule. I typically took it off as soon as I got home.

Some aspects of ashram life were familiar. I became a vegetarian when I was sixteen and stopped shaving while I was working at The Good Earth. The book *Are You Confused* by Paavo Airola had acquainted me with the practice of taking cold showers.

There were aspects of Sikhism that I loved: reading from the Sikh holy book and singing Sikh hymns was uplifting and joyous. I wanted to learn how to read Gurmukhi so I could read and sing in the sacred Sikh script. But the requirement to do sadhana was a constant and miserable struggle.

As I continued to falter at this practice, Kirtan Singh's frustration grew. We had fights about what he called "my lack of devotion."

By Thanksgiving, I had missed my period. My gynecologist confirmed I had a honeymoon pregnancy from our one sexual encounter. We knew when I conceived because we hadn't had sex since returning. Yogi Bhajan advocated having sex once a month, and we'd passed the month mark.

I was devastated to have another accidental pregnancy.

Kirtan Singh did not hesitate to tell me he wanted to abort. He felt we were too young and unprepared to be parents. His position baffled me. I begged him, "But, we're married. This is what married people do, they have a family!"

He was immovable. The next day, to further drive home his point, he read from a lecture by Yogi Bhajan, saying, "The Siri Singh Sahib says we must be prepared physically, mentally, spiritually, economically, psychologically, intellectually, and socially before having a child."

The more he talked, the more I heard his subtext: We would never be prepared enough to have children. The ridiculous list was unattainable. The fact that he was fighting with me over having a family was hard to bear, but we had never discussed having children, until now.

The abortion with Michael took an emotional toll on me. It wasn't something I wanted to experience again. It saddened me that my feelings and desires had no impact on my husband. What's more, it was becoming clear that if we disagreed on important topics, his viewpoint would be the one we honored. He tried to reassure me there was nothing wrong with having an abortion because Yogi Bhajan said the child's soul did not enter the womb until the 120th day of pregnancy.

Reluctantly and with a heavy heart, I resigned myself to his unwavering position. When the day for the procedure came, I was inconsolable. Kirtan Singh went with me and afterward he lovingly massaged my feet for two hours while I slept. When I woke up he had made me a masala that Yogi Bhajan recommended for women's health. A deep sadness lingered in my heart, but I felt Kirtan Singh's relief that the ordeal was over.

At Christmastime, I couldn't wait to be with my family. We gathered at my mom's for Christmas dinner—our big and boisterous family. We played charades and spoons, laughing and entertaining ourselves for hours.

Kris's boyfriend, Vince, fit right in. He was naturally theatrical, with a charming, funny personality. Through their shared Italian heritage and love of theater, Kirtan Singh and Vince got along well and provided great entertainment for the family as they riffed spontaneously while we played.

Midway through opening gifts, Vince announced he had a special present for Kirtan Singh. He handed the gift to him with a flourish, indicating he wanted us all to pay attention.

Kirtan Singh opened it, lifting a white t-shirt out of the box. Only Kirtan Singh could see the front and he had an odd look on his face. He turned the shirt around so we could see the lettering that read:

FUCK OFF IF YOU
DON'T LIKE MY TURBAN

We all howled with laughter, except Kirtan Singh, who was struggling with how to respond. Vince found a way to inject humor into the awkwardness around the big changes in my life.

Vince asked us if we were planning to have children, saying, "When you do, I sure hope you have a boy!"

"Why?" I asked.

"Well," he twinkled, "then you can name him Rod."

"Why Rod?" I responded. "That's not a Sikh name."

Vince grinned, ready for his punchline, "Because… then you can call him Kirtan Rod!"

We were all laughing again—except for Kirtan Singh. The irreverence was too much for him to find it amusing.

Not quite making the grade.

20
cucarachas everywhere

Sadhana continued to be the bane of my ashram experience, as I knew it would be. When the alarm went off at 3:30 a.m. I usually ignored it. Understandably, Kirtan Singh was frustrated and intolerant of my lax attitude, especially since I was aware of this requirement prior to moving in. My battle with sadhana made me a walking contradiction—I was fighting against the lifestyle I had agreed to.

Each morning began with him insisting I live up to the lifestyle I signed up for. I knew I was disappointing him, but my body was in full revolt. I could offer no rebuttal to his strenuous complaints.

One winter morning, he was so miffed he threw cold water on me while I was sleeping. Another incident occurred one night after I'd gone to the main house to use the bathroom, which I hated doing because it was freezing outside. It was close to sadhana time so Kirtan Singh locked me out of our bedroom to force me to stay up. I stood in the yard, shivering in my pajamas, screaming at him to open the door. His tactics enraged me. I picked up a huge boulder and threw it at the window, shattering it, then crawled through the broken window and went back to bed, sliding deep beneath the covers to avoid the frigid air now flowing into the room.

Other than his intense approach to yoga, I hadn't seen this side of him prior to our wedding day. But once we married, Kirtan Singh became a watchdog of my behavior, which I interpreted as his desire to control me. We were fighting more and more over his complaints about my deficiencies as a wife.

One day I happened to overhear him venting about me to the Didars. It was painful to hear him describing me as lazy, uncommitted, and lacking in devotion. After badmouthing me, Kirtan Singh went into the sadhana room to play guitar and chant. The dichotomy between his negative rant about me followed by pious chanting made my blood boil. I went in to confront him. His eyes were closed, so when I grabbed the guitar it gave him a start. I called him a phony and accused him of acting "holier than thou" after disparaging me to the Didars.

Without a word he reached out one hand, grabbed my glasses off my face, and crushed them. He knew my vision was terrible and that I could not drive a car or work without my glasses or contact lenses.

My temper flared. I saw a *kirpan* (a dagger) on the bookshelf and grabbed it. Kirtan Singh's eyes widened. He took off running and I chased him, cursing all the while as we tore through the huge front yard. His turban came loose and hit the ground leaving his long hair flowing behind him. Unable to catch him, I ran until I was out of breath. As I bent forward, gasping for air, I couldn't remember a time when I felt so enraged. I was out of control, no different than my father. Kirtan Singh's treatment of me made me feel violent.

Didar Singh witnessed my actions and intervened. This was the first time I ever saw him upset. He made it clear that my behavior was unacceptable and would not be tolerated. Any more violent outbursts and I would have to leave the ashram.

I apologized, feeling ashamed of losing my cool like that. He strongly suggested I meditate more to find some inner calm.

Feelings were disapproved of in the ashram. In fact, Yogi Bhajan made up a catchy alliteration to make clear his beliefs on the subject, "Emotional is commotional, be devotional." Kirtan Singh repeated this to me often, but I was at a loss as to what it meant for me, because I am, by nature, an effusive person.

Fearing that I would be thrown out (once again) from my new home, I did my best to comply, stuffing my feelings and editing my responses so that I appeared to fit in. It didn't work, of course. I became more pent up—a proverbial ticking time bomb.

Things crescendoed three months into our marriage when Kirtan Singh charged into our bedroom and declared, "Kirtan Kaur, I want a divorce. You are not living up to your agreement as a Khalsa woman."

"Wow," I shot back, "I didn't know our wedding vows were so conditional."

"I mean it," he said. "I'm done."

He walked out of the room and I fell apart on the bed.

Honestly, I should not have been surprised. His proposal to me was as dry as the parched soil of the Nevada desert. Our marriage was transactional. It revolved around living the teachings of Yogi Bhajan and nothing more. I was fooling myself to think otherwise. We were at cross-purposes: I wanted to be in love, to enjoy our lives and our community, while he was dead serious about the teachings and wanted nothing more than to exemplify them perfectly.

Not wanting to fail or face being homeless, I pleaded with him to reconsider. He was unwavering: Our marriage was a mistake. We should just admit it and divorce.

Desperate to change his mind, I talked with Didar Singh,

who, while sympathetic toward me, understood and agreed with Kirtan Singh's point of view. After giving it some thought, Didar said there might be a way to turn things around. He told me if a person was really struggling, it was sometimes possible for them to go to Los Angeles for a forty-day sadhana. In this arrangement, I'd be under the supervision of a teacher who would decide a corrective course of action for me and monitor my progress.

It was radical, but maybe going to Los Angeles would change me, maybe I could train myself to do sadhana. If so, most of the tension and fighting between us would stop. Maybe I could save our marriage. Didar gave me the phone number of The Secretariat, the headquarters in Los Angeles, and I called to learn more about this kind of arrangement. A secretary put me on hold after telling me I would need to speak with Mukhia Sardarni Sahiba Krishna Kaur, the secretary who had come to Reno who ran the regional office there.

Her lengthy name was the result of her status as a top minister in the organization. When Krishna picked up the line, her commanding voice intimidated me. I told her what was going on and asked if I could come to Los Angeles to improve myself. Krishna told me she was not convinced I would be worth her time or effort. Challenging me repeatedly, she drew attention to the shortcomings which produced the situation I was in. She asked why she should take a risk on me. Feeling I had no choice but to get help if I wanted to save my marriage, I assured her I'd do anything she asked of me.

Finally she relented and said she'd be in touch. She stressed this was not going to be a vacation and that a great deal would be required of me. When I told Kirtan Singh of my plan he responded pessimistically, expressing little confidence that I could change.

This was my first time going to Los Angeles. I had been on a plane once, nine years before, when I flew to Washington to attend Camp Field. The date of my departure was set, my mother booked my flight and I was on my way.

I was picked up at LAX and driven to the ashram (formally referred to as Guru Ram Das Ashram) on Preuss Road. Krishna's office was across the street and a secretary informed me that I would be employed there for the duration of my stay. I received brief instructions on phone protocols, how to use the copy machine, and was put to work.

As the day went on I grew hungry and tired. No one offered me lunch and I had no idea when Krishna would arrive. By the time the others left to go home, the reality of not having any control over my life sank in. I was now in Krishna's charge. I laid on the floor and dropped off into a hard, fast sleep.

Krishna showed up around eight o'clock waking me with her strong voice, "Get up, Kirtan Kaur, we're heading out now."

Scrambling to my feet, I obeyed, following her as she handed me things to carry.

Krishna was the head of the Broadway ashram in Watts, about half an hour away from Preuss Road. The further east we drove, the more Los Angeles looked dirty and derelict. An urge to go home gripped me.

As she drove Krishna laid down the rules: In addition to working at the regional office, I was to be her personal assistant and fulfill any task or requirement that she set forth. This included cleaning, cooking, and ironing, running personal errands, and giving her massages late at night.

Additionally, I was required to complete a perfect forty-day sadhana. This meant getting up with her at three o'clock to take my cold shower, dress and to be ready to drive to the yoga studio precisely at 3:25 a.m. Should I falter and sleep a*t all* during the two and a half hours of sadhana, my forty-day count would reset, with no exceptions. Swallowing hard did not remove the huge lump that had formed in my throat.

When we arrived at the ashram, Krishna cautioned me that the neighborhood was unsafe. The huge house was home to more than a dozen students including Krishna and me. Her bedroom was on the third floor and my room was a little cubby space adjacent to hers with no door for privacy.

A bedroll mattress about three inches thick was placed on the linoleum floor, so I opened my sleeping bag on top of it. There was no dresser, no furniture at all, so I placed my suitcase next to the bed. Krishna said the bathroom was down the hall as she handed me bath towels and a washcloth. I could do laundry on Sundays.

With that she excused herself and I stood motionless taking in my new living space. This attic room had a low ceiling and was dimly lit. It felt dank and the house had a musty smell that I suspected emanated from decades of wet floorboards. Compared to the crisp Nevada air I was accustomed to, this air was sticky and heavy on my skin.

Putting on my nightgown, I was glad to be alone. As I got into my sleeping bag, three large cockroaches scurried across the floor. I'd never seen a cockroach before except on TV in bug spray commercials. Suppressing a scream, this development unraveled me completely. Was I really expected to sleep on the floor with the roaches with no protection to keep them from crawling on me as I slept? I hurried into my sleeping bag and tightened the mummy sack, pulling the drawstring as much as I could to seal myself in the bag. Using my jacket as a pillow, I cried myself to sleep.

It seemed like a few minutes passed before Krishna was shaking me awake. And so began my routine for the duration of my stay. Krishna watched me like a hawk and if I seemed to be drowsy during sadhana, she would smack me on the head or I'd feel the heel of her foot in my low back, jolting me to stay awake.

The next day I walked to 7-Eleven on my lunch break to purchase a couple of cans of bug spray. Each night I sprayed the perimeter of my bed making sure not to miss any spots as I soaked the floor with insecticide. Each morning I woke to find anywhere from three to ten dead roaches that croaked at the poison line. After a while I got used to falling asleep in a cloud of chemicals.

My duties grew more and more with each passing day. Never had I worked so hard or had so much been demanded of me.

One Saturday we planned an ashram party at the beach. I was excited to see the ocean. As we were getting ready to leave, Krishna stopped me in the foyer and handed me a box of razor blades. "You're not going to the beach," she informed me. Instead I was told to scrape all the recent paint splatter off the hardwood floors that sloppy painters left behind. I hid my disappointment and spent the day alone reminding myself that I was there to save my marriage. Krishna had warned me that my time with her would not be easy, though some of the hardships she threw my way seemed unnecessary and excessive.

One thing was for sure, this was an unending marathon of sleep deprivation. Not a thirty-six hour marathon like the one at Omega House—this was a daily deficit that accumulated into chronic exhaustion.

Being with this large community served as a crash course in all aspects of 3HO. Yogi Bhajan taught that he was a Saturn teacher. It was explained to me that astrologically, Saturn, the ruling planet of Capricorn, is called "the sign of the father." Saturn teachers were direct, tough-love teachers—confrontational both in language and manner.

When I told a few people that I saw him strike a student at Ladies Camp, they nodded knowingly, saying this was an example of his teaching style. They said his actions, though outrageous, were beyond our understanding because he was working with people on karmic levels that we did not have access to.

Krishna's tough-love demeanor toward me was painfully reminiscent of Omega House and it was difficult to once again be subjected to this harsh approach.

Once a week, Krishna and I stayed in town to attend Yogi Bhajan's evening lecture. Still struggling to understand his accent, I often dozed off while he spoke. At one lecture, Yogi Bhajan talked about survival training, saying we needed to prepare for the possibility of atomic war. Fears about nuclear war were accelerating. The recent Three Mile Island partial nuclear meltdown in Pennsylvania in the spring of 1979 caused alarm about the safety of nuclear reactors in the United States. Yogi Bhajan's response was something he called *Jai Taygang;* it was his plan for surviving a world crisis.

As a result, we were instructed to fast on wheatberries one day a week to prepare our bodies for eating a diet of only this food. Our morning schedule changed as well. Sadhana now consisted of marching in the streets of Watts while carrying rifles. We learned to keep cadence while chanting. Being outside in the middle of the night in Los Angeles was frightening. Helicopters with searchlights flew low overhead like the ones I'd seen on the news in Vietnam. They scanned our neighborhood, while across the street from the ashram, women turned tricks and argued with their Johns.

The survival program fizzled out after a few weeks. I never heard why. By then I had made it to the thirty-ninth day of my forty-day sadhana. I was proud of myself and knew I'd be going home soon.

However, on day thirty-nine, fatigue got the better of me and I dozed off for several minutes toward the end of sadhana. The woman sitting next to me gave me a gentle nudge to wake me. When I realized I had passed out, fear gripped me and I sat up straight hoping Krishna hadn't noticed. Sadhana ended and no one congratulated me on completing forty days.

Krishna waited until I was opening her car door to announce, "Kirtan Kaur, tomorrow you begin again on day one."

She may as well have body slammed me to the pavement. I wanted to throttle her for dismissing forty days of sadhana over a few mere minutes. It was ridiculously unfair, but it was also exactly what she said she would do.

While we had breakfast and got ready for work I was fuming inside. I purposely dragged my feet, lagging behind until I told Krishna I felt unwell and couldn't work. She raised an eyebrow but said nothing and left without me. I swept the morning's dead roaches into the corner of my room and went back to bed.

The stress from the horrible living conditions, sleep deprivation, and unending workload pushed me to the brink. The whiplash change from believing I was about to go home to starting over was harsh. I wanted to leave.

That morning I called my mother and relayed how untenable the situation was. When I asked her to book me a flight home, she refused, saying, "You are a married woman now, honey, and this is something you should discuss with your husband."

"What?" I exclaimed, my voice escalating rapidly. "Mom, I am your daughter and I am telling you I need to get out of here today! You have no idea what I am going through."

She reiterated that I was a married woman, adding she didn't feel it was her place to interfere. I became unglued, screaming at her to buy me a ticket. Nothing I said mattered.

"Thanks for nothing, mom!" I yelled and hung up on her.

Just like when I tried to come home after running away from Omega House, I felt wholly betrayed by my mother. I wondered if she had been warned that I might call. Kirtan Singh may have anticipated this moment of desperation.

Taking a deep breath, I composed myself to call my husband. I didn't want to sound upset when I spoke to him, because neutrality was valued above all else—any kind of emotion would cause him to invalidate anything I said.

Kirtan Singh eagerly told me he was on yet another Yogi Bhajan mono-diet. This time he was restricted to forty days of eating nothing but bananas. He was on his twenty-first day, and clearly, he was losing it.

He was fixated on talking about food and the impact of the fast. The man was obsessed with cravings, the foods he longed for and desperately wanted to eat. Specifically, he went into surprising detail about the creamy peanut butter he craved, the incredibly realistic food dreams he was having and how he woke up in a cold sweat, not sure whether he had really eaten or dreamed it.

He had developed a gag reflex each time he put a banana in his mouth he was so repulsed by them and his bowel movements had stopped after three weeks of loading up on nothing but bananas. Finally, he asked me why I was calling. I told him what had happened on the 39th day of my sadhana practice and let him know I wanted to come home. Kirtan Singh coldly replied,

"You will come home when Krishna Kaur and I determine that you are ready to come home."

He spoke to me like I was a child. Obviously, he was already aware that I had dozed off because he and Krishna were regularly conferring. A sinking feeling came over me. I felt trapped like a mental patient that had been committed.

Before slamming the phone down, I told him I hoped he would choke on a goddamn banana.

I went back to bed and bawled my eyes out. Neither my mother nor my husband would help me. How I regretted instigating all of this. It didn't take long before resignation set in. I would have to complete the perfect forty-day sadhana in order to get back home.

Hearing footsteps climbing the stairs, the ashram housemother banged on Krishna's bedroom door, calling my name. Hoping my mother had rallied to my cause, I went to the door.

"You have an urgent call," she said.

Racing downstairs, I grabbed the phone, eagerly saying, "Yes? Mom? Is this you?"

There was a pause, then I heard Krishna's voice, "No, sorry. Not mom. Since you missed your ride you will take the city bus to work today. The housemother will tell you where to catch it. Be here by noon."

She hung up before I could speak. I stood there, stunned, as I was handed a piece of paper with directions to a bus stop a few blocks away. The housemother warned me, "You best get a move on or you won't get there on time."

I'd never used public transit in my life. Not in my little town, not in a big city, and certainly not in a high crime neighborhood. I knew I couldn't refuse, so I showered, dressed and made my way to the bus stop.

Walking through Watts, I had never been so aware of the color of my skin. As I walked, my sheltered life in a white bubble was unmistakable. My grade school and Manogue each had one black student. The fact that I was wearing a white costume with a headdress that made me look like a card-carrying Ku Klux Klan member was painfully awkward.

Stepping onto the bus I locked my gaze onto the floor rather than meet the stares of others. I could not have been more self-conscious. Once we got moving, I looked out the window watching for my stop: La Cienega Blvd.

More than an hour passed, stop after stop went by, and I began to panic. Sweat was forming on my forehead and my heart was racing as I kept a vigil on the street signs. When we began to roll away from our latest stop, I spotted the La Cienega street sign and screamed, "Stop the bus!"

The driver kindly obliged and I rushed onto the street holding another paper with instructions on how to get to the regional office. It was a half-mile walk but it felt like it took forever. When I arrived, I was strung out, drained from the stress of the morning. Still, I made it. Krishna would be glad.

She wasn't. As soon as I arrived I was called into her office. Instead of a friendly welcome, I got dressed down. She called me a spoiled brat and a whiner. She said I was lucky she had taken me on and that the time had come to quit sniveling and show some gratitude. Then she looked at me with dogged eyes and said, "I suggest you get on board, Kirtan Kaur, if you ever want to go home again."

Her message came through. I dug in for the duration, whatever that would be.

Incredibly, I achieved another thirty-nine days of a perfect sadhana and again briefly dozed off during my fortieth sadhana and started over for the third time. At this point I'd been in Los Angeles for eleven weeks. This time I didn't rebel. I kept my mouth shut and began again.

Eventually, I began to enjoy living in Los Angeles despite the hardships of living under Krishna's thumb. The city felt alive with its own unique momentum. It had a dynamism and energy that crackled in the air. I loved the warm weather, the palm trees and the openmindedness of nearly everyone I met. This larger 3HO community had solidarity and purpose and I felt proud to be a part of it.

Many of Yogi Bhajan's longtime followers lived there. The community was rich with creative, magnetic individuals, and amazing musicians. They were the celebrities of the community, the ones who started it all.

It was much easier living this lifestyle among a large group of people. It normalized what we were doing, as we had strength in numbers. I was making new friends with people who welcomed me warmly. This camaraderie would be hard to leave when the time came to return to our tiny outpost ashram.

Reno was largely unwelcoming to our alternative lifestyle. Shortly before I left, I was driven off the road by a cowboy in a truck who saw my turban after we both drove past a billboard designed to get Americans to conserve oil. Based on the 1973 OPEC oil embargo and the Iran hostage crisis, it featured Ayatollah Khomeini with the message GET REVENGE, DRIVE 55.

"Go back to Iran, towelhead!" he shouted out the window as his truck swerved toward me. It was difficult to deal with the ignorance of people like him.

Halfway into my third attempt, Kirtan Singh called to let me know that he and the Didars were coming to Los Angeles in April for the springtime Sikh holiday, *Baisakhi*, and a tantric course.

During our phone call my mood careened from excited anticipation to irritation. He couldn't stop gushing about Krishna and their phone calls discussing my progress. It was all the more off-putting because I sensed that he was infatuated with her. When I hung up, I wasn't sure I wanted to see him at all.

The regional office was busy with all manner of preparations for the Baisakhi weekend. The Reno ashram members arrived Friday afternoon just in time for the first evening of tantric yoga. It was awkward seeing Kirtan Singh again. He had lost weight on his banana fast and looked thin and strained. It was weird how much he felt like a stranger to me, but in his presence, I could feel how much being away had changed me.

For one thing, my appearance had significantly improved. I had new clothing, generously donated by women who could see I didn't have much in the way of bana and I tied my turban now with more expertise. This increased my esteem and identity in the organization.

The biggest change was my consistent sadhana practice, though one could argue my adherence was more forced out of fear and my desire to return home, making it a performative rather than genuine practice.

Personally, what I had gained most was an understanding and knowledge about the Sikh faith. My proudest achievement was learning to read Gurmukhi, which allowed me to read from the Sikh holy book and to recite the five daily prayers of the Sikhs. Through my studies I realized that Sikhism, in fact, had nothing to do with Yogi Bhajan; it preceded him by 500 years. This was important to me because it provided me with a sense of involvement in the community that was independent of him.

Ironically, my problematic attitude toward Yogi Bhajan had improved somewhat as well. As I heard stories of other people's interactions with him, it was clear that they all accepted his erratic, temperamental nature as part of being a Saturn teacher. This group mindset affected my view of him, though I still didn't look to him as a spiritual teacher the way Kirtan Singh did.

This time at tantric yoga, I was flawless. I held each position to perfection, practically daring Kirtan Singh to falter. He had not met this version of me. When he learned that I could read Gurmukhi, a subtle power shift took place in our marriage. The fact that I had surpassed him in knowledge and skill was beneficial to our relationship.

I wanted to go home. I missed my family and wanted to be out of Krishna Kaur's clutches. In my estimation, she had exploited my situation for her personal gain.

Kirtan Singh was staying at an ashram in West Los Angeles while I was still at the Broadway ashram. On Sunday morning, I discreetly packed my things and tucked them behind my seat before Krishna and I left. It was the last day of the tantric course. Krishna told Kirtan Singh and I to meet her afterward at the regional office.

When we arrived, Kirtan Singh puffed himself up and addressed me, saying, "Krishna Kaur and I feel it is not yet time for you to come home. There is still more work for you to do, especially because you haven't completed a perfect forty-day sadhana."

The condescension in his voice was unmistakable. Neither one of them had anything positive to say to me. I knew what I had accomplished and how I had persevered through every challenge Krishna had thrown at me. At this point I had over 100 days of sadhana under my belt with maybe six minutes of snoozing. As far as I was concerned, I had succeeded brilliantly.

Krishna said nothing, watching for my response.

"That's nice," I said sarcastically. "But, I don't care what either of you think because I am going home today."

Keeping my temper in check, I picked up my suitcase from behind my desk and went out the door to where the Didars were waiting.

Kirtan Singh did not come out right away and I wished I could hear what he and Krishna were saying.

Krishna and I said no goodbyes. If I had spoken at all it would have been in anger. She had put me through her gauntlet, excessively at times, and never offered me any kind of praise or acknowledgement. It was unfortunate to leave Los Angeles under her disapproving gaze. This, combined with my husband's arrogance, was extremely aggravating.

Kirtan Singh was fuming when he got in the car. The tension between us was thick. After three days together I was sick of him. Watching him suck up to Krishna, when he was clueless as to how I had been living, felt like a betrayal. Worse yet, I was going home under what he would consider a cloud of failure because I disobeyed her recommendation to stay.

The drive back to Reno was long and mostly silent. Every fiber of my being wanted to rebel and so my first morning back I skipped sadhana. I could have gotten up, but after months of little sleep, I was exhausted. In the spirit of retaliation, staying in bed was an effective way to say "fuck you" to Kirtan Singh.

Because of my newfound knowledge and skills, Kirtan Singh got off my back about sadhana. What started out as a means to strengthen our marriage created a chasm between us that would take time to mend. Even though I was inconsistent with sadhana, Kirtan Singh never brought up divorce again. We reconciled without discussing the matter and carried on with our lives, eventually finding moments of togetherness in our shared religious beliefs.

One of my two years at Khalsa Children's Camp in New Mexico.

21

suffer the little children

When Yogi Bhajan received close to one million dollars from the inheritance of one of his young female students, it caused some turbulence in the community. Her mother fought her inheritance in the courts, petitioning the court to declare her daughter insane. She claimed her daughter had undergone a drastic personality change under the influence of Yogi Bhajan because she was in a cult. Yogi Bhajan sent the woman to India for the better part of a year, essentially to hide, until her mother gave up the fight.

Subsequently, he used a portion of his windfall to purchase 160 acres of land in the Jemez mountains near Española, New Mexico. This land would serve as the gathering ground for what became the annual Summer Solstice celebration. He named the land Ram Das Puri. At an elevation of 9000 feet, one could expect wide temperature swings with cold nights and early mornings followed by hot, sunny days. Monsoon season was more intense at higher altitudes as well, with rapid, but short-lived, downpours a near daily occurrence.

It had been eight weeks since my return from Los Angeles and money was tight. My original forty-day stay had extended to three months and though I worked full time at the regional office, I wasn't paid. As a result, going to Women's Camp was not in our budget, but Kirtan Singh and I would both attend Summer Solstice.

We found out there were opportunities available to work as counselors at the Khalsa Children's Camp, which would provide a means for me to still be away for the summer. Kirtan Singh had recently graduated from UNR with his Bachelor of Fine Arts degree and unexpectedly decided he wanted to spend the summer in New Mexico as well. We applied and were hired to be camp counselors despite neither one of us having prior experience working with children.

Each of us would be paid $900 for the four-week camp with meals included. Counselors were responsible for four to five children. The job was demanding—we would be on duty twenty-four hours a day, six days a week. We thought the pay was generous, but, in fact, it worked out to be a measly buck and a half an hour.

Once again I took the long drive to New Mexico. Road-tripping with Kirtan Singh was easier and more pleasant as he did most of the driving. I was filled with anticipation about experiencing my first Summer Solstice.

Toward the end of the trip, after we left Albuquerque, I had to pee, so Kirtan Singh pulled to the side of the road. As fate would have it, I lost my wedding ring in this nondescript potty spot. I'd taken it off earlier in the day because my hands were swollen, no doubt from eating salty sunflower seeds. It was in my lap when I exited the car. When we got back on the road, it wasn't long before I discovered it missing and we exited the highway to backtrack. With miles of road to search, it was hopeless. We gave up after about thirty minutes.

That weird feeling of yet another bad omen washed over me.

Kirtan Singh said the first thing he wanted to do when we

arrived at Ram Das Puri was to kiss the ground. As soon as the car was in park, the doors flew open and we both were on our knees doing just that. We hoped the summer would be a blessing.

Yogi Bhajan claimed if you stuck a pin through a globe starting at Ram Das Puri it would pop out the other side in Amritsar, India at the location of *Harimandir Sahib*-the Golden Temple.

This was a story he told to emphasize the sacredness of the land. Perhaps he was taking poetic license, but he was wrong. Ram Das Puri's latitude is north of the venerated temple. Regardless, to us it felt like hallowed ground.

The site hosted an industrial-sized open shelter on a concrete pad which provided shade and some relief from the elements. Most attendees camped on the periphery of the shelter where sadhana and other activities were held. Some of the more privileged fat cats (old timers) stayed in trailers on the property.

Slowly but surely, performance pressure from Kirtan Singh resurfaced in our marriage. With hundreds of people getting up for sadhana at the event, I felt like I couldn't miss it. At precisely 3:30 a.m., a scrawny man named Guru Singh walked through the encampment strumming his guitar and singing to wake us for our morning ritual.

A rudimentary communal shower was constructed with corrugated aluminum walls and dozens of plastic, orange backyard sprinklers attached to two-by-fours that substituted for shower heads. The sprinkler attachment produced a sharp stream of icy mountain water that made cold showers even more unpleasant than usual. The ground was covered in small pebbles.

Showering together with other women, all rubbing themselves down with almond oil and chanting was yet another unusual aspect of life in 3HO that added fiber to the weft of our shared purpose.

Out of modesty, I packed some of Kirtan Singh's cotton briefs to wear during cold showers. They were thicker in the front than women's panties and mitigated the shock of cold water hitting my nether regions. My appearance in his underwear garnered a few laughs and raised a few eyebrows.

After showering, we climbed the small incline to the shelter for sadhana. My favorite part was when we chanted together. The exquisite sound of a thousand voices in unison created blissful moments of utopia for me, generating cascades of electricity that ran up and down my spine. I even forgot momentarily that I was chilled to the marrow. I shivered through sadhana until the sun came out to warm me.

We had three days of White Tantric yoga, which I still had not taken to. Yogi Bhajan's explanation of how it was supposed to work was still far-fetched to me, plus I never had the stupendous results I heard others claim. It was supposed to clear out your subconscious, but because the subconscious (by its defined nature) is not something a human can ever be consciously aware of, how would you know if it worked or not?

It seemed similar to the rote teachings of Catholicism that I was raised with. We were supposed to believe because we were told to. The same was true for me with regards to kundalini yoga, especially because I'd injured my back doing it more than once. My focus remained on the Sikh faith and the community of like-minded people I was sharing my life with.

The solstice diet was spare. We ate mostly broth made with cayenne and potatoes along with a quarter head of iceberg lettuce and a few oranges. We were encouraged to drink gobs of water to avoid dehydration.

In the evenings we had entertainment on the stage under the shelter. With music, dance, and hilarious skits, it was my favorite time of day because it was relaxed and fun. We could cut loose a bit and enjoy one another. It was during these evenings that I discovered I was in a group of highly talented people. I loved listening to the live renditions of music we listened to at the Golden Temple restaurant.

Groups with names like The Khalsa String Band and The Adi Shakti Choir performed at length, uniting us with their songs and voices. I was often moved to tears listening to them. The music that they created became the backbone of my life, the ever-present soundtrack that informed my experiences and wedded me ever deeper to our shared vision of a life of godliness and service.

On Sunday afternoon it seemed everyone washed their hair at the same time. For a few magical hours I felt transported back in time to images I'd seen of the Woodstock Festival. The sight of so many beautiful people of all ages walking about with their long flowing hair was incredible. This gathering, being together in this way, made me fall in love with who we were and strengthened my commitment to the life I had chosen.

The ten days of Solstice flew by. Jiwan Jot, the director of Children's Camp, scheduled an orientation meeting before Solstice ended to familiarize the new crew with the running of the camp. When we applied, we were given the opportunity to request the age and gender of children we'd like to care for. Both of us selected boys. I wanted four-year-old boys specifically. I'd always loved that age when kids are starting to become independent but still remain cuddly.

Encampments were set up by age and gender. The four-year-old encampment consisted of three tents arranged in a semi-circle up a small hill not far from the shelter.

On the first day of camp, I waited at my tent for the boys to be dropped off. Some of the children were terribly upset about having to attend, and who could blame them? I was a complete stranger. I noticed that two of the boys (both from large ashrams) seemed accustomed to this kind of hand-off, but the others pleaded with their parents to take them home amid lots of tears. As the parents retreated, I did my best to comfort them.

My tent had four boys. Jiwan Jot came by to tell me one of the boys (let's call him Dev) had some behavioral issues and pointed him out, but she didn't share any other details about what that meant. She said she was available if I needed extra support.

The head of the Española ashram (and top minister), Mukhia Singh Sahib Wha Guru Singh, also came to see me because his son was assigned to my tent. Known for his intense personality, he reminded me of Yul Brenner in *The Ten Commandments*. He was checking me out while also making me aware of his expectations regarding his son's care. I found him intimidating. He had a self-important air, a characteristic he had in common with other top ministers I had met. Listening intently, I assured him I would do my best with his son.

Children were expected to get up at sunrise for a short version of sadhana starting with a cold shower. Cold showers were achieved by throwing a five-gallon bucket of cold water on each child while encouraging them to chant wahe guru.

I struggled with this. They were four years old. It was brutal. More than that, it was borderline torture. Seeing them shiver and wince and cry each morning really got to me.

Trying to think of a reward for them to perhaps make it less painful, I found someone who was going to Española and had them pick up a couple of bottles of *Flintstones* chewable vitamins. I couldn't believe how well it worked—you would have thought I was giving them chocolate sundaes. They were over the moon to get a chewable vitamin and bravely braced for the cold water to hit their skin. I hated doing the showers, but with my husband's tent next to mine, he would have called me out if I didn't uphold the expected routine.

Next the kids ate breakfast and went to classes. Their days were filled with learning Yogi Bhajan's teachings and hearing historical stories of Sikhism. They enjoyed activities like swimming and archery classes, along with short hikes on the property.

It didn't take long before I was overwhelmed with the demands of caring for so many children at once. The relentless twenty-four hour, six-day work week was incredibly taxing.

Still, my struggles were nothing compared to the homesick children I was looking after. My boys cried at night for their mothers and I ached for them. How could this be a good thing, I wondered, for children this young to be separated for so long from their parents?

One day I made the connection that this was also the schedule for the counselors at Omega House. I'd never thought about how demanding that must've been for them, made even more so because they were dealing with troubled teenagers.

Dev, the little boy who had been labeled difficult, was bold in expressing his dissatisfaction. Labeling him seemed unfair to me, but he was strong-willed and sometimes uncooperative.

I saw in him a younger version of myself at Omega House. How well I knew the feeling of being placed somewhere I did not want to be. All I felt I could offer the boys was lots of affection and moments in the day where they had fun. But regardless, when the sun went down, the mood changed to sadness.

Despite my ability to relate to their circumstances, my patience ran thin as I struggled to keep up with the demands of non-stop childcare. Halfway through the session, I was exhausted and irritable, wishing the whole thing was over.

One afternoon we were getting ready for an activity but Dev did not want to go. I told him he had no choice because we all had to stay together. We went back and forth but he would not listen to me. As it was, we were going to be late. I told him if he didn't cooperate, the consequence would be a time-out in the tent. My threat had no impact and so a time-out was enforced.

It had rained and there was mud everywhere. He promptly unzipped the tent and jumped off the platform into the muck, hollering at me that he wasn't going with us. Exasperated, I put him back in, repeating that he was in a time-out and had to stay in the tent for five minutes. Dev defiantly came out again.

It occurred to me to try a technique I learned the year before at Ladies Camp, something Yogi Bhajan called *bundling*. He recommended it for when a child was having a tantrum, saying it contained them, making them feel safe, which thereby had a calming effect on the child. It was usually done with a blanket, but it was much too hot for that. I improvised, taking some rope from my trunk to wrap around his torso, arms, and legs.

In hindsight, it was idiotic to think that roping a child would feel anything like being wrapped in a blanket, but I was alone with the boys and desperate for a solution that would give me a moment of peace.

I left him in the tent, lying on his back. He was silent so I thought maybe it was working. When five minutes passed, I yelled to Dev, "Okay, your time-out is finished," and unzipped the tent.

Dev had freed himself from the rope, taken a shit in the tent, and smeared his feces all over my trunk, sleeping bag and cot.

"Are you kidding me?" I screamed, before grabbing him by the arm. I yanked him out of the tent and off the platform. Buckets of water were lined up along the platform, ready for the next morning's showers. I took one and poured it over Dev as he sat in the mud.

"Clean yourself up, you're covered in shit!" I yelled.

I went into the tent to figure out how to clean up the mess. Kirtan Singh had been walking up to the tents and saw what I had done. In a flash, he was on me. He grabbed me and threw me off the platform. I fell on the ground near Dev, who was wet and crying. Kirtan Singh dumped a bucket of water over my head, then threw the bucket at me. It hit me hard and caused a deep gash on the top of my right hand. He collected my boys and stormed down the hill with them, saying he was reporting me to Jiwan Jot.

Feeling humiliated and ashamed, I sat in the mud, crying. I was inept at this job and I had abused a child. Like the children, I wanted to go home.

Jiwan Jot was coming up the hill, calling my name. I scrambled to my feet to face her. "I'm so, so sorry," I cried. "I have no business being around children."

"Kirtan Kaur, didn't you come to me for help?" she asked, sounding exasperated.

"I don't know," I blubbered. "I didn't want to bother you."

She took my bleeding hand into hers saying, "Let's get this fixed up. Kirtan Singh is looking after your boys and someone has taken Dev to get washed."

I couldn't believe she wasn't yelling at me.

She took me to her trailer, which seemed like the height of luxury, and I sat in a cushioned chair while she bandaged my wound. She asked me what had happened and I tearfully told her the difficulties I was having and my lack of ability to handle the circumstances. She asked me if there was violence in my childhood home. I guess that much was obvious.

Her voice was kind and caring as we spoke. While she did not approve of what I had done, I never felt judged. She said someone was cleaning up the tent and providing me with a sleeping bag while mine was sent to the cleaners. She offered me ways to deal with feeling overwhelmed and made sure a couple of other counselors were available at a moment's notice if I needed help.

When I saw Kirtan Singh later that night, I told him I didn't think I ever wanted to have children. Being at camp had shown me I wouldn't be any good at it.

I apologized sincerely to Dev, who like most children, forgave easily. Jiwan Jot suggested I practice empathy and kindness toward Dev for the duration of camp. He became my special focus. We didn't have any more difficulties together; in fact, we got along well and I enjoyed how gregarious and funny he was.

Because of this experience, I found myself reflecting on the way Bill and other counselors had treated me at Omega House and how I had never received any apology from them. It would have done me a world of good to hear them admit when they crossed the line, but none of them ever felt they went too far.

Returning to the ashram in Reno was harder than ever. The support of Jiwan Jot and the friendships I found at camp reinforced the importance of living among a larger sangat. Living in a tiny ashram had become unsatisfying.

As soon as we got home from Children's Camp, I told Kirtan Singh that I wanted us to move to southern California. He was not interested in living in a big city and told me he was fine with the way things were. For months I made my argument, citing the support and fellowship I had experienced in Los Angeles. This did not persuade him, but I discovered what did: proximity to Yogi Bhajan. This was an enticement he could not ignore.

Finally we began making plans to move the following year. In the meantime, Kirtan Singh said we had to lighten our load and raise money to make this happen.

We began selling everything we could. Regrettably, our self-absorption obscured the incredible insensitivity we demonstrated when we sold the beautiful oak bedroom set my mother and Kirtan Singh's family had given us as a wedding gift. My mom would still be paying on that loan for another two years *after* we sold it for eight hundred dollars. Kirtan Singh sold our Dodge Dart and bought a little Toyota hatchback called the Starlet. We would move with what could fit in our car.

In my efforts to pull together some funds, I sold an antique, sterling silver cuff bracelet given to me by my paternal grandmother, Lucille. This upsets my mother to this day, because according to her, I was the only grandchild Lucille ever gave anything of value to and I sold it for a mere fifty dollars.

Kirtan Singh's natural inclination toward an ascetic life rubbed off on me as I gave away the last bits of secular clothing that I possessed. I even threw away my Camp Field memorabilia, thinking I should let go of any remnants from my former life.

The hardest, most agonizing part of moving was leaving Grandpa. He was my favorite man in the whole world, someone who was always there for me and my siblings. At seventy-six years old, I was afraid he would die soon and I would regret leaving him.

We were heading to Los Angeles on a shoestring with no employment lined up and no set place to stay. On a quiet morning in August of 1981, we jammed what we could into the hatchback and slowly drove out of the ashram driveway. My tears began almost instantly. I was emotional for hours. As we drove further and further, it felt like my deep roots in Nevada were slowly ripping out of the ground.

As hard as it was to leave my family, I was now twenty-one years old. My life thus far had been in a bubble that extended from Milwaukee to Reno to Richland. Keen to experience more of the world, I exited the bubble of my childhood.

22

city of angels

With my hopes pinned on a better life in The City of Angels, surrounded by like-minded devotees, we arrived at the ashram on Preuss Road. There was always a guard posted out front, called a *sevadar.* He put us in touch with a woman named Satkirin Kaur who offered to put us up for a few nights. She and her family lived on Pickford Avenue, a stone's throw from the ashram, so close we could walk to sadhana.

We were expecting a spare room to sleep in, but instead Satkirin took us to see her tiny, empty kitchen nook. When we opened our sleeping bags they covered all the available floor space. At least we had our sheepskins to put underneath them for some cushioning against the hard linoleum floor.

It always seemed odd to me that Yogi Bhajan recommended sheepskins for practicing yoga because we were vegetarians. But, according to him, striking a yoga pose on a butchered animal's tanned pelt was doing the animal a favor. He claimed we were "burning the animal's karma." Some of his teachings were preposterous, but, nonetheless, accepted as truth by his followers simply because he said it. I made mental notes about such things, but kept my opinions to myself.

We unloaded our car, stuffing our belongings in the cupboards that flanked one wall. There was no door, just a thin curtain hung between the nook and the kitchen. We had no privacy and mealtimes were noisy. It was a humble beginning to our new life, but it was temporary until we found a more suitable place, or so I thought.

Days later Kirtan Singh negotiated for us to rent the nook at a rate of three hundred dollars a month. The price blew my mind. We could rent a two-bedroom house in Reno for that much money. It annoyed me when he made unilateral decisions that affected both of us, but what bothered me more was seeing how much Kirtan Singh reveled in meagerness.

We both applied and were hired as food servers at The Golden Temple Restaurant on Fairfax Avenue. Having one car, it made sense to work at the same location. The restaurant was popular and had a menu full of delicious offerings with familiar dishes we served at The Golden Temple in Reno.

One of Yogi Bhajan's sons was managing the restaurant, though it seemed he was largely unqualified. My time there was brief, because I discovered the restaurant had a serious rat problem and quit. These were terrifying rats on steroids, the biggest, ugliest rodents I'd ever seen. They grossed me out and killed any desire I had to eat there.

Luckily, I found a job close to home at the Golden Temple Health Food store on La Cienega Boulevard. I could walk to work, allowing Kirtan Singh to use our car. The store was owned by Siri Ved Singh, one of Yogi Bhajan's earliest followers. He had a boyish quality to him and somehow managed to be sweet and affable while rendering astutely sarcastic remarks to all he spoke to. His sardonic humor cracked me up. I liked him immediately and enjoyed the store's more mellow pace.

We lived in the nook for months while waiting for a vacancy in one of the nearby ashrams. Within the sangat, some people lived in ashrams, while others had their own homes or apartments. Kirtan Singh firmly believed ashram living was an essential component of the 3HO lifestyle.

The dress. Kirtan Singh bought seven of these so I had one for every day of the week.

We were gradually becoming acquainted with people in the community and I reconnected with people I knew from my stay there. I was happy to be back and loved feeling connected with other seekers on our spiritual path.

Initially, Kirtan Singh did not take to city life. Coming from a town with pristine air, we were suffering from terrible headaches due to the smog. The noise of traffic during the day and helicopters at night was an assault on the senses. Still, I found it thrilling to be in the midst of so much activity and stimulation.

Kirtan Singh was well known and loved in Reno. It was challenging for him to start over in a new place. He was now a little fish in a big pond.

After waiting for what seemed like an eternity, we got word that an opening was available at *Siri Gurbani Sadan*, (less formally, Siri Gurbani) an ashram on Preuss Road headed by Ram Das Singh and Kaur. We swiftly packed our things, psyched to vacate the nook. My excitement petered out, however, once I saw our new accommodations.

Siri Gurbani was a huge three-story house. The top floor had two bedrooms and a bathroom. The ground floor had another three bedrooms, bathroom, kitchen, and large living room. The lower level, accessed by the back door and down a flight of stairs, led to two dingy, makeshift rooms with poor insulation and thin, cheap carpet spread over cement. We were offered one of these rooms. The other was the single men's room.

A key characteristic of our room involved the ashram's neglected doberman pinscher named Lady. She lived in the backyard and was there strictly to function as a guard dog. All of her time was spent outside with absolutely no house privileges. The permeating backyard odor was a repulsive mixture of wet fur, urine, and dog crap.

My disappointment was quickly expressed in a stream of complaints. Kirtan Singh countered me, stating flatly that we should have an attitude of gratitude. Further, he informed me, he had already signed the lease, paid the deposit and first month's rent. Once again, he had not consulted me whatsoever before making this decision. This was becoming the norm. Puffing up his chest, he spouted that *he* was the husband, *he* was the man, and it was my job to support him.

This attitude went against the grain of my core beliefs of equality between the sexes, which had been informed heavily by *Ms.* magazine. Since the age of fifteen, I avidly subscribed to and read every page of every issue, cover to cover.

When Billie Jean King beat Bobby Riggs in *The Battle of the Sexes* tennis match in 1973, I was jumping up and down in our living room, hollering with delight. I supported the Equal Rights Amendment and considered myself an equal to any man, yet here I was, expected to play the role of an obedient wife. It was not a comfortable situation for me. Having to make internal adjustments to fit into this life, I continued to weigh the pros and cons of my spiritual path.

We moved into our scuzzy room while I carried a mile-wide chip on my shoulder toward both my husband and the ashram. I hated where we were living and was embarrassed by our state of affairs. I was in a bad mood about it for months.

That winter, nighttime temperatures were often in the forties. Reno was much colder, but somehow the humidity of Los Angeles was a game changer. It was surprisingly and bone-penetratingly cold. We had a small space heater, but no amount of blankets could get me warm. During those long nights we discovered we had a flea infestation as well, thanks to the poor, wretched dog.

Navigating the distance from our room up the stairs and to the back door was a perilous undertaking. Lady was starving for attention. The appearance of any human caused her to go bananas. As soon as she heard the door open, she would bound toward me. Jumping with glee, she'd push against me, no doubt trying to feel some kind of physical connection. In the process, my white clothes were completely sullied. I felt sorry for that dog and I hated that dog. Wrapping a beach towel around myself became routine as I rushed the dog gauntlet to get inside.

The ashram was also infested with cockroaches. When turning on the kitchen lights in the morning, dozens of them would scuttle across the kitchen counters to flee death. It was repulsive to think of cooking and eating in there, knowing they were crawling all over our dishes and utensils.

Bizarrely, no one else seemed to care at all about the roaches.

My whole body shuddered, remembering the bug spray line around my bedroll at the Watts ashram. I bought diatomaceous earth and lined the cupboards with it to get rid of them.

My motivation to attend sadhana increased—at least the ashram was warm and I hadn't seen any roaches or fleas there. Unlike most of my peers, I went to sadhana to sleep. Within thirty minutes of arriving, I would curl up on my sheepskin with my blanket. Sleeping at sadhana, however, was so not cool. Those who did were seen as weak and undisciplined. I felt the disapproving gaze of my fellow seekers as the lights went up, jolting me awake.

One particular morning I was in a deep and blissful slumber. When sadhana ended, we turned to face the other end of the room where the Sikh holy book was kept. As I hurried to rise and turn, I didn't notice my right leg was completely asleep. As I stood, my leg buckled and I fell flat on my face. Then an agony of prickles rushed through my leg as the blood started flowing again. Wincing in pain, I tried to seat myself quickly. With all eyes upon me, my embarrassment painted my face scarlet red. The pressure to keep up with the teachings was ever present and some people never failed to clock the deficiencies of others.

It didn't take long to realize that in spite of our spiritual focus and practices, plenty of judgments populated the subtext of our gatherings. Every person's behavior was held up against the voluminous teachings of Yogi Bhajan.

Kirtan Singh was determined to carve out a place for himself in Los Angeles. His musical talents were a perfect way for him to get involved in the community. He also embraced the concept of seva (selfless service) and signed up at the main ashram to work as a sevadar. He answered calls and was responsible for protecting the ashram. As Kirtan Singh took on more responsibilities, we saw less of one another.

After several months of this, I became concerned that the man I fell in love with might slip away. I believed some of his best qualities were being sacrificed on the altar of his growing devotion. He rarely did Tai Chi anymore and we no longer had a piano he could play. I missed his improvisational talents on the keyboard. His serious demeanor was evident when he declared one day, "I want to devote my life to being an example of the teachings of Yogi Bhajan."

In that regard, we were worlds apart. The strategy I concocted at Ladies Camp (to relegate Yogi Bhajan to a back burner) after watching him strike Sangita Kaur, had been working well. I saw Yogi Bhajan at his weekly lectures at the main ashram, though peer pressure and continually observing others in their sincere adoration of Yogi Bhajan were influencing me. Sometimes I felt jealous of people who garnered his attention. He'd come outside after his lectures, typically surrounded by his staff, his doctors, and a few upper echelon students. During this time he would take notice of people in the crowd, calling attention to some with a comment here and there, or have a whispered conversation. It was easy to feel left out and insignificant.

It angered me that I wanted his attention. His early students were all so familiar with him; clearly, they loved and revered him. Yogi Bhajan's fondness for them was evident. Was I missing something? I began to have questions: Was he my spiritual teacher? If so, why was I resisting the full experience? I decided maybe I needed to give a little bit and try to become more devotional like Kirtan Singh.

One afternoon I came home to the sound of raised voices upstairs. Sat Nirmal Kaur and her husband, Swami Singh, were fighting. As I stood in the foyer listening, her husband abruptly rushed down the stairs and out the door. With no thought for their welfare whatsoever, my heart leaped in my chest. Maybe a room would soon be vacant!

The next day, we were told Swami Singh left 3HO for unspecified reasons. Sat Nirmal Kaur and I had been getting to know one another, and I'd never met anyone like her. She was from an Italian family of New Yorkers with the accent to prove it. Her deep brown eyes and wide smile competed with the constellations of moles on her face for attention. I'd sit on her bed, combing and braiding her long hair, while she told the most entertaining stories, the melodic rhythm of her voice adding to the richness of the tale.

After the scandal of her husband's departure, Yogi Bhajan arranged a marriage for her with a man from the Española ashram. Eureka! We moved out of our hellhole and into Sat Nirmal Kaur's room while she relocated to New Mexico.

At last, I felt like we had arrived.

Our new room was enormous with beautiful hardwood floors and a bay window that looked over the front yard and street. Sadly, we could not afford to furnish the room in any way that would have pleased me. Filled with regret, I thought of our beautiful oak bedroom set. As it was, our furnishings consisted of an egg-crate foam pad for a bed, a small crappy cardboard dresser with quilted fabric that Kirtan Singh found next to the trash bin in the alley, and an old dresser someone donated to our cause. It was meager—the way my husband liked it.

Once we moved into a proper room at the ashram, Kirtan Singh and I got along better and we began to enjoy our new home. The way we prayed and worshiped together made me feel intrinsically connected to everyone. As I got to know more people, my social life blossomed, which I found fulfilling.

My conversations mainly revolved around the teachings of Yogi Bhajan, but with close friends, we also shared about our marriages, personal struggles, and families. I had longed for this kind of fraternity of shared values and ideals. These were my people, my sacred family. My commitment to living as a Sikh deepened and ushered in a time of great happiness.

We now shared the top floor with the ashram heads. Ram Das Kaur had an attractive and effervescent personality. Yogi Bhajan had given her the title of Secretary of Religion, and as such, she travelled to India at least twice a year on spiritual pilgrimages called *yatras*. Always warm and welcoming, she was clearly a beloved member of the community.

Our improved living conditions did not change the fact that we were struggling financially. One day I asked Kirtan Singh for money to buy a bra.

"Why? he asked. You already have one."

"Yes," I said, "Exactly. I have *one*."

I tried to explain, "I'd like to purchase another bra so I have one to wear when I put my current bra in the wash."

"One is all you need," he decided. "Wash your bra at night, hang it up, and it will be dry in the morning."

That would have been true in the dry Nevada air, but in Los Angeles it would still be wet. Regardless, I had my answer.

While we were on the topic, he let me know that it bothered him tremendously when he could see my nipples through my clothing. Something had to be done about it, because he did not want me floating about in the sangat with my nipples on display.

It was impossible to disguise my incredulity.

"What do you suggest I do about it?" I asked. "I mean, I don't know what to tell you, Kirtan Singh—but these are my nipples. I'm wearing a bra, a dress and a *chunni* (veil) right now. I am under three layers of fabric and wholly covered up."

"It doesn't matter, I can still see your nipples," he complained. "They are erect and it's sexual. It's not graceful."

"Well, that sometimes happens," I stated. "It's not necessarily sexual. It could simply be a response to the cold."

Displeased with my lack of enthusiasm to find a solution to my protruding nipples, Kirtan Singh purchased a box of little round bandaids and insisted I place them over my nipples from now on. His fanatical tendencies were growing more worrisome.

Our food budget was strict. Kirtan Singh gave me $25 a week for groceries. We mostly ate yogurt, fruit, rice and steamed vegetables. In the kitchen pantry everyone had a crate to store their food supplies. When I was hungry, I often visited the pantry to munch on other people's food, especially the shelled pistachio nuts Ram Das Singh bought at Trader Joe's.

Being hungry was an unpleasant reminder of my childhood. As far as I was concerned, we were in a commune, therefore, all of us deserved to feel well-nourished. Each time he noticed his food had been devoured by someone else, Ram Das Singh got so ticked off, he'd call a meeting to harangue about it. I never copped to it, but he ended up buying a box with a lock on it.

After less than a year at Golden Temple Foods my job ended. The manager and I clashed on a daily basis until Siri Ved Singh nicely suggested I find a better fit elsewhere.

After I quit, Kirtan Singh applied for a job at GRD, short for Guru Ram Das Enterprises. It was a telephone sales company that sold office supplies, owned by Mukhia Singh Sahib Hari Jiwan Singh, and Mukhia Singh Sahib Baba Singh. They were close to Yogi Bhajan and longtime leaders in the organization.

One Sunday after gurdwara, GRD hosted a job fair to share employment opportunities that were available. Kirtan Singh and I attended along with about thirty other people. Hari Jiwan lectured on elements of success followed by a Q&A session. As if to test how well we were listening, Hari Jiwan posed a question to the crowd. At first shy to respond, eventually a couple of people raised their hands to answer.

"No and no," came his reply.

The answer was obvious, so I raised my hand and took a stab.

"Yes!" thundered Hari Jiwan, so pleased.

He asked another question. More people attempted but failed to answer correctly.

Again I raised my hand and answered the question.

"Yes!" Hari Jiwan roared.

He asked a third question. Again, I answered.

"Yes!" Hari Jiwan was enthralled, "What is your name?"

"Kirtan Kaur." I replied.

"How do you know all the answers?" he demanded.

"It seems like common sense to me," I replied, shrugging my shoulders.

Catching my husband's face out of the corner of my eye, he was annoyed. He'd tried to answer a question and didn't look too happy with me being praised as a possible business savant.

Hari Jiwan insisted I fill out an application, and so I did. Kirtan Singh applied as well. He got a job in the sales room. For my astute business acumen, I got a job procuring phone numbers for the salesmen to call.

Using old school directories, we called to verify phone numbers and confirm that the school was still operational. I would be paid $0.25 per phone number. After my first two weeks on the job, I received a hefty paycheck with a note from the manager that read, "Come see me in my office."

Entering the room, he praised me saying, "No one has ever

collected so many numbers so quickly. Your earnings for this two-week period are unprecedented."

"Thank you," I said, smiling from ear to ear.

Clearing his throat, he continued, "Therefore, we find it necessary to reduce your per call amount to ten cents going forward."

"What did you say?" I demanded. He repeated himself.

"What kind of incentive is that?" I asked, fuming. He had no answer.

I quit on the spot.

Kirtan Singh continued on at GRD while I applied for a position at the Khalsa Medical Clinic located in the Cedars Sinai Medical Towers. Doctors Saram Singh and Jaswant Singh owned the clinic and it was considered a prestigious place to work. As such, they rarely had positions available. I was thrilled when I was hired to be Dr. Jaswant's medical assistant.

The doctors could not have been more divergent from one another. Saram was a by-the-book diagnostician with a conservative and serious demeanor. He was rapidly becoming famous for his successful treatment of celebrity clients. Carrie Fisher, Marlo Thomas, and Richard Harris were all patients. Rod Stewart's ex-wife, Alana, was also a patient and the rudest woman I'd ever dealt with. Entitled and abusive, we all hated when she was on the schedule.

Richard Harris breezed in one time from London, reciting Shakespeare as he walked the hall to the treatment room. While getting his supplements at the front desk, he offered me a bar of soap from his last hotel room. I decline his offer, put off by his stratospheric arrogance.

Jaswant was free-spirited and unconventional in his approach to medicine. He was more oriented toward exploring the connection between emotions and illness, which did not always seem to meet with Saram's approval. Somehow they managed to coexist despite their obvious incongruities.

As Jaswant's medical assistant, I had several responsibilities: reading the patient charts, which was challenging until I learned to decipher his chicken-scratch writing; giving injections; collecting all supplements recommended for the patient; and keeping the treatment rooms clean. I had no formal training and from time to time had to remind him of that, but he preferred training people and believed those with conventional experience clouded his approach.

The quiet, restrained setting at the clinic was a challenge for my personality. I was prone to bursts of unbridled energy, kind of like a cat when it darts all over the house, which was not conducive to an upscale medical setting. The office manager showed a lot of patience with me. For example, she didn't fire me when I ran full bore down the hallway to get an I.V. drip and slammed right into the slight frame of Dr. Saram. He was a skinny fellow with a long red beard (I always thought he looked like Rip Van Winkle) who weighed less than I did.

As I helped him off the floor, he scolded me, saying, "Kirtan Kaur, this is not a place where we run down the halls!"

In time, I came to understand more deeply how the clinic operated amid the obvious schism between the two doctors. Saram was considered an excellent internist with his allopathic training serving as the backbone of his diagnosis. What made him unique was that he complemented this in pioneering ways, adding holistic treatments (like acupuncture) and natural supplements that achieved dazzling, highly effective results. Patients came from all over the world to see him—his reputation was sterling.

By contrast, Jaswant's reputation was as a healer. Unorthodox and charismatic, he was equally cherished by his patients.

My inexperience was on full display the first time he instructed me to do an ultrasound. I'd been there for about a year and without question was resistant to performing this treatment due to my lack of proper training. Jaswant told me I'd be performing an inter-rectal treatment for an elderly woman with cancer. I stated as strongly as I could that I didn't want to do it. Jaswant insisted, saying he would guide me through the process.

As we entered the room, Mrs. Cafezeira was already in position, kneeling on all fours on the medical table with her paper gown open in the back.

I felt sick.

Dr. Jaswant picked up a big tube of K-Y Jelly and squirted it into my palm. He told me to pick up the wand and coat it with the lubricant. Then he said, "Now, insert the wand into Mrs. Cafezeira's anus."

"Please be gentle!" Mrs. Cafezeira cried out, but I couldn't move. She reminded me of my grandma. I stood there frozen.

Dr. Jaswant put his hand over mine and lifted the wand into position. With his other hand, he pulled her butt cheeks open and then swirled the tip of the wand around the opening of her anus to apply the K-Y Jelly. My body temperature was rising and I felt certain I was going to vomit. Then he squeezed my hand harder as he pushed the wand forward into her anal canal.

Mrs. Cafezeira was huffing air in and out of her lungs like she was in labor. My forehead was cold with sweat as Dr. Jaswant instructed, "Now, Kirtan Kaur, you want to begin to move the wand in a circular motion to achieve optimal benefits."

He demonstrated the motion several times and then let go, nodding for me to continue. I tried my best to go slow and to be gentle, but Mrs. Cafezeira began to moan, especially at one point in the rotation.

"Go back," Dr. Jaswant told me. "Go back to where she moaned—let's put more attention in that location."

I followed his instructions even though Mrs. Cafezeira's moans sounded like a dying animal and my head was starting to spin. About ten minutes had passed when Dr. Jaswant said, "Okay, Kirtan Kaur, that's good, you can remove the wand now."

"Please, oh please, do it slowly!" Mrs. Cafezeira pleaded, adding, "It's painful if you go too fast."

"Of course," I replied, going as slowly as I possibly could.

Ignoring her plea, Dr. Jaswant became impatient with my turtle-like pace and once again put his hand over mine, pulling the wand out quickly.

As he pulled it out, a loud suction noise occurred and Mrs. Cafezeira let out a deep, horrendous groan.

I fainted dead away.

Dr. Jaswant revived me with smelling salts. I opened my eyes just in time to see Mrs. Cafezeira leaving the room.

"Never again," I said to him.

He agreed.

Giving injections was another area where I was an ignoramus. Incredibly, I was cleared to give injections after a five-minute lesson on how to fill and aspirate the syringe and a demonstration on how to flick my wrist while aiming the needle at the intended site. Needless to say, I had zero confidence. I gave injections to infants, who wailed and looked at me like I was a monster, gave homeopathic injections to women for female troubles, and when 3HO'ers were going to India, I gave hepatitis-C vaccinations.

Once, while giving an injection to Guru Singh, I flicked my wrist aiming for his glutes but felt the needle hit his pelvic bone. He was so skinny, there wasn't a lot of flesh to work with. He didn't seem to notice, though I was cringing inside.

Dr. Jaswant had a bevy of adoring female patients. After many of his sessions it was typical to find tissues everywhere in the treatment room and a patient soggy from crying. They all gushed about his tremendous healing powers. I couldn't help but notice that yeast infections were a common diagnosis. In their charts the doctor's instructions always said the same thing: Discontinue underwear.

Dr. Jaswant numbered instructions in the charts for me to write down and give to the patient along with whatever supplements he was recommending.

While he was unusual in his methods, he was also warm and personable. I felt lucky to work there and was learning so much in the process, plus the pay was good and the workday went by quickly. Being proud of my job, I began to feel more confident and loved that we were more financially abundant.

This coincided with a period of increased happiness and harmony in my marriage. Kirtan Singh stopped hassling me about sadhana. He knew it wasn't possible for me to get up that early and work a full day. Others managed to do it, but I wasn't built that way.

We were enjoying new friendships and the joy of being in a large community. There were many events to attend, from birthdays and weddings to religious ceremonies and political protests. It was engaging and rewarding to participate with our spiritual comrades. Those kinds of occasions were far more relaxed and gave people a chance to cut loose. We needed space to lighten up and have fun amid all the strict teachings.

For my birthday, Kirtan Singh wrote a lovely book of Haiku poetry for me. He also gave me an embroidered woolen shawl from India and a private session with one of Yogi Bhajan's several astrologers, named Anita. Kirtan Singh insisted on going with me to the astrologer and wouldn't let me have the session without being present. This visibly irritated Anita, who bit her lip and scowled before she made him regret his gift. She began my reading saying, "Oh, I see right away that you are going to be married three times."

His jaw hit the floor and before long he was grinding his teeth because it got worse.

"You have the energy of women like Eva Gardner and Bette Davis, which is to say, you're a real broad. Men love you. You will have a daughter that will inherit your moon in Scorpio and she will be a lover of the occult."

Kirtan Singh's eyes were bugging out, shocked at the suggestive way she was describing me. I was giggling because I thought she was terribly amusing. But, what a conundrum this posed for my husband—this person was recommended by Yogi Bhajan himself and Kirtan Singh despised every word coming out of her mouth. He ended the session early, filled with buyer's remorse. He was in a bad mood the rest of the day and we never discussed it again.

At work, Kirtan Singh was struggling doing telephone sales. At GRD, no one used their 3HO names when calling customers. They called themselves Bob Thomas, Mike Johnson, Bill Jones, and the like. I understood the use of simple names avoided the confusion of our spiritual names and kiddingly suggested he use the name Peter Sellers, in reference to the Pink Panther actor, riffing on his last name Sellers. Kirtan Singh thought it was a great idea and began to use that name.

We discussed his job on one occasion when Kirtan Singh was particularly low about the challenges he faced. He described GRD as a boiler room, saying they used high-pressure tactics along with false and misleading information to sell typewriter ribbons and toner.

GRD cold-called businesses hoping to get someone new or not particularly smart to run their script on, saying how it was time for them to renew their regular order, when in fact the company had never purchased from them. The script was designed to override any concerns or objections, and those who fell for it paid escalated costs for the products.

One night, Kirtan Singh changed his clothes after dinner, appearing in all black clothing with a black ski mask pulled over his face. This was how I learned that GRD employees went dumpster diving at night to steal leads from competitors. I asked him how he could possibly go along on these outings, acting like this was a legitimate practice. He calmly replied, "Don't worry, Kirtan Kaur, it's fine. The Siri Singh Sahib says *there is no karma over the telephone.*"

He looked satisfied with his explanation, but the sheer idiocy of what he said floored me. Staring at my husband, I replied, "You've been tying your turban too tight, Kirtan Singh. I mean, how do you think that would work?"

"It is not for me to ask questions," he replied. "It is for me to obey my teacher."

His mother's prophetic words came to mind. This was the Saturn teacher's dogma—the refrain that excused moral turpitude: "Yogi Bhajan knows more about you than you do yourself."

There was nothing I could say, no comeback that would be effective in the face of his beliefs. The quandary I had faced from the beginning resurfaced as I tried to juggle my reasons for being in my marriage and 3HO. I thought of my father's insightful counsel on my wedding day when he looked into my eyes and said, "Don't lose your discernment." Those four words became the precept through which I observed everything around me.

When my father first met Kirtan Singh, he expressed his concerns about 3HO being a cult and asked him why he believed anything Yogi Bhajan said. My husband replied that initially, what he learned from Yogi Bhajan was that a vegetarian diet would make him feel good. He tried it and found it to be true. Kirtan Singh then said he was told that yoga would make him limber and give him energy. In the same way, he tried it and this also turned out to be true. Kirtan Singh explained a series of experiences like this led him to have complete faith in whatever Yogi Bhajan taught.

My father pointed out that he had removed any healthy questioning of Yogi Bhajan—blind faith had replaced his capacity for analytical thinking. Kirtan Singh strongly disagreed, saying the term "blind faith" did not apply to him. He told my father he probably couldn't understand the concept of devotion that led to unequivocal dedication to a spiritual teacher.

Living in Los Angeles, I was noticing how the devotion lavished on Yogi Bhajan combined with the Saturn teacher premise gave him carte blanche authority—he had unconstrained permission to behave in any way he chose.

My first example of this was when Sangita Kaur explained being struck by Yogi Bhajan as an aura adjustment. Since that time there were other examples where Yogi Bhajan behaved outrageously: He had a quick-to-flare temper and sometimes lashed out at his students publicly, cursing and shaming them. He physically attacked people, grabbing, slapping, or pushing them. No one ever questioned his behavior because it was all explained as his method of testing a student: "Poke, provoke, confront, and elevate."

After two years of greater access to his teacher, Kirtan Singh was changing in alarming ways. He wrote letters to Yogi Bhajan soliciting advice about insignificant things, cherishing every reply. At one point, he wrote to Yogi Bhajan to ask if he should continue to do Tai Chi, which he had practiced for five years. Two weeks later, Yogi Bhajan's reply arrived and said, "My son, Tai Chi is not a complete discipline. Don't give it more, don't give it less."

When Kirtan Singh shared the letter with me, I could see he was completely let down and disheartened. I believe he was expecting Yogi Bhajan to praise him for his practice. The stark indifference of his response was a shock by comparison. Even more surprising, Kirtan Singh did not follow his instructions. Instead, he filed the letter and abandoned his practice. I tried to talk with him about it, but Yogi Bhajan's words annihilated his love of Tai Chi. I never saw him do it again.

This decision capped off several years of watching my husband relinquish aspects of his personality that I loved: his humor and spontaneity, his love of theater, his blues riffing, and now Tai Chi. All was replaced by his oxymoronic holy ambitions.

Witnessing his and others' dependency on Yogi Bhajan irritated me to such a degree that when I witnessed it firsthand, I began to make derisive comments like, "People in 3HO write to Yogi Bhajan if they have a hangnail." My criticism was not well received, but I had to say something to make it clear I did not think that way. In my assessment, the community had an unhealthy fixation on Yogi Bhajan. I was tired of hearing, "Yogi Bhajan says..." at the start of most conversations. After a recent lecture, I overheard two women comparing the length of time and the number of words he had uttered against past interactions they'd had with him. At this point, red flags were flapping in the breeze, but if I wanted to be in the community, I knew I better stay silent.

A recent sangat meeting raised bizarre topics for discussion that knocked me sideways. This had been deemed a mandatory meeting of the utmost importance and was therefore well-attended.

The first matter on the agenda was the ongoing problem of farting during sadhana. Specific details ensued to let us know that, in particular, curry farts were extremely unpleasant to endure while performing breath of fire. It was also believed that people who slept through sadhana farted more freely, which I found disturbing for obvious reasons.

We all knew that one particularly rotund man, Siri Ram, was the main offender. He deserves mention for his natural ability to issue spectacularly long bouts of wind. It was nearly impossible to keep a straight face.

A new, two-pronged fart protocol was voted on and passed. Part one: step outside to accomplish all farting. Part two: wait a sufficient length of time before returning to avoid bringing your fart into the room with your slipstream. I wondered if fart police would be roaming through sadhana to enforce the rules.

The second matter was women's attire during sadhana. Women were discouraged from wearing yoga pants—*while doing yoga*—because they were determined to be ungraceful, even offensive, when it came time to bow before the Sikh holy book. A woman in yoga pants, it was explained, upon assuming the bowing position was inadvertently displaying her genitalia to the congregation. Bowing down lifted one's butt in the air and the cotton fabric sometimes rested in the vulvar region, creating an outline, if you will.

Huh, I thought, *has no one noticed that when the men bowed you could see their dangling balls through their yoga pants?*

The meeting exposed our unspoken policy of scrutinizing one another, right down to our farts. I was guilty of it too. We judged one another while claiming that we cultivated a state of higher consciousness. Our judgments fit under our unspoken, arrogant guise of righteousness—we thought we were better than everyone else. In fact, I heard people refer to those who were not in 3HO as "people on the outside," making it clear that we lived in a special bubble of rarified, otherworldly air.

My work at the Khalsa Medical Clinic was going well, until the day came when Dr. Jaswant asked too much of me. He was running behind schedule because he had spent a long time with one particular patient, an attractive woman in her early thirties. Back at my station I opened her chart and read the following:

1. Continue to discontinue underwear.
2. Discontinue cat.
3. Put a green dot in the center of everything.
4. Duck when going through doorways.
5. Walk backwards for five minutes, three times a day.

I stood motionless, staring at his instructions in disbelief. Jaswant approached me saying, "Let's go, Kirtan Kaur. Finish up her chart so we can get the next patient in."

"I can't do it." I half-whispered.

"What did you say?" Jaswant replied.

"I said, I can't do it." I repeated. "I can't. I *won't* do it."

"This is a part of your job, Kirtan Kaur. Now finish up with this patient," he said, his voice growing angry.

"But these instructions are insane!" I countered. "Who tells someone to put a green dot in the center of everything?"

Jaswant was adamant and now I'd insulted him. His voice raised as he threw down the gauntlet, "For the last time, Kirtan Kaur, I'm telling you to finish up or you will lose your job!"

I was in a pressure cooker, having to make a choice. While I loved my job, I had reached a threshold with Jaswant's unorthodox methods and was too uncomfortable to comply.

"I won't do it, Jaswant." I decided. "So, I guess I quit."

That was my last day working at the Khalsa Medical Clinic.

A moment of reverence.

23
as you wish

When I got home, I told Kirtan Singh I quit my job, he responded enthusiastically. I was expecting him to be upset, but instead he proposed that I remain unemployed, saying this was an opportunity for us to make some important changes.

Based on his interpretation of Yogi Bhajan's teachings, Kirtan Singh believed the correct arrangement for our marriage was for him to support me financially, while I supported him spiritually. He described in detail how he wanted us to live going forward: my wifely duties would include the mundane chores of marketing, cooking, housecleaning, laundry, and ironing. He alone would be in charge of our financial affairs.

To spiritually support him, Kirtan Singh said it would be my job to attend sadhana, recite five Sikh prayers each day, as well as eleven recitations of a prayer called *Sopurkh*. Yogi Bhajan said this Sopurkh prayer had the power to transform a man into a saint, a giver, or a hero.

Kirtan Singh's urge to overhaul our marriage hurt my feelings because I thought we were in a pretty good place. His proposal that we take on traditional roles, as if I was a 1950s housewife, was disconcerting. I already struggled to perform well and complete all the obligatory requirements of Yogi Bhajan's teachings. While it was my idea to move to California, in unforeseen ways the Los Angeles sangat was proving to be an intense pressure cooker, mainly because the expectation level of what it meant to be in 3HO skyrocketed.

We even joked about it, tongue in cheek, saying things like "it takes three days to accomplish the daily teachings of Yogi Bhajan," highlighting the fact that failure was a constant companion. The endless demands often left me feeling bad about myself for what I did not get done.

I wanted to have a solid marriage and to be a good wife, but I wasn't convinced the direction he wanted us to go would be beneficial. A question formed in my mind—*If I do whatever Kirtan Singh asks of me for a full year, will that make him happy?* That question turned into a promise I made to myself. In that spirit, I decided to commit myself wholeheartedly to his plan.

With this new routine, I rose at 2:30 am to read *Jap Sahib* before sadhana. Our established bathroom routine at Siri Gurbani was that ashram heads used the bathroom first, followed by Kirtan Singh and me. When I asked Ram Das Kaur if I could use the bathroom earlier, she suggested we switch to women in the bathroom first, followed by the men. I had the weird sense she favored this arrangement because she wanted to see me naked. We had never discussed it, but it was obvious to me that she was gay.

Not long after we moved upstairs, Ram Das Kaur invited me to come by one afternoon "to cuddle," which I thought was a curious invitation. When I arrived, she had music playing, candles lit, and a couple of sheepskins on the floor in the corner of her bedroom.

Ram Das Kaur motioned for me to follow her and we sat side by side. Reaching for a blanket to throw over us, she snuggled close to me. Nothing threatening was happening as far as I was concerned, so I put my head on her shoulder. That seemed to encourage her and she began to stroke me, caressing my arms and hands. Her touch felt nice. She sighed, indicating she was relaxing and enjoying our time together. I was enjoying it as well. I felt sad for her, because clearly she had needs that were not being met. At the time I didn't see the parallels between us—I also had unmet needs in my marriage. Our comfortable embrace ended abruptly when her husband angrily charged into the room. "What's going on here?"he asked in an unmistakable, accusatory tone. She told him, "We're having a cuddle and listening to music."

When it came to sex, Yogi Bhajan's prolix teachings precluded any spontaneity, making the entire enterprise wretchedly forced and unnatural. Because of this, our sex life was close to nonexistent. We had serious problems in our intimate relations.

Here's a sampling of Yogi Bhajan's teachings on sex that I learned at Ladies Camp:

- Men should only have sexual intercourse once a month.
- The best time for sex must be calculated using astrology.
- The sexual experience must start seventy-two hours prior to intercourse, somewhere outside of the bedroom.
- The woman must give herself an enema before sex, so that her lower colon and rectum are empty. Also, she must bathe and douche if her vagina has any odor.
- The male must clean his organ, especially if he is uncircumcised, afterward he should apply oil to his organ and his leg pits, because they secrete a lot of acid.

- Foreplay should last one to two hours until the man can smell his sweat. Always rub your sweat back into your body, don't wash it off.
- Day One: Begin in the kitchen. Make some yogi tea and sip it together, then enjoy a delicious meal.
- Day Two: Move into the living room where you have cozy time to talk and share.
- Day Three: Proceed to the bedroom.

Yogi Bhajan declared, "A man who cannot pleasure a woman is not a man." Toward this end, it was crucial that five moon centers on the woman be satisfied before the man could penetrate her. Yogi Bhajan said women did not have orgasms, they had *tidings*. I never understood what he meant by that other than he used a different word to describe the same thing.

In my naiveté, I assumed everyone in 3HO was following his sex protocol. I could not have been more wrong. These were, after all, ex-hippies from the free-love era. In retrospect, I never heard anyone say they followed the overbearing to-do list for sex.

An unpleasant side effect of our new arrangement was that our lives became ruled by Kirtan Singh's insistent need for perfection. He expected each and every teaching to be followed to the letter.

For example, when I was ovulating and wanted to have sex, he rejected me, since thirty days had not passed. Conversely, when I suffered from PMS, was bloated, or simply uninterested in sex, it didn't matter if it was our scheduled time for sex. Kirtan Singh's rigidity and perfectionism plagued our sex life.

Once a month we attempted the three-day rigamarole and more often than not, we ended up having a fight. On the rare occasions when we did have sex, I found it joyless and unsatisfying.

Yogi Bhajan also taught that men should never masturbate. It's not difficult to imagine that one ejaculation a month for most men would create a high probability for lightning fast orgasms. Yogi Bhajan even had a fix for this predicament: at White Tantric courses you could purchase his premature ejaculation cure in the form of multiple packets of sap from the banyan tree in India.

Unfortunately, it was impossible for wives to be discreet as they made the walk-of-bad-sex to the banyan sap table. To add insult to injury, the sap was a completely ineffective remedy. The sap only benefited those who sold it, as they profited from Yogi Bhajan's claim, not the saps who bought it.

After going through this for years, my frustration was at an all time high. I had to deny the rush of hormones during ovulation that would have given us a family to instead suffer through three days of bullshit to do the deed. When the moment arrived, it was over in a flash. Most of the time my moon centers didn't get diddled at all. Sex ended with my husband asking me the preposterous question, "Did you come?"

When I answered with a bewildered "no," my husband would scowl and declare I was frigid.

Conversely, Sunday gurdwara, our religious service, was my favorite part of being in 3HO. Gathering together to sing devotional songs and pray was always uplifting. One Sunday, I left early to walk to gurdwara to make sure I could sit in the front. The pool of talented musicians and singers in the community was deep. I loved being close to them as they played and sang. I was pretty sure I was ovulating that day, which often made me feel a full and powerful sense of myself. Everything felt right in the world and I was feeling in sync with the pulsing rhythm of life. It was a gorgeous spring day in the City of Angels: clear skies with a light breeze that carried the sweet, musky scents of jasmine and gardenia into our room of worship.

Complementing the aromas in the air, the music transported me into a feeling of oneness. I found myself recalling my blissful moments of peace in the meadow at Camp Field. In my reverie, I was oblivious to those around me. I floated in this joyful state until I became aware of a far-away thought descending toward me… a thought that wanted to be recognized.

In my heightened awareness, I thought that surely this would be some kind of divine message, perhaps a fortuitous directive about my future. I patiently observed as the thought came closer and closer, until at last it revealed itself to me.

The thought was: *This cannot possibly be the only sex that I am ever going to have in this lifetime.*

A truth bomb from the ethers had gone off in my mind. I quietly laughed and then I wept. There it was. An unfiltered, brutally honest thought that changed my perspective and cracked open the veneer of my marriage. I made a note to get back to this thought because I had a few months left in my promise to Kirtan Singh.

During this time, a friend of mine gave birth to a precious and stunning little boy named Gurmukh. I loved spending afternoons watching her make Indian sweets while I held her son. Cradling Gurmukh and smelling the sweet scent on the top of his head launched every hormonal desire in me to have a baby.

Approaching Kirtan Singh one evening, I told him I was ready to be a mom.

"No, no, it's not time yet. We're nowhere near ready," came his quick reply.

"But, I'm twenty-three now," I protested, "and we've been married for four years. This is the perfect time."

"No, we're not ready," he repeated and walked away.

It didn't seem like Kirtan Singh would ever be ready. Sikhs embrace what they call the householder life, the life of family, but Kirtan Singh's need to be in control was not an agreeable agenda for having a family. I found myself at my friend's house more and more, loving that little boy, trying to fill the growing emptiness inside of me.

How I missed the man I met and fell in love with in Reno. He was full of life, passionate, and charming. Kirtan Singh had changed, becoming humorless and rigid. His singular goal in life was to be an example of the teachings of Yogi Bhajan.

I couldn't let it go and brought it up again a few days later. Attempting to make the case that no one feels prepared when they have children, I told him, "It's like stepping off a cliff, you go with it, trust, and do the best you can."

Kirtan Singh veered off subject to question my loyalty, asking, "If Yogi Bhajan asked you to jump off a cliff, would you?"

"What? No! What are you even talking about?" I asked.

"Well," Kirtan Singh continued, "I would jump off a cliff if he asked me to. I'd do anything he asked me to."

"Well, you're a dumbass then," I replied, "and still tying your turban too tight."

His declaration was distressing. This was a chasm between us I didn't know how to bridge. I found his blind devotion to Yogi Bhajan frightening and delusional.

Then he returned to the subject of having a baby—dropping a full-on crazy bomb in my lap:

"If you want a child so badly, why don't you become holy enough to immaculately conceive? That way we can give the Siri Singh Sahib a child that is a saint, a giver, or a hero."

Come again? The absurdity of his suggestion sent me reeling.

Oh my god, I thought, *he's dead serious.*

Huge blocks of understanding were moving inside my brain as I let his words sink in, followed by a painful realization that hit me like a ton of bricks. The man I had fallen in love with was gone. I was completely alone in my marriage. In seconds, Kirtan Singh's distorted quest to impress Yogi Bhajan with my immaculate conception shook the earth beneath me.

It is more than thirty-five years later, and I am sobbing at my keyboard remembering the colossal impact of that day.

I shared some of what I was going through with close friends, but mostly I tried to keep it together and carry on with the promise I made to myself.

Then our community was rocked to the core when a 3HO woman was raped at knifepoint in her home, blocks from the ashram. It drove home the lack of safety in our neighborhood that was confirmed regularly by crime reports in the paper.

A martial arts instructor was hired, in response to the panic and fear that ensued, to teach us the basics of self-defense. Her name was Graciela Casillas and she held world championship titles for kickboxing and western boxing. She held a class at the Robertson Recreational Center, across from the ashram.

Graciela had a no-nonsense approach. She had us all line up in pairs. We went through a series of warmups, and then did drills that covered an array of effective responses to being attacked. Next, we did push-ups, so many push-ups, all kinds of push-ups. When we got to the one where you push off the ground and clap, I landed on my elbows over and over until they were bleeding. Then we did kicks in the air and kicks on a pad that our partner held.

At one point, she came up to me and thumped me hard in the center of my chest with her fist, exclaiming, "Come on, Tiger! There's a fire in you that's about to go out."

I was shocked. She just met me. Her words landed as hard as her fist and with prescient significance. Time slowed and I felt like I did when I had the dream about meeting my Benefactor. She was calling me toward a new future, though I didn't know it yet.

After the class, I went home and laid on my bed, not moving. In fact, I was unable to move for four hours. I had never felt that spent, like every cell in my body needed to recover. I was hooked. In the name of self-defense, I told Kirtan Singh I wanted to take her classes at a gym in West Los Angeles. He said yes.

Not long after that, I began taking classes at the Inosanto Academy in Marina Del Rey. I trained six days a week, two to three hours a day, while keeping up all my wifely duties.

A desire for change began to stir inside of me.

The Academy was owned by Danny Inosanto, a friend of Bruce Lee's back in the day. The Academy's philosophy was unique in that it had no belt system and taught many different styles of fighting. We trained in Filipino Escrima and Kali stick-fighting, Western boxing, French Savate, Muay Thai kickboxing, Wing Chung, and Bruce Lee's Jeet Kun Do.

I loved how my body felt as I grew stronger and more confident. Something else was happening—it was freeing to wear my hair down and put on regular clothing. I liked feeling normal.

I'd never been enthusiastic about kundalini yoga. I had no affinity for it. Martial arts, on the other hand, felt like dancing. It had rhythm and grace.

Graciela was right: a tiger was awakening.

A handful of other people were serious about self-defense and attended classes; Shanti Shanti Kaur, Awtar Kaur, Veda Kaur, and her husband, Veda Singh. Their presence made it easier for Kirtan Singh to support my desire to train and I liked

Graciela and I at the Inosanto Academy in Marina del Rey, California.

relating to people from our community in a different setting.

Kirtan Singh and I began to socialize with the Vedas, having Saturday game nights at their apartment. They were older than us and had one child, a daughter named Pooja. We enjoyed one another's company and I particularly loved being with them because we didn't talk about the teachings or our lifestyle. As I observed how laid back they were, the strains of our uptight life came sharply into focus.

They had a two-bedroom apartment which was huge compared to our single room. I couldn't help but envy the amount of space, privacy and freedom they had. Later on, when I mentioned to Kirtan Singh that it would be cool to get our own place, he crushed that notion saying, "We will always live in an ashram."

After a few months of training, Veda Kaur stopped coming. It was hard for her to make it after a long day of work, plus, she had asthma and was having breathing difficulties during class.

Veda Singh and Swami Singh (Sat Nirmal's ex) had a business called Body Buddies, selling a massage roller device. Veda Singh worked part-time and still went to class, so he and I decided to carpool to make things easier and save on gas costs.

As summer approached, Kirtan Singh expected me to go to Ladies Camp because I had missed the year before. I didn't want to go because I'd been training with Graciela for nearly six months and was thrilled with the progress I was making. We fought about it for weeks until he blew up, reverting to his *I am the husband* argument that was meant to put me in my place. I was livid.

One afternoon, when Veda Singh picked me up, I told him about my fight with Kirtan Singh over attending Ladies Camp. This began a confidence between us, where we talked about things other than martial arts or 3HO life. He was a sympathetic listener and made helpful suggestions about how I might improve my relationship with Kirtan Singh. He pointed out that pretty much everyone was going to Solstice and Ladies Camp. Participation was an expected aspect of our lifestyle.

"Anyway," he said, "it's only four weeks and then you can get back to martial arts classes."

He recommended that I train while I was there to keep up my strength. I liked his idea. It made me feel better about going.

One day he gave me an unexpected compliment as I got in his car. He greeted me with a big smile, saying, "You are always so fresh and clean, and you smell good, too." The specifics of his praise made me slightly uncomfortable. I responded by giving him an informative explanation, "Well, that's because I shower before class. The hot water warms up my muscles. What you are smelling is Jean Naté, my favorite cologne."

"Veda Kaur always has an oily sheen on her skin when she comes home," he lamented.

His comment irritated me and I snapped at him, "No kidding? She's worked a long day. What do you expect?"

It was an unkind observation from him. Veda Kaur and I were friends. She was talented and independent in a way I longed to be. She worked full-time as a graphic designer and drove a brand new Toyota Cressida.

We had been friendly with another couple who were the same age as us, Mani Singh and his wife, Kartar Kaur. Sadly, our friendship with them didn't last because Mani Singh left 3HO. We heard Yogi Bhajan had brutally outed him as gay.

Yogi Bhajan's teachings about homosexuality were strange. He condemned gay men, saying they were stuck in their first chakra but that it was an easily curable perversion. However, when it came to women, he declared there was no such thing as female homosexuality. What's more, their status was neutral: lesbians wouldn't grow spiritually, but they wouldn't backslide either. His teachings made it clear gay people were not welcomed in 3HO.

The date for Summer Solstice was approaching. On the way to class one day, Veda Singh asked me if Kirtan Singh was going.

"No, he has to work." I replied. "I'm taking our car so I can get around for the summer at Ladies Camp."

"Oh, so you acquiesced?" Veda Singh teased.

"Yea, I did. I'm still angry about it, but I'm going to keep training like you suggested. Graciela is putting together a program for me to maintain while I'm there. Anyway, I'll enjoy being back in the Land of Enchantment."

"Is Veda Kaur going?" I asked.

"No, she needs to work, same as Kirtan Singh."

He paused briefly, then continued, "We should caravan. It will be safer for you and better than driving all that way alone."

"That sounds good, I'll talk to Kirtan Singh about it." I said.

For nearly a year I had kept my promise, abiding by Kirtan Singh's new vision for our marriage, but in my estimation it wasn't working. I missed having a job and missed the autonomy of having my own money. Living on one income was difficult and made no sense to me. It created unnecessary financial tensions. Though he refused to talk about it, he obviously did not enjoy his job.

The most unfortunate development, however, was that my new role of serving Kirtan Singh had landed me squarely on the microscopic slide as a specimen to be scrutinized and evaluated, which encouraged one of his most negative tendencies: blaming me for anything that was going wrong.

Though I was putting forth considerable effort to please him, he still found something to complain about. For example, he said my recitation of the Sopurkh prayer wasn't having the effect it was supposed to (to make one's husband a saint, a giver, or hero) and accused me of not doing it right. I was tired of being criticized and regretted agreeing to his plan. Being dependent on him for every penny I spent angered me. Something was going to have to change.

I knew he was struggling at work. When I deposited his paychecks, even though he worked solely on commission, they were always the same amount. When I asked him about this, he blew up and told me it was none of my business. I was shut out of anything to do with money and whatever it was that was making him so tense and cross. I was glad I was going to be away from him for the summer.

The day came for my roadtrip. I was packed and ready to go. Kirtan Singh left cash for the summer on the dresser before he left for work. Veda Singh and Pooja arrived in their Volkswagen Rabbit, while I drove our Toyota Starlet. The drive time to Flagstaff was approximately eight hours. We'd spend the night there.

We had frequent breaks due to bathroom, food, and fuel needs. I brought my favorite music as a kind of emotional companion—a soothing balm for my hurting heart.

My quest for "something more" had been ignited by the lyrics of Cat Stevens, so I played his music for hours, singing along to every song. How I wanted to connect with the girl I was when these songs moved me for the first time. Next I listened to Neil Diamond, Loggins and Messina, and The Guess Who. I sang my heart out for hours as I drove away from Kirtan Singh toward the otherworldly light of New Mexico.

We arrived in Flagstaff right at dinner time. After checking into the motel, we found a nearby vegetarian restaurant. After our meal, we settled into our separate rooms. Veda Singh had booked the arrangements, choosing rooms with an adjoining door. He said he thought that was wise in case he had to run to the car or something, then Pooja wouldn't be alone. She was out like a light after dinner and we sat in the doorway between our rooms, talking.

I told him how frustrated I was in my marriage and how I never seemed to measure up to Kirtan Singh's standards. As always, he listened attentively. When I finished, I waited for him to say something but he was silent. Eventually, he leaned forward and put his hand on my leg to comfort me.

"It's going to be okay," he said.

We sat in silence until a big yawn overtook me, signaling time for bed. We said goodnight and closed the door.

Sleep was immediate. Even the frequent rumble of Flagstaff's locomotives, patiently crisscrossing the country and sounding their five-chime whistles, didn't disturb my slumber.

Performing sword form on stage at Summer Solstice in New Mexico in 1984.

24
quivering paradigms

Nine undisturbed hours in the Land of Nod. It had been years since I had such a nourishing night of sleep. The glow of sunlight, persistent through the heavy curtains, woke me. With a satisfied inhale, I opened my eyes, looking forward to the day ahead.

I had the peculiar feeling that someone was touching me. The next moment, I was thunderstruck to see Veda Singh sitting at the end of the bed with his hands resting on my feet. Was that what woke me? Tilting my head like an inquisitive puppy, I smiled at him. He smiled as well and then whispered a life-altering sentence:

"The hardest thing I've ever done in my life was not making love to you last night."

I was astounded to hear the words come out of his mouth. In an instant, a colossal shift in perception occurred inside of me.

Love named and recognized changes everything.

Prior to that moment, I had never thought of Veda Singh romantically. He was simply my friend's husband and my training partner. I knew only too well the pain my mother suffered from my father's betrayal. Perhaps that was why the thought had never entered my mind. Perhaps I'd even held it at bay, in a latent state, because of my parents' history. In our community,

Yogi Bhajan encouraged and bolstered our sense of familial connection, telling us we were all siblings of destiny. I had always thought of him as a brother.

Then he uttered that remarkable, provocative sentence, which I received as an invitation. Like a magical incantation, his words ushered forth my every unmet need and all the sad shreds of loneliness and heartbreak that my nearly five-year marriage had produced.

A tidal wave of feeling rose up in me to meet his sentiment fully, though I didn't speak. I had no idea he felt that way about me. My skin was tingling as I took a deep breath, keenly aware that our relationship had transformed completely.

Yes, yes, my mind said soothingly, *this feels like nourishment and I have been starving for years.*

Without breaking eye contact, I slowly pulled back the covers to move toward him. He came to my bedside and we embraced. Stress poured off of me like rushing water in a heavy rainstorm. All the sadness that ached inside me softened into a lovely feeling of ease. As we held one another close, we heard the sounds of Pooja waking up. It was time to have breakfast and get back on the road.

I remember nothing about the drive from Flagstaff to Española, other than my exquisite state of euphoria. I smiled so much my face hurt. With me moving through time and space in my own little capsule and Veda Singh moving through time and space in his, I had hours by myself to lean into what he said and to ponder my feelings for him. More importantly, what would we do about it?

Of course, I thought of Veda Kaur. She was a good and loyal friend. I admired her immensely. She was artistic, sensitive, caring, and she was loved in the community. As I thought of her, such a bizarre feeling came over me, a real paradox. I was incredibly flattered that Veda Singh cared for me *precisely* because he was married to Veda Kaur.

My mind couldn't work out the big picture of it all, so I focused instead on the surging love I was feeling. Like Scarlet O'Hara, I'd deal with the rest on the morrow.

Veda Singh had been my confidant for months. He knew my intention to serve Kirtan Singh and improve our marriage. He also knew how stringent Kirtan Singh could be and that I had been unhappy for months.

Veda Singh was the opposite; relaxed and easy-going. He liked to laugh and have fun. He liked to tease me. He even referred to Yogi Bhajan casually as *dad*, which, besides being psychologically revealing, was the most informal way I'd ever heard anyone refer to him. In many ways he was a perfect antidote to the wound-tight perfectionism of my husband.

The drive to Ram Das Puri took all day. The final stretch was an elevation climb on unpaved, rocky road. At last, we saw the welcome sign at the gate and parked. I jumped out of the car and kissed the ground, as Kirtan Singh and I had done our first time there.

A woman with a clipboard approached to get us registered and situated. We were handed a paper with general information and a map designating tent areas.

Veda Singh would tent in the family area and I would be with the single ladies. My tent mate, Melissa, had already arrived. I set out to find her and get situated.

At that time, Summer Solstice attracted about a thousand people who came from around the world for ten days of sadhana, chanting, and tantric yoga. I considered it a chance to participate in a utopian experiment in higher-consciousness living.

While we were having dinner, Veda Singh asked me if I would take Pooja to the showers before sadhana, since he obviously couldn't enter the women's bathing area. As I learned at Children's Camp, kids weren't exempt from 3HO's disciplines.

He dropped her off at my tent and we made our way down the hill. The chilled air at that elevation made undressing an act of bravery. I showered first while she waited, wrapped in a blanket. Quickly rubbing almond oil over my skin, I turned on the sprinkler head and jumped in, gasping and chanting *wahe guru*. As I toweled off, I looked over and saw Pooja, shivering in anticipation. She was six and a petite little girl. I didn't have the heart to make her shower because it felt too unreasonable and cruel. Instead we went straight to the shelter for sadhana.

A light breeze was blowing as we hunkered down to get warm. Veda Singh found us and we sat together. After that day, Veda Singh decided Pooja could skip the showers altogether.

After sadhana, we ate the same breakfast each day, spicy potato soup with bananas and oranges, then children and adults went to their separate activities.

During Solstice, Veda Singh and I made the radical choice to spend time alone together in his tent. I'd join him in the afternoons, combing his hair while we talked. That simple act was incredibly intimate. On one of those afternoons, he started calling me *Keke*, geminating my initials. It made me smile because this was also intimate, something special between us.

We were aware that we were being observed. A few folks from Los Angeles had already given me disapproving looks, suggesting that the gossip mill was in full production. We had that swooning energy going on and no doubt many could feel it.

On about day six, while rushing to the shelter, I nearly crashed into Kirtan Singh.

"Whoa, Kirtan Singh?" I gasped. "What are you doing here?"

"Sat Nam, Kirtan Kaur," he said formally. I decided to come for a few days, last minute," he added in a distinctly gruff tone.

"Oh. Wow. Were you going to let me know you were here?" My response was agitated, so I changed the subject, "Where are you tenting?"

"I've got that worked out," he said, without telling me where. "Obviously, I know you're tenting with Melissa."

We stood there, not looking at one another in awkward silence until he announced, "I've signed up for a lot of seva, I have to go."

With that, our unexpected nano-encounter ended.

My hackles went up and stayed there because Kirtan Singh's appearance was definitely suspect. Veda Singh and I met at his tent and agreed someone must've reported us, prompting Kirtan Singh to get on a plane. Defensively, I wanted to argue that we hadn't technically done anything wrong, but energetically we had—we were both married.

Kirtan Singh said nothing about Veda Singh and didn't ask me any questions either. If he was upset about the possibility of my involvement with another man, he kept that to himself.

As a result of his snubbing, I carried on meeting Veda Singh and Pooja each morning. When people scowled at me, I gave them a huge smile. Since discovering that Veda Singh cared for me, I felt bolder. More than that, a defiance was rising in me, loosening emotions I'd been suppressing for years.

Solstice featured a shopping bazaar where you could purchase myriad items direct from India; turban material, shawls, prayer books, prayer beads, jewelry, you name it. 3HO-related businesses also had booths to sell their wares.

Veda Singh was selling 100 percent cotton sweatpants and

sweatshirts in earth tone colors. I'd been helping him and they were selling well. He generously gave me a cut of my sales.

On the last day of Solstice, he asked if I wanted to sell the remaining inventory while I was at Ladies Camp. He preferred not to haul the boxes back to Los Angeles, and I could earn money for the summer. I happily agreed.

Melissa caught a shuttle to Albuquerque and someone in passing told me Kirtan Singh had left the day before, without so much as a goodbye.

A massive problem in our community was that no one talked about their feelings because emotions were pretty much taboo. As a result of this condemnation of matters of the heart, most of us were pretty constipated when it came to our feelings.

It was safe to assume that Yogi Bhajan had been apprised of what was going on. Like Richard Nixon, he had informants everywhere. It was naïve to think otherwise.

As the event was ending, I realized I hadn't made any plans for lodging that night. Somehow, Veda Singh read my mind.

"Let's go," he said brightly. "I've booked a casita for us at the El Rey Inn in Santa Fe."

I was tickled pink.

The El Rey Inn was a charming adobe motel sprawled out over several acres of land. When we checked into our casita, I was amazed at the beauty and feel of the place. Gorgeously decorated in southwestern style, it had a kiva fireplace, lodgepole furniture, colorful native textiles, and warm lighting. There was a sitting area with a comfortable loveseat and recliner in front of the kiva and one king-sized bed.

We went out for dinner and enjoyed the absence of prying eyes. Veda Singh made a wise choice booking a motel in Santa Fe rather than Española.

Once back at our casita, Veda Singh tucked Pooja into bed. After an exhausting ten days at Solstice, she was pleased as punch to be on a comfortable mattress. We had the TV on low while she slept.

A fire had been lit in the kiva while we were at dinner. Veda Singh plopped down in the cozy recliner.

"May I sit on your lap?" I asked.

"Get over here, Keke," he purred.

His invitation was incredibly arousing. Slowly walking across the room, I eased into his lap, relishing the feeling, as we had never been this close before. To be pulsing with desire while maintaining restraint was a new kind of pleasure—or was it an exquisite torture? As we leaned into one another, touching foreheads, I whispered, "What are we going to do?"

"Well, I am heading home and you are at Ladies Camp for the next month," he replied matter of factly, killing the mood.

"You know what I mean!" I said, nudging him.

"Let's figure that out when you are back in Los Angeles," was all he would say.

His response was disappointing. I'd been bursting with the conversations I wanted to have and now we had the privacy and opportunity to have them. Inexplicably, Veda Singh was unwilling to engage in any talk about the future. I was frustrated and deflated but didn't push it.

We sat in that comfy chair for hours, talking about everything but our future. Eventually, we began nuzzling one another. Then we progressed into kissing, which was nice, except that Veda Singh kissed me like we were Jimmy Stewart and Katherine Hepburn in *The Philadelphia Story*. For the record, it was my first polite, circa-1940s, lip-press kiss, mouths definitely closed.

"Why won't you really kiss me?" I asked.

"Pooja," he said with conviction. "If I kiss you like I want to, I won't be able to control myself."

"I want to make love," I whispered.

"Keke, I can't," he said softly, "my daughter is present."

Pure agony.

Of course, I understood. I didn't like it, but I understood. I was amazed at his self-control and admired him for putting Pooja first. But, my god, I wanted to. My body was surging with a veritable tsunami of sensations that craved a response. It had been years since I felt this sexually charged, and so, I persisted, shifting my position on his lap so I could straddle him. Now I could press my pelvis into him, like I was riding a horse. He was hard. We both amplified. He stroked my face and arms and then my breasts, over my bra and shirt. My breathing accelerated even more. He let out a groan, saying he had blue balls, which made both of us laugh. This was definitely torture.

He was leaving in the morning and I wanted more. Had he been willing, I would have had sex with him that night. As it was, his boundary had to be honored.

That's how we passed the night: keyed up, flirting, and nuzzling. When fatigue took over, he crashed in the chair and I slept on the loveseat.

The bright light of the new day instantly brought the pain of separation. A month was going to feel like forever. Over breakfast, he gave me pointers on selling the sweats and went over his work and training schedule back home. Handing me his office number, he said to call him there. We promised one another we'd write.

We stood in the El Rey parking lot. Pooja was already in the car, as he was taking her to Children's Camp before leaving town. No matter how much I wanted to smother him in kisses, it was impossible. We said a quick goodbye and he drove away.

Heartsick, I made my way to Ladies Camp. My tent mate for the month, Awtar Kaur, was also a housemate from Siri Gurbani. Though we lived together, we had never connected in any kind of meaningful way. She was a ginger-headed intellectual who loved listening to public radio, especially while ironing. In some ways she reminded me of my husband, so I wasn't excited about sharing close quarters with her.

Once I located her tent, I unloaded my belongings from the car. As always, I had minimal accoutrements but had brought the bathroom rugs from home to fancy up the place. Whoopee. Awtar had an altar set up that she invited me to use.

After that I walked the dirt footpath that led to the kitchen, a short walk up a slight hill. There was always yogi tea on the stove and a mug of warming spices sounded comforting. On the way I saw Guru Meher Kaur, the mother of a boy I took care of at Children's Camp, who lived in Española. We stopped to chat. I told her I'd gotten into martial arts and was determined to keep training while in New Mexico. Serendipity blessed me as she told me she had an empty garage, which we happened to be standing right in front of. She took out her key and showed it to me, saying I could use it for the summer. It even had an overhead light and an electrical outlet. I was ecstatic. I offered her fifty dollars rent for the four weeks and she gave me the key.

This unexpected boon energized me. I was all set for my training, plus I had a place where I could go when I wanted to be alone. Abandoning the cup of yogi tea, I went to the car to get my gear. I'd brought my training notebook, boombox and an extension cord, custom-mixed cassette tapes, a jump rope, my yellow boxing gloves, Kali Sticks, and an exercise mat. My training would begin in the morning.

It was easy to get doughy under the mountain of clothing we wore. Thanks to Graciela and my training, I had never been more fit. Weighing in at one-hundred and twelve pounds, I was lean and strong. Graciela wrote out specific workouts for me to rotate, including jumping rope, shadow-boxing, push-ups, and stick-fighting drills. My boombox would be vibrating with top eighties hits by Madonna, Michael Jackson and Culture Club, to name a few.

Undeterred by the fact that Kirtan Singh had forced me to attend camp, I had planned my rebellion. My internal battlecry was to do *exactly* what I wanted and *nothing else.* His attempts to control me would fail.

Unbeknownst to my husband, before leaving town I had purchased some civilian clothing to wear. When I wasn't in my black martial arts clothes, I had a perfect summer outfit consisting of cuffed shorts, V-neck muscle tanks, scrunchie socks and L.A. Gear high-tops. Because of my enthusiasm for this look, I bought the identical outfit in mint green, yellow, sky blue, and lavender. It was remarkable how much had changed in under two weeks.

My feelings for Veda Singh invigorated me in unexpected ways. There was no doubt I was going to ruffle a lot of feathers with the choices I was making, but being a provocateur suited me fine.

My first decision was to allow myself the luxury of waking up naturally. No sadhana for me. I didn't attend Yogi Bhajan's lectures either. For the first three weeks of camp, I practically lived in that garage. It became my refuge.

The footpath to the kitchen was often busy with women far more devout than myself walking by the garage each day. My scandalous behavior caused some of them to glare at me as they went by, but I also noticed that more than a few seemed curious about my independence. Being ridiculed for liking girls and participating in The Game at Omega House had prepared me well for this moment in time. I'd spent a good portion of my teenage years being a topic of gossip and rumors. At this point, I didn't care what people were saying. In fact, I felt carefree for the first time since I had joined 3HO.

Sometimes I went to Sat Nirmal's house to visit with her and a few other friends, combing and braiding each other's hair and talking. Sat Nirmal said Yogi Bhajan knew I was skipping his lectures. I suspected Awtar Kaur was the snitch. It was really odd to think Yogi Bhajan had any idea who I was.

He'd certainly never noticed me in Los Angeles, but I had certainly been watching him. Ever since he struck Sangita Kaur, I had been watching him. My observations taught me that Yogi Bhajan was interested in people with money, power, and position. Those were the people he kept company with.

Regardless of Yogi Bhajan, my summer was unfolding as I intended it to. I had to admit, it was such a relief being away from Kirtan Singh because he wasn't around to criticize me or make me feel bad about myself.

On Sundays after gurdwara, I sold apparel for Veda Singh, mailing him the checks I received. He wrote back sending my cut in cash, wrapped in his love letters to me. We were writing to one another frequently. As a precaution, I mailed my letters in town rather than at the Ladies Camp office. Ours was yet an unrequited love. Our letters grew more steamy the longer we were apart.

Veda Singh even sent me a package with a photo album he created, called *A day in my life without Keke*. It was quirky and sweet: him on the sofa, napping with a teddy bear; in a martial arts pose looking fierce; leaning against the door of his office waiting for the mailman to bring him a letter from me; and one in the shower, tastefully cropped from the waist down.

All my correspondence from him was secreted away in my car, safeguarded, in case Awtar or anyone else decided to snoop through my belongings.

Someone handling the incoming mail did notice the letters I was receiving from Veda Singh. A few days after I got the package from him, I was heading to the garage to train. To my surprise, Veda Kaur and another woman were walking toward me on the footpath. The woman held a letter and was waving it in the air.

"Oh, Kirtan Kaur!" she yelled, her voice pinched with insinuation, "A letter arrived for you today from Veda Singh, you know, *Veda Kaur's husband.*"

"Oh, great, thanks," I said, ignoring her as I nonchalantly took the letter.

"Well, aren't you going to open it?" she insisted.

When I didn't respond right away, she commanded, "Open it now! After all, his wife is right here before you!"

Clearly, this woman had it in for me.

"Sure, I can open it." I replied, unperturbed. "I'm sure it has something to do with the clothing I'm selling for him."

I opened the letter, scanned it, and saw that it was not suitable for sharing. Reading the business references that were in it, I said, "Oh, yes, he's asking if there's any inventory left and if so, he wants to know if I'll have room in my car for the boxes to bring back to Los Angeles when camp is over." Hoping my delivery was convincing, I folded the letter and returned it to the envelope. I didn't know what I would do if they demanded to see it, but Veda Kaur seemed to accept what I said at face value.

Changing the subject, I told Veda Kaur I was stunned to see her, as she said she wasn't coming (like Kirtan Singh wasn't going to be at Solstice). She said it was a last-minute decision and she was staying for a week. An unspoken strain replaced the usual rapport between us.

Seeing Veda Kaur filled me with guilt and shame. Although I was trying to come off cool and unflustered, this was the friend I was betraying. I'd mulled over my dilemma for weeks, and at some unknown point, I selfishly justified my needs over hers. After years of severity and judgment living with Kirtan Singh, I wanted to receive the love that Veda Singh was offering.

Days later, I was at Sat Nirmal's house during Yogi Bhajan's afternoon yoga class. She found my defiance amusing, but cautioned me that I wasn't going to get away with it. It was ironic how she chided me for not attending class but didn't go herself.

We heard someone pounding on the front door. One of Yogi Bhajan's secretaries let herself in yelling, " Kirtan Kaur, Yogi Bhajan says you are to come to the Big Tent this instant!"

Sat Nirmal's face broke into a smug I-told-you-so smile.

I was wearing my lavender outfit that day and had no time to change into white clothing. This worried me a bit as I grabbed my sheepskin and headed to the Big Tent.

I heard later that as soon as he arrived, Yogi Bhajan asked if I was present and became irritated when told I was not. This produced a search to locate my whereabouts. Not knowing any of this at the time, I walked toward the stage looking for a place to put down my sheepskin. Yogi Bhajan saw me but didn't know me well enough to recognize me.

"What's your name?" he asked.

"Kirtan Kaur," I replied.

Hearing this, he made a face, declaring, "You're an idiot."

Placing my sheepskin on the ground, I mimicked what everyone else was doing. At first he told me I was doing it wrong, but moments later he complimented me, before he switched gears again to ridicule my clothing. His mercurial disposition reminded me of a bratty child.

It had long been evident to me that Yogi Bhajan loved food way more than yoga. He was overweight and out of shape, yet criticized me for missing class while he sat with his big gut hanging out. That day, he was even eating while he taught. At one point, he tossed a chunk of food in his mouth, briefly chomped on it, then spit it into his hand and threw it to the side of the stage. He also belched into the microphone repeatedly. I seemed to be the only person disgusted by his crude behavior.

For the next exercise, he told us to grab our ankles and put our nose between our knees, adding if we could achieve this posture we were normal. He looked at me and commented that I was doing well and that I had the right posture. This gave me great satisfaction, because as he praised my execution of the pose, I knew it did not stem from practicing kundalini yoga.

Moments later, he extolled my posture, telling the audience, "Look at this girl, see how good she is." He told me to get on stage to demonstrate how the pose was to be done. Joking with the audience, he claimed this was my punishment for missing his classes. All the women had a big laugh at my expense.

Turning to me, he asked, "What happened? Where is your turban? Why are your clothes different?" He didn't wait for an answer. Again, he made note of my flexibility, then gestured toward me, declaring I had perfected the pose. "This is it!" he exclaimed. Well, this was one hell of a development.

The experience left me perplexed. On the one hand, I thought Yogi Bhajan was a hypocrite who certainly did not practice what he preached. On the other hand, it felt good to be noticed and praised by him in front of everyone. The idea of being more esteemed in the community appealed to me. These disparate points of view had me in knots.

Then, something else happened that gave me clarity. Getting noticed and praised by Yogi Bhajan skyrocketed my Q-rating at Ladies Camp. All of a sudden, so many people were friendly and solicitous of my attention, asking me about my martial art training and telling me they wanted to hang out.

Women who never noticed me before were lavishing me with praise. I could see right through them. Their insincerity made me want to puke. I felt like I was back in high school where popularity was fickle and absolutely everything depended on it. I wasn't about to be seduced by liars and fakes.

A brief moment of escapism before the storm. Sailing off the coast of Malibu.

25

cavorting with chaos

Despite being made a spectacle at Yogi Bhajan's class, I was not deterred from my training. However, I did want to get away from camp more often, so I took little excursions to Española. I'd written to Veda Singh, warning him not to write again as his letter would likely be confiscated if his name was on the envelope. As usual, I mailed my letter to him at the post office in town.

One weekend, a group of us went to a spa outside of Santa Fe called Ten Thousand Waves to enjoy the hot tubs. We spent a couple of hours soaking and relaxing. As hard as I was pushing my body, the hot water worked magic on my sore muscles.

Afterward, we went into Santa Fe and parked near the Plaza. I'd never been there and was charmed by the ambience of the place. While exploring the shops, I discovered that Santa Fe was savvy about the white-clad seekers who came to town each year. Catering to our demographic, several clothing boutiques had racks of white cotton garments imported from India.

For years I'd had a small, unremarkable wardrobe. I called Kirtan Singh to tell him I wanted to buy some new clothes, but he said we couldn't afford it. He sternly reminded me that our American Express Card was for emergencies. I had a little cash from my commissions from Veda Singh and bought myself a summer dress.

Once I discovered Santa Fe, I continued to visit and walked through town taking in the art and culture that was on display everywhere you looked. No one could reach me in Santa Fe and I loved being anonymous on those cobbled streets, making them familiar as I traveled along them.

Nonetheless, Yogi Bhajan's emissaries were still hunting for me. I was given notice one day to come for a private audience at the ranch, referring to the complex that featured a number of buildings, including the Española ashram, Hacienda de Guru Ram Das. First the yoga class and now this. The idea of a private audience filled me with dread. I'd never been alone with Yogi Bhajan. My nerves frazzled at the thought of it. He was a huge man with an imposing personality. I laid down on my cot, glad to have the tent to myself. Being summoned meant I was busted. The intensity of the situation altogether overwhelmed me.

Ever since my first Ladies Camp in 1979, I kept my distance from Yogi Bhajan. As a result, I didn't have a strong sense of him as my teacher. Contemplating this upcoming meeting, I wondered if maybe that was part of the problem. In so many ways, I'd always been a fringe follower when perhaps it would have been wiser to be like everyone else. At this particular moment when I needed help, I decided a different approach was called for. I would be completely honest with him and hope something good would come from it.

When I arrived at the ranch, I was shown into a small room. Yogi Bhajan entered with some urgency, demanding, "Kirtan Kaur, is this true that you are having an affair with Veda Singh? This is what I am being told."

"Strictly speaking, no, sir, I am not." I began. "We haven't had sex yet."

"No? No sex?" Yogi Bhajan asked.

"No, sir," I repeated.

He asked me what was going on that would make me consider such a terrible course of action. Bursting into tears, I told him I was miserable in my marriage to Kirtan Singh.

"Tell me more about this," he said, leaning forward. "How is your sex life?"

Yogi Bhajan proceeded to ask me detailed, invasive questions about my sex life, not only with my husband, but all of my sexual history. Honestly, this felt sleazy to me from the get-go, but because his words *sounded* like someone who was looking out for me, I didn't name or act on what I was feeling.

As our conversation progressed, I could feel the energy in the room change. It was obvious to me that he was sexually aroused by the discussion we were having. He may have sensed this, because he changed direction, asking, "You are writing to one another? You and Veda Singh, yes?"

"Yes, sir." I replied.

"Sexy letters?" he pried.

"Yes, sir," I admitted.

"You will bring these to me," he ordered. "I have my Ph.D in humanology. I will make a study of these letters to understand the situation."

He continued in his typical, fragmented sentence structure, "Anything else he has sent you?"

"Yes," I replied, "he sent me some photos."

"You will bring those to me also."

Then he picked up a framed photo of himself and handed it to me, telling me to put it on my altar.

"Whenever you think of Veda Singh," he said, "you will look at this picture and think of me instead."

His advice turned my stomach, adding to the already queasy

feeling I had from our interaction. Yogi Bhajan was no substitute for the way I felt about Veda Singh. What really riled me up was his implication that I think of him romantically.

He ended the meeting abruptly with a wave of his hand, gesturing toward the door, "Now go, Kirtan Kaur. Try to be a good girl. Try to live as a Khalsa woman."

Those words: *Try to be a good girl*—it was such a parental thing to say. Looking back, this comment managed to hook me into wanting praise from Yogi Bhajan in the way I had always wanted it from my father. Maybe if I yielded to his orders, I would win his admiration. If I could correct my bad behavior and find favor with him, I might finally fit in.

And so, though I was filled with trepidation, I obeyed his instructions and returned to the ranch with all my correspondence from Veda Singh. It wasn't easy to relinquish because I was torn between maintaining the life I had known for nearly five years versus a life that might be possible with Veda Singh at my side.

Ultimately, guilt won over and I decided to try and right my wrongs. I can't recall who I handed my precious letters to, but I certainly didn't kid myself that Yogi Bhajan would be alone in reading them. I was now utterly exposed.

I told myself I should feel good because I was trying to do the right thing, but as soon as I complied with his wishes, I was filled with distress and foreboding. As I walked back to camp what really shook me up was that "doing the right thing" did not feel good at all. Doing the right thing for who and based on what? By the time I got back to my tent, I was upset and filled with regret. I laid on my cot and cried. The more I thought about the inappropriate way Yogi Bhajan had grilled me about my sexuality, the angrier I got. He had manipulated me and I was miserable that I had given away my letters and photos. My actions probably cost me whatever future I might have had with Veda Singh.

A few days later, on July 25, 1984, I received a message that Yogi Bhajan expected me to be present at his lecture that afternoon, in full bana. I was too afraid to defy a direct order and so I did as I was told. Wearing my turban, dress, churidars, and veil felt confining after weeks of living in shorts and sleeveless tees.

The lecture topic for the day was "The Art of Communication" and Yogi Bhajan wanted volunteers to participate in an exercise. He said that in fifteen sentences, the volunteer should convince the audience that Yogi Bhajan was the dirtiest person on the planet. He emphasized that we had to be poised and graceful—you couldn't criticize him angrily—it had to be done with a smile, in the most charming way. This was a tall order as all interactions with him required the utmost respect and reverence. Essentially, he was giving us permission to break code. A gauntlet had been thrown down.

The first volunteer opened weakly, stating that what he was asking for was simply not possible. Yogi Bhajan instantly put her on the defensive, claiming he knew the secrets she was most ashamed of. It was game over for her.

Yogi Bhajan asked if we understood how he'd created insecurity in her, proclaiming, "When you want to ruin someone, create doubt about that person."

What a bizarre, disturbing lesson to be teaching, I thought.

Another woman volunteered and failed. Yogi Bhajan claimed victory saying, "Butt in and you can always win."

Obviously, most women were too nervous or uncomfortable to follow his instructions. Yogi Bhajan reiterated that we must communicate in a most refined manner, not getting flustered by him, but instead, it was our job to fluster him.

The next woman did better. She challenged him on his policy of sending our children to India for schooling. When she concluded he said, "Come on, come on, it's your day. Take any subject, don't worry. Communication is an art. There is no reality in communication anyway."

Watching the others, I was irritated that no one was doing what he asked. I wanted a chance. More than that, the anger I felt toward him made me want to take him down and embarrass him in front of his students. My heart was racing. I knew I couldn't show my anger or he would say I failed the exercise. In order to succeed, I would have to keep my feelings hidden while I let him have it.

I raised my hand as high as I could to get his attention. It worked. Walking to the mic, I took a deep breath before beginning:

Me: "Sat nam, sir, I would like to talk to you about your weight."

(This opening line sent a loud gasp through the audience.)

Yogi Bhajan: "Oh sure. This morning my weight was two hundred and thirty-three pounds."

Me: "Mmm, how tall are you?"

Yogi Bhajan: "I am six feet, two inches."

Me: "I think around the belly…"

(nervous laughter from the audience)

Yogi Bhajan: "I am thirty-three pounds overweight."

Me: "Yes. I would like to put you on a program, streamline your diet and get some more exercise for you."

Yogi Bhajan: "Oh, for that you have not to bother. You have to call Dr. Saram. He is my medical doctor. Talk to him. He's really investigating things and you can really help him."

Me: "But, that doesn't matter, because if you don't have the commitment to do it, it doesn't matter what Dr. Saram says."

(groans from the audience)

Yogi Bhajan: "My commitment is within me, plus the help of my doctor. That's a fact."

Me: "But he's an excuse at this point. You need to just lose the weight."

Yogi Bhajan: "No, no, it is a reality. I am very serious about it."

Me: "Then why haven't you lost the weight? I think you should get another doctor or..."

Yogi Bhajan: (cutting me off) "Oh, basically, what I want to explain to you, it is a fact, that I've been to another doctor too."

Me: "Oh, you have? Who's that? Which doctor is that?"

Yogi Bhajan: "And I am also with a third doctor also these days."

Me: "And, they don't seem to make any difference. I think you should entrust yourself to me."

Yogi Bhajan: "Well, that's the fact of the situation is I am just working it out, it is not my weight which is in trouble."

Me: "Oh? What is in trouble?"

Yogi Bhajan: "It is the jet lag."

Me: "The jet lag. Well, see, we can take care of that."

Yogi Bhajan: "How?"

Me: "Through your diet and exercise. I think you probably sit a lot of hours, you could do more things on the plane: isometric type exercises to lose weight."

Yogi Bhajan: "You are absolutely right."

Me: "Do you want to discuss now how we're going to do that?"

Yogi Bhajan: "It is absolutely up to you. I'm just…any good suggestion will be so wonderful."

Me: "Okay, well I have…"

Yogi Bhajan: (interrupting) "You mean I should start flying on the magic carpet?"

Me: "No, I think you should fly on the plane, but I think you should get some weights, ankle weights and free weights, to work on to help you lose the weight."

Yogi Bhajan: "You mean, put two pounds on the ankle to walk?"

Me: "And do 108 leg lifts, 108 frogs…"

Yogi Bhajan: "To be very honest with you, this morning I did five more than the 108."

Me: "Five more? I think you should do three sets of 108. You have to let those muscles burn."

Yogi Bhajan: "You mean to say I was one hour late, I should have been two hours late?"

Me: "No. You should keep your responsibilities, but you have to be creative. When you're counseling people and things, you do your exercises."

Yogi Bhajan: (laughing) "You mean to say, when I counsel people I should start doing leg lifts?"

Me: "Exactly. They'll be impressed. That's when you should do it."

Yogi Bhajan: (laughing more) "That is a fantastic idea! I will be extremely impressive! I do my ups and downs and start talking?"

Me: "Yes, and as you get your stamina you'll be able to talk without any problem."

Yogi Bhajan: "Well, that will take care of all the counseling, I can assure you! Nobody will ever come to get counseled. And you want to give me a title of a jumping yogi?"

Me: "No, not really. I just think that it would help your image a lot if you would streamline your physique a little better."

(At this point everyone was laughing and Yogi Bhajan was nodding his head up and down)

Yogi Bhajan: "You mean, I should get to be skinny?"

Me: "No, lean and mean."

Yogi Bhajan: (asking the audience) "What she say?"

The audience yells "lean and mean!"

Yogi Bhajan: "Lean and mean! That's very affectionate. Lean and mean. Like that of a meat?"

Me: "No, not like meat."

Yogi Bhajan: "Like an avocado?"

Me: "Yes, lean and mean like an avocado, without the pit."

Yogi Bhajan: "Really, you are very suggestive, and your understanding is very affectionate."

Me: "I have your best interest at heart."

Yogi Bhajan: "Oh, I know, I know, I agree. I'll do my best to carry your best interest. I agree, 100 percent. Very sweet of you."

Me: "Thank you."

Yogi Bhajan: “Keep talking dummy.”

Me: “Keep talking dummy? Okay.”

Yogi Bhajan: “You should not come to thank me.”

Me: “I appreciate the compliment because I know that I have a lot to offer you.”

Yogi Bhajan: “That is the other way to shut you up.”

Me: (emphatically) “I think that I’m still talking. I would like to set up a schedule of six days a week exercising, and Sundays you can have off.”

Yogi Bhajan: “Oh, I basically will agree to that in the sense, you know I have a secretary, and if you train her into it, it will be a great communication and I shall be personally very grateful.”

Me: “Well, she’s not the point. You are. I don’t think I need a go-between.”

Yogi Bhajan: “No, no. It is not a question of going between, but it’s a question of she will keep the record.”

Me: “Of your weight and measurements?”

Yogi Bhajan: “Weight and measurements and run all that program you are running. The best thing will be to convince her you can put her on that program. She can have that perfect personal experience.”

Me: “I would like to know how long of a goal you’d like to set before we take the thirty-three pounds off.”

Yogi Bhajan: “Oh, till my death, I don’t mind.”

Me: “But, that’s too long.”

Yogi Bhajan: “I think that the moment I see my secretary getting skinny it will psychologically…”

Me: (interrupting) "No, she wants to see you getting skinny, you're going to inspire her."

Yogi Bhajan: "Let us not get into catch-22. The fact is, that if you can get her to be skinny..."

Me: "But, you're trying to change the point of this discussion."

Yogi Bhajan: "No, no, I am with you. There's no difference of opinion at all. The problem is, the secretary."

Me: "No, the problem is you!"

Yogi Bhajan: "No, no. I definitely agree with you as far as I am concerned. I want to be lean and mean and green and all that. And I'll be just talking, sitting, standing, jumping, whatever you want, but if you can give her a little experience that way, then all the time she will be just an inspiration."

Me: "I think your staff generally looks very good."

Yogi Bhajan: "They are?"

Me: "Yeah, they look pretty healthy."

Yogi Bhajan: "I am the only one who looks bad?"

Me: "About thirty-three pounds."

Yogi Bhajan: "I think you have to change your opinion a little bit."

Me: "In what way?"

Yogi Bhajan: "I think I do not look very good, but I don't look very bad either."

Me: "No, you don't look bad. You have a good stout physique, but I do think that you need to lose the weight."

Yogi Bhajan: "Oh, how do you know I have a stout physique?"

Me: "Oh, well, because I can see. I've been trained to see that kind of thing."

Yogi Bhajan: "Is that true?"

Me: "Yes, it's very true."

Yogi Bhajan: "So what you intend to employ that if I lose all the weight I have to lose, and I do what I have to do, in which way can you help me?"

Me: "The way you'll be helped is you'll sleep better, you'll have more energy..."

Yogi Bhajan: "Oh, I sleep well. I sleep well. There's no problem with my sleeping, with my eating."

Me: "We're just going to maximize..."

Yogi Bhajan: "No, no. My problem is I need somebody trained to remind me all the time."

Me: "I'd be happy to do that."

Yogi Bhajan: "Oh, damn. You know Sat Simran?"

Me: "Yes, I do."

Yogi Bhajan: "Get on her."

Me: "Get on her about what?"

Yogi Bhajan: "Train her."

Me: "Train her to do what?"

Yogi Bhajan: "To keep reminding me, inspiring me and if she loses thirty pounds, I lose fifty!"

Me: "I'd be happy to train her sir."

Yogi Bhajan: "Thank you."

Me: "Thank you, Sat nam."

Yogi Bhajan: "Again you have stopped!"

Me: "What else is there to say? I am satisfied! We're going to get the weight off you, I'll train Sat Simran..."

Yogi Bhajan: (To the audience) Without offending people you can satisfy them in shortest possible time, but the greatest mistake is don't make them go satisfied in a small pace if they want to take the long phase.

Yogi Bhajan: (to me) "Okay, thank you."

Me: "Thank you."

The manner in which I spoke to Yogi Bhajan during this class was unprecedented. During the time that we were conversing, I went through a few different emotions. While I had started out angry, even surly inside, as we began to have our back and forth, I enjoyed myself. I knew he would try to throw me off my topic, and so he did, attempting to distract me or create humor with his comebacks. I had the briefest glimpse into Yogi Bhajan as a mere man, someone I could have a casual conversation with.

This was an unusual sensation, conversing and even laughing with him. I felt powerful and loved how much the audience was responding to what I was saying. That changed, however, when he said I was being "very suggestive" followed by his comment that I was being "very affectionate." Both comments made me uncomfortable and felt like he was trying to manipulate me.

When we concluded, I felt victorious.

As I collected my things, a secretary approached me, saying, "Yogi Bhajan wants to see you. Right now."

Still amped from our conversation, I headed to the ranch. Why did he want to see me? Did I anger him by bringing up his weight problem?

It was a stunning day, the kind that made it easy to enjoy the beauty of New Mexico, with her bluest of skies and magnificent clouds. The snows of summer fell from the cottonwood trees and floated against the cobalt sky. I walked slowly, trying to relax a bit before I arrived.

I was greeted at the door by Guruke Kaur, a pink-hued, bird-faced woman with a prominent beak where her nose should have been. She lived in Los Angeles, and seemed to me to put on airs, broadcasting her superiority as one of Yogi Bhajan's chosen secretaries. We had never spoken before, but she greeted me with excessive, gushing energy.

"Sat Nam, Kirtan Kaur," she cooed. "Come in, Siri Singh Sahibji is waiting for you."

So gross. I stifled the urge to punch her in the beak.

Yogi Bhajan was in a recliner, eating masala. The aroma of Indian spices had greeted me long before I entered the house. Seeing me, Yogi Bhajan commanded, "Kirtan Kaur, rub my feet."

Ugh, I thought, *not those massive dogs.*

There was a bottle of hand lotion on a tray table next to the recliner and a towel on the floor indicating where to kneel. Walking to where he was, I pumped some lotion into my hands, knelt on the towel and began massaging his feet half-heartedly.

Yogi Bhajan was eating while talking to people on the phone. This was the second time I'd seen him out of the public eye and both times were disarming. Behind closed doors he was a completely different person, obnoxious and crude, farting and belching while he devoured his food.

I tried to keep my attention on his feet but my mind was moving fast, taking in my surroundings. Yogi Bhajan barked his commands to the air and people appeared to do his bidding. Eventually, he stared at me without saying a word. It was creepy and made me extremely uncomfortable.

Then he started flexing and pointing his feet, alternating left and right. It made it difficult to massage him, so I stopped what I was doing. I lowered my head, keeping my eyes on the floor until he stopped moving, then I resumed the foot massage.

After a few minutes of silence, I looked up and was perturbed to see he was still staring at me. He shifted his weight, side to side to maneuver himself lower in the recliner. His legs slid off the footrest. He resumed pointing and flexing, but now, with his legs extended, his feet could reach my body.

In an alternating motion, he pressed his feet into my chest, using the balls of his feet to palpate my breasts. He silently stared at me, goading me to respond. Staring back at him, I said nothing.

Disturbed by his gall, I leaned back on my heels so that my breasts were out of reach and looked at him quizzically.

Yogi Bhajan's face broke into a massive shit-eating grin.

I was in danger.

Cranking the side lever, Yogi Bhajan got out of the recliner and walked toward a room, motioning for me to follow. I stood up and saw Guruke giving me a knowing smile like we were about to become sister wives, nodding in encouragement for me to follow him.

I had not realized that his wife Bibiji was in the house. She entered the room and walked past me, raising her arm in slow motion until her palm was facing me. It was a weird semi-wave accompanied with a weak smile before she exited the room. The facial expressions of both women made me feel substantially more ill at ease. I felt like I was back at Lake Tahoe and about to be harmed by another bad man. I walked forward, my heart pounding harder with each step.

When I reached the doorway, I raised both my arms at right angles, placing them on the wall outside the door frame, bracing myself there.

Yogi Bhajan was in a small bedroom that appeared to be his wife's room. He had pulled the covers down and was sitting on the edge of the bed, waiting for me.

I didn't move an inch.

In an attempt to entice me into the room, he started patting the bed with his hand, as if to say *this is where I want you.*

Simultaneously, he puckered his lips and made kissy-face noises at me. I was gobsmacked watching him make a fool of himself. He looked ridiculous. His big belly was sagging forward, undulating as he thumped on the bed.

Had I not been frightened, I would've laughed out loud. Fear glued my feet to the floor. I remained frozen in the door jam. Finally I spoke, my disgust evident in my tone: "My god, do you mean to tell me that all the rumors I've heard about you are true?"

He said nothing, so I continued, stating loudly, "I am *not* going to have sex with you. I think of you like an old grandpa!"

Yogi Bhajan's sexy face crashed to the floor. He was instantly enraged. Getting off the bed, he roared at me, red-faced, "You look like shit, Kirtan Kaur! Go buy yourself some new bana and make yourself worthy to be my lover!"

I was already hauling ass past a stunned Guruke and was halfway out the door before he finished yelling. I didn't hear anything else he was saying. I was getting the hell out of there.

Without speaking to anyone, I drove to Española to find a phone booth. I hadn't called Veda Singh once, but still had his office phone number. Hoping he would be there, I dialed his number. Thankfully, he picked up. As soon as I heard his voice, I became emotional, "Oh my god, Veda Singh, you are not going to believe what happened."

Talking fast, I recounted the last couple of weeks, first telling him about being called onstage at yoga class, and then about the creepy, private audience that resulted in my giving Yogi Bhajan our letters and photos. I apologized to him, saying I gave in at a moment of weakness.

Then I told him what had transpired at the ranch, fully expecting him to be as stunned and outraged as I was. When I finished speaking, I heard Veda Singh chuckle and say, "Wow, so *dad* is into you?"

"What did you say?" I asked indignantly.

"There's nothing funny about this, whatsoever, Veda!" I roared into the phone. "This is so fucked up."

"No, you're right," he corrected. "I know it is. I've heard rumors for years."

"Yeah," I said. "Me too. Apparently, they are true."

Yogi Bhajan's abusive behavior and unwanted sexual advances changed everything. Nothing was the same after that. Nothing could be the same.

Veda Singh asked what I was going to do. I said I was done with camp and wanted to come back to Los Angeles. He agreed. I told him I would let him know when I was leaving.

When I returned to camp, Awtar was in our tent. I told her what had happened. I couldn't keep it to myself. She was taciturn after hearing my account, like she could not figure out what she wanted to say. I had the feeling she maybe didn't believe me. I did not tell her I was leaving camp because I wanted time to think through the best way to make that happen.

The next day, I drove to Española to buy some things I needed before leaving town. Then I went to Santa Fe. It had occurred to me that since Yogi Bhajan ordered me to buy new clothes, Kirtan Singh could not object. Taking advantage of this, I used our American Express card and treated myself to a shopping spree.

This was a memorable day of pleasure and I had a bounty of clothing to choose from. I bought beautiful dresses made in

India from smooth pima cotton and gauzy summer dresses that were more sheer. I found an outfit made of raw silk which had a distinctive earthy scent to it. Adding to that, I couldn't pass up the stunning native textiles and got several striped, brightly colored sashes that could be wrapped as a cummerbund. I was in heaven. All in all, about four hundred dollars went on the American Express credit card. This put me in a tremendously good mood.

Afterward, I made phone calls to Veda Singh and Graciela, telling them I was leaving in the morning. Before returning to camp, I tucked my purchases behind the seats and parked close to our tent. This way, I could load up quickly in the morning while Awtar and most everyone else was at sadhana.

It was still dark when I was ready to go. Unfortunately, the road out of camp went right by the Big Tent. Anyone paying attention would know I'd flown the coop.

Sure enough, phone calls were made to alert both Yogi Bhajan and Kirtan Singh once I had fled.

Not surprisingly, I can't remember much of the drive back to Los Angeles except I was scared to do it alone. When I got to Flagstaff, I got a room at the same motel Veda Singh and I had stayed at on our way to Solstice. This time the hourly trains going through town kept me awake. After a restless night, I got an early start back on the road.

My mind was alert with an avalanche of thoughts about what I was going to do. It was already taxing thinking about my feelings for Veda, but Yogi Bhajan's shocking breach was staggering. It made me question the credibility of the entire 3HO organization.

Based on how Guruke had behaved, I was convinced that Yogi Bhajan was having sex with all of his staff (no pun intended).

I was also convinced that the secretaries colluded with and protected Yogi Bhajan from being exposed. This made my refusal of him all the more extreme, even dangerous. I had to proceed cautiously.

The miles went by quickly, in a blur really, as I cried and yelled in my car. So much emotion was pouring out of me. All my stifled feelings, the confusion I had about the life I was living, coupled with the horrible feeling that I had gotten it wrong, flooded to the surface.

When I told Graciela what had happened, she invited me to come to her apartment in Santa Monica rather than go home. It was early afternoon when I arrived. Graciela greeted me warmly, shaking her head at the bizarre developments that had transpired in New Mexico.

Using her phone, I called Kirtan Singh. He was irate that I left camp and even angrier that I hadn't communicated with him for three days. We hadn't gotten into the details of what had gone down with Yogi Bhajan, but he was full of indignation from the rumors about Veda Singh and I.

After berating me, he asked, "When will you be home?"

"I'm not sure." I said. "I need to think."

He began another rant, so I hung up.

Then I called Veda, but he didn't pick up. Looking at her watch, Graciela said he was probably in class at the Inosanto Academy in Marina Del Rey.

I wanted to freshen up from the long drive, so I showered and washed my hair before splashing on some Jean Naté. Wearing one of my favorite new dresses with a pretty latticed back, I put on my new sandals and left my legs bare. I wore my hair down in public for the first time in years, which felt amazing.

Graciela offered to drive, and sure enough, as we entered the parking lot I saw Veda Singh's Rabbit. He was there.

To this day I vividly remember how his face lit up with a humongous smile when he saw me. In a scene fit for a movie, he rushed over, picked me up, and twirled me in the air. It felt magnificent. I was over the moon to be in his arms again.

Graciela went out for the evening but gave me her spare key with a wink, so Veda Singh and I could be alone. *Finally,* I thought, *we will be able to make love.* I was shimmering with anticipation. We drove to her place and I sat on his lap again, like I had at the El Rey Inn. We cuddled and kissed a little, but our conversation turned serious as we talked about what to do next.

Veda Singh's opening comment was, "*Dad's* gonna be mad."

His personal sobriquet for Yogi Bhajan really annoyed me. It was odd and off-putting, but I kept quiet about it, preferring to talk about us. I told him I wanted to leave as soon as possible, but he didn't agree, mainly out of concern for his daughter. He said he needed more time, even though it had been a month since this all began.

"How much time?" I asked.

"I'm not sure, but I can't do this hastily," he said.

What could I do but acquiesce? It wasn't for me to tell him what pace to go at. Our conversation killed any sexual desire I was feeling. We agreed to return to our respective homes until we knew what we wanted to do. Saying goodbye to Veda Singh, I shuddered with dread. I didn't want to spend one more second living with Kirtan Singh. I stayed at Graciela's that night, not ready to see my husband yet.

In the morning, I thanked Graciela for her help and drove to Siri Gurbani. Kirtan Singh was outside waiting for me with his arms folded tightly across his chest. Seeing him caught me off guard in the sense that until that moment I had not realized how drastically my perception of him had changed. There was no love between us. What I saw was a man with a pinched face, shut-down heart, and clenched asshole, ready and waiting to let me have it.

He didn't speak until I had unloaded and parked the car. Once we were in our bedroom he launched at me, "What were you thinking, taking off like that, Kirtan Kaur? You showed no respect to anyone, especially the Siri Singh Sahib." I was in no mood for one of his diatribes.

"Lay off, Kirtan Singh, I mean it," I shot back at him, adding, "Why is it that you haven't even bothered to ask me why I left? What is wrong with you?"

"Fine," he responded. "Why did you leave then?"

"I left, Kirtan Singh, because Yogi Bhajan tried to have sex with me! He molested me."

Without missing a beat, Kirtan Singh replied, "He is our spiritual teacher. If he wants to have sex with you, *he can*."

His outrageous pronouncement smashed my heart to pieces.

How could a sentence like that even come out of his mouth?

I finally got it—my husband would *always* choose Yogi Bhajan over me. I was his wife, but the painful words he said on the day he proposed came back to me, "You could be any woman."

But, there was only one Yogi Bhajan.

Kirtan Singh's fidelity to this man was so warped it made him think he had the right to tell me what Yogi Bhajan was entitled to do with my body. I made another attempt to get him to understand, "Listen to me, please. I'm telling you, he is a different person behind closed doors. He is *not* who you think he is, Kirtan Singh. He's a pig."

Hearing this, my husband stuck his fingers in his ears and began loudly chanting:

"You are slandering a saint, I will not listen...

"You are slandering a saint, I will not listen...

"You are slandering a saint, I will not listen..."

Coming home to a husband who *did not* and *could not* care for me was crushing. Kirtan Singh slammed shut all communication between us about what had happened to me in Española.

For days, I barely functioned, staying in bed and sleeping as much as possible. At least sleep allowed me to temporarily disown my reality. It provided relief from agonizing days where time lumbered along as a punishment. Kirtan Singh worked all day and mostly kept away from me. Veda Singh was always on my mind. What was going on with him? What was he thinking? I hated being in the dark.

Like an answer to my prayers, about a week later Veda Singh called with delightful news. He had cleverly planned a sailing excursion with classmates from the Academy, so he and I could spend some time together. Our privacy would be granted by the limitless expanse of the ocean. Writing down the details of where to meet, I let Kirtan Singh know the day I would be gone, telling him I was taking an all day self-defense seminar. He didn't object. I assumed he was glad for any reason to be rid of me.

August in Los Angeles can typically be hot and muggy, but the day we went sailing the weather was exceptional—a sunny, breezy, lovely day. We met at the docks in Marina Del Rey. This would be my first time on the ocean in any kind of vessel. We were a small group, five of us including our teacher from the academy.

Seeing Veda Singh made me so happy. He brought music and got the tunes going right away. Sailing north toward Malibu, Veda Singh and I found a spot to ourselves. I told him Kirtan Singh's infuriating response to Yogi Bhajan's behavior toward me at the ranch.

I laid down on some cushions with Veda Singh beside me, stroking my back. I was holding back tears, not wanting to attract any attention. Even on this stunning day, I was melancholy. While I was on cloud nine to see Veda Singh, it also pained me because nothing was in motion to bring us together. When I asked him when we would make our move, he still didn't have an answer.

Veda Singh sat with me as the motion of the water lulled me to sleep. When we reached Malibu, we dropped anchor and jumped into the water to swim. The shore line of Malibu with its pricey beachfront properties was amazing to see. Playing in the water lightened my mood considerably and I was able to stop worrying for a while and enjoy myself.

Veda Singh played the song, "Sailing," by Christopher Cross on the way back to the marina. It was the perfect song to align with the gorgeous day. Veda Singh and I took pictures of one another to commemorate the day, but no pictures of us together.

With nothing decided, the outing was a short-lived reprieve from the crap state of my marriage. I was sadder than ever to say goodbye.

By nature, I'm an impatient person. Waiting for Veda Singh to make a decision was frustrating, but I was tolerant because I did not want to leave by myself. He was nine years older than me and I hoped he would know what to do. For years I had seen how people were ostracized and shunned when they left. I had a pretty good idea of what was coming.

This unkind treatment of people by our community always mystified me. One day we loved them and the next they were outcasts. Discussion about why someone left was forbidden, as if the act of talking about their reasons for leaving would infect us, putting us in peril. It was disheartening to see how quickly our love for people was abandoned and turned to hate.

From the early days of 3HO, Yogi Bhajan fabricated a perfect catch-22 which perpetuated a dangerous belief in the community: leaving your spiritual teacher was never acceptable.

This catch-22 was predicated on an internal state of crisis Yogi Bhajan called *shaktipad.* Shaktipad was an affliction of faith, an egotistical state of mind a seeker could get caught in which would convince them they no longer needed their spiritual teacher. To survive it required prayer, yoga, meditation, and dedication to the master. Thus, criticism of Yogi Bhajan or his teachings was forbidden. Criticizing him was a sure indication a person was in shaktipad. Any complaint or honest feedback was labeled as slander against our teacher. The indoctrination on shaktipad *guaranteed* no possible way to leave without being labeled a slanderer. If you had taken Amrit vows (a sacred Sikh initiation ceremony) you were given the additional label of being a *patit*: one who turns their back on the Guru. In authentic Sikhism, this term is applied to someone who breaks the Khalsa code of conduct; in 3HO, it was weaponized to mean anyone who left the community.

If you left, you lost everything, and ironically, you were immediately and cruelly slandered by the community that would not stand for slander. It was a preposterous double standard. All of this ensured division and polarization when someone left.

Yogi Bhajan controlled the narrative.

No one could leave on good terms, so no one was ever able to tell those of us who were interested why they left. As a result, 3HO operated as a toxic, insular system that brutalized anyone who dared to leave.

Sharing with Megg during her visit to Los Angeles on the beach in Santa Monica.

26
boomerang

Within days of our covert sailing trip, I was relaxing with a morning cup of tea in my bedroom when the phone rang. It was Veda Singh, breathing so fast he was nearly gasping.

"Keke," he said urgently. "I told her. I told Veda Kaur everything. I'm at my office. Come over here now."

"What? Right now?" I stammered, knocked for a loop. "Veda, you said you needed time!"

"I know," he replied. "But, I can't do this anymore, I can't live a lie."

Then he repeated, emphatically, "I told Veda Kaur *everything*."

Those words made my heart lurch, like I'd been hit by a shockwave. This was now blood-and-guts real. My zen morning took flight out the window.

"Oh my god, Veda Singh, oh my god. Jesus, you didn't give me any notice!"

"I know. I'm sorry," he said. "But you should get over here as fast as you can."

Within minutes, I was driving full throttle to his office on Overland Boulevard.

He heard me practically skid into a parking spot and opened the door, looking scared. We were both agitated. This wasn't anything like my daydreams where I imagined the momentous occasion when we both would declare our love and our freedom. I didn't know how quickly the soft flourishes of romantic love could disappear under the microscope of reality.

We went inside and, as per our usual, he sat in a chair and I sat on his lap, except this time his right leg was vibrating with nervous tension. Veda Singh was no longer silent; it was time to talk. This meant the end of our marriages and, as far as I was concerned, the end of our involvement with 3HO.

Our conversation was disjointed as both of us struggled with how to move forward. "I'm going to leave everything with Veda Kaur," Veda Singh stated. "Since I'm the one ending our marriage, it's the right thing to do."

"Okay." I responded.

"What I think will be best is for us to move to Oregon. We can live with my parents," he continued.

"Oregon?" I repeated, taken aback. This was news to me.

"That sounds tricky," I suggested. "I mean, aren't your parents going to hate me for ruining your marriage?"

Of course they would. I had no doubt they loved Veda Kaur and would resent me from the start. I silently clutched. Moving to Oregon was completely unappealing to me. I couldn't help but flash on Bill Dansie living at home at the age of twenty-six. Veda Singh was thirty-four years old. Why did he think this was our best option?

Switching subjects, I asked, "What will you call yourself? Will you use your birth name? What is your birth name?"

"What do you mean?" he said, "We can still be Sikhs."

Goddamnit, I thought, *this is exactly why we should have been talking long before this moment.*

I had no idea he would feel this way.

"Um, wow, no. I don't want to be a Sikh anymore," I replied.

I did not know how Sikhs in India lived, but Yogi Bhajan's version of a Sikh lifestyle was intensely disciplined and required vast amounts of time and energy. I didn't want to live like that anymore. My response wasn't what Veda Singh expected to hear. We sat in awkward, stilted silence.

This moment of togetherness that I had longed for now felt grim. Sadly, it was dawning on me that we really didn't know each other at all. Like all marital affairs, we gravitated toward one another out of a need and longing for something better, or maybe something different. We were wholly unprepared for the conversation we were attempting to have. Our newly found flirtation needed to rapidly concretize into an actual relationship under extreme circumstances.

The phone clanged loudly, causing us to jump out of our skins. We looked at each other and I practically screamed at Veda Singh, "Do not pick it up!"

But like a moth to the flame, Veda Singh disregarded my advice. Lifting the receiver he held it so we could both hear. Unbelievably, it was Nirinjan, one of Yogi Bhajan's staff.

"Veda Singh? Sat Nam, Veda, are you there? This is Nirinjan."

"Yes," he confirmed.

Speaking like a member of the royal family, she continued, "We want you to know that we are fully aware of what is going on and we know you are with Kirtan Kaur. May I speak with her?"

"Okay."

Veda Singh extended the phone to me. This really pissed me off. I didn't take the phone from him. I was gesturing like a wild woman, trying to get an indication from him about how to respond to this intrusion. He gave me nothing. He held the phone in the air, waiting for me to take it from him.

My mind was too amped. I couldn't think straight.

The pressure was immense. I raised the phone to my ear and said in a most unfriendly tone, "What do you want?"

"Sat Nam, Kirtan Kaur. Yogi Bhajan is aware of all that has happened. He has spoken with Veda Kaur," she began.

"Yogi Bhajan would like to marry you and Veda Singh, this weekend in front of the whole sangat. He asks that you and Veda Singh come to the ashram to personally speak with him so that he may give you his blessing."

Let me address an obvious question: No, I did not know at that time it took six months to get a divorce. Because of my ignorance, this proposal of marrying us in a few days felt real and more like a threat than a happy occasion.

Nirinjan's voice was fake. She was acting ridiculously upbeat, as if to say, *It's a miracle! You and Veda Singh screwed over your spouses, but we still accept you completely.*

My bullshit detector was humming. I covered the phone and repeated what she said. Veda Singh shrugged his shoulders sheepishly, "I think we should go and see what he has to say."

"That is not a good idea," I flatly stated.

"Why? What's the harm in it?" he countered. "Aren't you a little curious to hear what he has to say?"

No, I wasn't. I had zero interest in what Yogi Bhajan might say. My frustration level was rising because I didn't know how to get through to Veda Singh. As vehemently as I could, I told him, "I'm not curious at all. Please listen to me, this is a terrible idea."

He didn't respond. Things were moving too fast. This was going to be a trap. I put my hand on his shoulder, pleading with him, "Veda, this is a set-up. Hang up the phone, right now."

"No," Veda decided, ignoring my plea. "I think we should meet with him. We owe him that much."

My heart sank. I didn't owe Yogi Bhajan a fucking thing.

Our difference in perspective was maddening. Talking into the phone I said, "Okay" and hung up.

We had just made a deal with the devil.

Nirinjan was on the sidewalk waiting for us when we pulled up. She escorted us through the side door where Yogi Bhajan was lying in wait.

"Oh, there you are!" He said in a lyrical voice I'd never heard come out of him.

"Come in, come in! Veda Singh and Kirtan Kaur, sit, let us sit and talk together."

We sat on the floor in front of him. *He's too chipper,* I thought.

"Let us discuss this. You want to leave your spouses and get married? Yes?"

"Yes, sir," we both chimed.

"Good, very good. Let us discuss some things. You are my son and daughter and it is my utmost duty as your spiritual teacher to make sure you understand this path you are taking."

Yogi Bhajan turns his attention to me and says, "Kirtan Kaur, of course you are aware Veda Singh is not making any money and you know it is Veda Kaur who is the breadwinner in their family. You are aware of this, yes?"

Hard gulp, accompanied by a huge lump in my throat.

No, I didn't know.

I knew Veda Kaur worked full time as a graphic designer, but I didn't know Veda Singh wasn't earning anything. I remained silent and Yogi Bhajan continued in a discouraging tone, "Yes, yes, Veda Singh has not provided for his wife and daughter. He is playing at various enterprises, this and that, but no real money is coming in. He has failed to be a householder for his family."

Yogi Bhajan was shaming Veda Singh while putting me on alert that we would be starting out with nothing. This explained why Veda Singh suggested we would live with his parents in Oregon. Was he really a financial disaster? I already had a husband who filled that position.

I was accustomed to not having much, but hearing Yogi Bhajan characterize Veda Singh as an incompetent husband didn't feel great. Still, I said nothing. A sinking feeling was growing in the pit of my stomach, like a trap door was about to open. I knew this was a set-up, but it was more than that—it was a demolition mission.

Veda Singh's head was hanging down like a dog who had been beaten. Having been exposed as a failure by his Yogi Bhajan, he was silent.

We were lambs for the slaughter.

Then it was my turn, "Kirtan Kaur, why do you want to divorce Kirtan Singh?" That was an easy question to answer, "Because I am unhappy, because he doesn't meet my needs, because he is severe..."

Yogi Bhajan interrupted, "Oh, I see. So, Kirtan Kaur, I am prepared to marry you to Veda Singh this Saturday with the entire sangat present to witness my blessing. On this you have my word."

He paused for dramatic effect before saying, "But, my daughter, I have to ask you one thing."

I didn't want to know the question.

"It is this," he said somberly. "You have promised to love and serve Kirtan Singh until you die, yes? You took Amrit vows also, yes? You made vows. And now you want to marry Veda Singh."

Yogi Bhajan then dropped his voice to a more measured tone, "In five years, if you should find yourself in this same place with Veda Singh, the place you are right now with Kirtan Singh, should Veda Singh expect that you will divorce him also?"

Now my face was hot with shame.

The Amrit vows he spoke of refer to the Sikh initiation ceremony, which I had taken the year before under unrelenting pressure from Kirtan Singh.

I could hear my father's voice in my head calling me *flighty* and *capricious*, words I heard too many times.

From the time I had moved into the ashram at nineteen until now at the age of twenty-four, I had changed everything about who I was. From my name and my religion to the way I dressed, how I thought, and where I lived. Up until now, my allegiance was to my spiritual community. A community where I had made dear friends and found a sense of belonging that I cherished.

Yogi Bhajan's words pulled me outside the bubble of tenderness and love I had been savoring with Veda Singh. What would the community think of me? I'd already hurt Veda Kaur. How would their daughter look at me? We might be married by Yogi Bhajan, with his blessing, but there was no doubt in my mind I would be reviled.

We were silent for a long time while I thought about his question. It seemed logical to me that if I was willing to leave Kirtan Singh at this level of unhappiness, then if Veda Singh and I also reached this level of unhappiness, I probably would leave.

This whole situation had arisen because I was finally able to declare to myself that I was not willing to live in a miserable marriage. Anyway, Yogi Bhajan's hypothetical scenario might never materialize. It was a big *if*. I mean, who was to say we would be unhappy? We hadn't even had a chance to start our life together.

But Yogi Bhajan was clever. By naming it as a possibility, he had given this hypothetical weight and validity, not to me, but to Veda Singh, who was already a wreck. I didn't want to answer yes, but it was there in my head. Finally I said, "Yes, I probably would leave, *only if* we were as unhappy as Kirtan Singh and I are now."

I looked at Veda Singh. Hearing my answer, all the color drained from his face.

The death knell was tolling.

For a few moments we were all still. The thought occurred to me to grab Veda Singh and say, "Let's get out of here while we still can, we've been duped!"

But Veda Singh spoke first, breaking the silence and my heart. Quietly he said, "Sir, I think I'd like to go back to my wife now."

His words sliced the air with their certainty. Tears streamed out of my eyes while Yogi Bhajan smiled triumphantly.

"Are you sure, my son? Because I am prepared to marry you this weekend."

"Yes, sir, I'm sure," he confirmed.

I was dizzy from the velocity of the pendulum swing—the flip-flop of my fate that Yogi Bhajan manipulated with ease.

Veda Singh stood up. Without even looking at me, he walked out the door to go back to his wife. My head was pounding so hard it made my ears ring. I felt like I was going to explode. I wanted to smash Yogi Bhajan's smug face in. What an easy mark Veda Singh was, weak and pathetic. My whole body tensed as I thrust my fists into my thighs, pushing as hard as I could to steady myself. In less than ten minutes, Veda Singh and I were over. I sat, stunned at the outcome.

"Go, Kirtan Kaur," Yogi Bhajan said dismissively. Nirinjan came in to escort me out. She had a look on her face that said she had seen this kind of situation play out many times before.

Yogi Bhajan had exposed the shaky ground of our relationship and destroyed my hopes of leaving with Veda Singh. Was this his revenge because I sexually rejected him at Ladies Camp?

As the door was closing behind me, Yogi Bhajan delivered one more instruction, "You should go and tell Kirtan Singh."

Once outside, I stood alone on the street. Huge gulping sobs of defeat shook my whole body. My brain hurt. I went from being on my way out to feeling stuck again.

The hard truth was I didn't know how to leave on my own. I was too scared and couldn't see the first steps I would need to take. I may have been twenty-four, but inside I still felt like a teenager.

Now what? I didn't have a plan B. I made my way across the street to GRD to come face-to-face with my husband.

I thought about what I should say to Kirtan Singh, should I be contrite and apologize so we could begin again? That might have been a possible intention as I entered the building, but then I heard Kirtan Singh's voice talking loudly to his co-workers.

I stopped to listen. He was holding court with his cohorts in deception, bragging about how I had left with Veda Singh and how glad he was to finally be rid of me. He and his buddies were whooping it up at my expense. Any feeling of contrition I had was replaced by rage. Rounding the corner, I confronted him.

They all jumped at the sight of me. I nearly laughed at the look of shock on their faces. I yelled at Kirtan Singh, "Don't get too excited, mother fucker, because I'm back!"

That shut them up. Grabbing our car keys off his desk, I stormed out.

His gleeful celebration over being done with me filled me with hatred. He was cruel. An egotist wrapped in cloaks of fake humility. I'm sure it never occurred to him that my betrayal was fueled by his poor treatment of me.

I decided to drive to the Vedas' apartment to apologize to Veda Kaur. I owed her that much.

My feelings were pouring out of me before she opened the door. Her anguished face when she looked at me was the hard slap I needed. Looking into her eyes, I suddenly couldn't conceive how I had been so thoughtless and selfish. I hugged her, saying over and over how sorry I was.

She was crying too and said, "My friends suspected what was happening, but I said no, there's no way Kirtan Kaur would ever do that to me."

"We never had sex, Veda Kaur, never. We only kissed," I hurriedly said, thinking somehow that would be a consolation.

But what meaning could it have? Betrayal is betrayal. Truly, I hated myself for wounding her so deeply. It was sickening to acknowledge that I had done to her what Mrs. Carlson did to my mother. The words *I'm sorry* seemed like the most meaningless, empty words in the English language.

We hugged one another and cried. My tears held regret and sorrow but also sadness that Veda Singh and I were over and I was left with my unhappy life with Kirtan Singh.

I went home completely spent. As I entered our bedroom a crushing feeling of depression came down on me hard. I collapsed on the bed. The agony of being back in our room was unbearable. I thought Veda Singh and I would be driving away together, not this. Longing gripped me in his absence. I had no idea how I was going to be able to continue on in my marriage. I wanted to be with Veda Singh, feeling loved and alive again.

The last six weeks felt like a flimsy joke. It had seemed so real to me, but now it felt like Veda Singh and I built a house of cards made of nothing, so it took nothing for Yogi Bhajan to knock it down. This abrupt about-face of everything that had occupied my thoughts and fortified my heart ripped a gaping hole in me. Emptiness replaced hope. I laid on our shitty egg-crate foam mattress, crying, yawning, and sleeping, like I did that first miserable night at The Omega House Residence.

Kirtan Singh came home later than usual. I assumed he went to see Yogi Bhajan after work. When he climbed into bed he moved to press his body up against me. My body revolted and I leapt up to get away from him. I immediately suspected Yogi Bhajan put him up to this. There was no way Kirtan Singh was touching me ever again. I went downstairs and laid on a couch in the living room.

Though he left me, I still found it soothing to focus on Veda Singh. Maybe he would come around, I told myself. Maybe I could talk to him and we still could leave together. Honestly, I didn't know how I could leave without him by my side. I didn't have a job, we had one car, and my contacts in Los Angeles were the 3HO community, and Graciela. Veda Singh had been my best ticket out.

As soon as I woke, I called his office. When he answered, I was so pleased. I told him we'd made a mistake and I was ready to meet him so we could leave together.

He responded curtly, "I can't talk to you anymore. Please don't call here again. Keep up, Keke."

Click.

He sounded dead. I stared vacantly at the phone as the bottom fell out of my life. No wavering, he was done. He would tuck himself back in and be a good boy for *Dad*.

Those first few weeks after Veda Singh changed his colors were godawful. The whole community knew what had happened. Mostly, I stayed at Siri Gurbani, keeping a low profile. If I did go out, I was snubbed, receiving scornful glances and disdainful grunts as I walked by. The public shaming had begun.

One morning, I walked into the kitchen to discover Kirtan Singh and Awtar Kaur knee deep in a shit-talking session about me. I told them both to fuck off.

Make no mistake, Kirtan Singh came out of this looking good. In fact, my poor behavior had won him the attention of Yogi Bhajan, the thing he lived and breathed for. He seemed high as a kite, energized from it all.

Since I did not feel capable of leaving on my own, I found myself in a terrible predicament. Veda Singh remained contrite in his marriage to Veda Kaur, while Kirtan Singh and I suffered under the strain of my betrayal.

On the heels of many weeks of chaos, the Inosanto Academy was my place of refuge. Against my husband's wishes, I continued my regular training schedule with Graciela. She had become a friend and was concerned about me staying in 3HO. The example she set as an independent single woman sparked a longing in me for a different kind of future.

In the meantime, I needed to try to repair my reputation, even though I thought it was an impossible task. The most obvious place to begin was to volunteer my time and effort doing the ubiquitous practice of *seva*; selfless service.

Kirtan Singh joined the effort and volunteered me for a few hours of ironing at the Estate. This was formally called Guru Ram Das Estates. Yogi Bhajan's secretaries and wife lived there.

The iron was hot and ready for me when I arrived, along with a couple of large baskets of clothing next to the ironing board. As I reached for my first garment, I saw the first basket was full of Yogi Bhajan's underwear. Jockey brand tighty-whities.

You have got to be kidding me, I thought to myself. *He needs his underwear ironed?*

Because I was hoping to improve my standing in the sangat, I reached down and grabbed a pair. Setting them on the ironing board, I saw one of Yogi Bhajan's pubic hairs sticking out of the frontal area.

Oh hell no!

I walked straight out the front door without so much as a word to anyone. Kirtan Singh was pissed off to hear I bailed on my commitment, so I clearly let him know there was never going to be a time when I would do that particular job. My idea to do seva fizzled along with my efforts to be a good Khalsa woman.

Kirtan Singh and I barely interacted. Most of my time was spent trying to figure out what to do now that Veda Singh wasn't an option. I knew as long as I didn't leave, Kirtan Singh would put up with me. He was far too holy to instigate a divorce.

My efforts to improve my standing in the community failed. The whole enterprise was forced. Honestly, I couldn't remember a time when I did something simply because I wanted to. My life was nothing but rules to obey and try to live up to.

The next day, I slept in. I hadn't gone to sadhana since coming home from Ladies Camp. Being alone in our room, I relished the quiet space where I could be alone with my thoughts. On this particularly peaceful morning, I pondered the idea that if there was a god or a source of the universe-whatever you want to call it-it was certainly something far beyond our comprehension. As I imagined this source of everything, it struck me as truly ludicrous that puny humans constructed beliefs about what this unfathomable source would want from us.

Why did I believe god would give a rat's ass whether or not I got up in the middle of the night, gagged myself with alum powder, took a cold shower, or did sadhana? Why had I allowed myself to be controlled by Yogi Bhajan's daily to-do list?

This led to a marvelous epiphany. My life had been taken over by mono-diets, disciplines, pressure, and judgment. No more. I was done. I decided I would no longer participate in any kind of teaching unless I authentically felt moved to do so. Because let's face it, I was one miserable person in the Happy, Healthy, Holy Organization.

This revelation felt so right, it brought me comfort and resolve. With perfect timing, Kirtan Singh came into our bedroom and made a snarky comment about my missing sadhana. He gave me the opportunity to share my epiphany and let him know *his idea* of who I was supposed to be meant nothing to me anymore. My barometer would be to do things I genuinely wanted to do. If he didn't like it, too bad. Exasperated by my speech, he went to work, shaking his head.

Shortly after this significant shift, I received a call from Kirtan Singh's boss, Hari Jiwan, asking me to come to the ashram for a meeting with Yogi Bhajan. I had not seen him since the day he decimated my relationship with Veda Singh. Why he wanted to see me was a mystery. I certainly did not want to see him, but staying in the community required a certain capitulation to the demands of Yogi Bhajan.

It turned out to be a business meeting. Yogi Bhajan was starting a skincare company named Oriental Beauty Secrets. Hari Jiwan and Baba Singh, two of 3HO's most illustrious mucketymucks, were also investing in the endeavor. The cosmetic formulations were created by Kartar Purkh, one of his secretaries. It would be a multi-level marketing company like Amway, which I was familiar with because my father sold it when I was a kid. They wanted me to demonstrate how to use the product at the company launch party in a couple of weeks.

Yogi Bhajan complimented me, saying I was chosen for this job because of my beautiful, radiant skin. He promised I would make a million dollars "by the end of next year" and would be able to afford a Jaguar.

Furthermore, after the launch, a three-week tour around the country was planned. They invited me to come along. Hari Jiwan said I would have to pay fifteen-hundred dollars to cover my airfare and expenses, but not to worry because I would earn that money back before the tour was over. They hired a multi-level marketing expert, Eileen Kirkbride, to guarantee our success.

Because I was too afraid to leave on my own, I accepted their offer. I was flattered to be chosen to participate on the ground floor of such an opportunity. I hoped it was a sign that things were looking up for me. Hari Jiwan said to bring him a check before the end of the week. The additional bonus for me was the tour would give me a vacation from my husband.

Kirtan Singh and I did not have any savings, so I asked my father for a loan. I lied, telling him we owed back taxes because I didn't think he'd help me if I told him the truth. He phoned to tell me a check was in the mail.

On the heels of this unexpected development, my little sister, Meg, now eighteen, came to town for a visit. Being with her was a balm for my aching heart. She was observing my ashram life in Los Angeles for the first time, staying in the guest room at Siri Gurbani.

The best part of her visit was being alone together. We went to the movies in Westwood, did some shopping, and spent a day at Santa Monica beach. I didn't want to burden her with all that was going on, but I did tell her I was thinking about leaving my marriage. She was comforting, saying I had some big decisions to make and that she'd be there for me no matter what.

The last day of Meg's visit was going to be a scorcher, with temperatures in the hundreds. We were taking her to Universal Studios in the San Fernando Valley. With the weather in mind, I put on a summer dress and churidars, and tied my hair in a bun.

Displeased with my appearance, Kirtan Singh stated I was not leaving the ashram without a turban. When I refused, he grabbed my arm, insisting I do as he said. With a hard jerk, I freed myself from his grip, running down the stairs to Meg who was waiting in the foyer. We went to the car as I apologized, telling her Kirtan Singh and I were fighting. We were always fighting. Our relationship had become a battle of wills. His goal was to break mine.

Kirtan Singh begrudgingly capitulated and we went to Universal. Like a sniper, he made harsh comments throughout the day to communicate his disappointment in me.

A photo taken that day encapsulated the state of our marriage; Kirtan Singh's arms encompassed my waist with his fingers firmly interlocked at my abdomen. This was not a gesture of affection, it's a man holding his wife like a hostage, a hostage he desperately wanted to constrain.

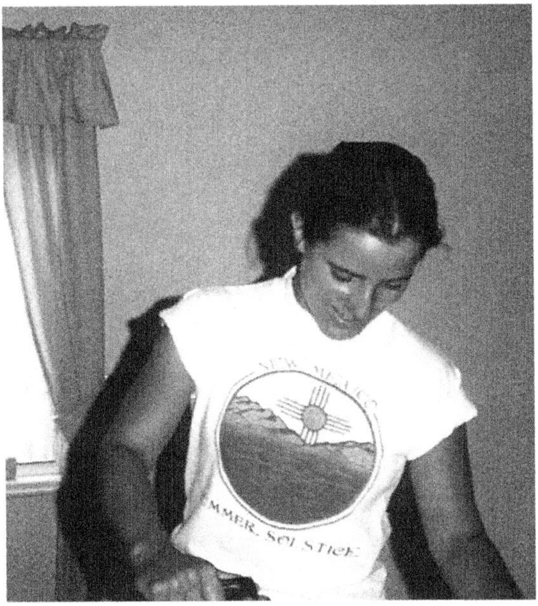

After Solstice at the Vedas' apartment.
No turban, full rebellion.

27
crescendo

Vowing to get over the loss of Veda Singh, I was glad to have the distraction of Oriental Beauty Secrets. I was given product samples to use so I could personally speak of its efficacy.

Yogi Bhajan exuded confidence about the future of his new company. He told me I would be rich, saying he was looking out for me and he wanted me to have my own wealth. All of this was attractive to hear. It would be my secret that I would use my earnings to leave 3HO.

During one of our meetings he began asking me questions about Graciela. He commented that her self-defense lessons were a great benefit to the community. I agreed. Then he mentioned another company that was starting up in New Mexico called Akal Security. Yogi Bhajan wanted to meet with Graciela to offer her a job as the head of this company. He asked me to convey his wishes to her, adding he would pay her $50,000 a year and buy her a Mercedes Benz.

This was unacceptable. There was no way in hell I would stand by and watch Graciela get sucked into this organization.

On another visit, Guruke approached me with some masala she had made and wrapped in aluminum foil. Extending it to me like it was the sacred food of the gods, she said Yogi Bhajan asked her to prepare this food especially for Graciela. Could I deliver it to her?

I refused. Guruke stared at me in disbelief. She couldn't fathom anyone saying no to Yogi Bhajan. Again she asked and I refused. I was not going to be any part of enticing Graciela into the fold.

At my next class, I told Graciela what was going on, warning her how manipulative Yogi Bhajan could be. The job offer in New Mexico made her curious. She assured me she could handle herself and decided to schedule a meeting with him.

Before I knew it, the day of the Oriental Beauty Secrets launch party arrived. My demonstration went well and I was given feedback that I was a natural at public speaking. We left on the tour visiting Albuquerque, St. Louis, Atlanta, Herndon, Virginia, and New York City. Each ashram provided food, transportation, and lodging. I slept wherever I was told, sometimes in a bed in the single ladies rooms, but more often than not on sofas and floors.

We had our longest stay in New York City. I was looking forward to seeing the Big Apple for myself. My excitement, however, was snuffed out rather quickly. It's safe to say nothing could have prepared me for the rudeness I encountered on the streets of New York. I had never been in a public setting where people were so comfortable shouting insults. Most popular among the many epithets hurled at me were the visually powerful *Q-Tip* along with *The Walking Wounded.*

The high and mighty muckety-mucks made reservations for dinner at Il Nido, a chi-chi Italian restaurant. The menu was pricey so I ordered a cup of soup and a small salad to stay within my budget. The grand poobahs ordered multiple appetizers for the table. When I told Baba Singh I wouldn't be eating any of that food because it was too expensive, he chastised me, saying, "This is why you'll never have any money, Kirtan Kaur. You have scarcity consciousness."

When the bill came, it was split evenly for the table. Baba Singh demanded one-hundred dollars from me, even though he knew damn well I only had soup and salad. He insisted I chip in like everyone else. I resented paying for their appetites and felt Baba Singh was a jerk for taking advantage of me.

On a much happier note, Dustin Hoffman and John Malkovich were playing on Broadway in Arthur Miller's *Death of a Salesman*. I desperately wanted to see my first Broadway play, but no one would go with me. With some help I managed to buy a ticket and find my way to the theater, even though I was terrified to be alone in the city. Once inside, I found my seat and sat down with a sigh, glad to have made it. The man behind me groaned and said my turban was blocking his view. Removing it wasn't an option, so I scrunched down in my chair until the play was over.

The play was the best part of the tour. I was transported out of my personal misery and right into the misery of Willy Lohman. Dustin Hoffman was mesmerizing, masterful even—with the slightest nuance in his voice or gesture, you could hear the rippling sound of women opening their purses to reach for a tissue.

As the Oriental Beauty Secrets tour was coming to an end, and despite repeated assurances that I would be "growing my downline" during the tour, nothing was happening. After each presentation when I was supposed to be signing up recruits, there was always some task that needed attending, a task always assigned to me. They signed up recruits and I did menial work.

I had been played. They were all liars. I had been invited on the tour as free labor. I believe this was Yogi Bhajan's plan all along. He was a conman and his promises were crafted as part of the manipulation. Resentment and hatred toward him replaced my foolish notions that he ever wanted to help me.

One chance remained for me to grow my downline. Eileen and I planned an event in Reno so I could invite all the people I knew to support my new business. While everyone else flew back to Los Angeles, I went to Reno. My brother, Peter, was getting married on the third of November and my presentation was on the eighth. Eileen would arrive in the morning that day. She booked a room at the Airport Plaza Hotel where the event was scheduled.

Just like the good old days, my mother and I went shopping. Knowing there would be live music at Peter's wedding reception, I wanted something fun to dance in. It was sobering to think I had not danced since my days at the disco five years earlier. It had also been years since I was in a department store. The styles were so different from anything I'd ever seen. I found a pair of French designer jeans that cost a whopping eighty-six dollars and a blue and white striped top. Though my workout sneakers were pretty grungy, I decided they would have to make do. I didn't want to charge too much on our American Express card. Kirtan Singh was already going to be fuming when he got yet another unexpected bill like he had in the summer.

Being home felt indescribably good. All of my white clothing remained in my suitcase. I wanted to look like a normal person.

Kirtan Singh came up for the wedding. With his jaw clenched for most of the visit, he endured my flagrant disregard for the rules and regulations of 3HO. He was outraged at what I was wearing and angrier still that I wore my hair down in a braid.

But he was on my turf, with my family, and therefore couldn't muscle up on me like he did in Los Angeles.

I was on the dance floor for as long as the band played. My god, it felt good to cut loose. My mother and siblings were aware that my marriage was on the rocks, but as always, were friendly and loving toward Kirtan Singh.

Before leaving town, he demanded to know when I was coming home and was dissatisfied when I told him I didn't know. He left right after the wedding, much to my relief.

Eileen arrived for my presentation. We were polite with one another but not friendly. I considered her complicit in my ill treatment during the tour.

As luck would have it, a massive snowstorm hit the Sierra Nevada on the day of my event which made driving a hazard. I had been so confident I could fill the banquet room and secure a downline, but the adverse weather swayed a different outcome.

I met up with Eileen, who had brought product, pamphlets, and sign-up forms while I brought the items I needed to demonstrate how to use the product.

The event was scheduled for six o'clock. Watching the clock, my tension level climbed as no one came through the door. At 6:05, my mother and Meg arrived followed by my father and his wife. Four people in total.

I marched over to Eileen and bitched at her saying the fact that I had no downline was her fault, along with her cohorts, Hari Jiwan and Baba. She came right back at me in a nasty tone and called me a loser. She demanded I go out and do my presentation for my four family members. She said it was the only thing, as well as the professional thing, to do.

I did my presentation. I signed up no one. Eileen left the ballroom before I was finished and I never saw her again.

My father had a doomed look on his face that said "I don't think I'm going to get my loan back."

This outcome was hard to take. I hate feeling stupid. I hate feeling like someone got the best of me, but that is exactly what happened with the three musketeers and Yogi Bhajan.

Sitting with the glaring truth of all that had taken place since June when Veda Singh sweetly held my feet, I was filled with rage: rage about my marriage, rage at Veda Singh for not sticking with me, rage at the never-ending constraints of Yogi Bhajan's teachings, and rage at the community that judged relentlessly while acting like they were spiritual.

Another two weeks passed and I was still in Reno. My days went by as I did nothing but sleep, watch TV, and eat my mother's cooking. I put on weight and felt gross.

Kirtan Singh hounded me to come home. The decision I had to make was looming, and I was avoiding it with all my might. Inertia held back the tide that was rapidly rising, the tide that would wipe away everything familiar. If I didn't say the words, I could pretend it was all going to be okay.

My mother took me shopping again. I bought some gorgeous pecan-colored jeans with a matching striped sweater. Regular clothing felt so good to me and it was a pleasure not to stand out.

One day my mother and I went to the airport to pick someone up. While we were waiting at the gate, who should step off the plane but Brian, the beautiful man who had drawn me the Happy Birthday message at The Golden Temple years before. His hair was cut short and I almost didn't recognize him. He looked tense, but nevertheless I approached him, "Brian? Hi! Remember me, from The Golden Temple? I was Suzy, and then Kirtan Kaur?"

Ugh, I was nervous. He gave a little smile and nodded yes.

"Wow. How are you? It's really good to see you. Do you still live in Reno?" I rattled off enthusiastically.

"I'm just now moving back from Colorado after a lousy breakup," he replied.

"Oh, no kidding," I said, "I'm heading that direction as well."

I tried to think of something upbeat to say, because I was genuinely excited to see him, but his heart seemed as broken as mine. Then he made a pessimistic comment, something about the stupidity of falling in love that conveyed the bitterness he was feeling about his breakup. I felt unbelievably discouraged when he said it. After a few awkward sentences, we said goodbye and he went on his way.

Seeing Brian flooded me with memories of my days at The Golden Temple. How different we were five years later. A sadness filled me, thinking both of us were downtrodden from love. I remembered his soulful deep eyes and the ready smile he always had for me when he sat at the counter. Now, here we were, kicked to the curb, sour about love.

Brian's artwork is a lovely snapshot in time, when he was somewhere in northern Nevada on a job, drawing me a beautiful sky as a way to say hello. Pangs of regret moved through me, thinking what might have been if I had felt good enough to respond to his fondness for me.

Off in another world, my mother tugged on me to leave. On the way back to her house, she gently suggested that perhaps it was time to return to Los Angeles, saying softly, "You have a big decision to make, honey."

She was right. It was time to go home.

She booked my flight and I called Kirtan Singh to let him know when I was arriving at LAX. Then I called Graciela to tell her I was coming back. I asked if she ever met with Yogi Bhajan and she told me she did, adding that I was right on the money to warn her.

When she went to see him, he told her she needed a back adjustment. Lying on the floor on her stomach, Yogi Bhajan, all two hundred and forty pounds of him, sat on her back. She said he rocked his pelvis and rode her spine all the way up to her neck.

Then he told her, "You have a very fuckable body."

His efforts to seduce her included a classic Yogi Bhajan statement, "When you come to me naked, devoid of ego, I will adorn you in diamonds and pearls."

Graciela saw right through him.

It was efficient, I suppose, in one meeting she was done with him for good.

Saying goodbye to my mother, I didn't want to leave. All that was waiting for me in Los Angeles was pain. The last five months had been non-stop chaos. My brain hurt from trying to work out what I needed to say and do.

The captain's voice was loud as he announced our descent. Looking out the window at miles and miles of concrete, the brown layer of smog, and thousands of cars below, my eyes filled with tears. Like a zombie, I walked through LAX not even able to manufacture a smile when I saw Kirtan Singh. Then again, he had a sour expression for me. Ironically, our tension level was exactly where we'd left it when I departed for the Oriental Beauty Secrets tour.

Kirtan Singh asked me how the tour went. I let my anger fly about how ill-treated I was and how I had not secured any downline. He didn't respond and didn't ask me anything more. My body ached with fatigue. It was late and all I wanted was to go to bed. The circumstances of my life were too overwhelming.

As we passed the oil rigs on La Cienega Boulevard, I said to myself, *Hold on, you're almost home.* But, Kirtan Singh had other plans. When we got to Preuss Road, he made a left instead of a right turn.

Oh, you mother fucker, you're taking me to see Yogi Bhajan.

"Kirtan Singh," I snapped. "What are you doing?"

"The Siri Singh Sahib wants to see you," he said.

"Well, I don't want to see him!" I screamed.

Of course he would blindside me like this. No doubt, they had been scheming about my return.

"You have an audience with him right now," he replied, pulling over to the curb outside the ashram.

"You're such an asshole, Kirtan Singh," I said, slamming the car door. I had to be red with rage, I was so goddamn angry.

I was wearing black martial arts pants and a short-sleeved white shirt. My hair was in a braid down my back. Here was yet another curve ball. My body was surging with a bizarre cocktail of fear, fatigue, and indignation that got stronger with each step I took. Yogi Bhajan's lies to me, his deception, his disgusting sexual advances toward me-and now Graciela-were blazing in my mind as I knocked on the door. Adding to my foul mood, bird-beaked Guruke opened the door.

Oh good, this bitch again.

She didn't smile. I didn't say hello. She motioned with her head to follow her through the kitchen into a small sitting room.

Yogi Bhajan wasted no time firing insults at me, "Oh my god, Kirtan Kaur, look at you, you've gotten fat. How much weight you have gained? Ten pounds? Twenty pounds?"

What a joke, the fat yogi is commenting on my weight.

I gave no response. I wanted him to know his words meant nothing to me. He continued ragging at me, "Where is your bana? This is how you come to meet your spiritual teacher? In black? Wearing your hair down?"

"I had no idea I was coming here. I thought I was going home," I responded tonelessly.

"And this is how you represent yourself, as a daughter of Guru Gobind Singh?" he continued. "Hair down, neurotic American woman, sexual woman, walking through the airport like this, as a disgrace."

He was baiting me, begging for a response. I gave him nothing. I sat down on a small bench across from him.

He always seemed to be in a La-Z-Boy recliner. He always seemed to be eating as well. This time he had a bowl of chana masala, which thankfully stopped him from talking as he scooped up a big mouthful with his chapati.

Always in a recliner.

Always stuffing his face.

Then he leaned to one side, farted and belched. More of his revolting behaviors I wished I was not familiar with.

He ate for several minutes while I sat silently. When he'd had enough food, he set his plate down on an end table while making forced guttural noises to clear his mucus-laden throat. He could not have been more repulsive if he tried.

He scowled at me in disgust. I stared back at him, not caring. I was worn out and wanted to leave there as quickly as I could.

Then without warning, he shouted, jolting me into a hyper-alert state, "How dare you sit across from me like this and not on the floor beneath me!"

My mind tumbled backward, until I was back in the hot seat at Omega House at fifteen years old. But instead of Bill reaming me abusively, it was Yogi Bhajan.

A feeling came over me like nothing I had ever felt before. It was an electrifying indignation that said, *I have fucking had enough of this bullshit.*

The menace in his voice told me I was in jeopardy. I answered him insolently, nonetheless.

"I AM NOT going to sit on the floor beneath you," I declared.

This pissed him off. He was pulling the lever on his La-Z-Boy to bring himself upright in the chair, yelling again, "And you dare to come in here and not touch the feet of your spiritual teacher!"

"I AM NOT going to touch your feet," I shot back.

That was it.

Yogi Bhajan launched his huge body out of the chair.

As he stood, I stood as well. He was a foot taller than me. We were standing maybe two feet from one another. I saw him raise his right arm, his fist clenched as he swung hard at me, trying to smash me in the head.

My eyes must have been enormous. I instinctively ducked under his intended blow and jumped into a fighting stance with both my fists up, at the ready.

He swung at me again with his left fist, furious he had missed his target, again, trying to smash me in the head.

I dodged his second attempt as well.

I was on full alert, agile and strong. Regaining my stance, fists up, I stared at him. I kid you not, in my head I heard myself say, *Come on, fat man.*

In those moments of witnessing his violence, I knew, without any doubt, that Yogi Bhajan representing himself as a spiritual teacher was an absolute travesty.

I was in the best shape of my life despite the few extra pounds, and, holy crap, he was no yogi. He was huffing and puffing from the exertion of trying to punch me.

He stood there, catching his breath, looking frustrated. I remained in my fighting stance, anticipating his next move. He decided to change tactics, however, since he couldn't beat the shit out of me and began to speak in a softer, more fatherly tone.

Sitting back down, he used a soothing voice, saying, "You are my daughter, Kirtan Kaur, you are the daughter of Guru Gobind Singh. I am trying to make you a graceful Khalsa woman. What I can do? You came to me and said you wanted to leave your husband. I said okay. I sent you on the Oriental Beauty Secrets tour because I want you to be rich, to drive a Jaguar, and have money. I predicted in 1984, many will leave and here you are, so defiant, so ungraceful. What I can do?"

"Sit down Kirtan Kaur, sit down," he said.

I sat further away from him in case he became violent again. He continued in this vein, predicting my future with me at the center of a successful, happy, holy life in the dharma. The intensity of our initial interaction had flooded me with fight-or-flight instincts, but his caring, fatherly voice reached out like a hook to grab me.

He told me he knew I hadn't signed any recruits on the tour. He said it was regrettable and blamed Hari Jiwan and Baba Singh for not paying attention to me, adding that he would personally make sure it was corrected right away.

Yogi Bhajan knew how to manipulate me, I will say that. After hearing this, I said, "Thank you sir."

"I am your spiritual teacher, Kirtan Kaur. It is your destiny. You are my daughter, do you see?"

I cringe to remember that I bowed low on the floor and put my third-eye on his big toe.

"Yes, yes, go now," he said, dismissing me.

The second I was outside, the spell broke.

Goddammit, he got me again! I said to myself, severely disappointed after I had started so strong. At that moment, I realized the flaw in my thinking. I had been convinced there should be a last time when we would meet so all that needed to be said would be aired and then I would depart.

But it never went that way. He always won in the end. I was too young and inexperienced to match him. Yogi Bhajan was an adept con-artist and a masterful manipulator.

Walking to the car, I smelled like I had worked out. The threat of his violence had produced a huge rush of adrenaline in my body. Until I was in the cold air, I hadn't noticed my armpits were soaked. A chill ran up my spine as I contemplated what would have happened to me if his punches had connected.

I made a promise to myself, *never again*. There would be no final meeting between us.

I never saw Yogi Bhajan again.

Kirtan Singh and I drove home in angry silence. I went straight to bed. In the morning, I met with Graciela to tell her about my near brawl with Yogi Bhajan. She was stunned to hear of his unhinged behavior.

"We have to get you out of there," she said.

"I don't know how," I replied.

"My family is telling me to come home, but I don't want to move back to Reno. I want to stay here."

"So stay here," she said, like it was no biggie.

"I don't have a job," I tried to explain. "I don't have any money...I..."

"Oh shut it," she said, smiling. "These are all problems with solutions. We'll figure it out. But first, you've got to get away from this group. It's a cult."

Her words were like magic, lifting my spirits and making a different life seem possible. Driving home afterward, I was in a good mood, feeling hopeful for the first time in months.

With an abundance of energy, I did the laundry, ironed, and made dinner. He wouldn't know why, but Kirtan Singh would be the beneficiary of Graciela's support and encouragement.

28

fate escape

Kirtan Singh came home from work and received the warmest greeting I had given him in ages. I told him dinner was ready but could sense that weird dynamic going on where my natural cheerfulness irritated the crap out of him. I ignored it, assuming he had a bad day at work. Ever since he took the job at GRD, his general mood was lousy. He was a creative person and I believed it was a soul-sucking choice for him to be there, but he never spoke to me about his job.

When I entered the dining room the atmosphere around my husband was thick and heavy.

"Sat Nam, Kirtan Singh, here is your dinner," I said, placing his meal before him

"What's this? Heavy food, again?"

"No, not heavy," I said, tensing up. "I think you'll like it."

"You weighed it?" he asked.

Yogi Bhajan said a man should weigh his meals and they should never exceed a pound. We had a scale for this purpose in the kitchen.

"Yes," I answered. "I weighed it."

"Did you weigh the plate first and subtract it?" he inquired.

"Yes," I answered, a bit crisply.

Fortunately or unfortunately, I don't have a poker face. My feelings are pretty much transparent. Kirtan Singh caught my anger even though I was doing my best to hide it.

"I don't like your vibration," he began accusatorially. "Is this the energy you cooked my food with?"

"No, Kirtan Singh, it isn't," I replied, at first trying to contain myself. But then I was more honest, "I'm frustrated that I made this meal for you and you are so dissatisfied, why can't..."

I didn't finish, because Kirtan Singh stood up, plate in hand. Walking into the kitchen, he looked at me before throwing his meal in the sink, saying, "There is no way I am eating *that*."

I said nothing and went to our room to get away from him. As I paced the floor, I decided to work out in an effort to release the anger I was feeling.

Our room still had almost no furniture in it. The hardwood floors were perfect for jumping rope and training. I used our full-length mirror to practice kicks while watching my form.

I took off my turban and put on my martial arts clothes.

I put in a mixed tape in the boombox and hit play. Madonna's hit song, *Lucky Star* played while I shadowboxed to warm up. Ten minutes into my workout, Kirtan Singh came in, walked over to the boombox and turned off the music.

"Sat Nam, Kirtan Singh," I said through clenched teeth, "I'm working out right now."

"Well, I want to meditate," he stated flatly.

"That's fine, you can meditate in the gurdwara or the sadhana room," I responded.

"I know," he persisted, "but I want to meditate *in here*."

"Okay. Well, I'll be done in an hour."

'No, I want to meditate *right now*," he insisted.

Turning on the music, I ignored him, and went back to my workout. He turned it off again.

I turned it on.

He turned it off.

His audacity had my blood boiling. I paced the floor, breathing hard. All my efforts to please him during the last year were racing in my mind. I turned to walk back to the boombox and saw Kirtan Singh removing my cassette tape. He was going to have it his way.

Maybe I was still juiced from Yogi Bhajan's violence toward me, I don't know, but I had to stand up to Kirtan Singh. The way he tried to control me was infuriating. He wasn't a husband, he was my oppressor—a vice grip all around me, suffocating me.

All the pent up emotion from five years of being told I was crazy because I had feelings and five years of trying my best to meet his unreasonable demands erupted out of me. I front-kicked him from behind, right in the tailbone.

He hit the dresser and swirled around, coming at me. Swinging his arm around my neck, he had me in a headlock and ran my head into the wall.

Unlike the beating I received in Dixie Valley from Michael, I initiated this attack. I'd reached my breaking point. We proceeded to beat the shit out of one another.

Everything in me cut loose. I cussed and screamed, "You asshole, I hate your guts!"

Back and forth we landed kicks and blows.

I picked up every framed photograph we had of Yogi Bhajan, including the one he gave me at Ladies Camp, and punched the glass, breaking it. My knuckles were bleeding, but I felt no pain.

I wanted to hurt Kirtan Singh like he hurt me. This man who did nothing but criticize and blame me for his failings.

This man who rarely said anything kind or supportive. The long suppressed, deep-seated frustrations of our marriage ran wild as I attacked him again and again.

I could feel his hatred toward me as well. I was a shitty wife, a lousy Sikh, and a betrayer of my vows. He didn't respect me and he didn't like me. I was the worst thing you could be in 3HO: an emotional woman who was entirely out of control.

We were both sucking wind, trying to catch our breath. Our blows became weaker. His turban was off and I had a handful of his hair in my hand.

As my energy crashed, my anger subsided and was replaced with tremendous sadness. I started heaving with grief and collapsed to the floor, as did Kirtan Singh. We were both spent.

Still breathing hard, I pleaded with him, "Can you please just admit you will *never* be happy with me, no matter what I do?"

He was looking at the floor when I made my request. He raised his head to look at me. Tears welled in his eyes as he spoke, "You're right, Kirtan Kaur, I won't ever be happy with you."

The pain of those honest words, both validating and decimating, released an avalanche of emotions. What I had suspected but never dared to say out loud–that I could not match his seriousness and discipline–was now a palpable truth.

I couldn't admit it before, but my ambition to marry Kirtan Singh was always tangled up with how untethered I was at that time. Underlying it all was my desperate need to belong and the ashram was the one solution I could come up with.

And now, here I was, untethered again. Five years of trying to conform in order to be loved and accepted had failed. The time I invested in the 3HO lifestyle felt like a colossal exercise in avoidance. I'd been hiding out, avoiding my pain, playing house while trying to connect with this alternative family. New levels of awareness were emerging in my mind, but I needed to get up off the floor. I needed to say something to my husband.

Already feeling the bruises that would hurt like hell tomorrow, I stood up and managed to speak the words I'd been avoiding for months. They came out in broken sobs, "I am leaving you."

At last we told the truth. For the first time, I saw Kirtan Singh cry. Whatever I hoped for with the man I married was dead and gone. Never could I have imagined we would come to this.

"I'm sorry, Kirtan Singh," I said through my tears. "I think I have been a terrible wife to you and not at all the kind of wife you wanted." I said and meant it.

If I had not been in love with Kirtan Singh, I don't believe I would have lasted three months in 3HO. I was never there for Yogi Bhajan or to be a spiritual aspirant, not really. I was looking for security and thought I could get it with Kirtan Singh. In that respect, I had duped him, pretending to be more into the lifestyle than I ever was. I was filled with remorse for all of it.

The weight of the moment made me want to go outside for some fresh air. I hadn't thought about who had heard our fight, but I knew that another one of Yogi Bhajan's idiotic teachings was that no one was ever to interfere when a husband and wife were fighting. Without a doubt, anyone who was home heard our brawl.

No matter what, he taught, do not interfere—wait until the fight is over and then offer the woman a big glass of water.

As I opened our bedroom door to leave, there were the ashram heads, Ram Das Singh and Kaur, stiffly standing at attention. Ram Das Singh reached toward me with a big glass of water he had in his hand.

"Oh my god, go fuck yourself!" I yelled, rushing past their stupefied faces, down the stairs, and out the front door.

I went to bed right after dinner. I needed to check out and my body hurt all over. When Kirtan Singh got in bed, I was asleep.

Opening my eyes with the sunrise, the house was quiet and I was alone. Every muscle in my body hurt. My first thought was, *What now? How am I going to leave?* But, I quickly realized my brain wasn't up for thinking. I was hungry and needed food.

Ram Das Kaur came into the kitchen while I was making breakfast. She gave me a hug and asked if I was okay. Wanting to talk with her away from the ashram, I asked her to have dinner with me. We made plans to meet at the Old World restaurant in Westwood.

Knowing her marriage was also strained, I hoped to connect more deeply. Was she aware of Yogi Bhajan making sexual advances toward anyone? Like many people in the Los Angeles sangat, I'd heard rumors, but nothing was ever confirmed.

As soon as we were seated, I wasted no time telling her all that had happened since Ladies Camp. I didn't bother with small talk; there was too much to say and I didn't want to leave anything out. I barely ate the split pea soup the restaurant was famous for.

Ram Das Kaur listened attentively, but when I reached the part about Yogi Bhajan's inappropriate sexual advances she became uncomfortable. She was squirming in her chair and I was afraid she would get up and leave. I took her hand, saying, "I need a friend right now. I love you and I trust you and I need your help."

She smiled and squeezed my hand but didn't speak. She seemed to be struggling about how to respond to me, but I also felt she had understood what I was saying. It occurred to me she might feel she couldn't talk for fear of being punished. So I asked, "If I ask you *yes* or *no* questions can you nod to answer?" This way, if interrogated, she could honestly say she said nothing. She liked this suggestion and looked relieved.

My first question was, "Do you have firsthand knowledge of Yogi Bhajan having sex with his secretaries?"

Her eyes widened, shocked by my directness. She gave the smallest nod, affirming my suspicion.

Then I asked, "Does Yogi Bhajan order his secretaries to have sex with one another?"

Again, her eyes widened, and again she gave a small nod.

I fucking knew it.

Even though I had my suspicions, Ram Das Kaur's rapid confirmation was a colossal shock to my system. As we sat together, I wept from the sheer relief of knowing the truth. Now I knew for certain Yogi Bhajan was a fraud.

I hugged her and thanked her for being honest with me. My next thought was, who else could confirm his behaviors?

Back at the ashram, Kirtan Singh didn't bring up the fact that I said I was leaving. We didn't talk about our fight or what was said, which was typical of our marriage. I was glad he wasn't demanding I get out, since I had no plan yet. We kind of carried on normally, but talked even less than usual.

On Sunday, I went to gurdwara and noticed Siri Ram, one of Yogi Bhajan's secretaries, staring at me during the service. She was being flirtatious. I'd noticed her making eyes at me before, but dismissed it as my imagination. Now I knew differently.

After the service, I approached her. She was all smiles, telling me I should come to work with her, serving Yogi Bhajan.

"Are you all having sex with him?" I asked point-blank.

"Are you crazy?" she replied, her smile vanishing.

Another secretary, Surya, was nearby, so I asked her the same question.

"Are you crazy?" she said, mimicking the first woman's reply.

On my walk home, I saw a woman I knew in passing who had recently become a secretary. We struck up a conversation and I told her I was molested by Yogi Bhajan at Ladies Camp.

She did not have a reaction, but simply replied, "I was raped by Yogi Bhajan."

"Oh my god, no!" I replied.

She told me what happened and said she was planning to get out. She wasn't emotional, just matter of fact. I told her I was leaving too. It was an intense communication between strangers.

Back at the ashram, I found Ram Das Kaur and told her what I had learned. I was upset, insisting we had to do something. Ram Das Kaur tried to calm me down, telling me we would talk about it later.

My sleep that night was uneasy, thoughts of Yogi Bhajan's secret life weighing heavily on my mind. Shortly after waking, I got a call from the woman I'd spoken to on the street. She had gotten a call that morning from Yogi Bhajan. He chewed her out for speaking with me. She was infuriated to discover I shared what she told me and said I had caused her no end of trouble.

"I'm so sorry," I said before explaining that I wanted the truth about him to come out. She cut me off, told me to fuck off and never speak to her again and ended the call.

I deserved her outrage, but I wouldn't change what I had done. Raping someone and getting away with it? Yogi Bhajan had to be exposed. I was sorry that I harmed her, but my god, what was going on in our community that this could happen to her?

Ram Das Kaur called Yogi Bhajan and relayed our conversation. Now it was my turn to feel betrayed. I couldn't believe it. Her loyalty to him trumped everything—truth, rape, you name it. Ram Das Kaur turned out to be a painful disappointment. Her perverse allegiance to Yogi Bhajan ended our friendship.

Yogi Bhajan was now on red alert that I was someone who was willing to talk about his ugly secrets.

After my next class with Graciela, I told her about the huge fight with Kirtan Singh and that Yogi Bhajan had raped someone. When she asked what my plan was, I told her I still didn't know.

"Well, I've given it some thought," she said, "and I've decided you can come and live with me while you get on your feet."

My shoulders dropped a few inches. Her words gave me tremendous comfort. If ever anyone needed to be thrown a bone, it was me at that moment. I was lucky to have her as a friend. I gave her a huge hug, saying, "Graciela, you are a lifesaver."

Back home, I began to think about what to take with me. We had a cubby space in the back of our closet where we kept photo albums and other storage items. Looking through our photo album and seeing the beginning of our life together was sorrowful considering the current state of our marriage. It didn't feel right to take the whole album, so I selected a few pictures I wanted to keep.

All of a sudden, the bedroom door flew open and a small group of people walked in.

"What do you think you're doing?" they asked.

"What are you doing barging into my room?" I demanded.

"Yogi Bhajan has assigned us to be a *panj pyare*, to keep an eye on you so you don't leave," one of them said.

The term "Panj Pyare" translates to the "Five Beloved Ones. This revered title refers to the five individuals who offered their lives to Guru Gobind Singh in 1699. They became the founding members of the Khalsa. Yogi Bhajan's use of this term to describe enforcers or watchdogs represents a deliberate misappropriation of a sacred concept in Sikhism.

I'd never heard of him trying to prevent a person from leaving before, but surmised he was afraid I might speak about his corrupt behavior. But, how did they know I was starting to collect my things? Paranoia gripped me. Did someone place a hidden camera in my room?

Another strange thing occurred that week. A housemate from Siri Gurbani gave me an envelope of photos from Veda Singh. It contained the pictures from our sailing voyage to Malibu. When I could be alone, I opened the envelope and discovered he had given me the negatives as well. My heart hurt looking over that beautiful day, when I was clueless what lay ahead. I got to the end of our photos and saw that he had more pictures on that roll of film. Pictures of him and Veda Kaur after he had left me. They were at a beach on horseback having a getaway with a couple who lived at Siri Gurbani. My heart hardened seeing him smiling without me.

Later that week I tried once more, quietly removing my suitcase to pack. I'd checked to see that no one was around to disturb my efforts. I was sorting through a box from the cubby when my door burst open again.

"You can't leave. We won't let you,"one of them said. All I heard was the usual 3HO platitudes:

"This is your destiny. If you leave, if you turn your back on the Guru, you will be a *patit*. You will have a million incarnations as a cockroach for this!"

As they lectured me, they took my clothes out of the suitcase and stuffed them into drawers. They put the box back in the cubby and stood like sentries at my door.

Once again, I didn't understand how they knew I was packing. I lied to them, so they would leave, saying, "I hear you, truly. Thank you. I'm okay now."

They weren't convinced. I was lectured more on the bug life I would dwell in for eons if I left. They firmly believed I would be a cockroach, the lowliest of creatures for my sins against Yogi Bhajan and the Guru.

It took some doing, but they finally left.

Being watched was unsettling. I floated through days, not grounded, not present, numbly going through the motions.

The weather turned cold and gloomy. It was November and my birthday was approaching. This urged me on because I did not want to wake up on my twenty-fifth birthday in the ashram.

The morning before my birthday Kirtan Singh got up for sadhana. I faked being sick, coughing and moaning profusely. I told him I was staying in bed, since I was for sure contagious. Everyone went to the main ashram for sadhana. In order for my plan to work, I had to get out before dawn.

I hadn't packed because I was being watched, so I grabbed an armload of white clothing from the closet and raced down the stairs and out to the car, throwing them in the back. Then a second trip for another armload. Lastly, I grabbed the boombox and my training gear. My heart thundered in my chest. I had to make it out this time.

As soon as I started the car, I exploded with emotion. My eyes flooded with tears. I didn't know how I was going to drive or read the directions Graciela gave me to her apartment. Jerking the car roughly out of the parking space, I floored it and sped toward the freeway. An anguished howling drowned out all other sounds as I drove. God help me, it was frightening how much raw emotion was moving through me. Screaming and pounding the steering wheel, all the feelings I'd shoved down for years rose to the surface to be witnessed at last.

Fortunately almost no one was on the 10 that early in the morning. Despite my condition I made it to the Lincoln Boulevard exit in Santa Monica.

Pulling up to the curb on California Avenue, it was over. I had done it. I left my husband, my community, and 3HO.

Graciela opened her door half-awake in her pajamas. I flung myself at her, hugging her as hard as I could. She helped me to do what I could not do alone. My family urged me to come home, but I was too ashamed. Going home would have felt like a failure, me with my tail between my legs. Something compelled me to stay in Los Angeles. Graciela went back to bed and I slept on her sofa until it was time for breakfast.

Later that day I called Kirtan Singh, who immediately stated he wanted the car back. He told me Ram Das Singh, who was an attorney, was preparing our divorce papers. I was to meet them at his office the next day to sign the papers. He was all business as he communicated what he expected of me. I hadn't had a moment to speak with anyone or to get any advice. He concluded saying he would drop me off at Graciela's afterward.

Next I called my three closest friends in 3HO. The first two hung up the phone as soon as they recognized my voice. The third one, a woman named Sat Guru said, "Why on earth are you calling me?" before hanging up.

Graciela saw a 3HO person at the dojo that week. They told her when Yogi Bhajan announced my departure he characterized me as a lesbian, a home-wrecker, and a whore.

Later that day I called Meg and my mother to tell them I had left. Hearing my mother's voice elicited the little girl in me to come forward and I bawled incoherently while trying to tell her what I was going through. She was gentle and kind and told me everything would be okay. She talked about the day I was born, commenting on my breech birth, "You came into this world feet first, honey. You will land on your feet again."

She and my sisters were putting together a care-package of clothing for me so I would have something other than white bana to wear. In hindsight, why did I bother to load the car up with my bana? I didn't want to wear any of it ever again.

Graciela and I were the same size, so she loaned me something to wear for the meeting with my husband. I hated feeling rushed by him, but as I had no counsel on the matter, I did as he requested.

When I arrived, I expected my emotional state would be judged by them. Kirtan Singh was stiff and cold as our eyes briefly met in the office. He didn't look at me again. In matter-of-fact tones, Ram Das Singh went over the divorce stipulations that Kirtan Singh and he put together; I was to get no money whatsoever, except what I had on me, which was about fifty dollars. I gave him my three credit cards which were cut up in front of me. He was taking the car and keeping the belongings in our bedroom. Regarding finances, we had credit card debt that he wanted to split 50/50 with me. Then he dropped a huge bomb.

It turned out that he owed a large amount of money to his employer, which he had never divulged. He expected me to pay half of this debt.

Incredulous, I said to him, "I asked you about this, do you remember? I asked you why your paychecks were always the same amount when you worked on commission, and you got all blustery about how you were the husband and you were the householder. You said it was your job to provide and my job to serve you. So how is this now falling to me?"

"You benefited from the advances I was getting from Hari Jiwan," he replied.

"I am, for goddamned sure, not going to pay on a debt you concealed from me," I exclaimed.

"You don't have a choice, Kirtan Kaur," Ram Das Singh retorted. "California is a community property state."

Ignoring Ram Das Singh, I addressed Kirtan Singh, "So, you've earned no money there? All of your paychecks were advances?"

"Yes, so far," he confirmed. Unbelievable. What a sham.

"I'm not giving you a dime on this debt. I refuse."

"You don't have a choice," Ram Das Singh repeated.

"Oh, I most certainly do. I'd rather file bankruptcy than give him one cent for a debt he hid from me!" I said.

Nonetheless, I signed the papers as they were, knowing I'd be seeking advice from a bankruptcy attorney in the near future.

The physical act of signing the papers was awful. The finality of it had me shaking and in tears as I wrote my name knowing it was the last time I'd ever sign anything as *Kirtan Kaur.* I felt demolished and grief-stricken while the two men in turbans sat stoically, like heartless pillars of stone.

"How is it that you are feeling nothing, Kirtan Singh?" I blubbered at him. "Why don't you have any emotions about the end of our marriage?"

"I'm doing two and a half hours of stretch pose a day," he replied, referencing a kundalini yoga exercise. This was his explanation for feeling nothing, the perfect tiresome response.

We drove to Graciela's. Kirtan Singh filled some boxes with items I left behind. He carried my things inside and was gone.

A woman from martial arts class came by and took a polaroid of Graciela and me that night. I'm wearing a *Ghostbuster* T-shirt I bought at the Dreamcatcher theater in Santa Fe along with a pair of the sweatpants I sold for Veda Singh. My hair is in a braid and I still have on Playtex gloves from cleaning. I'm sitting on a box with Graciela behind me. Both of us are smiling even though I was blown out from crying.

With fifty dollars to my name and some white clothing, bleak doesn't begin to describe how I was feeling at that moment.

Graciela made room in her closet and bathroom cupboards for my things. Her sofas were big cushions, so she gave me sheets to put over whichever one I wanted to sleep on. She cooked up some delicious enchiladas and after we ate, I went to bed.

Closing my eyes, a photo I loved came to mind from when I was a little girl. It was from a family outing. As we were traipsing through the countryside, I found a small piece of a broken branch in the shape of the letter "Y." This struck me as a special thing to find, so I picked it up, right when my father was calling us to gather for a photo. We all assembled and I held my stick up for the photo as if to ask the existential question—*Why?*

This miffed my father who hollered at me to get rid of the stick. No way. I was determined to ask my question and so I refused to drop my stick. He yelled at me again, but saw the look on my face and gave up. He snapped the picture, as I held up my *Why?* I didn't smile for the photo, I was too intent on what I wanted to convey.

The *Why* was everything.

It was the impetus to explore spirituality so I could feel connected again like I did in the meadow at Camp Field. My need for answers led me to believe in signs, like my dream about the old wise man and believing Yogi Bhajan was he, even though

Me and my "why?" stick. My siblings and I somewhere in California around 1967.

he was nothing like the sage in my dream. The *why not* was my adventurous side that said yes to a Beefalo cattle ranch and an ashram in the same year.

Ever since that day in the meadow when I'd experienced oneness, I had been seeking it, trying to do the right meditation or yoga pose to find my way there again, but I overlooked such an important fact: That younger me didn't "do" anything that day. I was there. I was quiet. The experience, as far as I could surmise, emerged because I was receptive, nothing more. Maybe it was that simple.

All the efforts I made meant nothing. In fact, effort moved me further and further away from feeling connection. I thought I'd find it in Kirtan Singh, then Veda Singh, or maybe Yogi Bhajan, always looking for solutions outside of my Self.

Looking up at Graciela's mushroom brown ceiling, my mind assessed the damages. My marriage failed. I betrayed a friend and worst of all, I did not believe I could trust myself. After all, I said I would be married to Kirtan Singh til death. I thought I'd be in 3HO and a Sikh for the rest of my life. How could I trust myself when all I had believed in now meant nothing?

Amid the fallout, a glimmer existed as well. I also felt euphoric because getting out was nothing short of triumphant. I stood toe to toe with Yogi Bhajan and he failed to corral me. He failed to rape me and he failed to beat me. A smile lit my face in the dark. That was something to hold onto and be proud of.

I drifted into slumber in a swirl of thoughts and feelings that would be with me for many nights to follow.

In the morning, Graciela suggested I check out Palisades Park along Ocean Avenue, half a mile from her apartment. It was stunning. Green expanses of grass with long rows of palm trees reaching for the sky combined with the calm, soft blue ocean before me, soothing every cell in my body.

Heading down to the beach, I found a spot near the shoreline. I had a working theory that it's nearly impossible to have small thoughts while taking in the monumental beauty of nature. As sad as I was, sitting before the Pacific Ocean and her lulling waves, I felt my mood lifting.

To my right and left, I packed down the sand until it was firm and smooth. Then I wrote the name Kirtan Kaur in the sand on my right and Suzanne in the sand on my left. Under Kirtan Kaur, I put the word *dogma*. That said it all: being her meant discipline and rules and practices. Under Suzanne I wrote *freedom*: she could be or do anything. Those two words summed up all that I needed to know I made the right choice.

I was calm but emotional. Tears rolled down my face as I sat with the enormity of change that was upon me.

The melancholic lyrics from "Kathy's Song" by Paul Simon played in my head:

And so you see I have come to doubt
All that I once held as true
I stand alone without belief
The only truth I know is you

Everything I had ardently believed for the last five years poured out of me as if I was a broken hourglass emptying into the sand. There were no words to accompany my nothingness. Nothing existed beyond my deep sense of loss and succumbing to the moment I was in.

My eyes shed the tears of who I used to be. That girl no longer existed. Looking up at the sky, I imagined myself catapulted high into the air, breaking apart into zillions of pieces. There were particles of me floating everywhere.

Sometime soon, I would reassemble.

In the meantime, all those particles that belonged to the past, or to someone else's heart, or to tired beliefs, could fall away. A vivid picture emerged in my mind: all the useless pieces, big chunks and tiny bits, falling away, falling away…

I did not know the *me* that would reassemble, not yet. I was in between worlds, gestating. Everything was going to be unfamiliar for a while. This understanding gave me peace. My eyes cleared and my heart softened with hope.

My mother was right, I *would* land on my feet, and more than that, I would never fall prey to that kind of control again. Though I could not know what lay before me, or how my life would unfold, on this beach, on this day, I was Suzanne again and I was free.

epilogue

After many years, I was able to reconnect with some of the folks from my younger days. I found Gail from Camp Field and my friend, Lisa, from Richland both on social media. While I haven't seen them in person yet, I hope to in the near future.

After Becky drove away in her van, it was twenty-nine years before we saw one another again. She married my best friend from the fourth grade. We had a nice evening together and then they both stopped communicating with me.

Rita and I are still in touch. She became a Mormon and had seven children. Her daughter, Nicole, has become a dear friend.

I recently heard Bill died last year.

Michael, my ex-boyfriend and I connected briefly on social media before he died in 2019 from complications of diabetes.

My dear brother Mike passed away in 2022. My father followed him a year later.

Graciela and I remain close friends and are planning a get together this year.

Yogi Bhajan was in poor health for years and died in 2004. Incredibly, he never had to answer for his many crimes or the harm he inflicted on so many.

My escape from 3HO took place in November of 1984. Thirty-six years later, in January of 2020, I was reacquainted with the 3HO community that shunned and slandered me.

1985 in Santa Monica. I cut my hair and got a perm.

In the more than six years since then, a tsunami of revelations have made clear the true nature of Yogi Bhajan. He was far worse than I ever could have imagined: a perverse, corrupt lifelong criminal, child abuser, rapist, and serial sexual abuser of women.

The private Facebook group that I started called *Beyond the Cage: The 3HO | Yogi Bhajan | Kundalini Yoga Aftermath* has thousands of members, some of whom have shared the shocking details of their abuse by Yogi Bhajan. We gather in solidarity, having survived him and his corrupt organizations.

In 2022 VICE TV produced a series called, *True Believers.* The first episode, *Empire of Yoga*, focused on the allegations, scandal, and debauchery surrounding Yogi Bhajan.

Hayley Pappas and Smiley Stevens produced a docuseries that aired on HBO in 2024, called *Breath of Fire.* It captured the early years of Yogi Bhajan in America, though its main focus was the abuses of a popular kundalini yoga teacher named Guru Jagat Kaur.

Music producer Rick Rubin practiced kundalini yoga at the Golden Bridge Studio in Los Angeles in the 90s. He and Leila Mattimore executive produced a docuseries through Fifth Season called *Long Time Sun.*

I was hired as a consulting producer on the project. It was powerful and gratifying to be part of an effort to make the truth about Yogi Bhajan available to a wider audience.

Unfortunately, Yogi Bhajan is still revered, especially in parts of the world where the truth of his actions are not well known. Many of his early students and some of their now adult children refuse to acknowledge his crimes and instead continue to perpetuate his toxic teachings. Yogi Tea (now called Yogi) was started by a Yogi Bhajan devotee and supplies vast amounts of money in the form of grants to a number of nonprofit organizations in the 3HO empire.

Regardless of this, the stark truth remains. Yogi Bhajan was a sexual predator and abuser who deeply harmed many of his students and sexually abused countless women. His abuse extended to the second generation of children who were either born into the cult or who joined it by proxy through their parents at a young age.

Because of the pressures caused by the truth coming out, the Siri Singh Sahib Corporation board got around to initiating a reparations program they said would address the harms done. They made sure not to mention Yogi Bhajan while doing so. However, they ignored many others who were harmed. My understanding was that this was a prophylactic move to try and avoid an avalanche of legal problems. Several lawsuits have been filed on behalf of some of the survivors.

A reconciliation program was also initiated with a company called Just Outcomes. I participated in this program for nearly two years and, in my opinion, it failed miserably. What's worse, it retraumatized myself and others who were abused by Yogi Bhajan due to a lack of appropriate boundaries and their ignorance of the workings of the cult who employed them.

Many people have left 3HO and discarded the practices taught by Yogi Bhajan. The chasms between family members that remained and those who have left are deep and painful. Through the Beyond the Cage group, I was able to reconnect with people I had not spoken to since my departure.

Kirtan Singh still professes his love for Yogi Bhajan and follows his teachings. Veda Singh and I spoke in 2020. He has little recall of those days long ago, saying he moved all those memories to a compartment in the back of his mind.

Transformation. Six months after my departure.

About the Author

SUZANNE JORDAN is an activist and advocate dedicated to supporting survivors of predatory systems and institutional abuse. As a survivor of both the troubled teen industry and the 3HO movement, she has turned her personal history into a catalyst for systemic change. Suzanne served as a consulting producer for the Fifth Season docuseries *Long Time Sun*, produced by Rick Rubin and Leila Mattimore. Beyond her work in film, she founded and moderates a private advocacy group for survivors of Yogi Bhajan and 3HO, offering support to those reclaiming their lives. A vocal critic of the darker side of the spiritual, New Age, and wellness industries, she works to expose the mechanics of manipulation hidden behind the veneer of spirituality. *The Deviant Daughter* is her first book.

Printed in Dunstable, United Kingdom

84302399R00282